Mr. Prime Minister, 1867-1964

Mr. Prime Minister

By the Same Author

The Unknown Country

The Incredible Canadian

The Struggle for the Border

Canada's Lonely Neighbour

Canada: To-morrow's Giant

The Fraser

The Hollow Men

BRUCE HUTCHISON

1867-1964

LONGMANS CANADA LIMITED

Printed in Canada by
The Hunter Rose Co. Limited

*To my Mother, Constance
Hutchison, a citizen of
Canada who well remembers its
first Prime Minister.*

Contents

Adventure at the Apex

This book has one modest purpose. It was written to view Canada's inner politics (as distinguished from the public legend) solely from that central listening-post and engine room, the Prime Minister's office. It is not a formal book of history, a constitutional essay or an economic thesis. It does not argue any political doctrine or advocate any theory. Rather it is a tale of adventure at the apex of Canadian power.

Having studied the lives of all our fourteen Prime Ministers and personally known six of them, I thought it would be useful to trace their work, to examine their characters and to analyze the successive management of a mysterious institution, as a single narrative. So, indeed, it is—a narrative of alternating success, failure and sometimes bitter sorrow, much less plausible than fiction.

Thus focused on the Prime Ministers, such a book must drastically condense some great events deserving better treatment and ignore others of importance because they do not directly involve these men. No attempt is made to record the collective evolution of our society, which directly conditioned its leaders and was more decisive than any of their achievements. Though politics are only the changing reflection of a nation's habits and, at most, the clumsy apparatus of its will, politics alone, as directed and sometimes misdirected from their true centre, are considered here.

Concerning the years and personalities before my time, I have relied on countless books, newspapers and other documents, the original Confederation Debates, the magnificent biography of John A. Macdonald by Donald Creighton, the equally excellent biography of Alexander Mackenzie by Dale Thomson, the memoirs of Robert Borden, the diaries of Mackenzie King and our old Canadian treasure chest of mixed gold and dross, the parliamentary Hansard.

After King's arrival my own recollections over a period of forty-six years in political journalism are mingled with the public record, occasionally denying it.

I am indebted for all this information to innumerable men, illustrious and obscure, living and dead. My highest debt is owed to Jean Ellis, who prepared the manuscript and, I hope, removed its worst blemishes.

Bruce Hutchison
Victoria, B.C.
July, 1964

The Land, Its Leaders and Its People

Fourteen Prime Ministers, from Macdonald to Pearson, have governed Canada in constant flux of fortune, good and bad. All these men, so different as private persons and public figures, have confronted, but seldom dared to utter, the same question that none knew how to answer.

Could a nation conceived in vague compromise and dedicated to the defiance of continental logic long endure? Would Canadians permanently pay the price set by nature for their endurance? Or, rejecting the price—especially the price of biracial toleration between themselves—would they admit defeat, accept the logic, liquidate the national experiment and fall piecemeal into the embrace of their rich American neighbours?

In 1964, as in 1867, the unanswered question is unlikely to trouble a world where democracy is on trial for its life after a brief pilgrimage. It necessarily troubles the people of Canada and must soon be answered. Pearson's predecessors assumed an affirmative answer. He differs from all the others because he can no longer be sure.

Like Macdonald, Pearson and his successors must see that the great imponderable is not economic, financial or legislative but emotional, psychic, human. It therefore centres in the Prime Minister not as a constitutional instrument but as a human being.

The Founding Fathers of the United States, in their noblest illusion, conceived a good society under the government of unerring laws. The makers of a second North American nation could afford no such sanguine postulate.

From its birth to this day Canada has been governed by fallible men who practised politics as the art of the impossible. Considering their unique Canadian circumstances, it is not surprising that among our Prime Ministers before Pearson only Macdonald, Laurier, Borden, King and St. Laurent succeeded, that most of the others ended in frustration and despair, several in tragedy.

No group of fourteen could be more disparate in origin, temperament and ability; yet all, with perhaps two exceptions, were animated by a common motive, an insatiable appetite for power.

Seeking it, as necessary to the nation's welfare, every Prime Minister has found that politics is not the lofty symposium of moralities or the chivalrous debate of principles described in textbooks for the young. It is a clash of greedy interests to be reconciled somehow before they convulse the State, a civil war without violence but war nevertheless, with supreme power as its prize. And when the prize is won it usually becomes a cup of poison in the winner's hands.

All the Canadian winners were honest men, as this world goes. None profited financially from his office. A majority of them left it poor, unhappy and broken in health.

None had ever known precisely what he sought. All had often done the reverse of what they said. None could even be truly classified as a Conservative or a Liberal, since each of these proud names was never more than a handy alias and both are now totally intermingled, indecipherable. All spoke, perforce, in two languages and thought in two separate compartments to make themselves understood by their sophisticated followers and by a public which, as Laurier said of Quebec, usually has no opinions, only sentiments.

Nor has any Prime Minister ever told the whole truth to the nation or to himself. He could not tell it, if by chance he knew it, lest he infect the nation with his own dread of the future and confess that he was frequently mistaken in his judgments.

Every Prime Minister made his own mistakes and suffered his own penalties.

Macdonald's campaign funds, accepted in drunken desperation from shady railroad contractors; Laurier's reciprocity agreement, a masterstroke fatal to his career; Borden's well-meaning breach with the French-Canadian race; King's gross, almost comical misjudgment of the contemporary world; Bennett's Conservative apostasy and futile New Deal; St. Laurent's bungled pipeline scheme; Diefenbaker's weird self-destruction; Pearson's start as the opposition and then as the government leader in a double fiasco that humiliated him but deceived his enemies and masked his real purposes—these adventures, and others to be told here, have demonstrated that a Prime Minister must live in ceaseless hazard steadily increasing at a time of world-wide revolution incomprehensible to all men, large and small.

Despite the solitude and the miseries of office, only three Prime Ministers voluntarily abandoned it. Power made a few giants and they helped to make a fortunate society but the best of them could not quite escape power's agreeable corruption.

These things are never publicly acknowledged. Politics throughout all times and places being in large part a denial of obvious facts, the few successful Prime Ministers have jealously guarded their intentions, hopes, fears and confusion from the people. But their record may help the people to examine themselves in the shifting mirror of leadership. That self-examination is long overdue. For the people, not their leaders, must finally answer, by their little, unknown lives, the question so often evaded by the famous practitioners of politics.

Men, however large and durable, soon pass. The earth of Canada remains, wondrously broad and fair. The crops sprout in the springtime, the forests rise again from man's butchery, the rivers run forever to their three oceans, autumn sets the mountains aflame and the cruel winter asserts our common creaturehood in a lonely northern land.

All the cities piled together would make a narrow scar on this immensity. All habitation gleams in tiny specks of light through the darkness as the traveler flies from one coast to the other. Half a continent is ours, with its wealth, its stark splendour and its limitless chance of human contentment. Yet the treasure, both physical and spiritual, which our fathers possessed for us, can be lost if we lose their old, unuttered dream. The land can be despoiled, the dream betrayed by our folly and ours alone.

Of itself the land is not enough, the treasure barren without man's intelligence, above all, his goodwill, his tolerance among his fellows of different blood and race. In the Prime Minister's office, and the layers of government beneath him, we have built the machinery of a nation. We have still to build its inward fibre, its *sense of unbreakable community, its instinctive agreement that the nation, though formed of many parts, is one thing or nothing. After nearly a hundred years of joint experience we are in peril from no one but ourselves.*

Great men have led us thus far. Greater will be needed to lead us on the unmarked road ahead but none can rise above his source, the people who, in greatness or meanness, in generosity or greed, must save the nation or surrender it.

As the nation approaches its hundredth birthday the time for that decision is at hand. And when a disordered world is watching our experiment as a clear test of men's will to bridge the chasm of blood and race, we hold in our keeping a trust much larger than we know.

1: The Myth Maker

The captains and the kings, or the nearest equivalents that Canada could muster, had departed at last. From Fundy to Huron the bonfires were burned out, the last rockets discharged, the bands and the orators silent. Queen Victoria's proclamation, read in every village square, was filed away, seldom to be read again.

On the night of July 1, 1867, John Alexander Macdonald, an improbable midwife, felt satisfied that his Canadian Confederation was decently born, even if the grandeur of its birth had been somewhat marred by a nasty little quarrel in the Cabinet chamber and a rather shocking affront to the Queen's Governor-General.

Fortunately Lord Monck accepted colonial bad manners with British phlegm. He was evidently bored by the vulgar din of Ottawa and did not take the occasion seriously enough to wear anything more impressive than a business suit, when his ministers had expected plume, gold braid and sword in deference to a great landmark of Empire.

At least he had promulgated the union of Ontario, Quebec, New Brunswick and Nova Scotia, and sworn in a makeshift government under a Prime Minister whose reputation was slightly scandalous, to say the best of it. Any experienced statesman from London must regard the whole Canadian experiment as fragile, pathetic, almost unnatural. Still, given a bit of luck, the thing might work, though God and the Imperial Privy Council, in their long, intimate association, knew it was doubtful.

No one perceived the dangers ahead as clearly as Macdonald, who had undertaken, with the deepest misgivings, to rear an infant

State. The battered portmanteau of his mind carried all Canada's business but there were some things that he did not know and could not learn in his remaining years.

A hopeful constitution had established and awarded to him a new focus of power without defining it, and thereby had changed everything as neither he nor any other man foresaw. His successors, down to Lester Bowles Pearson, have not fully explored, even now, the possibilities of the Prime Minister's office. Their lives, eight in failure, five in success and one yet to be judged, cannot measure the nation's life; but they have pervaded, articulated, unified or disrupted it from the beginning.

No past event of any importance can be understood, no contemporary problem can be solved outside the context of these men's work. Without the presence of the Prime Minister and his authority (most of it invisible) our collective affairs are meaningless.

Some seventy-two years separate the departure of Macdonald and the arrival of Pearson. With all this experience behind it, the Prime Ministry remains mysterious and uncodified but constantly enlarges its unwritten prerogative and subtle sovereignty.

So it must when the nation constantly moves to what is glibly called the left, expands its socialism under opposite labels, vests more and more of its business in the State and mocks the solemn doctrines of its political parties. The party system may be splintered and deranged, as it is today, the public's business grossly bungled, but while the State grows its general manager, its chief legislator, and sometimes its executioner, must grow with it.

The singular man resting his half-sick body after Canada's birthday celebration was long used to power, settled in his ways but still capable of unlimited growth. Far better than the men around him Macdonald understood the public postures and secret tricks, the rewards and heartbreaks, the victories and defeats, the unwritten but inexorable laws of his trade. Lacking his factual knowledge and, above all, his sixth sense of politics as human nature roughly organized, he would not have come thus far and could not hope to survive the unknown perils now ahead.

What, the first Prime Minister must have asked himself, did he really possess in addition to his title and office? Nothing more, as he well knew, than a dubious gamble and a myth to disguise its fragility. The two things were inseparable. A rudimentary State must live thenceforth mainly on myths, assuming that it could live at all.

Macdonald knew that, too, as an experienced maker of myths.

He was mostly a myth himself, the largest myth in Canada. The knighthood, just conferred on him by a grateful sovereign who would never see Canada, added nothing to the gaudy, home-made image of his own creation.

The office now in his tenure was a very different thing. It must remain partly mythical but it must also grapple with facts, or post-pone them if they could not be faced. No contemporary was as able with facts as Macdonald, none so skilled in the trick of blurring them. For all his knowledge, and still deeper intuition, even he could not accurately gauge his task and, failing to gauge it, was about to ruin himself.

Meanwhile, having endured the day's weary ritual with a fair pretence of enjoyment, Macdonald was alone to contemplate the Dominion's prospects and his own. Both looked equally sombre. In truth, they were worse than he suspected. His first grave blunder, his public disgrace, and the latest, the harshest, the least endurable of many private griefs were hidden on the evening of his triumph.

To all appearances he was the same jolly, bantering, some-what disreputable personage known to all Canadians; but with him appearances were deceptive. Natural talent and long practice had made him a master of deception.

He was also a personal institution, predating the official in-stitution of government, his presence worn by the Canadian folk as comfortably as an old pair of shoes, every wrinkle in his homely face and, so they supposed, every cranny of his mind as familiar as the landscape at their door. He might seem a little tired now, worn out by labour and dissipation; but actually, at the age of fifty-two, he had entered the flood-tide of his powers and twenty-four years of active life lay before him.

The tall, loose figure decked out in flashy clothes, the swarm of black curls, the deep, melancholy eyes, the jutting beak empurpled by whisky, the thin mouth twisted in jest or pain, rather resembled a quizzical stork of exotic plumage always poised for flight yet strangely immovable.

Most Canadians had watched him for a long time. They were accustomed to the careless, conversational style of his speeches, so unlike the endless, over-stuffed rhetoric of the Victorian age. They liked his winking sallies and sly retorts, his most serious arguments phrased in simplest language, his quick lunge at the heart of the matter: and they were unaware that the material had been supplied by others, the notes for the most important occasions scribbled on an envelope and usually mislaid.

He was no orator. His speeches could never become literature and would seldom be quoted afterwards, but they accomplished their purpose. They convinced voters and won elections. With an ear as sensitive as his political nose, he attuned his words to his listeners. Before Parliament or caucus the speeches were tightly organized, factually documented, a fine net of reasoning. Before a country audience they sounded, and were deliberately contrived to sound, like neighbourly gossip over a rail fence, though sometimes they were oddly sprinkled with Latin quotations. You never knew what this unpredictable man might drag next from the cluttered attic of his mind.

For the most part his parliamentary speeches read better now than those of any successor except Laurier, the opulent painter, and Meighen, the antiseptic surgeon, with words. Beside Macdonald's, the speeches of King (who was at least his equal in ability) are diffuse, redundant and mushy; those of Bennett pompous and gushing; those of Diefenbaker theatrical and chaotic; those of Pearson literate but short of muscle.

Macdonald often used what he called "good buncombe arguments" and supplied them regularly to his supporters. Like all political leaders in all lands and ages, he preached the current superstitions and mouthed the native prejudices, and that was easy in his case because he believed most of them.

Still, his general aim was grand and prophetic. Every word supplied some casual fragment in the nation's edifice. He would laugh at such a fancy word but Macdonald had a private dream of Canada, a boy's streak of Scottish romance rarely admitted even to himself. For any successful Prime Minister that was essential equipment, the lack of which spoiled several more promising careers. Macdonald hid it carefully in public and never made the mistake of assuming, like Bennett and Diefenbaker, that eloquence was a substitute for policy.

Friends and enemies could readily understand such a man—or so they thought, quite wrongly. Macdonald's contradictions and sinuosities were beyond the people's grasp and they reflected the same qualities in a divided nation. The contour of his disposition was smoothly rounded, presented no sharp angles, and gave his rivals no chance to come to firm grips with him. His enemies could only hate, without comprehending, the artful dodger. A large minority of the voters also hated, or at least distrusted him, but a majority took him for what he was, a kind of natural phenomenon like the weather.

4

This strange creature, unique, alone and lonely, contained depths and shoals, weakness and strength, virtue and vice, genius and blindness that almost a century of research has failed to reveal. The man is so deeply embedded in sedimentary layers of myth that he will never be pried loose.

No matter, the myth served him and the people well in his time, being one of Canada's few negotiable assets. On the country's natal day, however, Macdonald must reckon with much larger liabilities.

Less than four million Canadians inhabited the new State and it was split by the empty space between the old community of the St. Lawrence and the two Maritime provinces. Moreover, Nova Scotia already was trying to escape from the union, mainly because Joseph Howe had not invented it. Prince Edward Island and Newfoundland had rejected Confederation outright.

West of Ontario stretched the cold vacuum of the Prairies, the ancient fief of the Hudson's Bay Company, all of it outside Canada's jurisdiction. Beyond the Prairies stood the appalling barrier of the Rockies, penetrated by a few summer trails, impenetrable in winter. Beyond them the impoverished little colony of British Columbia, the flotsam of a recent gold rush, seemed likely to accept Manifest Destiny by joining the United States and giving it a convenient corridor to its new territory of Alaska.

Canada's internal tensions were serious enough and would soon grow, but the ravenous republic beside him was Macdonald's overriding anxiety. More than anything else, American threats had driven Canadians into Confederation. Now, for Macdonald and all his successors, the United States posed the opposite risk of friendly attraction. That was to be a permanent and primary fact of Canada.

All these geographic, economic and political facts overcrowded Macdonald's first agenda. He must join the St. Lawrence to the Maritimes by railway, seize the Prairies, and somehow lure British Columbia into the union. The first steps of Canadian expansion were imperative. Prince Edward Island and Newfoundland were needed too, but their adherence could wait.

As though the agenda were not sufficiently full, perhaps impossible, another item had lately appeared. Britain was planning some kind of omnibus deal with the United States, now reunited by its Civil War, and the deal, Macdonald surmised, would probably be at Canada's expense.

The whisky-nose in Ottawa was a highly sensitive instrument. It smelled trouble in London years ahead, but it failed to detect graver trouble much closer in distance and time. The Prairies, their half-breed inhabitants and the chemicals of an early explosion were and would remain the great lacunae in Macdonald's survey. He could never understand them.

Thus by every rational calculation the Canadian State was not viable—a creation of paper only, and the frail written words of its British North America Act must surely be expunged without much delay by the historic forces of the continent. If Canada was to be saved nothing but an irrational instinct among its people and a strong government in Ottawa could save it. Here was another primary fact, as true today as in 1867, and perhaps just as doubtful in its outcome.

Macdonald might count safely on the Canadian people's instinct, for the project of a Canadian State had always been irrational, its only foundation no more than a wild surmise in a people who were determined, against all continental logic, to be themselves. Could he count on a strong government to unify the people and resist the logic?

Certainly the Government established on Confederation Day was not the government Macdonald wanted. He had wanted a centralized system with the provinces subordinated, in all except purely local concerns, to the national authority. Instead, he had been forced to accept a federal system of provinces sovereign in uncertain but wide areas which they were evidently determined to stretch.

He had wanted Canada to wear the shining name of Kingdom. Instead, it had been given the ambiguous title of Dominion because Britain feared to affront the Americans who rejected kings in America, even by remote, semantic association.

Though all the arrangements were inadequate, possibly they could be improved and centralized by gradual stages. Thus, for a time, it would turn out. In the early days a strong leader like Macdonald could disallow provincial statutes and make power flow increasingly to the federal Government. Then the tide changed, the use of disallowance almost ceased before the twentieth century was long under way and the Imperial Privy Council repeatedly interpreted the constitution in favour of provincial jurisdiction until the British North America Act would hardly have been recognized by its architects.

Two world wars and the Great Depression of the nineteen-thirties reversed the tide again. Federal power reached a new peak but in the last few years the provinces reasserted their old prerogatives and began to erode the centralized structure built for times of emergency.

Yet beneath the surface of events, apparently in rapid centrifugal motion, such instruments as the gigantic federal budget and the Bank of Canada enabled the national Government to manage the Canadian economy from the centre in a fashion quite incredible to Macdonald and his generation of truly free enterprise.

While the Government has lately surrendered much revenue and some functions to the provinces, the primary fiscal, monetary and economic weapons are still in its hands, which plunge ever more deeply into the taxpayer's pocket and the affairs of private business. The two wings of the State will continue to quarrel but together they have amassed a collective power over the citizen that would have been unthinkable in the last century.

As power has flowed from the individual to the State so, in its federal sphere, it has flowed from the legislature to the executive and hence to the Prime Minister as the centre of the executive.

All this lay ahead of Macdonald, but the cold-blooded realism behind his jovial, romantic exterior must have told him that the Government's strength was no greater than his own. Since there had been no true Prime Minister before Confederation Day, only two co-equal leaders of Upper and Lower Canada, without any reliable control of an ambivalent legislature, the powers of the new office had yet to be fathomed, its laws tested and codified by trial and error. The trial had begun now. The errors would soon follow.

Of one thing and no more could Macdonald be sure. The Prime Ministry must be built of native materials without any precedent or plan. It had been easy to write down in the constitution that the Canadian system would accurately reproduce the British original. Of course it could not.

The unitary British government on a small island was organically different from the apparatus devised for a State already sprawling over a quarter of a continent and likely, in time, to cover half of it. Under the federal system imported from the United States, the Canadian Prime Minister's position opened a new venture in the British Empire.

Much more decisive than constitutional distinctions was the difference between Britain and Canada in geography, race, character and attitude. The awesome words on parchment could never bridge that transatlantic gulf.

No Canadian government, as Macdonald said, allowed room for "overwashed Englishmen, utterly ignorant of the country and full of crotchets as all Englishmen are." His office was uniquely Canadian, like the national embryo in its charge. So was he, for all his Scottish nostalgia.

Canadian, yes, but what did that mean precisely? No one knew or could know until the experiment was launched, and no one is quite sure about it today. As to the office, with all its legal restraints, it would be what Macdonald and his successors made it by expansion and contraction, advance and retreat, success and failure, according to the courage of the occupants and the mere luck of the game.

Yet none of the thirteen men who followed Macdonald in the office could alter much the basic shape he gave it. He had stamped his own peculiar lineaments on it; and after the lapse of ninety-seven years his mark remains legible, if somewhat faint, in the work of his present heir, Pearson. The problems of the office and its secret methods have not changed much either. They were permanently fixed by Macdonald's queer rationale. His mould could be broken only at the cost of breaking any Prime Minister foolish enough to disobey his precepts, as several did.

The first law of the office is clear in retrospect, though always hidden, if possible, from any Prime Minister's contemporaries as it was hidden from Macdonald's. Like him, every Prime Minister must appear to be a typical Canadian, the ordinary man writ large to flatter the groundlings, a composite portrait of his people, a mirror of their life.

Macdonald was nothing of the sort, despite his amiable public posture. Neither were any of his four successful heirs, or they would have failed. In most of them the mirror might be reliable but each could give it varying angles of reflection, or cloud it, as circumstances demanded.

If he is to succeed, a Prime Minister must be set apart by nature at birth and then by his own design. He must be inscrutable —often baffled, sometimes afraid but he must not *show* a moment's uncertainty or fear. He may not win the people's affection, as King never did, but he must have their confidence. And to win that he must show an unvarying air of confidence himself, however he may feel inside. At all times he must seem to ride the events that invariably ride him.

In the craft of confusion Macdonald had only one superior, King, and one close competitor, Diefenbaker. In the craft of delay Macdonald was supreme. Before he reached middle age he had won the revealing title of Old Tomorrow.

In Macdonald the contrast between the leader and the led was particularly marked. The inhabitants of Canada were for the most part farmers, woodsmen, country folk, living by the labour of their hands on a raw frontier or in squalid little towns. Macdonald never worked with his hands. Though an immigrant, he felt the substance of the Canadian earth more urgently than most of its natives; but he felt it intellectually and emotionally, not physically as his compatriots felt it. Among a rural, labouring people he was urban and sedentary. Like all his successors, with one exception, he was a man of the town, not of the country; of the house, not the outdoors.

His indoor habitat was the smoky caucus room, the Cabinet chamber, the clamorous election platform, the saloon or the quiet study. His talent lay in smooth, effortless paper work, in the manipulation of men, in patient conspiracy or ruthless war. His relaxation was a French novel on a couch, with his family around him. His relief, when all else failed, was drink.

He lived symbiotically with the political process, as every competent Prime Minister must. He loved the game as the propulsion and passion of his life; but, outwardly gregarious, he lived apart, a solitary enigma. The men around him seldom could tell where the lines of laughter ended in his face and the lines of sorrow began. He was, as he said, "a rum 'un to look at but a rare 'un to go." Lacking better, that verdict must serve.

A second unwritten law of the office, incarnate in the first Prime Minister, was codified much later by John Wesley Dafoe, the great prairie editor, who had watched Macdonald and nine successors. According to Dafoe's law, any Prime Minister must of necessity be an egotist and an autocrat, and "if he comes to office without those characteristics his environment equips him with them as surely as a diet of royal jelly transforms a worker into a queen bee."

Of all our Prime Ministers Macdonald was the least spoiled by that diet, but an egotist he had to be. Otherwise he would not have sought office in the first place. After half a lifetime in government, he would not have accepted on Confederation Day a second term of imprisonment when he was jaded, disillusioned and broke— worse than broke, bankrupt, if his creditors pressed their debts of some eighty thousand dollars.

Misfortune and vanity alike were melted and healed by Macdonald's merciful gift of humour. He could laugh at his own follies because he had no illusions about himself or any human being.

Having sinned so much, he would not cast the first stone unless it was necessary to destroy an enemy in self-defence. If possible, he preferred cajolery, flattery and gentle persuasion to overt power, though he could use it, brutally, if kinder methods failed. Even that ultimate tool, the razor, must sometimes be employed; but, unlike King, who most resembled him in method, Macdonald never supposed that the Deity was guiding his hand as he cut an unsuspecting throat.

His fingers seldom itched for the enemy's jugular. Perhaps only in the case of George Brown did he strike with any pleasure; and the treatment of his lifelong enemy—in the wretched Double Shuffle and the venomous Kingston Penitentiary scandal—was the worst blemish of his life.

Those youthful outbursts of fury and rancour were behind him now; only a few more would mar his record, and he could say from the platform, in undoubted truth, that the country preferred him drunk to Brown sober any day. The country, in fact, preferred him just as he was, with all his failings. He fitted those rough times when an election was commonly a riot, politics a kind of tribal religion and whisky abundant on polling day.

Macdonald also fulfilled a third law of the office as once codified, or rather spoken off the cuff, by King to me. A Prime Minister, King said, contemptuously dismissing the claims of a certain colleague, must be a gentleman.

By the hereditary British tradition Macdonald was not a gentleman, but he was a gentleman by nature and the more democratic tradition of North America. The same was true of all his successors. Canada's government has come from that sure source of energy, the middle class.

Besides, in Macdonald's time the people did not want a hereditary gentleman, having suffered too many of them already. They liked a leader who got drunk with his fellows at the bar, called them by their first names, bought them drinks and told them bawdy jokes. A nice balance between familiarity and remoteness, restraint and intimacy, was Macdonald's secret which no successor could exactly imitate.

A fourth unwritten law declares that a Canadian Prime Minister must be bred, apprenticed and long trained in his profession. Unlike his British counterpart, he cannot be helped by family connections and social pull. Unlike an American President, he cannot be invented. Then, in addition to ability and experience, he must have luck. Otherwise talent is useless, as proved in Meighen's classic case.

Macdonald's life thus far had been almost a codification of all the laws, written and unwritten.

To begin with, it was no political disadvantage to be born in Glasgow when a Scottish strain had coloured the life of Canada after the Conquest and now a new tide of British immigration was submerging the original United Empire Loyalists from the States.

It was no permanent handicap to be the son of a tradesman who had a weakness for liquor, could seldom make ends meet and, by his failures, drove the son to success. A larger blessing was the thrifty mother of good Scottish granite whom the boy adored. These ill-assorted parents brought Macdonald to Kingston at the age of five and there he stumbled into the perfect setting for a public career.

The town was small, hardly more than a village, but a hive of politics and for a time the Upper Canadian capital. Its schools and those of the surrounding hamlets where the family moved from one losing enterprise to another gave the boy a rude education, and only five years of it, but he educated himself by immersion in books —history, biography, travel, fiction, anything he could lay hands on.

Another boy, not far away, read omnivorously in the same fashion. Abraham Lincoln was preparing himself to save one union while Macdonald prepared to build another. The lives of the two men would never touch directly but their work, in curious parallel and indirect conflict, would finally bisect the continent between two countries.

"I had no boyhood," Macdonald wrote in later years. "From the age of fifteen I began to earn my own living." It was a poor living for the lawyer's clerk of quizzical, mobile face and gangling frame, and yet it was the best possible training for politics. He became a sound lawyer, even though his trumpery examinations at York proved nothing, and he had become an apprentice politician before he passed them. The jaunty youngster, a roisterer and something of a fop in his flamboyant dress, could do the election chores of the local Tory machine.

He was excessively fond of drink and the company in saloons. Once, it was said, he had gone off to the States and played a concertina while a friend, dressed as a dancing bear, solicited pennies from the yokels. A fellow of such habits obviously could not be elected himself but he might help to elect better men. Everybody liked his merry, offhand ways, his coarse stories, his dutiful support of an impecunious family. No one saw him as a leader of men.

That there might be more to Macdonald than a blithe spirit Kingston began to suspect when he shouldered his musket against the Rebellion of 1837 and, next year, took a first irrevocable step, unnoticed outside his town. Since no other lawyer would defend Nils Szoltevcky Von Schoultz, the gallant Polish-American who had invaded Canada and fought the battle of Prescott's Windmill, Macdonald was roused from his bed at dawn, accepted the case, knowing it to be hopeless, refused any fee and escorted his client to the gallows.

The incident left an indelible mark on Macdonald, a fear of American power which lasted the rest of his life. It also left a mark on Kingston. The young man ready to defy public opinion in the interests of justice might be worth watching.

Kingston's Tories watched and, finding no better material, elected Macdonald to the Canadian Assembly. At first he was neither distinguished nor much interested in government business, though he soon learned to do six men's work with careless ease. Scoffing at detail, he nevertheless demolished mountains of paper, quickly acquired the lore of the political back room and became the ablest administrator of his time.

The Assembly afforded a good school for aspiring politicians. Equally divided between Upper and Lower Canada, it was usually in uproar or deadlock and thoroughly corrupted by jobbery and graft. These things were routine, expected and far less hypocritical than our modern politics where the higher crimes of bribery are committed under the law, the whole nation bribed quadrennially on the grand scale with its own money.

Macdonald assisted in the regular purchase of votes and constituencies, but he could not be bought. Poverty was the best proof of his honour; and his main complaint, as he wrote later, was that men well paid often failed to stay bought. Politics, however, came second to private life. His heart, his work and soon his anguish were all committed to his first love affair.

The cousin, Isabella Clark, whom he had met on a trip to Scotland and married in Kingston, could give him devotion but in the quick collapse of her health could not give him a home. For the next dozen years the harassed husband, by day a rising politician, sat by night at his wife's bedside when he should have been sitting in the Assembly, and watched her slowly die.

Even to himself he denied the inevitable end, carried Isabella to American health resorts, lived with her in the dingy boarding-houses of Toronto while the Assembly met there, neglected his law practice, overspent his income, found brief refuge in bouts of liquor and more than once decided to leave politics altogether.

The wife marvelously survived the birth of a son, giving the parents a few months of happiness. He died in infancy and left on the father a scar that would never heal. In his old age Macdonald still clung secretly to a box of the child's toys. A second son, Hugh John, brought another short reprieve. For Isabella death came as a merciful release, for Macdonald as the beginning of nine years' lonely widowerhood.

His private life, so far, had been all misery and despair to a man naturally domesticated, uxorious and deeply wounded under his outer show of cynical cheer. His public life and the experience of the Assembly seem trivial against his later achievements but laid their foundation.

The tawdry record of short-lived governments, crooked elections, cabals, treacheries and shifting combinations, in which Macdonald played by the rough rules of the game and with few scruples, produced final paralysis. It also produced the makings of Canada's first coherent political party. Macdonald was its maker.

His Liberal-Conservative Party might be a loose coalition of opposites, a marriage of convenience, a compromise of many conflicting principles held together mainly by patronage and hunger for office, but it had described the basic pattern of successful future parties, all of them coalitions, all internally at war.

Macdonald's coalition with George Etienne Cartier united the moderates of the two Canadian races, the English-speaking Protestants of Ontario and the French-Canadian Catholics of Quebec. It had isolated and enforced the only principle on which Canada could ever be governed. It had found the one durable base of power in a diverse country—the centre. And as soon as Brown, the Reform leader, joined it, in a mixture of loathing and patriotism, it had achieved Confederation.

Here another myth emerged and is still indestructible. Macdonald had not conceived the idea of Confederation. He had opposed it when Brown, Galt and others advocated it. He had failed especially to see the opportunities of the West when they saw them and he had written as late as 1865 that "the opening of the prairie lands would drain away our youth and strength. . . . I am perfectly willing personally to leave the whole country a wilderness for the next half century."

Nevertheless, the myth gives Macdonald credit for the invention of the Canadian State and perhaps he deserves it. Once persuaded that Confederation could be built, he alone had the ingenuity, influence and political expertise to build it. The Quebec Resolutions, the first draft of the British North America Act, were mostly devised in his mind and recorded in his handwriting. They represented the true title deeds to the supreme office.

No one disputed his possession, even before the Act became the constitution of the State. The choice of the first Prime Minister was made, in theory, by Queen Victoria but was actually the unquestionable choice of the Canadian people. Brown could not seriously quarrel with it. He could only resign from the coalition and plan to defeat Macdonald in the first election a few months later.

For some time anyway, Macdonald was politically invulnerable and his private affairs were marvelously improved. He had married his second wife, a family friend of his youth, immediately after their chance meeting on a London street. Susan Agnes Bernard was now a handsome, serene woman just short of middle age, and the ideal mate. The marriage had been hurried, the honeymoon in England lasting only two days, but Macdonald never regretted his choice.

Susan Agnes adored him, gave up wine to set him a good example, prayed morning and night for his soul and wondered in her diary whether she could ever be worthy of this paragon. At the end of the day she was waiting to drive him home in summer carriage or winter sleigh. She entertained his political friends at cozy little dinners in his ugly, comfortable house, "The Quadrilateral." If Parliament sat late she was waiting for him with a midnight snack. She mothered and raised his son, Hugh John, and hoped for a child of her own.

After those bitter, grinding years in mean lodgings beside his beloved invalid, the Prime Minister had his first home. The problems of government were intractable, his creditors pressed for money but he could lay aside his trouble as he stretched on a couch in the upstairs study and Susan Agnes read to him.

These moments of relaxation alone preserved his health from the depletion of work and the abuse of alcohol. With his wife and little boy he could forget the turmoil of Parliament Hill, a mile distant, drop his official papers, pick up a book or instantly fall into a nap. Thus pampered and pleasantly spoiled at home, the frail-looking man would live long.

His official family cared little for his health or comfort. Like the constitution, the Cabinet which he had finally assembled on the eve of the nation's birth was not the Cabinet he had wanted or even a Cabinet of the best men. Such counsels of perfection were negated by another law of his office.

No Cabinet, according to this law, could ever be anything more than an agglomeration of racial, religious, geographic and economic divisions as represented by their quarreling ambassadors under the transparent fiction of solidarity, that most useful of all myths inherited from Britain.

Every minister in the first, as in all subsequent Cabinets, spoke for a distinct interest, held a morsel of local power and drew on the Prime Minister's political bank account. If the minister brought real ability with him, so much the better; but it was by no means necessary and, indeed, quite exceptional.

The ceaseless warfare and polite hatreds of the Cabinet chamber, the shifting alliances and coalitions within the general coalition of the ruling party, did not surprise or alarm Macdonald. He had known nothing else for the last twenty years.

So it would continue to his last day. He must always live in adulation, betrayal, bad advice, excessive expectations and false alarms, knowing that the settlement of any problem in Cabinet would probably spawn at least two new problems equally grave.

Fortunately, under the ancient oaths of Cabinet secrecy, then as now, the organized quarrel known as a unanimous Cabinet could be kept from the eyes of the people or otherwise the democratic process would be shattered. The people must never know too much. They must never suspect that the major decisions of state were frequently taken at the eleventh hour in the most casual, *ad hoc* fashion, contradicting today everything said yesterday and invariably announced as the Cabinet's lifelong convictions.

The broad, equivocal statement to be interpreted either way, the decisive public stand hiding a void of indecision, the aura of certainty around the absence of ideas—these were, and are, only the day-to-day tools of the Cabinet maker's trade.

In making the first Cabinet Macdonald was baffled by the inadequate and refractory material at hand. The old lumber of Ontario and Quebec could not be glued to the new lumber of the Maritime provinces. Within two days of the July 1 deadline he had been at the point of desperation and retirement; but of course he could not retire, often as he talked of it. He must go on or the national experiment could not begin. After he had set it in motion, he told himself, he could hand it to younger men. That, as he must have known, was impossible. He must go on to the end.

"If I had my way," he said of his colleagues, "they would be highly respectable parties whom I could send to the penitentiary if I liked." Respectable or not, the colleagues available at the moment and later gave him no such choice. And adequate or not, the Cabinet was the supreme court by which the laws of the Prime Minister's office must be enforced.

In most affairs Macdonald (like a handful of successors) could have his own way and usually veto a majority since votes were seldom counted. He could sum up "the sense of the Cabinet" as he saw fit, with no questions asked. In great affairs, however, he must carry a majority; more than a majority, for he could not quarrel with certain colleagues even if they were a minority. Every ambassador of a sufficiently powerful area or interest held a personal veto. John C. Calhoun's Law of Concurrent Majorities applied, and still applies, more effectively to Canada than to the United States.

On the other hand, the Prime Minister possessed an ultimate veto and awful power denied to an American President. He could dissolve the legislature at will and by the threat of dissolution generally whip all except the strongest rebels into line. Few ministers would face a sudden election and the disruption of their party.

Given all these elements of strength and weakness, the first Macdonald Cabinet was essentially the great coalition which had created the Dominion, but with one profound change. Brown was not in "the concern," as he disdainfully styled it. To Macdonald, who detested him after their brief fair-weather friendship, their shipboard card games and their famous frolic with champagne and peashooters at the English Derby, Brown's absence was more welcome than his presence—yet far more dangerous.

Actually it was not as dangerous as it looked. The opposition leader, a red giant of flailing arms and torrential speech, could excite the passions of the mob. His integrity of soul, the virtue of his private life, the potent though narrow machinery of his mind, had made him Macdonald's only serious rival; but Brown's political touch was awkward, heavy and destructive. He could smash; he could not create. Like Meighen, he approached every negotiation with unanswerable logic and at the last moment broke it with his heavy hand. Besides, like Meighen, he had no luck.

Even without the embarrassment of Brown, the construction of a Liberal-Conservative Government was difficult, almost impossible, and gave Macdonald the worst hours he had ever known so far.

In the first place, he must pay a high price for the ambassadors of Ontario. The Reformers in the coalition, now calling themselves Liberals, demanded three portfolios, leaving only two for the faithful Conservatives, Macdonald's original friends. As the Prime Minister alone would be comparable in power to several colleagues, this arrangement was eminently fair in the opinion of the Liberal boss, William McDougall, who had earned the name of "Wandering Willy" by his erratic loyalties and would soon wander into an ultimate act of madness, dragging the Government with him. McDougall's price was paid.

Quebec belonged to Macdonald's almost equal partner and *alter ego*, Cartier. The two men had built the coalition together. They had been interdependent administrators in a series of pre-Confederation governments and their personal friendship was as strong as their public alliance.

Cartier's stiff pompadour, his brisk, Gallic face, pugnacious jaw and barking, staccato speech had become as familiar to Quebec as Macdonald was to Ontario. For the support of the country's second man, who assured the support of French Canada, Macdonald had long suffered in Ontario the charge of treachery to the English-speaking race and the Protestant religion, heaped upon him by Brown's furious invective.

This abuse must be borne, as it would be borne long afterwards by King and, in reverse, by Laurier. The Prime Minister was satisfied to let Brown "ride his Protestant horse," sure that it would end in the ditch. For Macdonald had learned—ironically enough, from the early Reformers, Baldwin and Lafontaine—the paramount law of Canadian politics which, if broken, must destroy any political leader. It was destroying Brown now and would destroy other hopeful statesmen later on.

Macdonald had phrased the law in his own version of 1856: "Treat them [the French Canadians] as a nation and they will act as a free people generally do. Call them a faction and they become factious."

So long as Cartier stood with him, Macdonald could enforce the law of equal partnership with French Canada. The absence of such a partner would be fatal to the experiment, in its first days anyway, and it was to prove fatal for Meighen, Bennett and Diefenbaker in our time. Unhappily Cartier would not be available for long. Death had marked him already.

Meanwhile his price of three French-Canadian portfolios was

reasonable. Nevertheless, it left an insoluble problem of arithmetic.

The English-speaking, Protestant minority of Quebec must have a minister—obviously Alexander Tilloch Galt, the apostate Rouge, now purged of his reforming Liberalism, whom Macdonald had lured into the coalition long ago. Galt was "as unstable as water," Macdonald said, but he had been the first advocate of Confederation, the maker of pre-Confederation tariffs and a competent minister of finance.

If Galt must have the same portfolio in the new Government, there was no room for the ambassador of the Irish Catholics, now too large a community to be unrepresented. Thomas D'Arcy McGee, the darling of all the Irish, the peerless orator of Confederation and Macdonald's old drinking companion, justly claimed the ambassadorship. Unfortunately there was no place for him in the Quebec delegation.

As July 1 approached, Macdonald saw that the jigsaw puzzle simply would not fit together.

The answer came at the eleventh hour from an unexpected quarter. Charles Tupper, a man of bulldog look and similar courage, who had led Nova Scotia into the union against the brilliant megalomania of Howe, withdrew his own undeniable claim in favour of Edward Kenny. This obscure Nova Scotian could represent his province, and the Irish Catholics elsewhere.

McGee withdrew also, in an act of generosity to be rewarded a few months later by the bullet of a Fenian assassin in an Ottawa street, where Macdonald knelt in tears over the body of his friend.

New Brunswick would naturally be represented by its veteran premier, Samuel Leonard Tilley, a compact little man with a bright, knowing face, who had pushed his province into the union after some costly but honourable intrigue. The jigsaw was complete.

So the first Cabinet came from the maker's work-bench, ostensibly representing on an equal basis all the vital divisions of the country. In fact, it was ruled by Macdonald, Cartier, Galt and Tilley. All subsequent Cabinets would be ruled by a similar inner group, some ministers being more equal than others.

Such as it was, Macdonald must live with this Cabinet, tolerating his colleague's mistakes, forgiving their sins as they forgave his, mending their quarrels and maintaining as best he could the fable of solidarity. That work had begun, under the worst of circumstances, on the day of Confederation.

Macdonald had been appalled when, without consulting him, the insensitive Monck announced that, on the Queen's instructions, the Prime Minister had been elevated to the Bath as a Knight Commander while Cartier, Galt, Tilley, Tupper, McDougall and W. P. Howland were to be only Companions. At this moment of dreadful silence, Cartier and Galt decided to refuse their second-class honours.

Macdonald knew that he must placate them with higher titles at the first opportunity but nothing could be done now. Despite this unseemly rebuff to the Queen and her Governor-General, the opening show of July 1 proceeded as planned, the public ignorant, as always, of events in the East Block.

The show was a splendid success yet it lacked an essential actor. Macdonald's gravest worry from the start was the absence of Howe who, unappeased and half mad with envy, was determined to take his private kingdom of Nova Scotia out of Confederation because other men had built it.

This extraordinary person—statesman, orator, editor, poet, duellist and minor genius—was in London denouncing "The Botheration Scheme" to the British Government, which would not listen, and to any street-corner acquaintance who would. Though a drinking man himself, as his coarsening but still potent features revealed, he was quoting Brown's editorials that condemned with moral fervour and cheap sarcasm the drunkenness of the Prime Minister.

Macdonald was used to these unspeakably low blows in the Toronto *Globe* and had long since written them off as the penalties of the game. The demonic tribune of Nova Scotia could not be written off. He must be brought in.

Knowing that a Prime Minister must seldom indulge the luxury of revenge, Macdonald sent Tupper, the bulldog, on the trail of Howe, the bear, and meditated another seduction. Howe in his present humour was impossible, "a pestilential fellow," but there was another side to him, a side of greatness. Properly handled, the man could be had.

All these men around the Prime Minister, while important to him, were only the levers by which he controlled a larger apparatus, the party.

Then as now, a party was not, as it claimed to be, a natural association of like-minded citizens promoting a common doctrine in the national interest. It was a rigidly disciplined state-within-the-state promoting itself. It had its unwritten, immutable laws, its rewards and punishments, its devils and its heroes, from the major oligarchs of Ottawa down to the petty oligarchs of the urban ward or the village saloon. It was also a church of sorts with its high priests and acolytes, whose creed was victory, sometimes tempered by assassination, whose worship was a dark Oriental mystery, whose deity was power.

For any party the ultimate objective must be power. Little men wanted power because it meant the loot of office. Big men like Macdonald and Brown wanted power for its own sake. They believed, quite sincerely, and so their successors believe today, that they could use power more competently than any rival, always for the nation's good.

Hence for a good party man, then as now, the right of the secret State to govern the public State was a right given by God. While He might err occasionally in transferring power to the wrong party, His error could be corrected at the next election. To which end the State-within-the-State was kept mobilized for instant assault or defence.

In Macdonald's time even the ruling Liberal-Conservative coalition was primitive and unreliable, the Liberal Opposition hardly yet a party at all. The "loose fish" of Parliament might cross party lines and vote the wrong way at any moment. Then as now, many men who regarded themselves as Conservatives were Liberals, many Liberals were more Conservative than Macdonald and others on both sides had no settled loyalties, much less convictions.

Party management has been much improved, or at any rate stabilized, in our time. A modern Prime Minister seldom has to count the friendly noses in Parliament. Macdonald never ceased to count them.

He kept three lists of Members on his desk—the dependable supporters, appropriately ticked off with a blue pencil, the certain enemies noted in red and, in between them, a third group of wavering men whom he flattered, wined and dined shamelessly in preparation for doubtful parliamentary divisions.

His management did not end there. More sedulously than any Prime Minister except King, he kept in direct touch with the local oligarchs in endless hand-written notes of encouragement, advice, warning and joke, realizing that the appointment of a postmaster, a customs clerk or a ferryman might be more important in the next election than some large public policy.

The high, abstract appeal of his personality had given him a public aura among independent voters; his low, concrete methods of organization had constructed a machine. But it was primarily a Macdonald, not a Conservative, machine and without him it was nothing, as his departure would eventually demonstrate.

Like all successful leaders of men he knew that the public could be safely given only a few simple ideas, most of them irrelevant. Lincoln's ideal, lately proclaimed in the trumpet call of Gettysburg, was for Macdonald and all his successors an ideal only. There might be government *for* the people; never of and by the people.

Brown's notion—as implicit in his long struggle for "Rep by Pop"—that a majority would always, or usually, be right had never appealed to Macdonald or any real Conservative and had been denied by all human experience. In opposition the Liberals worshipped the subliminal wisdom of the majority. They seldom relied on it in office. As much as they, Macdonald wanted a majority only because it meant power, not because it was sure to be right.

The Lincolnian ideal was physically impossible anyway in anything more than a small pastoral community, had been rejected by the American Republic's founders and was only a remote aspiration in Lincoln himself, the elected wartime dictator.

More by instinct than by conscious thought, Macdonald accepted Burke's contrary dictum to the electors of Bristol—that government must consult the people but in protecting their real interest must not be bound by their ignorant opinions. Macdonald wanted a party that could give him a majority because a majority was required to establish the only government likely, by its own decisions, to be more or less right—*his* government, of course.

Though he could not foresee it fully, government of, by and for the people would become less realistic as society became more complex and more unmanageable until, in our time, it is only a pious ritual when half a dozen men the world over can finger the buttons of humanity's destruction and an equal number in Canada control the national State.

Macdonald was quite aware that if party organization was essential to victory and power, elections were then, as now, mainly contests between two men, the Prime Minister and the leader of the Opposition—a human struggle, a gladiatorial combat, a sporting event which invariably dwarfed decisions of far greater importance.

Then, as now, the political process must be generally circular, a wheel revolving in perpetual paradox, a curve disguised as a straight line, most governments advancing stealthily when they

21

seemed to retreat or waving the banners of advance when they were in full flight. An expert, therefore, must usually read the signals in reverse. Happily for Prime Ministers, there are not many expert readers.

Macdonald's enemies were wrong, however, in saying that he had no principles. He was exactly what he called himself—a Liberal Conservative. His policies of national progress were more Liberal in practical affairs than those of the Liberal opposition. He was Conservative in his skepticism of human nature. Never trusting the people's wisdom completely, he often deceived them; but he loved them and a majority returned his love. A minority abominated him with a frenzy unknown today.

Whatever his private principles might be, Macdonald led the party of business. It represented especially the manufacturing interests of Toronto and Montreal and its policy was generally shaped to suit them. The Liberal Party also represented business, but mainly the exporting industries, and found its political base in the farm vote whose need was export markets.

On that rough division the Conservatives were bound to become the party of high tariffs, the Liberals of low. Both parties painted the issue of Protection versus Free Trade in black and white, when, of course, it could never be settled except in mixed and changing tones of grey.

The Conservatives were accepted and attacked as the party of the rich, respectable and privileged. The Liberals claimed to represent the underprivileged and exploited. In fact, both shared a right-wing economic conservatism and a strict financial orthodoxy, as judged by modern standards. The Liberal Party's conversion to King's boyish *Industry and Humanity* and the welfare state lay more than half a century ahead. The Conservative Party's attempt to outdo King in radical Liberalism must await the coming of Diefenbaker.

Macdonald's coalition had descended from the aristocratic Family Compact of Upper Canada and the Chateau Clique of Lower Canada. Long before Confederation, however, it had been moderated by middle-class leaders like him. Brown's Liberal Party of "Clear Grits" was the offspring of William Lyon Mackenzie's Rebellion, though most of its leaders had opposed it.

Both parties supported the British connection and the Empire, the Conservatives somewhat more ardently than the Liberals. The difference of emphasis between them was narrow but sufficient to

supply Macdonald with the vital ammunition of his uninterrupted
war and the telling argument at the final crisis of his life.

Unless they could be used for political purposes Macdonald
concerned himself little with these fine distinctions. He was not a
logician like Brown. He was much more an operator, a manager
and improviser than an original thinker. How could a Prime Minister be anything else? Office left scant time for philosophic reflection. The fundamental ideas of politics have always come from
obscure men far outside government and, pre-empted by the politicians, have been remodeled, smoothed and tamed to fit the
necessities of the time.

This intricate process of thought transference and intellectual
larceny, learned by Macdonald in his youth, made his own synthesis of other men's inventions difficult to follow. As early as
1860, for example, he had thus described himself in a rare feat of
double talk: "It is well known, sir, that while I have always been
a member of what is called the Conservative Party, I could never
have been called a Tory, although there is no man who more re-
spects what is called old-fogey Toryism than I do, so long as it is
based on principle."

That tortured circumlocution, based on anything but principle,
was designed to work both sides of the street and accurately defined him as a Liberal Conservative. He continued to move in
circles until his end but his purpose in government was as straight
as an arrow. He would do anything to preserve the new union.
And if possible he preferred to let his greatest decisions pass unnoticed, as they commonly do in Canadian politics, while the
public was agitated by something quite unimportant.

Against all his liabilities Macdonald possessed, in addition to
the priceless asset of his own reputation, some other assets denied
to his modern successors.

He presided over a unit of the imperishable British Empire
whose sun had not begun to set on palm or pine—a unit not yet
stabilized, certainly not recognized as the birthplace of a still larger
experiment, the modern Commonwealth, but meanwhile loyal to
Britain, strongly monarchial even in Quebec and safe under the
wing of its mother.

Whatever it was or would become, the Empire then possessed
regnant power not yet challenged by the American Republic. It
guaranteed Canada's protection. Above all, it was governed by the
Victorian law of inevitable human progress. The later repeal of

that law throughout the world would make the fundamental difference between Macdonald's age and ours.

Moreover, the Empire and Canada were guarded not only by British arms, money and progress but personally by God. He was still an active participant in imperial politics, *ex officio* a member of the Government in London, a fond patron of the Government in Ottawa. When human resources failed, a Canadian Prime Minister could appeal to Him in honest conviction and often did. God remained in His Heaven and all must be right with the world, at least the English-speaking world, possibly including the United States, though that was rather questionable.

Macdonald's task thus appeared simpler in some ways, as it was more complex in others, than that of any successor. For on the ultimate ends of Canadian society and the purposes of human life virtually all men agreed. Separation from Britain was unthinkable. Any alternative to capitalism and the iron laws of the free market was a heresy for a few fatuous dreamers who had no power in society. The work of Darwin had not yet invaded religion and few Canadians had heard the name of Karl Marx. That the future of the Empire and of capitalism and even the existence of mankind would become precarious within eighty years had occurred to no living Canadian.

All the moral assumptions of the day entered, consciously or unconsciously, into Macdonald's plans. The practical assumptions were still more comforting.

He now led the only organized party in the business. The Liberals had been fatally split when some of their leaders joined the Government and received their recent excommunication from Brown, with Protestant bell, book and candle. Apparently the Opposition had been split again by Brown's attempt to rebuild it in his own mighty image. Moreover, while he did not know it then, Brown already was near the end of his political career and would soon abandon it, after long bachelorhood, for the arms of a Scottish lass, the world well lost.

Lately the chiseled and handsome face of Brown's political heir had appeared but Macdonald did not recognize the laborious stonemason's talents of his new rival. Alexander Mackenzie seemed to offer no threat in 1867. His following was hardly more than a congeries of wrangling sects and gibbering conventicles, all arguing about the number of angels who could dance on the needle point of a doctrinaire Liberalism.

No such schoolmen's logic restricted Macdonald's freedom of

manoeuvre. He had plenty of elbow room. Any man who would support the coalition was welcome whether he agreed with it or not. As Macdonald wrote in a famous letter, he wanted men who would back him not only if he was right but if he was wrong. Then he added wistfully: "Send me better men to deal with and I will be a better man." And again: "We are all merely petty provincial politicians at present. Perhaps bye and bye some of us will rise to the level of national statesmen."

That must wait. At the moment he had mastered the old party but he had not mastered the new nation. The Dominion's first election was only a few weeks off.

2: The Heights and The Depths

In the first national election, which stretched through the late summer of 1867, Macdonald did not extend himself. The result was guaranteed in advance. His personal power, the power of his party, the general opinion in favour of Confederation, above all, the chaos of the Opposition, easily swept the Government back to office. It won a handsome majority in Ontario and Quebec and a narrow margin in New Brunswick. But in Nova Scotia the anti-Confederationists, led by Howe, carried every seat except that of the indestructible Tupper.

"The great reason why I have always been able to beat Brown," Macdonald had once written, "is that I have been able to look a little ahead while he could on no occasion forgo the temptation of a temporary triumph." The victor was looking ahead now, though not as shrewdly as he supposed. Across the central aisle of the first House of Commons the prospect, except for one clear and present danger, seemed almost too good to be true.

Best of all, Brown was not there. He had been defeated at the polls, had summoned his elected followers for a council of war in Toronto and then promptly deserted them to enjoy a holiday with his wife in Scotland, leaving his party divided and leaderless. He would never seek election again.

Without Brown the Liberals were not even ready to choose a new leader. For reasons not explained by the Prime Minister, his namesake, old enemy and recent friend, John Sandfield Macdonald, was recognized as official opposition leader; but this once powerful personage, his influence exhausted, could no longer be a menace to anyone. The unled Liberals, as Macdonald thought, were in no better case. That comfortable judgment was wrong already and later would prove disastrous. In his present mood of hubris the Prime Minister failed to see his nemesis in the unlikely figure of Alexander Mackenzie.

For the moment that man of the future appeared awkward in his formal clothes, overawed and silent. Mackenzie had always been underestimated. He was Macdonald's fatal mistake. Yet the mistake was natural enough. No one imagined that the stonemason and building contractor from Sarnia could become Canada's second Prime Minister, the only opponent able to defeat the first.

Mackenzie's long, angular face with its naked upper lip and massive, reddish beard, looked stern, impassive and humourless—a dry, small, literal-minded man, as Macdonald thought. A closer glance might penetrate the blue, metallic eyes and detect the raging fire behind them. The story of Mackenzie's life, if anyone had bothered to study it, would have revealed a curious parallel to Macdonald's private grief and a similar streak of romanticism, always well hidden.

Even less imposing than Mackenzie was the new arrival at his side. Edward Blake, in his middle thirties, already had been judged the ablest legal mind of Canada; but his round, chubby, boy's face, his absurd little spectacles and his squat, ungainly figure, lacked any presence. Blake, as Macdonald assumed, was not cut out for politics.

That assumption would prove correct in the end. In the immediate future, however, Blake, not Mackenzie or Brown, was the most dangerous opponent that Macdonald had yet encountered. The man of intuitions had met the man of facts. As always, intuition must defeat fact; but a long, doubtful contest between them was only beginning.

To Macdonald, warily eyeing the Opposition with an outward show of languor and boredom, the real threat was Howe. The rough, bulbous face of that arch-enemy, the hotspring of invective, the jealousy and the regret of a man who had begun to see that he was wrong, suggested formidable dangers. Howe had come to Parliament only in the hope of disrupting it—a vain hope, as it was to turn out, but Macdonald could not be sure of that.

The secession of Nova Scotia, if Howe and his little band of anti-Confederationists could manage it, must break the union. Still, there was greatness in Howe and a giant's generosity, if it could be reached. For the present, Macdonald must listen patiently to his threats, though they were almost treasonable, and wait for the chance to annihilate or embrace him. Either method would do.

Like so many of his successors, Macdonald had completely misjudged the centre of his public troubles. They seemed to lie in Nova Scotia when actually they lay far off on the western Prairies and the Pacific coast where everything, quite unnoticed, was starting to go wrong.

Something had gone wrong in Ottawa, too. Cartier, still brooding over the inferior title offered to him by the Queen and indignantly refused, had opened a nasty little intrigue with Brown who at first encouraged it. The only purpose could be to unload Macdonald. These negotiations came to nothing, after an exchange of friendly letters, because Brown would not enter Parliament as Cartier's ally and Mackenzie distrusted both the cabal and the Conservatives.

All the same, this curious incident, known to few at the time and possibly unknown to Macdonald, exposed an erratic streak in Cartier which, before long, would assure much more serious mischief. A constant occupational hazard of the Prime Minister's office was also exposed. No man who holds it can be immune to Cabinet treachery. And now a final blow was about to fall on Macdonald's home.

Ignorant of it, he went about his public business systematically. The old cat, as Brown called him, was always on the prowl for game. Within two years Macdonald had embraced Howe at a well-staged meeting in Halifax after Tupper had skilfully tamed the Nova Scotian bear. With Howe in the Cabinet as President of the Council, and now opening the last struggle of his life to undo his work of disruption among his own people, Macdonald could be sure of Nova Scotia.

In early 1869 his mind was elsewhere. The baby girl borne by his wife in a prolonged agony just short of death appeared normal at first but then a frightening deterioration began. For some months the parents could persuade themselves that the child's strange looks and misshapen head would change. As they were soon compelled to realize, Mary's feeble-mindedness was incurable. For the rest of their lives the father and mother must treat her, even in middle age, as a physical and mental infant.

There could be no relief from Macdonald's latest heartbreak but he learned to live with it by throwing himself more and more into politics or seeking the anodyne of drink. In the record of Canadian Prime Ministers, often publicly tragic, perhaps nothing is so moving as the private picture of a man who bestrode the nation and came home at night to read nursery rhymes to a woman who remained in childhood. Without the courage and religious serenity of his wife, the burden would have been insupportable. Together they could carry it to the end by pretending that Mary was indeed a child.

While wooing Howe on the Atlantic coast, Macdonald had suddenly discovered an equally valuable and even more eccentric ally on the Pacific. Amor de Cosmos—a Canadian, born plain Smith but transformed into the Lover of the World by Act of the California legislature—had some of Howe's qualities and all of his egotism. Anyway, lacking better, he would serve. The tall figure and rather ascetic, bearded face were well known in the squabbling Assembly of British Columbia at Victoria. The Bird Cages there, as the local residents called their tiny wooden legislative buildings, had long echoed to de Cosmos' orations. His editorials in *The Colonist* were regarded by the dying Hudson's Bay hierarchy as sheer treason.

De Cosmos, in fact, was fighting on the other side of Canada Howe's old battle for self-government and, unlike Howe, he had grasped the meaning of Confederation from the start. Such a man, though erratic, brilliant, great-hearted and mean by turns, could be cultivated.

The first step, as Macdonald wrote to London, was to "put the screws" on British Columbia through a governor who knew his business. Accordingly, Anthony Musgrave arrived at Victoria and, even lying in bed with a broken leg, put the screws on so effectively that soon the dubious legislators, after inclining toward a more natural union with the adjacent American States, reversed themselves and sent a delegation to Ottawa.

To be sure, as a prominent anti-Confederationist protested to de Cosmos, British Columbians joining the Canadian union would fall under the rule of Canadian "politicians" in place of British "statesmen." Even the rule of an American Congress was better than that. More profitable, too, for the Pacific settlement of genteel poverty. But the continental axis of Macdonald and de Cosmos proved irresistible when the Canadian Government dangled a shining prize before the British Columbia delegates.

As finally negotiated, the price offered for the region west of the Rockies was incomparably higher than the price for Nova Scotia or any other territory—nothing less than the largest economic gamble ever undertaken in North America.

Macdonald, the man who had always doubted the value and distrusted the drain of the West, agreed to begin building within two years, and complete within ten, a railway from Ontario to the

Pacific Coast, though the colonists there had expected, at best, a wagon road. That promise ended all talk of annexation to the United States. The British Columbians, entranced by a railway when railways were guaranteed to cure all human ills and usher in the golden age of mankind, instantly accepted Macdonald's offer and prepared to join Confederation in July, 1871.

The Canadian Pacific Railway prospectus, impossible of fulfilment on its existing terms, contained an invisible clause guaranteeing Macdonald's ruin. Even if he could have read this clause perhaps he would have signed nevertheless, since he was now convinced that without British Columbia the new nation must fall, whole or by pieces, into the welcoming jaws of the republic beside it. For a transcontinental State, the only viable State, any price must be paid, even ruin.

At the moment, however, the peaceful deal with British Columbia was dwarfed by an event which looked very like war on the prairies. There Macdonald continued to misunderstand and botch everything.

Possibly if he had witnessed an obscure event near Fort Garry, on October 11, 1869, he would have recognized an enemy more dangerous than Mackenzie, Blake or any man in politics—an enemy in life and, long afterwards, in death, the posthumous wrecker of the Liberal Conservative Party. Louis Riel had stamped his moccasin on a surveyor's measuring chain and launched his queer epic.

Here, on the banks of the Red River, another law of the supreme office appeared—the best-laid plans of mice and Prime Ministers can be smashed by the humblest agents. In threatening the lands of Riel and his Métis people, Macdonald's agents unwittingly had threatened to smash the new Canadian State.

Of all Macdonald's enemies Riel was the strangest—a man of only twenty-four years, strikingly handsome with his olive skin, curly hair, drooping moustache and dark, hypnotic eyes, a man well educated in Quebec, but given to visions and frantic eloquence, driven by a mad dream, born for judicial murder on the gallows.

Of all the follies in Macdonald's life his treatment of Riel and the Métis was the least excusable. If only he had applied to Red River the lofty dictum which had served him so well in Quebec, if only he had seen in the Métis settlers a nation to be treated generously, not a faction to be coerced and made factious, the double calamity of the West might have been averted. It was too late now. Macdonald had decided that the Métis were only "miserable halfbreeds," requiring coercion.

30

He himself had planted the seeds of the first Riel Rebellion, so-called, by failing, when he bought the Prairies from the Hudson's Bay Company for $1,500,000, to assure the inhabitants that their property would be safe in Canada. Riel and fifteen armed horsemen drove the government survey party from the banks of the Red River because a distant, alien state apparently intended to seize their little farms; but they were not rebelling against Canadian authority. Canada had yet to take legal possession of the West. At this juncture no government existed between the Lakes and the Rockies. The Métis had stepped into a constitutional void.

All they wanted was their land, the free way of life built here by their fathers of mixed Indian, French-Canadian and Scottish blood; but, quite unintentionally, they had endangered the keystone of Macdonald's transcontinental arch. At last he grasped the fact that Riel might remove the keystone.

Of course the Métis could be quickly crushed. Some thirty thousand of these people must be helpless alone against Canadian power, but they were not alone. Macdonald's intelligence reports, delayed and fragmentary, told him that the Americans just south of the border saw in Riel their long-sought quisling. If he requested their intervention the United States might thrust its power northward in the virtuous rescue of an oppressed minority. Without much exertion, even without much criticism, Manifest Destiny would split the arch and flow to its natural boundary on the Arctic.

Macdonald saw that danger late but he saw it clearly in the news from Red River. The Americans, he wrote in sudden alarm, "are resolved to do all they can short of war to get possession of the western territory and we must take immediate and vigorous steps to counteract them."

What steps? Every step taken from then on led straight to debacle. Throughout that winter the news, as it moved slowly to Ottawa over the snowbound Canadian trails and the American telegraph lines, was beyond belief.

Riel and his horsemen had seized Fort Garry without firing a shot. Now, in boiled white shirt, tail coat, black trousers and beaded moccasins, the young Métis prophet was presiding over a provisional government. More disturbing, he was supported by an American fifth column whose spy and general manager, Enos Stutsman, though born without legs, galloped back and forth across the border on horseback, hopefully fomenting his country's intervention.

Macdonald's first vigorous step was to unload an inconvenient Cabinet colleague and send McDougall west as Governor of Rupert's

Land. "Wandering Willy," that man of impenetrable stupidity, wandered northward from St. Paul, his baggage in sixty wagons. At the Canadian border he was politely turned back by a band of silent Métis horsemen.

Still Riel had committed no crime. He considered himself a loyal subject of the Queen in part of her territory which had no government but his. That much Macdonald understood from the delayed telegrams. McDougall, cooped up in a log cabin at Pembina, understood nothing, consulted nobody and meditated a supreme idiocy.

Macdonald read the latest telegram with disbelief but it was true. McDougall had perceived his duty to the Queen, had written a royal proclamation, forged her name to it and driven across the border in a night of howling blizzard. While his companions held a tiny Union Jack in the wind and warmed themselves with neat whisky, he had read his proclamation, declared himself the legal Governor of Red River and retreated, half-frozen, to Pembina.

His farce, quickly reported by a chortling American press, was too much for Macdonald. He halted the purchase of Rupert's Land and fired Wandering Willy.

"Immediate and vigorous steps." The promise was only a bluff now and Macdonald knew it. He could not quickly suppress Riel, as he had assumed. No armed force could reach Red River until summer opened the overland Canadian trail. The "miserable half-breed" had defeated the Prime Minister.

Since Riel could not be coerced, he must be appeased. Macdonald sent his old friend, Donald Smith, to Red River, where that wily Hudson's Bay trader harangued the Métis for two days in the icy open air and persuaded them to negotiate with the Canadian Government.

The Government of Canada had thus given *de facto* recognition to the government of Riel. It was humiliating but better than a military adventure which might involve the United States. If the thing ended in a deal with the Métis delegates it would be worth the cost of humiliation. Riel refused to let it end there.

In a clash between the Métis and the loyal Canadians of Red River, Riel's horsemen had captured a blustering, loose-tongued fellow named Thomas Scott. The prisoner leaped upon Riel in the Fort Garry jail and tried to throttle him. This momentary scuffle was the flash-point long feared by Macdonald. The taut mind of Riel snapped. Scott was court-martialed and shot by a firing-squad. He had become the inevitable martyr and, from Macdonald's point of view, the worst possible martyr—a citizen of Ontario, a Protestant and an Orangeman murdered by a half-breed Papist.

Ontario's fury and the Liberal party's thirst for revenge produced a political fact that Macdonald, the master politician, instantly comprehended. It was counterbalanced, as usual, by another. Quebec instinctively supported the French-Canadian and Catholic Métis. The ancient racial clash had drawn blood again; not much, and that under strong provocation, but enough to revive the classic tension and expose the Achilles' heel of Canada.

A half-breed lunatic strutting across an empty empire much larger than most civilized states, a legless horseman riding on his mysterious American missions, a Canadian Governor forging his Queen's name, a Protestant martyr dead in the snow of a remote jail yard—it was enough to drive any Prime Minister to distraction. It drove Macdonald to drink.

He was drunk in his office. He was seen reeling to the bar of the Russell House. Then he disappeared altogether, as the Governor-General informed the British Government in a secret dispatch. Lady Macdonald, witnessing for the first time the depth of her husband's weakness, wrote her despair in her diary, but she stood by him.

So did the Government, since it had no one to take his place. As always, Macdonald soon pulled himself together and made his decision. Once spring opened the trail, an army would march overland to conquer Red River.

Riel had won just the same. His delegates, at first arrested by the Ontario police and hurriedly released on Ottawa's orders, arrived in Ottawa to lay down their own terms. Red River was to enter Confederation as the sovereign province of Manitoba. That name, as they proudly explained, meant in their mixed tongue "The God that speaks." Anyway, the West had spoken. The Métis had got what they wanted.

When Macdonald's army of twelve thousand men wallowed next summer across the continental portage and through the Red River mud, Riel watched from Fort Garry. As the soldiers approached, he crossed the Assiniboine on a raft to begin his exile of fifteen years in the United States.

He was still dangerous. Dangerous enough, at least, to refuse the Canadian Government's inadequate bribe of a thousand dollars if he would remain in exile. For an extra sum of six hundred pounds, provided from the treasury of the Hudson's Bay Company, Riel promised to make no more trouble.

Where was the rebel? Macdonald could only say that he wished to God he knew. Of course he knew. Riel had been elected to Parliament *in absentia,* had turned up in Ottawa and, with the connivance of his French-Canadian sympathizers, had signed the members' roll of the House of Commons. He had disappeared again but often lived in Canada and never lost touch with his race.

It was tantalizing for Macdonald to realize that he had stumbled clumsily into Canada's racial and religious dichotomy out West after managing it so well in the East. Still, the Red River bungle had passed off with remarkably little damage after all. American intervention had been avoided, thanks mainly to Riel, who had refused to invite it. Macdonald had soothed Ontario by denouncing a rebellion and exiling the rebel. Happily for the Government's position in Quebec, the rebel had departed in safety. For the present he was not a martyr but a phantom—for the present only.

Having pushed through Parliament an act establishing the Province of Manitoba almost precisely as Riel had desired, Macdonald persuaded the country and perhaps even himself that a defeat had been a victory, as it was for common sense. But these months of worry and alcohol had drained his energies. As he sat alone one day assessing his prospects, nature punished him. In a sudden convulsion of pain he fell, writhing, to the floor.

The doctors improvised a hospital in his office, diagnosed his illness as gallstones, expected him to die within hours and published daily bulletins to a grieving public. The patient surprised everybody by slowly recovering under the care of his wife until he could be carried on a stretcher to the train. After a summer of seaside convalescence at Charlottetown, while Cartier conducted the government, the Prime Minister seemed as healthy as ever.

That was fortunate for Canada. All his resources of body and mind were required for a desperate trial of strength in Washington.

When Britain and the United States met to settle the Alabama Claims and other residual disputes of the American Civil War, Macdonald appeared, rather ambiguously, as a member of the British delegation. Canada had no control of its foreign policy but the presence of the Canadian Prime Minister at the Washington conference entered a narrow wedge into the vital substance of the Empire. Once a Canadian had been admitted to the councils of the world's great powers, even by the back door, the Empire could never be the same again. Year by year the wedge must be driven deeper until Canada managed all its external affairs and the Commonwealth replaced the Empire.

Macdonald had begun to foresee all this, though vaguely. Already he knew for certain that the great powers intended to settle their conflicts at the expense of Canada. He could expect no sympathy from the United States and doubtless would be double-crossed by Britain. It was no time, however, to disclose his long thoughts. The British delegation would not understand them anyway.

It was composed of over-washed Englishmen full of crotchets and headed by Earl de Grey and Ripon, who concealed the depths of his duplicity under a noble aristocratic air and a bristling square beard. To him Canada was a minor appendage of the Empire and must be controlled from London for its own good, while Macdonald was a total enigma.

The British delegates had expected to meet a roistering caucus boss and backwoods rustic, knighted for necessary imperial reasons. Instead, they found a quiet, sober and firm negotiator, inconveniently intelligent. Certainly intelligence would count for little in a naked confrontation of power but how to deal with this curious man from Ottawa, so disarming, so illusive and so stubborn?

De Grey thought he knew. Macdonald must be bullied to start with, then deceived and finally bribed by the offer of a British Privy Councillorship.

The Americans understood Macdonald and Canada no better. Washington's perennial lunatic fringe was still howling for possession of the peculiar new Dominion which seemed to mock the divine logic of Manifest Destiny. President Grant had lately arraigned Canada as "this semi-independent but irresponsible agent" exercising "its delegated powers in an unfriendly way," while Senator Zachariah Chandler had "put on file a mortgage on the British North American provinces."

This bluster no longer worried Macdonald. He had just seen the last Fenian raid end in comedy south of Red River where Riel, the exile, had rallied with his Métis horsemen to support Manitoba's new Governor. No, the Canadian arch was safe from outright American interference. Its future perils were more subtle—and permanent.

Since its earliest days as a French colony, Canada had been a powerless bargaining counter in the power politics of Europe and America. So it was now. So it would remain. Macdonald had been caught in the old transatlantic vise.

Charged with responsibility but denied power, he must resist pressure from both sides, American and British, but he must try to reconcile them, at almost any cost to Canada and himself. For any serious quarrel between Britain and the United States would rend the Canadian nation. The two psychic heart-tugs, of British history and sentiment on one side, and North American geography on the other, must always keep the Canadian subconscious divided and continue as the major conscious preoccupation of all Prime Ministers.

Though the great powers would gradually learn to understand and treat Canada better, every Prime Minister to our time must occupy essentially Macdonald's position, wrestling with essentially the same forces, whether in the guise of codfish or of nuclear bombs.

As the latest transatlantic poker game opened at Washington, Macdonald held only one high card. Canada owned the rich fisheries off the Maritime coast from which it had recently excluded American fishermen and seized four hundred of their vessels. Free access to the fisheries was far more important to the Americans than the Alabama Claims against Britain or certain disputed islands off the Pacific coast.

With that single card, played at the right moment, Macdonald might save something at Washington. He would be satisfied to trade the fisheries for a revival of the reciprocity agreement angrily canceled by the United States during the Civil War. In the end, however, his single economic ace could be beaten by the cards of military power in the hands of two great players. Canada must survive beside the United States and, having no defences of its own, must have Britain's support.

Neither Britain nor the United States knew, at first, that Macdonald's position was even weaker than it looked. The delegates of the great powers were backed by solid governments and manageable legislatures. Macdonald's Cabinet was split between impractical men who were ready to defy Britain and timid men ready to surrender, while Brown was thundering again in his *Globe* against any sacrifice of Canadian interests.

The British soon learned the truth through their own chief spy at Ottawa. Lord Lisgar, the Governor-General, saw all Macdonald's secret dispatches to his colleagues and sent them on to London. Macdonald never saw the dispatches from the British delegation in Washington. The double-cross of Canada was conducted with impeccable manners, cold cynicism and that ponderous air of morality which distinguished the new London Government.

For Gladstone, the British Prime Minister, a higher morality justified this disagreeable business. Somehow he had to make permanent peace with the United States, now that it had emerged from its Civil War as a great power in its own right. After his own admitted mistake "of incredible grossness" in backing the South, he was determined to end the earlier civil war in the English-speaking family and liquidate the last liabilities of the American Revolution.

That necessity must override, then as now, the immediate concerns of Canada.

Foreseeing the outcome, and harassed by contractory advice from his wavering Cabinet, Macdonald masked his heart-sickness under a patient, cheerful mien at the conference table and his homely charm at the endless round of banquets and parties. He got around. Washington was soon snickering over his contretemps with an American senator's wife who, failing to catch his name, had told him that "a perfect rascal" governed Canada; and he had solemnly agreed until the lady learned, to her horror, that she was talking to the rascal in person.

Such incidents of comic relief were rare. By this time Macdonald had become thoroughly disgusted with the London Government and his own. He thought of resigning from the British delegation but that would probably worsen the terms of the ultimate settlement. He must stay and save what he could from the wreckage.

The Americans, who had hinted that they would buy the fisheries by reviving reciprocity, now rejected it and even refused to consider Canada's fair claim for damages on account of the Fenian raids. Very well then, if he could not have reciprocity, Macdonald would have the opposite, protective tariffs; but he said nothing about them now. His complete reversal and the first intimations of the National Policy, already crystallizing in his mind, must wait until his Government had been safely re-elected on a different policy.

As the spring days of deadlock on the Potomac stretched into weeks and months, Macdonald prepared to play his ace. If it could not be played against the United States he would play it against Britain. The Americans could have the fisheries provided Britain would compensate Canada for them.

He had chosen the psychological moment. The British were tired and baffled by his stubbornness, they accused him of "treachery" in their dispatches but they could not budge him. Exhausted at last, de Grey dropped a momentous hint—Britain instead of the United States might pay the Fenian claims. Macdonald leaped at the chance and forced a definite commitment from London.

Thus the Washington deal was made. American fishermen were to be admitted to Canadian waters for ten years. The cash value of this concession was to be arbitrated along with the Alabama Claims, and the western international boundary through Georgia Strait, where, as usual, Canada's claims would be rejected. The Americans were to have free use of the St. Lawrence, and Canada the same rights on three remote Alaskan rivers.

37

"There go the fisheries," Macdonald whispered when he signed the agreement. He had refused to sign it as a representative of Canada and signed only as a British commissioner. That gesture might help him a little at home but the fisheries were gone. So were his last illusions about over-washed Englishmen.

Even then the argument was not settled. London tried to welsh on the Fenian payment. Macdonald, attacked by the Liberals for surrendering the fisheries, dared not submit the Washington agreement to Parliament until the payment was guaranteed. Finally the Gladstone Government came around and, after half a year's wrangle, grudgingly underwrote loans of £2,500,000 for the construction of Canadian railways and canals when money was badly needed for the Intercolonial line to the Maritimes.

These advances blunted the Liberal attack on the Washington deal. The British-minded Conservatives were persuaded that Canada owed a sacrifice to Motherland and Empire. Macdonald rammed the treaty through Parliament just in time. A second national election must now be faced.

Preparing for it, Macdonald could look back on five years of work without parallel in later Canadian history, with few parallels in any nation. He had launched Confederation, pacified the rebels in Nova Scotia, assured Prince Edward Island's early adherence to the union, possessed the Prairies and the Pacific Coast, escaped from his blunder at Red River and laid the cornerstone of an independent Canadian foreign policy in the future. The nation which had been a document in 1867 was now a going concern from coast to coast, administered by a permanent political party. The Prime Minister's office had overtopped the constitution to become the central organ of the State.

Those massive achievements had exhausted their maker. Again he thought of resigning. It was no use. The concern might collapse without its manager. No one else could hope to lead the party. Another election must be got through somehow. Then, perhaps, retirement and release.

"There is some work left in me yet," he wrote to a friend, "before I make my final bow to the Canadian audience." Yes, nineteen years' more work, among them five of odium and disgrace. Mercifully unaware of these prospects, Macdonald plunged into the election with more than his usual cunning and too much liquor.

As he knew, the second election would not be as easy as the first. He had the assets of his personal power, a reliable party machine and a Cabinet which, with some stretch of the imagination, could be called Liberal-Conservative. Cartier was still with him to guarantee the Conservative vote of Quebec, and Howe, the reformed Reformer, could deliver Nova Scotia.

Lately Macdonald had captured another old-time Reformer of doubtful reputation and high talents. Francis Hincks, called "the Hyena" for his rapacity and his brutal style of debate, was home after long absence in the British foreign service, his lifelong feud with Macdonald and his pre-Confederation plunder forgotten. He had hardly landed at Montreal before he found himself in the Cabinet as Minister of Finance. With an election pending, a Prime Minister could not afford to be fussy.

Against all his assets Macdonald must reckon his liabilities and they were daunting.

The Conservative machine in Ontario was rusty and, like its creator, was broke. Besides, the Ontario Protestants were still angry at Scott's murder by a Catholic rebel. The farmers were alarmed by the final collapse of reciprocity. Everyone disliked the Washington deal. In Quebec the Catholics resented Riel's banishment.

Much more serious was the latest word from Cartier's doctors. Macdonald knew now that he must soon lose his oldest partner without whom the Quebec machine might disintegrate. Morever, the Liberal Opposition was organized for the first time under its new leader, Mackenzie, and its brain, Blake.

Macdonald began to repair his party by quiet overtures to the Ontario clergy and the offer of patronage to their flock. He seized a lucky chance to steal the working-man's vote from the Liberals by promising to legalize labour unions when Brown, by a fortunate coincidence, was fighting a printers' strike at the *Globe*. In sudden transformation the Tories had become the workers' only true friend and Macdonald was declaring himself, at a mass meeting in Toronto, a worker, too, "a cabinet maker" by trade, while his wife was presented with a jeweled casket in token of labour's appreciation.

These repairs could not win the election. Something else was needed to restore the Government's lost magic—a new doctrine, a new climate and a new hope.

All of them could have been created overnight if Macdonald had dared to announce his real policy of protective tariffs, as meditated at Washington, but it was too early for that. Only a few months ago he had been seeking a new reciprocity agreement with the United States. His private reversal could not be announced yet, openly at any rate. It must be insinuated into the public mind by masterly equivocation.

For the benefit of the farmers Macdonald preached the need of international trade, but he sympathized with the manufacturing industries and their workers in their fear of foreign competition.

His instructions to Conservative candidates and newspapers were devious but explicit: "The word 'protection' must be taboo but we can ring the changes on National Policy, paying the U.S. in their own coin."

The National Policy, core of the Conservative doctrine for the next ninety years, had entered the political lexicon but gently, unobtrusively, almost unnoticed by the voters. Even the word "Conservative," as Macdonald advised his newspaper friends, should be kept in the background until the polls closed. He preferred the semantically safer name of "Union Party."

Meanwhile any heckler who guessed the truth about protection was fobbed off with the assurance that tariffs for the manufacturers would be quite "incidental." The manufacturers, on the other hand, were told to wait patiently and they would get what they needed.

The double talk of the tariff debate, perpetual *leit motif* of Canadian politics, had begun and has continued into our time. No one (except, perhaps, King and Diefenbaker) could straddle the issue as nimbly as Macdonald, while poor Mackenzie spoke out honestly for free trade and antagonized at least half the electorate.

Macdonald's real difficulty in 1872 was not the party machine, not the tariff issue, not even the unfriendly political climate in the wake of the Washington deal, but the Pacific railway. That problem obsessed him day and night and soon appeared insoluble.

With Old Tomorrow, time had always seemed to be a friend. Now it became an enemy. Within six weeks of polling day he had no plan for the construction of the railway, no money to finance the election campaign and no physical strength to fight it.

The Canadian Pacific Railway Company, organized by Sir Hugh Allan, the respected shipping magnate of Montreal, was ready to undertake the largest engineering project in North American history but it was backed, perhaps secretly controlled, by American capital. Macdonald refused to sign Allan's contract unless his foreign backers were eliminated. Otherwise they might control the Canadian economy in the long run and, in the short, the Government would probably lose the election. Allan accepted those terms and immediately betrayed Macdonald by keeping his American partners, but well in the background.

There was another complication. David L. Macpherson, one of Macdonald's oldest cronies, had organized the Interoceanic Railway

Company in Toronto and demanded the Pacific contract. Having collected $67,000 to pay off Macdonald's private debts, Macpherson had an unanswerable claim on his friendship. Besides, Toronto business interests must participate in any railway syndicate if the Government was to hold its Ontario seats.

Obviously, then, Allan and Macpherson should amalgamate. Now began a domestic negotiation far more difficult than the foreign negotiations of Washington. Day after day, week after week, Macdonald tried to reconcile the Montreal and Toronto magnates by blandishment, argument and threat. He failed. Allan would amalgamate, provided that he and his hidden American partners dominated the joint company. Macpherson would do anything else for Macdonald but he would not accept Allan's control.

The election only a few days off, Cartier mortally ill and already under Allan's thumb, the railway contract unsigned, Macdonald's own seat of Kingston in doubt—was this fiasco to be the fruit of his five triumphant years?

The actor's settled pose of cheerfulness broke under the strain. At a dreadful moment in Kingston he lunged across the election platform and grappled with his Liberal opponent. The spectators saw only an angry man whom they knew and could forgive. They did not see the telegrams from Montreal with their mixture of blackmail and bait.

Allan said he must control the railway if he was to elect Cartier and the Quebec Conservatives, but the friends of the Government everywhere would be assisted with funds in the pending elections. Macdonald could resist the blackmail. He could not resist the bait.

Money he must have, and within hours, to match the Liberals' apparently unlimited resources—at least sixty thousand dollars for a start. The first instalment of that sum arrived from Allan one day before the Kingston poll of August 1. It was immediately spent there and in other seats. Altogether more than $350,000 was spent in Ontario and Quebec.

Macdonald had lost all count of it by now. He was staggering through the election, eyes glazed, grin fixed, like a somnambulist in a nightmare of speeches, conferences, telegrams and drink.

Still he rejected Allan's terms but he needed Allan's help. Drunk, sick, incoherent, he scribbled a final telegram to Montreal: "I must have another ten thousand. Will be the last time of calling. Do not fail me. Answer today."

It was an act of madness to put such a message on the wires but the money arrived in time. Macdonald spent it without scruple. Yet

41

he was sufficiently coherent to feel a gnawing doubt. True, all that Allan had been guaranteed was the presidency of the railway, not its control, and only if the Americans were eliminated. The bargain was quite honest but who would believe that? If the facts of the campaign funds leaked out everyone would say that Allan had bought the Government. Such was his own assumption.

Despite the stupefaction of these last days, Macdonald saw the possibility of trouble but he thrust it aside. The electoral sleep-walk must go on to its end.

It ended in a victory for the Conservatives, a Pyrrhic victory. They had won a minority of the Ontario seats and a bare majority in Quebec. Even Cartier, with all Allan's money behind him, Cartier the invulnerable, had been defeated in Montreal. The Government survived only on its support from British Columbia, Manitoba and the Maritimes where Howe and Tupper, the old enemies, had united to sweep Nova Scotia.

These narrow results were bad enough but they could have been worse. Macdonald took them philosophically, sobered up and was preparing to tackle the break-down of his railway scheme when George W. McMullen, an enigmatic financier from Chicago, arrived at the Prime Minister's office to table some interesting documents. They showed that Allan had never abandoned his deal with the Americans and McMullen expected the Government to honour it. If not, he proposed to publish the facts and the campaign-fund figures.

Hiding his own shock, Macdonald saw at once that Allan had lied to the Government, had told the Americans that they were to be excluded from the railway company on paper but "we can get over that some way or another." Nevertheless, as Macdonald realized, the Government, not Allan, would be blamed for selling out to foreigners. Was McMullen's blackmail a bluff? What else did he know? Had he seen those telegrams from Kingston?

Unable to guess, Macdonald played for time, promised to consider McMullen's demands and suddenly remembered Hincks. That was an inspiration.

The stealthy Hyena adjusted these delicate affairs, as he had adjusted so many others in the old days, by inviting Allan's coterie and its American partners to dinner in Montreal and persuading them to make some kind of settlement between themselves. He did not ask the details, nor did Macdonald, but apparently the Americans were paid off and Allan went to London in search of untainted British capital to finance his railway.

For the first time in six months Macdonald felt safe. At that very moment two unknown men were arranging his destruction.

The Montreal office of J. J. C. Abbott, Allan's solicitor, was carefully locked after business hours but George Norris, a confidential clerk, possessed his own key. Early in 1873 pressing duties brought him and a young helper to the office at midnight. They rifled the files, took what they wanted and drove off in a cab.

The ingredients of the Pacific Scandal, in their hands, were available to any purchaser at the modest price of five thousand dollars. Next morning a satisfactory sale was negotiated. Macdonald heard nothing of this prologue to Canada's classic melodrama and his own Greek tragedy.

The first act opened quietly in Parliament on April 2. Lucius Seth Huntington, a somewhat undistinguished Liberal member of the cast, rose to inform the House that the Canadian Pacific Railway was an American company under Canadian disguise. This charge did not greatly disturb Macdonald. He could easily prove that the Government had never condoned this foreign taint and it had been already removed. Then, as he waited, a single appalling sentence fell from Huntington's lips—Allan had bought his railway charter by a gift of election funds to the Government. Having said that, and no more, Huntington sat down.

Macdonald, listening with a careless air, knew that he confronted the watershed of his life, but how much did the Liberals know? Probably not much. They must be bluffing. All those telegrams from Kingston, which he could hardly remember himself, were in reliable hands. But as he looked across the House at the stone face of Mackenzie and the moon face of Blake a new fear gripped him. What had Cartier done in the election? What money had he accepted? What promises had he given? There could be no answer. Cartier was dying in London.

Blindly Macdonald walked into the Liberals' trap, voted down their motion for a committee of investigation, saw his mistake overnight, reversed himself next day, appointed a committee and waited, through weeks of procedural argument, for the return of Allan with British capital for his railway. Allan came home empty-handed. The Pacific Scandal had closed the doors of the British banks. Now, as if fate were telling Macdonald that the game was played out, he received the news of Cartier's death.

The essential French-Canadian partnership sundered, the railway scheme bankrupt, Confederation itself in peril, all the work of a lifetime shattered—such was the end. Almost unable to utter it,

Macdonald paid his last tribute to Cartier, stumbled from the House and deadened his pain with the old remedy.

While the railway committee wrangled, he remained drunk. It was pitiable, as the new Governor-General, Lord Dufferin, informed the British Government, to see "so superior a man" struggling "with desperate courage until fairly prostrate and broken down." Almost insensible in his bed, Macdonald knew only that he must resign.

The Cabinet would not hear of his resignation. If Macdonald went, the Government would go with him. No, he must fight on.

Perhaps, he told himself, it was not too late. The evidence produced before the committee touched only the correspondence between Allan and McMullen. It showed that Allan had deceived the Americans by pretending that the Government had connived at their participation in the C.P.R. but it also showed that the Government had been ignorant of Allan's conspiracy. If this was all the Liberals could prove then their case, though damaging, was not necessarily fatal.

Macdonald began to breathe freely again. The scandal, he wrote, "has ended in a fizzle as I knew it would." Brave words. He only half believed them. For the Liberals might know more than they had yet said. The boyish but implacable look of Blake as he argued before the committee was frightening. Rightly, Macdonald guessed that Blake held a secret. Was it the ultimate secret? Again the gnawing fear—could the Liberals have seen the Kingston telegrams? Surely that was impossible. All the evidence had been securely locked in Abbott's safe. Nevertheless, Macdonald must be ready for anything. Above all, his depleted strength must be rebuilt for the approaching battle.

He had just reached the sanctuary of his summer home at Rivière du Loup and begun to relax when the Montreal newspapers told him that Blake knew everything. It was all there on the front pages, documented, undeniable, devastating—Cartier's correspondence with Allan specifying the distribution of campaign funds, Macdonald's own pleas for money and that lethal telegram: "I must have another ten thousand."

Norris, the confidential clerk and efficient burglar, had done his work well. For five thousand dollars the Liberals had bought Macdonald's downfall. They had used a dirty weapon, never suspecting that the same sort of burglary would be turned against them in due time, but there could be no defence now.

Macdonald must have pondered another law of his office which holds that a Prime Minister, or any head of state, cannot always be expected to practise in a nation's affairs the morals applied to his own. By the nature of politics everywhere that is impossible. Politicians for the most part can be perfectly honest, politics never. Macdonald knew, too, that the Canadian people would not be surprised by the use of campaign funds from any source, but the present case stood outside these loose rules. The Government had been caught red-handed in a deal too rough even for politics.

Macdonald drank himself into oblivion again. Escaping his watchful wife, he slunk off and lay unconscious in the stews of Levis. For several days she searched frantically but could not find him. The Liberals spread the rumour of his suicide. His colleagues wondered if they would ever see him again.

He was not finished even yet. Immediately before the reopening of Parliament he returned to Ottawa, sick, shaking, hardly able to stand. With his last energies he presented himself at Rideau Hall and persuaded the doubtful Governor-General to adjourn Parliament for ten weeks while a royal commission took over the work of the railway committee.

One final chance remained. If Macdonald could convince the commission of his personal innocence its report might be just favourable enough to convince Parliament.

So the second act opened. Though quite unfit for work, Macdonald appeared before the commission as the Government's counsel, cross-questioned the Liberal witnesses but produced none of his own. He had none to produce. McMullen, who could prove the Government's ignorance of Allan's deal with the Americans, remained discreetly in Chicago. Norris, who could prove the Liberals guilty of buying stolen papers, had fled to the United States.

Macdonald was driven back to the defence that campaign funds were used by all political parties and implied no obligation to the donors—a pitiable defence but he had no other. And now the avalanche descended.

Sudden inquiries from the Governor-General as to the intentions of his Prime Minister; Macdonald's laborious hand-written reply, a masterpiece of legal reasoning, to prove the Government's integrity and its ignorance of Cartier's "insane course"; Dufferin's assurance of personal respect for Macdonald but his judgment that "your personal connection with what has passed cannot but fatally affect your position as minister"; a polite but deadly confrontation between the two men at Rideau Hall; the Governor-General's plain intimation that the Prime Minister should resign; the British Government's sharp warning to Dufferin that Parliament alone must decide Macdonald's fate; guarantees from the Conservative whips that they could muster a majority of sixteen in the House—so opened the third act.

The galleries of the Commons were crowded. Dufferin, eager to witness the denouement from some secret listening-post, "a closet no matter how dark or inconvenient," was compelled by Macdonald to remain at home. The chief actor sprawled listlessly in his chair. Blake, the inquisitor, remained ominously silent, perhaps with some final secret concealed behind that blank, pudgy face. What could it be? Macdonald waited, not daring to move until he knew. The Conservative back benches clamoured for his intervention but he would not speak before Blake.

Day after day their duel of silence continued while others spoke in a setting as artificial as any stage. One by one Macdonald's followers decided to vote against the Government and save their own skins.

The whips reported that the Conservative majority had fallen to half a dozen, then to two. Macdonald heard them vaguely. He was drunk again. At last, as he sat helpless, the truth dawned on him. Blake had no secret. He was only waiting for the Government's majority to melt away.

Once that flash of knowledge entered his misty consciousness, Macdonald knew what he must do. Drunk, feeble and shaking, he lurched to his feet, looked across to the silent Opposition benches, glanced up at the galleries, saw his wife there and seemed to draw strength from her presence. His voice was weak and hoarse at first, the words inaudible, his notes for a speech scrawled on a scrap of paper and discarded. The Liberals, eager for the kill, watched a man apparently broken in mind and body, a crumbling relic of Macdonald. They had never been so wrong.

Miraculously the mind cleared, the frail body straightened and expanded in power, the voice took on its familiar edge, the words poured out like a lawyer's orderly brief. As a feat of mind and body it was unbelievable. At his worst hour Macdonald was making the greatest speech of his life. All his steps from Kingston onward led to this summit, all his fifty-eight years had been only a preface to this climax.

For five hours the speech flowed on, logical, convincing, faultless, as if every word had been written in advance. The Government benches cheered. Lady Macdonald rejoiced in the triumph of her idol. The Opposition gaped, incredulous. Surely the spectacle was not in nature? Whence came the power of this depleted creature? It came from courage, from a sense of his own honour, and also from innumerable glasses of water, invisibly laced with gin.

Step by step he led his listeners through the labyrinth of the railway contract, answered every criticism, defended all his acts until he reached his peroration. It was past one o'clock in the morning when he uttered his last words of faith: "I leave it to this House with every confidence. I am equal to either fortune."

That night had been magnificent, in Macdonald's condition incredible. His wife hurried to Rideau Hall and told a delighted Governor-General that the Prime Minister was himself again. The country acclaimed its hero. Magnificent, yes, but not necessarily victorious war.

Next day Blake began his reply in a cold, factual style "as devoid of warmth as a flake of December snow" but murderous. Macdonald did not hear his young destroyer. He was stretched out, sober but impotent, on his office couch, scarcely able to grasp the whips' latest figures. The Government's vote was still falling.

When Macdonald's old friend, Donald Smith, appeared in the House with a burden of morality which had never troubled him before and would never trouble him again, everyone knew that his speech would be decisive. If Smith deserted Macdonald now, the game was up.

After a few unctuous protestations of loyalty to his chief, the sudden moralist announced that, for conscience' sake, he must vote against the Government.

It was all over. Macdonald drove out to Rideau Hall and presented his resignation; the Liberals would be called to office; the stonemason had won. The railway scheme might never be started. Without it, British Columbia might leave Confederation. The arch would then fall. All the labour of a lifetime had issued in failure for Canada, in disgrace for its creator.

Thus it seemed when Macdonald offered his resignation as party leader to the Conservative caucus, which instantly refused it, and was seen "tottering down the hill to the East Gate alone, others passing him with a wide sweep." In that harsh winter, a friend reported, he was wearing "a Red River sash and coat and the old historic mink-skin cap," the familiar uniform of many battles, now the garb of an outcast. In his hand he carried an unseen leper's bell. Its tinkle deceived Mackenzie.

3: The Working-man

When Mackenzie was summoned to the Governor-General's office on November 5 he could hardly believe that his chance had come at last. The road from the crofter's cottage had been so long, the barriers of ignorance and poverty so high, the sense of inadequacy so deep! Could an immigrant so inferior in origins, training and talent be Prime Minister of his country and set above the educated men born here? The thing almost accomplished still seemed impossible.

Besides, Dufferin was notoriously a Conservative partisan, a contemptuous critic of the Clear Grits, an intimate of Macdonald. What new cabal had these two cronies been hatching at their long interview that morning? Perhaps Dufferin would connive, as Governor Edmund Head had done, at a Double Shuffle of some sort? Surely Macdonald would not go without a last gambler's fling?

Mackenzie was wrong again about his enemy. Macdonald had gone, as he thought for good, and Dufferin received his successor with a mixture of cordiality and condescension. Not only was the Liberal leader asked to form a ministry but was offered a parliamentary dissolution and an immediate election to cleanse the "taint" of C.P.R. money.

The British aristocrat, for all his worldliness and the clever brain behind the handsome face and satanic moustaches, was wrong about the Canadian stonemason. So were most contemporary Canadians and later historians. The Mackenzie myth, beginning in Dufferin's office, would persist until Dale C. Thomson produced his superb biography of the unknown Prime Minister after the lapse of almost a century.

In his dispatches to London the Governor-General had called Mackenzie "a poor creature and under the thumb of George Brown," a mere "puppet" and pitiable substitute for Macdonald. Dufferin's verdict (which he was soon to alter) contained some superficial truth.

The man of fifty-one years, already gray and prematurely lined by toil, who now stood doubtfully at the vice-regal desk, had none of Macdonald's charm, cynicism or imagination. Mackenzie was a lesser but a more honest and, in some ways, a far better man. A brave man, too, faithful in his simple beliefs, intelligent in business, able enough for office in a work-a-day fashion. The straight plumb-line of his trade, the geometrically accurate square, the level foundation of integrity—these had instilled habits of mind that guaranteed upright government at any rate. They were big assets but the most essential one of all was lacking—Mackenzie had no luck.

Though neither he nor Dufferin suspected it, the decisive fact of the day was not a change of government; it was a change of economic climate. Two months earlier, a financial boom had broken in London and New York. The third, unseen presence in the Governor-General's office was that recurring ghost of Canadian politics and unerring killer of governments, a great depression.

As usual, Macdonald had all the luck. He left office at exactly the right time. And he left Mackenzie doomed from the start by a world economic convulsion which all his theories of free trade and the omniscient market somehow failed to cure.

No one saw them then but the social process and ideological conflict of our time were already under way. Here Mackenzie had picked the losing side, had bequeathed to a distant successor named King the task of reversing the Liberal position without notice. There was more to Mackenzie's ordained ruin than that. Fate had passed on him a private sentence brutal and undeserved.

The poor crofter's son was born among the Perthshire hills, his birth not far from Macdonald's in distance and time. He mastered his trade as a youth and managed to get six years of rudimentary schooling. At twenty he sailed for Canada with his tools, and with sixteen shillings in his pocket—not mainly to seek his fortune in the new world but to follow his sweetheart, Helen Neil.

Settling in Kingston, he must have often seen a personable young lawyer, already established at the bar, but the paths of the two men who later were to divide Canadian politics diverged for the next ten years. Macdonald rose fast to become a gentleman. Mackenzie remained a working-man.

He homesteaded for one winter with Helen's family in the Ontario wilderness, worked as a mason on the St. Lawrence canals and the Kingston fortifications, undertook small building contracts and slowly saved enough to bring his mother and six brothers to Canada.

As men saw him, he was industrious, reliable, competent and uninteresting—a devout Baptist who prayed morning and night, never touched liquor and spent all his spare time reading the English classics or his new discovery, the Toronto *Globe*. Such a man, rather too much the sea green incorruptible for a rough frontier society, might make some modest success in the business of a country town, no more.

So his few friends supposed. Another side of Mackenzie went unnoticed. The builder who built in stone worked inwardly with the same material. A character of stone was forming—hard, inflexible and dry, but the immigrant had brought with him from the highlands that flame of Scottish passion which also burned under Macdonald's banter. Mackenzie concealed it, except for rare outbursts, under a granitic look. Only his family knew the depth of his affections, tender to the point of sentimentality. Only Helen felt the warmth of his ardour. He courted her at Kingston by walking over the flimsy ice from Wolfe's Island every Saturday night, and once, falling into the water, was almost drowned.

Mackenzie had a playful side too, juvenile and crude—as when he stuffed the chimney of the Neils's cabin and watched the household driven by smoke into the winter snow, or when, on a trip of exploration to Lake Superior, he rolled a boulder down a cliff for the fun of it and, to his horror, almost killed his companion.

In growing Ontario Mackenzie prospered rapidly, married Helen and, settling permanently as a builder in Sarnia, soon became one of its leading citizens. Then, before he was twenty-five years old, he received the first blow of the same domestic sorrows that afflicted his future rival.

Helen's first child died. The second, a daughter, was healthy; but the third, a boy, lived only a few weeks and the mother's health was undermined. Like Macdonald, Mackenzie watched his wife die slowly. His own health was weakened by bouts of fever and dysentery but he drove himself with a quiet, demonic energy to earn money and support his new-found idol, Brown.

Idolatry, in fact, was to prove Mackenzie's incurable weakness. He never regarded himself as a leader but always as the follower of some bigger man. He long worshipped his genial brother, Hope, and planned for him a great career in politics. He worshipped Brown from the day of their first meeting, organized the far-western constituency of Lambton for the Reform Party and, inevitably, was himself elected in 1861 to the Canadian Assembly. There he watched and strongly advocated the birth of Confederation while acquiring an almost childish suspicion of all Tories and a dislike of public life.

Hope Mackenzie died young, leaving his brother involved for the rest of his time in politics, so deeply that his business was neglected, his savings drained, and his private life turned into an endless round of country meetings, speeches from wagons, conferences in the back rooms of grocery stores, all-night rides on horseback.

Brown had found a useful lieutenant and used him ruthlessly as a stubborn debater in the Assembly, a tireless organizer in the West, a student of politics who did his homework and was unquestionably loyal to his leader.

By now Mackenzie had married a neighbour's daughter, Jane Sym, had thoroughly educated himself out of books and spoke with hard, reasoned argument in his broad Scottish burr, often with compelling power and sometimes with searing wit. Accused on the platform of disloyalty to the Queen, he turned those metallic blue eyes on his Conservative opponent and retorted: "Loyalty to the Queen does not require a man to bow down to her manservant, her maidservant—or her ass."

These sallies were infrequent. Mackenzie might crack a pawky joke at a Burns Night dinner, drill with the local militia company in the days of the Fenian Raids or march with the local fire brigade on civic holidays, but his whole mind was given to politics as a science, almost as a religion. This was another grave weakness for a future Prime Minister—he had become the prisoner of principles in an amorphous country that couldn't stand them.

Liberalism, as he conceived it, would solve all men's problems. Free Trade and the divine mechanism of the competitive market, if they were only allowed to work, must make any nation rich. With him Economic Man, liberalism's favourite fiction, was a solemn truth.

Moreover, his generally balanced judgment was often distorted by his hatred of the corrupt but curiously invulnerable Government, by his naive opinion of Macdonald as a scallawag and "debauchee," by his loathing of Tory protectionism. All civic evils sprouted rankly

51

in the dark shadow of the tariff. Protection was "a monster when you come to look at it. It is the essence of injustice. It is the acme of human selfishness. It is one of the relics of barbarism."

Yet paradox and inconsistency, the hidden colleagues of all successful politicians, did not spare even this excessively logical man. His liberalism was passionate and sincere but confined for the most part to the Anglo-Saxon peoples. They were God's chosen agents, the natural missionaries of civilization. Britain was still "home."

The conflict between his Canadian nationalism and his distrust of British governors on the one hand and his nostalgic imperialism on the other—that old tension between geography and history which still splits the Canadian personality today—was never resolved in Mackenzie and perhaps never occurred to him.

Wherever the British Empire and the Anglo-Saxon race were concerned he generally thought with his blood. It boiled at the news of the Métis revolt and set him ranting, as a British Protestant, against Riel, a French Canadian, a Papist and a murderer, though Mackenzie learned later on that Catholics were people, voters and necessary allies of a Liberal government.

Where Canada's interests were concerned he thought as a Canadian and when they seemed to be sacrificed at the Washington conference he bitterly attacked the resulting treaty.

Where business was concerned he had a practical business man's grasp of facts and figures, a much better grasp than Macdonald's. Thus, while he had seen the possibilities of the far West much earlier than Macdonald, he also saw that the Pacific railway, as first devised, was financially and physically impossible—"a monstrous scheme."

Where politics were concerned he could not conduct a long guerilla war as well as Macdonald—no one could—but Mackenzie won many battles. In the election of 1872 he met the great warrior face to face on the Sarnia hustings and, with cool generalship, drove Macdonald to childish fury and cheap abuse. But then, Mackenzie had the advantage of the hometown audience that day and his own sobriety.

With a methodical stonemason's skill applied to politics, a painstaking care of party management and a modest view of himself as only an ordinary Clear Grit, "sand without a particle of dirt in it," Mackenzie had long since been recognized as Brown's chief aide and never expected to be anything else. He saw Brown much larger than life and Brown saw him much smaller. Nevertheless, Brown was the declining and Mackenzie the ascending man.

When Brown married late in life, neglected politics for his consuming love affair and was defeated in the first election of 1867, the Liberal Party expected him to return and refused to face the problem of its permanent leadership.

Meanwhile another star had risen in the person of young Blake. Some of Mackenzie's incurable hero-worship and sense of inferiority were transferred to this prodigy of pure intellect. After Blake defeated the Tory government of Ontario and became its Premier, Mackenzie—though an active Member of Parliament and an opponent of simultaneous membership in two legislative bodies—joined the new provincial government as its treasurer, governed the province during Blake's long absence in England and exhausted himself, sometimes, in his fevers and dysentery, using opium as Macdonald used drink.

Still there was no accepted Liberal leader in Ottawa, still there was the hope of Brown's return as the breaking-point of the Pacific Scandal approached. At last, after the election of 1872, since Brown refused to return, realizing, as he said, that he was not cut out for government, the elected Liberal Members were forced to make a choice.

Mackenzie favoured Blake or, as a second-best, his brilliant French-Canadian friend, Antoine-Aimé Dorion. They both preferred Mackenzie and, with days of wrangling in caucus, compelled him to accept the leadership.

Thus, on the morning of Macdonald's fall, Dufferin reluctantly called in the "poor creature," Brown's "puppet," to make him the second Prime Minister of Canada.

Even then Mackenzie was doubtful and disturbed by his own inadequacy. After leaving the Governor-General, he met Blake on the street and offered him the office. Blake refused to consider it or, at first, even to enter the Cabinet. That was the trouble with the greatest mind in Canada—it could never be made up. Its caprice and vacillation had begun the friendly but systematic work of Mackenzie's destruction. And as the new Prime Minister built his Cabinet that final destroyer, the Great Depression of the nineteenth century, was also at work.

Like Macdonald's, the first Liberal Cabinet could not be what the Prime Minister wanted. He was able to get Blake by arranging a hundred telegrams of pressure from leading Liberals, but only as President of the Council, without departmental duties, and only until the election was won.

To Mackenzie's disappointment and anger, his old comrade-in-arms, Luther Holton, would not leave Montreal to accept the Finance Ministry. As a questionable alternative Richard Cartwright, a reformed Conservative, was appointed and brought into the Government the flaring sideburns like misplaced antlers, the pugnacious jaw and battering-ram style that made him the terrible man of politics.

Far more satisfactory, since it established the vital link with Quebec, was the appointment of Dorion as Minister of Justice. Mackenzie himself took the Department of Public Works, where he could keep a builder's trained eye on the grafters and personally revise the C.P.R. scheme.

By the time he had fitted the lesser square pegs into the round holes of the other portfolios Mackenzie confessed himself "sick, really ill in fact" and sometimes he wrote longingly of his hope for peace in Heaven. Evidently there would be none here. He was learning, however.

He was learning, among other things, the cardinal lesson that all Prime Ministers must learn—the head of a Canadian government can never be exactly himself. He can seldom do what he wants to do. He must be a composite and amalgam of his diverse party, sometimes a chameleon, always a compromiser. This was easy for Macdonald, hard for Mackenzie, but he was learning.

To the public he showed at the beginning an air of quiet confidence and energy. Like all Canadian Cabinets, Mackenzie's was a mixture of talent and mediocrity, an egg of unknown contents to be hatched under the watchful eye of Brown as if it were the eye of God. Unable to live without his oldest hero, or to lure him into government, Mackenzie made Brown a senator and sent him, at his own wish, to Washington, where he expected to revive the reciprocity agreement lost by Macdonald.

With a brave show of strength, the Mackenzie Government went to the country on January 22, 1874, on "an honest, vigorous and economical policy" and won a majority of 60 seats in a House of 206. That day marked the high tide of Mackenzie's career. As if to remind him that the tide must change, he received Blake's resignation written at seven o'clock on the morning of the election. This was bad news but on the other hand the Pacific Scandal had wrecked the Tories for a long time to come and given the Liberals their great chance.

The Conservative leader of the Opposition, narrowly re-elected in Kingston, sat listlessly in the new Parliament, few of his old lieutenants around him. All except Tupper had gone down in the wreck. Macdonald could only wait for a successor to appear because, as he wrote Tupper, "my fighting days are over."

As a temporary caretaker of his party he soon moved his family to Toronto, set up a law firm and prepared to enjoy an old age of well-earned serenity. Yet the famous whisky nose already had begun to sniff something decidedly wrong in a Government so confident on the outside, so full of inward virtue. Well, he would watch it for a little while longer but a younger man must unhorse it. For the first time in his life the aging sceptic fooled himself.

What kind of Government had Mackenzie actually constructed? It was a Government of thin talents, to begin with, after Blake had withdrawn and Dorion had resigned to become Chief Justice of Quebec; a Government almost entirely dependent upon the single talent of its leader; a Government of Free Trade, strict Scottish thrift, maximum business competition, minimum state interference in the God-ordained market; a Government, theoretically at least, of Jeffersonian democracy fresh and pure from the frontier, and a Government which established for many years to come the image of Canadian Liberalism.

Here, perhaps, was to be Mackenzie's only important achievement—he had installed his theories of government so deeply in Liberalism that, often compromised or betrayed in practice, they remained as an ideal, a moral memory, a kind of enduring conscience. Even after they had become irrelevant in a changed society, they still persisted, and persist to this day among the few surviving, unreconstructed Liberals who live in the nineteenth century.

Mackenzie, in short, had tried to erect what he took to be the natural form of human government, unaware that nature had other plans. His high tide was beginning to ebb invisibly.

He could not detect its motion when, for the first time, he was tasting the sweets of success, the adulation of office and the comfort of a settled domestic life after all his years of hurry and scurry.

At his roomy house, within walking distance of his office in the West Block, he entertained Liberals and Conservatives alike with warm hospitality and a genial air too long suppressed. His wife, despite her humble upbringing, surprised everyone by her dignity and warmth. The teetotaler's table was well supplied with wines and spirits for guests who enjoyed them.

In this happy home the steel of Mackenzie's nature seemed to melt. Decked out in Windsor uniform at the opening of Parliament, he looked a striking, handsome and regnant figure. Even the snobbish Dufferin was altering his opinion. The Prime Minister, he wrote to London, "is a thoroughly upright, well-principled and well-meaning man." The Government was not merely strong but "very strong." If so, its strength resided in one man and came from toil, loneliness and pain, the breeding-ground of Prime Ministers. But strength alone would not serve. As in Macdonald's years of office, hubris was closely followed by nemesis.

The first intimation of change appeared in the Government's legislative program. It was easy enough to establish the secret ballot, against Macdonald's grumbling protest that all free men should vote in the open, to set up a Supreme Court and announce a policy of thrift. The locust swarms of Liberal contractors could be resisted, though they disgusted Mackenzie. He designed a secret stairway in the West Block tower to escape the hordes of job hunters in his anteroom. These details of administration he could manage handily but Cartwright's budget showed that the Government faced larger problems, almost insoluble. It was feeling the impact of hard times.

The Great Depression had done its work well. Revenues were falling, expenditures rising to the dreadful figure of twenty-four and a half million dollars and, without tax increases, the Government risked an unthinkable million-dollar deficit.

In that pre-Keynesian age no man had yet discovered the magic of cyclical budgets and deficit spending to prime the economic pump. More revenue must be secured somehow, but where? Regardless of his free-trade theories, Mackenzie was forced to accept the common lot of all Prime Ministers, reverse himself and raise the general tariff from 15% to 17½%. He might call this a "tariff for revenue only," the convenient Liberal excuse, but it was the monster of Protection just the same, fed by its enemies.

Mackenzie should have learned long before now that the Canadian tariff was not, as he had once imagined, and as his successors would long pretend, a sacred trial between good and evil. It was a secular contest of economic interests, a purely pragmatic attempt to satisfy manufacturers, exporters and consumers, a rough and changing compromise between them on grounds of expediency as the various pressures mounted or declined. The tariff was, and is, the Government's best guess of what the political traffic will bear. It registers the strength of the rival voting blocs as on a butcher's scales. For all the ritual postures of election times, it usually contains no more principle than a cash register.

Only two Prime Ministers ever put principle ahead of expediency and pushed the theories of free trade or protection to their logical conclusion. Both were defeated for their logic. The fate of Laurier and Bennett was a long way off as Mackenzie felt compelled by the Depression to commit his innocent apostasy, but only for the moment. A little later on Brown would deliver a free-trade agreement with the United States. Liberalism would return to the imaginary norm never existing in politics.

Meanwhile Mackenzie was driven by hard times toward another policy which would re-emerge exactly eighty-nine years later under the new name of "austerity" as Diefenbaker ordered his retreat from Moscow. The Great Depression, said Cartwright, must compel politicians and people to modify their demands on the public treasury. At which Macdonald scoffed that Liberal times were always bad times, and thus invented a political legend as false as the legend of the tariff.

Mackenzie had not made the hard times. They had been made by the world economy and for the most part by the state of the American market where Canada bought and sold. So it would always be; but the political parties have always used and still use the legend against each other with equal enthusiasm and deceit.

Macdonald was using it to discredit Mackenzie while a future Liberal leader, now an apprentice in Parliament, would use it to discredit the Conservatives, as King would use it again to discredit Bennett and Diefenbaker would repeat the same strategy to discredit St. Laurent.

The two-edged sword of Depression, wielded with sufficient lack of scruple, would always wreak enough havoc against any government to divert the public mind from the simple fact that Canada's prosperity rises and falls with the state of the world in as sure a tidal motion as that now going against Mackenzie.

Depression's most immediate effect was to demoralize the Pacific railway scheme. Mackenzie had never doubted that the contract to start construction within two years of British Columbia's admission into Confederation in 1871 was "a piece of madness, an insane act." Now, in the summer of 1874, the surveys were just getting well under way.

Blake, still a powerful, almost mystic figure in the Liberal Party, a lofty arbiter and *amicus curiae*, had taken an even darker view. He could foresee only "two streaks of rust across the wilderness," on which "a bushel of wheat will never go to England." The railway "will never pay for its axle-grease." If the British Columbians insisted on an impossible bargain let them leave the union, for it could not survive the cost of the C.P.R.

On the one policy where the great Canadian mind had been fully made up it was wrong.

A less talented and more practical man, with a life-long faith in the far West, Mackenzie knew that the C.P.R. must be built but in times of shrunken revenues and falling credit he must build it even more slowly than he had planned. And since Macdonald had lured British Columbia into the union by an impossible promise, Mackenzie must make the impatient settlers accept a long postponement of their hopes.

His railway policy, condemned by most future historians as piddling and cowardly, was the best that economic conditions would allow. Instead of attempting to lay tracks all the way across the continent at once, the Government would use steamboats on the "enormous stretches of magnificent water communication" between Lake Huron and the Rockies, and join the lakes and navigable rivers with a series of separate railway lines to be connected when money was available. In any case, the promise to complete the project within ten years must be extended, as the British Columbians had better understand.

They refused to understand. Mackenzie's private ambassador to Victoria, James Edgar, was insulted and sent packing by the bellicose provincial premier, George Walkem.

Here Macdonald saw his first chance to wound the Government and, blandly ignoring his own mismanagement of the railway scheme, protested that any change in the contract was a breach of faith which justified British Columbia's withdrawal from Confederation.

His old ally, de Cosmos, screamed the threat of secession across the House of Commons. A mob of angry citizens marched into the legislative Bird Cages at Victoria to protest Mackenzie's treachery, drove the legislators from their seats and, by a rather comical night's work, since celebrated in local legendry as "The Rebellion," reminded the Prime Minister that Confederation was still a flimsy structure, not a work of stone, the material he understood. Then the provincial government appealed directly to the Queen. British Columbia's withdrawal and the break-up of the union had become a positive threat.

Mackenzie tried to mollify the province by offering various financial concessions but its heart was set on the "iron horse" which would make everybody rich. It cared little for Canada anyway, and less for the Liberal Government.

Walkem came to Ottawa on a mission of blackmail and appealed to Mackenzie's "statesmanship." The Prime Minister, calling this bluff, replied that "we made no pretensions to statesmanship, we were plain business men" who knew that the railway could not be started until the surveys were complete, even if the Government owned "the wealth of India."

Walkem went off in a huff to London and evidently made some impression on Lord Carnarvon. The Colonial Secretary's offer to arbitrate the dispute between the two Canadian governments so irritated Mackenzie that he was sent to bed with a stomach upset; but in the end he reluctantly accepted the arbitration.

By the Carnarvon terms the Canadian Government agreed to press the surveys as fast as possible, to complete the railway by 1890 and to begin immediately the construction of a line on Vancouver Island from Nanaimo to Esquimalt, the ostensible terminus of the C.P.R.

This plan was implemented by legislation in the Commons (Blake opposing and Macdonald supporting it) but was rejected by the Senate. Mackenzie could do no more. He was off the railway hook for the moment while his other troubles still piled up and a man who seemed so independent of friends began to feel the awful solitude of office.

His only close friend in the Cabinet had gone. Excessive generosity had prompted Mackenzie to offer the chief justiceship of Quebec to Dorion whose retirement from politics weakened, and might well break, the essential coalition with French Canada. There was no one to replace Dorion as the necessary co-Prime Minister, though by chance or inspiration Mackenzie's eye had fallen, earlier in the year, on the man of the future.

Young Wilfrid Laurier, in his first parliamentary speech, had not ventured to use English, but his noble features, his eloquence, his power and his almost kingly presence had astounded the House —a youngster to be watched, apparently as intelligent as Blake and without Blake's maddening instability.

Laurier was too young, however, to replace Dorion. Mackenzie had stumbled into the problem solved for Macdonald by Cartier, the problem which all successful Prime Ministers must solve, or perish, the problem which, unsolved, would later smash Meighen, Bennett and Diefenbaker.

Dorion was gone. Brown was in Toronto. Blake was strangely silent, meditating revolt. Mackenzie's wife was at the seaside. He had taken a new house just west of the West Block after fire had destroyed his first house, his furniture, his clothes and all his personal belongings. From his porch in the evening he could look across the gleaming Ottawa to the Gatineau Hills after a day of exhausting business.

As he wrote to one of his brothers, he knew by now that his trouble came not from his enemies but his friends, the Liberal grafters who "dig trenches at a distance and approach in regular siege form." It came from the ministers unfit for office, most of all from the mysterious rumblings of Blake.

Mackenzie tried to forget the day's frustrations by working about the new house with the skilful mason's hands, so long idle and soft. He wrote every evening to his wife in a vein of pretended playfulness and a lover's longing. How the world would have laughed to read these clumsy but moving love letters from the man of stone!

He was about to advertise, he told Jane, for a wife "who left Ottawa on the morning of the 4th and has not since been heard of. Her age about—, skin fair, hair mixed, teeth good and nearly new, small, fat, docile disposition and $30 in her pocket. I saw the Sergeant last night. He told me he was going down today and I asked him if he saw you not to mention that I was crying when he came in. Mr. Buckingham and I use up a handkerchief daily. I think of using a towel after this for economical reasons. If you stay long away it may come to a sheet . . . I presume you are indicating your title to the Baptist profession by immersing well and thus at once sticking to your principles and laying in a stock of health for the winter."

A lonely, harassed and melancholy man but a stronger man than the world then knew or history would soon recognize. Mackenzie's stature was growing with his unhappiness. The local politician had become a national statesman. In these times of the Depression a shaky, half-built edifice called the Dominion of Canada rested solely on the stone foundation of his honesty. He understood that fact, and his own limitations.

"I see the Tory papers say I am eaten up with ambition," he wrote Jane. "I think I know myself and can honestly say I am not. I am ambitious to succeed in governing the country well and without any reproach but beyond that my ambition is of a very humble kind . . . I think I have ambition enough, however, to strengthen me to fight in, I hope, a manly way the base herd of hireling scribes who would for political gain write away a man's character, and courage to back up that ambition."

Mackenzie needed all his strength for the two blows now falling.

Brown and a British commission had negotiated a limited but satisfactory reciprocity deal with the American Government. The Senate had refused to ratify it and, in these sluggish times, seemed unlikely to encourage Canadian imports. This was a crushing disappointment. It struck at the root of all Mackenzie's free-trade hopes. While he knew that the trade between the two North American neighbours must be rationalized some day, the solution was postponed indefinitely and, indeed, would remain on the agenda, pressing for an answer, into our time.

Mackenzie must wait, suffer and still hope. The whimsical genius of Liberalism would not wait. Having refused to re-enter the Government, Blake had suddenly changed his mind and now, in an amazing letter, offered to take Mackenzie's place as Prime Minister.

The pressure on him was so heavy, Blake wrote, that "it might be my duty under certain circumstances to face my difficulties and overcome my personal reluctance to office." If Mackenzie wished to retain the Public Works portfolio, Blake would "add myself up to the effort of so arranging my professional and personal affairs as to enable me to . . . meet your views." Otherwise, if "you prefer to remain first minister I shall know that I can . . . retain my present position."

The meaning of these elephantine overtures was plain enough—Blake had decided to take over the Government and the nation from a sense of duty but if Mackenzie refused to surrender then he and the nation must accept the consequences. Blake's conscience would be clear.

Nothing else was clear. At first Mackenzie suspected a serious revolt in his party. Blake had been associating lately with the new Canada First group and its prophet, Goldwin Smith, the English professor who, living in Toronto, had undertaken to arrange Canada's inevitable marriage with the United States. That Blake would sink to conspiracy was impossible. That he had no clear intentions was likely. That he had the power to split the party and disrupt the Government was certain.

Mackenzie could not be sure, no one could ever be sure, about the wanton genius of Liberalism. Blake was given no answer to his letter for eleven days as Mackenzie considered this mysterious threat and felt his highland blood begin to boil. The two controlling minds of Canada had collided, the brilliant mind of plastic, the inflexible mind of stone. Mackenzie would not surrender. That much was clear, and only that.

Unable to restrain his impatience, Blake wrote again to say, perhaps more in hope than in anger, that the Prime Minister's silence "ends the matter for me." His generous offer had been made and ignored. Now Mackenzie must bear responsibility for the outcome.

As a local politician and proud Scot, Mackenzie would have let the thing rest there. As a national leader he realized, on second thoughts, that he could not afford to quarrel with Blake and split the party. The situation called for the methods of that disarming rascal, Old Tomorrow.

Mackenzie temporized, wrote Blake that "I am as yet unable to see my way to the right conclusion" and offered to talk the problem over. Blake was not to be fobbed off with flattery. He knew his offer had been rejected by an inferior mind and, smarting under the first serious rebuff of his life, wrote bitterly to "beg you will not add to your other cares, which are quite heavy enough, by devoting a moment's further thought to the matter."

Blake was sulking but he was not finished. He was only beginning. At an election rally in Aurora the great mind exploded and poured out its cargo of festering grievances.

The supposed free trader criticized reciprocity. He condemned the Government's appeasement of British Columbia, a worthless "sea of mountains," and added that if the alternative to a sensible railway scheme was the secession of the Pacific province, "I would take the alternative."

His thoughts ranged far beyond these immediate issues, the explosion flinging its debris in all directions. The British Empire, said Blake, must become a federation since otherwise Canada was only "four millions of Britons who are not free" and, by the policy of England, "might be plunged into the horrors of war."

Jove had hurled a thunderbolt from Aurora but it failed to shake the man of stone. As Mackenzie foresaw, the Canadian people, concerned only with the Depression, were little interested in Blake's cosmic speculations. The thunderbolt sputtered out like a child's firecracker.

Mackenzie made no public comment, telling Brown privately that the Aurora speech was "neither wise nor friendly, though it may be so meant."

A firecracker, yes, but did it perhaps portend a larger explosion? Were Blake and the young Canada First crowd seriously conspiring to remove the Prime Minister? Mackenzie did not know. Grimly he settled down to wait.

Macdonald also waited, and with high hopes. He was perhaps

the most interested reader of the Aurora speech. Having long watched Blake, he respected his talents and considered him the Conservatives' secret weapon in the Government—a genius, but a born disturber who must surely break the Liberal Party sooner or later.

Some of Macdonald's lieutenants, tired of his Fabian strategy, wanted to exploit Blake's rebellion at once, but Old Tomorrow knew better. If he attacked now he would drive the Liberal factions together for survival. No, let the boil ripen and he would prick it at the right time. Meanwhile he was persuaded, quite wrongly, that the Government must eventually fall into the old fissures of the Reform movement, the cracks of principle and prejudice that Brown had only widened, that Mackenzie had temporarily papered over.

Actually the Aurora speech was nothing more than an annoyance to Mackenzie, a brief distraction from his paramount problem. Over everything hung the horror of the Pacific railway like a bad dream—no money to build it, no company willing to undertake it, no choice of a route through the Rockies, no satisfactory route at all through the Coast range and no agreement with British Columbia.

On the other hand, the C.P.R. deadlock had produced one valuable asset, for the time being at least. The great mind, unmade again, had decided that its place was in the Government after all, if the Carnarvon terms were altered in one detail.

Overlooking the Aurora speech, Blake became Minister of Justice after Mackenzie, in an agony of conscience, agreed to abandon the Vancouver Island railway, as rejected by the Senate, and to pay British Columbia subsidies instead until the main line was built. Blake was an uncomfortable and prickly colleague, always threatening to resign, frequently bursting into tears, once writing a formal resignation and withdrawing it at Mackenzie's heartbroken plea, but he could share the Prime Minister's intolerable burdens.

Macdonald was surprised and shaken by Blake's return. He had counted on the rebel to demoralize the Liberal Party, had withheld his own fire while waiting for nature to do the Opposition's work. That strategy had failed. If Blake was loyal after all, the Conservatives must follow a strategy of open attack.

By 1876 the climate was propitious for attack. Mackenzie's abandonment of the island railway had set British Columbia shouting betrayal, breach of contract and secession, with a new fury. Dufferin had become restive and was playing his own game of local politics for the prize of a larger game, the viceroyship of India. If he could knock the colonial heads of Canada together, the Queen would look favourably on his claim. So he proposed to settle the quarrel with British Columbia himself by going to Victoria, drumming some sense into the provincial politicians and, unknown to the Prime Minister, promising them better terms.

Mackenzie objected indignantly to this interference by the Crown and doubtfully approved of the Governor's western safari on the strict understanding that it was only a formal gesture committing the Government to nothing. Dufferin promised to be discreet but in such an ambitious and subtle man discretion was a virtue for his colonial advisers, not for him. He made a triumphal entry into Victoria on a warship, delivered a flowery speech, and listened to the local politicians twelve hours a day, assuring them in one breath that he was powerless and, in the next, that he would fight their battle at Ottawa.

On his return he wrote the new British Columbia Premier, Andrew Elliott, to this effect and commanded that his letter be burned immediately. He also wrote to London, condemning the Prime Minister whom he had formerly praised and proposing to break the railway stalemate by an imperial arbitration.

Mackenzie did not know of this double dealing but, as a constitutionalist, he was scandalized by the threat of interference from London. He and Blake opposed the arbitration and endured a series of stand-up rows with Dufferin in Rideau Hall. They were dumbfounded to hear the Governor-General say that he could accept or reject the advice of his ministers; and when they insisted that he could not and offered to resign if he distrusted them, Dufferin apologized, only to reassert his constitutional heresy next day. Mackenzie stood firm. Blake argued the constitution. The Governor-General fumed and threatened. The railway, on island and mainland, remained unbuilt.

This struggle with the Governor-General for Canada's independent status was among the most valuable and permanent work of Mackenzie's life, though the public heard nothing of it then and has not appreciated it now. It laid the base for a final settlement of the nation's autonomy half a century later and incidentally gave Mackenzie King the answer to his constitutional crisis of 1926.

Dufferin could be managed with a mixture of toughness and tact. The political dilemma of the Government was becoming unmanageable.

In 1875 Mackenzie and his wife escaped it for a few weeks by returning for the first time to Britain. The former steerage passengers traveled first-class now—a measure of the immigrant's success—but the holiday was ruined by public engagements, speeches and inconclusive conferences with the British Government.

Mackenzie made a sentimental journey to his highland birthplace and delivered a series of eloquent speeches on the high destiny of the Anglo-Saxon race. Yet on closer inspection he found British society shockingly less virtuous than he had supposed in his youth. Its class system was an unmitigated evil quite alien, as he intimated in his speeches, to the pure democracy of Canada. Moreover, the smug British people seemed to have little interest in the Empire. Canada, he concluded privately, was "more British than Britain."

At any rate, by warmly praising Canada's American neighbours, he had assumed, almost unconsciously, the historic role of Canadian Prime Ministers as the honest brokers between Britain and the United States.

Mackenzie came back to Ottawa feeling refreshed, but not for long. He plunged into his arrears of business, fell sick, consulted specialists in New York and, told that his working habits were eroding his health, worked harder than ever.

There was nothing else for it, unless he resigned. Within three years of his electoral triumph the full impact of the Great Depression produced its inevitable effects—unemployment in the towns, poverty on the farms, mounting deficits in the treasury as Cartwright borrowed desperately in London and tried to keep the banks afloat in Montreal. All the news was bad but Mackenzie would not keep it from the public. Unlike a modern Prime Minister, he decided that "the truth must be told—I have no faith in pretensions of any sort." His words were to have a weird relevance in 1962.

Financial stringency obsessed him. An older, larger problem was destroying him. Depression pressed down on the weak joints of the nation and strained the weakest joint of all, between the English and French races. Mackenzie had encountered, in the naked realities of politics, the oldest and most durable Canadian dilemma. Lacking a Cartier, he was in no position to solve it. The Government might be strong, as Dufferin said. The Liberal organism was weak, as Macdonald always knew.

Already Riel had taught Mackenzie, *in absentia*, that the Quebec problem was not nearly as simple as he had imagined in his carefree opposition days. His own loose words about the murderer of Fort Garry could not be unsaid, but since Quebec and his French-Canadian ministers demanded an amnesty for Riel, as promised by Macdonald, Mackenzie realized that the unity of the races was more important than the punishment of a half-breed rebel. Anyway, Riel, now often living in Quebec after being elected to Parliament and actually signing its roll, could not be arrested without a French-Canadian explosion.

In this latest version of every Prime Minister's classic test, Mackenzie contrived an ingenious compromise—immediate amnesty for all the rebels except Riel and two others, and amnesty for them, too, after an exile of five years. Parliament agreed. Like the Government, the Opposition had no wish to quarrel with Protestant Ontario by excusing Riel, or with Quebec by persecuting him. The rebel was safely stowed away to smash the Conservative Party later.

For the present, Riel was only one element in a chemical reaction long producing explosions at regular intervals. As Canada was divided by race, religion and language, the Church of Quebec was divided within itself between the ultramontane clergy, more Catholic than the Pope, and the moderates who deprecated the old alliance between the hierarchy and the Conservative Government. The clash between the two clerical groups sent agents of both hurrying to Rome year after year, while Rome sent its agents of reconciliation to Quebec. The outcome of this "Holy War" could be foreseen. In the end the Vatican came down on the side of the moderates but the time of trouble lasted through a whole generation.

Meanwhile the conflicting social forces of Quebec found their contemporary symbols and their flash points. The ultramontane symbol was Bishop Bourget, of Montreal. Catholic liberalism was centered in the mildly radical Institut, of which Laurier was a leading member. A humble man, Joseph Guibord, provided the flash point by dying inconveniently.

Bourget had dedicated his life to curbing Canada's heresies and suppressing the new liberalism. Here, as in Europe, it was denounced as the enemy of the Church. A Quebec Rouge, said Bourget, could not be a good Catholic. He excommunicated many Institut members and, as one of them, Guibord was denied burial in sanctified ground. When his body was brought to a Catholic cemetery a mob of Bourget's followers turned it away.

The Catholic liberals saw this as a test case and carried it to the Privy Council. After five years of deliberation, the court of last resort ruled against the Bishop and the Vatican intervened with sensible advice. Guibord was admitted to sacred soil but Bourget placed his grave under interdict.

An ugly, preposterous incident, but it had kindled old flames and racial memories. The Conservatives knew how to fan them.

Mackenzie's Government was caught in the familiar squeeze—attacked in Catholic Quebec as anti-clerical, in Protestant Ontario as soft on Catholicism. Until it came to terms with the Church, and until the Church was no longer suspect in English-speaking Canada, the Liberal Party must remain fractured.

Mackenzie could not hope to heal the Quebec schism. He was too old, an ardent Baptist, the friend of Brown whose "Protestant horse," as Macdonald called it, and his anti-Catholic tirades, were well remembered in French Canada. The great work of conciliation must be left to younger hands, the soothing, physician's hands of Laurier. Even he could not win his struggle against the bishops for twenty years yet.

With an election in sight, one of Mackenzie's ministers, Lucius Huntington, who had used the stolen C.P.R. papers with such skill, now undertook another adventure. His public speech assailing the politics of the Catholic clergy infuriated Quebec and appalled Mackenzie. The Conservatives pretended outrage. Macdonald wrote a friend that this affair had "finished" the Liberals in French Canada. Mackenzie could only say that Huntington had spoken for himself alone, not for the Government.

Macdonald's prognosis was accurate. In desperation the Prime Minister sought a reliable French-Canadian colleague, foolishly decided that Laurier was too young and, on the advice of the party machine, accepted Joseph Cauchon, an ingratiating little newspaperman of doubtful reputation but, as he claimed, a good friend of the clergy.

The latest experiment was a failure. The Government lost its Quebec by-elections. Hector Langevin, Macdonald's chief French-Canadian lieutenant and indifferent substitute for Cartier, was back in Parliament and, as the brother of a bishop, was using the clergy to intimidate the Liberal voters.

Quebec, though Mackenzie could not believe it yet, was lost to the Liberal Party. Now the rot spread to Ontario. There Mackenzie took the stump himself, delivered the best campaign speeches of his life, was warmly cheered and promptly defeated at the by-election polls.

A few later victories could no longer mask the state of the Government. Behind its stone façade it was cracked beyond repair by the battering-ram of the Depression and the wedge of religious passion. And the one man who knew how to use these and every other instrument of demolition had reappeared—quietly, ambiguously but with all his unequalled cunning.

The old cat, as Brown had called Macdonald, was on the prowl again, his feline instincts sharpened by rest and sobriety. After two years' quiescence and apparent retirement, he had slid unobtrusively into active politics, stronger, more sober than he had ever been in office and now wiser also.

Mackenzie might have expected the return of the nation's ablest politician even if Macdonald didn't. Nature had decided that question from the beginning. Even if Macdonald could have subdued his natural appetite for power and for vindication, there was no one else to lead the Conservative Party. Tupper had tried hard enough to establish his claim in a perpetual round of horrendous speeches but the country was not ready to accept him.

Gingerly Macdonald tested the water and, still half determined to retire, recrossed his Rubicon by inventing a new art form of politics, the country picnic, where he spoke little of policy but entertained the happy, sweating crowds with jest and homely anecdote. His reception was heady wine. The experiment proved so successful, the public so enthusiastic that he was soon fighting by-elections in person.

There could be no further doubt about his intentions when he followed Mackenzie to Montreal, condemned the Liberals' "veiled treason" to the Empire and, seizing on the old credo of Upper Canada's Baldwin, made it his own forever—"A British subject I was born, a British subject I hope to die."

No sentiment could be more obvious, almost banal, and it was purloined from a Reformer, but it caught the public imagination. It could be used over and over again, a pure Tory doctrine to outlive the orator.

Macdonald was back. No mistake about that and Mackenzie knew what it meant. From now on he must meet the champion in open combat. Yet surely Macdonald could never live down the Pacific Scandal? Mackenzie thought it impossible. Without the Great Depression, it probably was. Nevertheless, Macdonald would fight with every weapon in his well-stocked arsenal, but on what precise issue?

Old Tomorrow was too cautious to reveal it yet. Though he continued to criticize the slow progress on the Pacific railway, the criticism was remarkably mild. He knew that eastern Canada resented the railway's cost and was tired of the British Columbians' absurd demands. In Parliament the blustering Tupper might talk about a "National Policy" of protection. With Macdonald that word was still taboo, as in 1872. He repaired to his old strategy of blur and ambiguity by urging merely a "readjustment" of the tariff to raise more revenue when direct taxes on income were intolerable and, with a sudden premonition of Keynesian economics, he argued that the Government must spend more money on public works to cure unemployment. But in a "readjustment" of the tariff protection would be merely "incidental," a happy coincidence for manufacturer and farmers alike.

Having sowed this seed, Macdonald waited for it to sprout, not without anxiety. As protectionist sentiment mounted among an impoverished people he feared that the Government would abandon its free-trade principles and steal the Conservative policy, such as it was. Then he would have no issue.

The test came in the budget of 1876. Half the Cabinet and probably most of the country wanted protection. The political prophets confidently predicted that the Government would turn a somersault and raise the tariff. Mackenzie said nothing in public while he fought off his protectionist ministers in private. The budget was a well-kept secret.

Macdonald awaited it in a sweat of suspense. Tupper, as he confessed to Mackenzie later, had written two speeches, one denouncing the Government's retreat from free trade, the other denouncing its refusal to adopt a wise policy of protection. To his surprise—for he had underestimated Mackenzie's courage—the opposition critic found it necessary to deliver the second speech.

Despite the pressure in his Cabinet, the demands of the business interests and the failure of Brown's reciprocity mission in Washington, the Prime Minister would not retreat. The tariff was left alone except for minor changes.

Macdonald breathed a quiet sigh of relief. He had his issue and knew how to exploit it. Some Liberal Members offered to support him on protection but he laughingly rejected their overtures. He was not ready yet to raise the protectionist banner openly. He would not even move a tariff amendment to the budget until he had pondered the prospects for a fortnight.

At last, in a masterly speech and a subtle, decisive manoeuvre, he proposed the National Policy without admittting for a moment that it meant more than a "readjusted" tariff of only "incidental" protection. The fisherman's net was flung wide enough to catch all the loose fish and alarm nobody but the incorrigible theorists of free trade. The lines of the next election had been laid down—vaguely, safely and with diabolic craft. The net was closing on Mackenzie.

Macdonald had another issue, or the appearance of an issue,

69

highly congenial to the victim of the Pacific Scandal. He began to accuse the Government of corruption and eagerly seized on any fragments of evidence.

One of Mackenzie's brothers, for example, seemed to be, but was not actually, involved in the Government's purchase of steel rails for the discarded Vancouver Island railway. This affair, presented with a mixture of leer and morality, was a useful little exhibit. Soon afterwards, like manna from heaven, came the publication of Brown's letters to a few friends in the 1872 election urging a "big push" for campaign funds.

The request was natural enough, the response amounted to less than four thousand dollars but the immaculate Dufferin was shocked, the public suspicious. With squeals of joy the minor Tory fuglemen declared that the Government which had come to office on the peccadilloes of its enemies was far more dishonest than its predecessor. On a minor, almost ridiculous scale, the Pacific Scandal began to operate in reverse.

No one could doubt Mackenzie's personal honour but what about his friends? Macdonald allowed other Conservatives to shout while he talked loftily about the evils of corruption, which he fully understood. The damage of the "big push" letters cost Brown a title from a disillusioned Queen, despite Mackenzie's repeated recommendation. The damage to the Government was much worse.

Its four years had been long, hard and discouraging. Now, as the election neared, ruin came with a rush.

Mackenzie could not see it, would not believe it, denied it even to himself. As Parliament entered its ferocious session of 1877 the long strain had made him cranky in speech, bitter in mind, sick in body. The doctors ordered him to bed but after a few days he was back in the House, old and haggard. The reddish beard had turned gray. The face was grooved and gaunt. This was a man physically at the end of his tether. Dufferin wrote to London that the Prime Minister looked like "a washed-out rag and limp enough to hang upon a clothes line."

Yet he must go on. No one could replace him. In his absence Blake could argue but could not lead the Government and Blake also was sick, haunted by the fear of a mental collapse, always writing letters of resignation that his leader refused to accept. Apart from the savage Cartwright, the rest of the Cabinet, as Mackenzie confessed to his brother, was useless. He had failed to create a team. He was a general without an army. Alone he must fight off the Opposition, answer the questions, manage the Governor-General and some-how find time, late at night, to prepare for the election.

Macdonald, fully restored to health, unusually sober and certain of victory, glanced across the House to recognize in Mackenzie his own anguish during the days of the Pacific Scandal. But it was no time for mercy, and revenge would be sweet.

Scandal in a dozen different versions, none of them very serious, none touching the Prime Minister but effective in combination, must be pressed upon the most honest man in politics. Mackenzie denied all these piddling charges, dared his enemies to produce evidence and, knowing his innocence, expected an intelligent public to believe him. That was another mistake. Mackenzie's liberalism always made him overestimate the public.

With a fine sense of irony, Macdonald increasingly blamed the Government for failing to build the Pacific railway which *he* had failed to build. No matter that the Government could not find a con-tractor willing to undertake the scheme; no matter that the surveys had been rapidly pressed by Sandford Fleming; no matter that Mackenzie had finally chosen a route through the Yellowhead Pass to Burrard Inlet, was ready to let a contract for the Yale-Kamloops section and was building the line between Lake Superior and Winni-peg; no matter that the Government's budget was still in alarming deficit and Cartwright borrowing heavily in London—still the Op-position complained of inexcusable delay.

All this was the normal infighting of politics, intensified with clamorous oratory and all-night squabbles in Parliament as the elec-tion year of 1878 arrived; but Macdonald was developing his larger design. The National Policy, still vague enough to attract almost everybody, was made to sound like an inspired cure-all, the salvation of manufacturer and farmer, the one answer to the Great Depression.

Macdonald's real meaning, higher tariffs, might (as he intended) not be clear to the public, but it was clear to Mackenzie who rose at once to the old angler's bait. Dragging himself through a series of by-election speeches, the weary Prime Minister denounced the "monster" of Protection as a conspiracy against the poor. The people, he still believed, would see the fallacy of restricting trade. It was incredible to him, even now, that the National Policy, once exposed in the open, could become the permanent policy of Canada, the warp and woof of its economy for the next eight decades, the monster that Liberals would always attack, sometimes modify but never remove.

Against the glittering, open-ended promises of the National

Policy all argument was futile. In vain Mackenzie condemned the delusion of the tariff. "Give us the chance and we will show you!" Macdonald retorted in the exact words to be repeated by his latter-day heir, Diefenbaker.

Briefly the falling Liberal tide seemed to rise in 1878 when Mackenzie and Brown, living together in Ottawa, organized the election campaign at all-night sessions. Business had improved a little in the first stirrings of recovery—too late. After long arbitration, the Government had received the precious windfall of $5,500,000 for American use of the Maritime fisheries. With easier times in business and public treasury, Mackenzie's hopes revived.

The session of 1878, one of the most savage on record, plunged Parliament into daily and nightly turmoil. Macdonald was fighting now with all his youthful ferocity, his wit, his subtlety and an old man's wisdom, knowing that within months he or Mackenzie must disappear from politics. The Prime Minister staggered to bed at dawn and, after a few hours' sleep, rose again to face the morning's business and the evening's barrage. Macdonald seemed to thrive on battle. A dozen oysters, a glass or two of sherry and a nap on his couch fortified him for another attack.

Even in the last moments of the session, when the Governor-General impatiently awaited the Commons Members in the Senate chamber, Macdonald and Tupper were still shouting at Donald Smith and damning his railway line from Winnipeg to Pembina. "Coward," bellowed the frenzied Tupper, "mean, treacherous coward!" The last recorded words of Hansard were Macdonald's. "That fellow Smith," he howled, "is the biggest liar I ever met!"

Such was the election overture but Mackenzie misinterpreted it as a sign of Tory desperation. The good news, the important news, had been coming from Quebec.

Where all the older men had succeeded only in antagonizing the Quebec Catholics, the young Laurier apparently was well advanced in his life-work of reconciling the two Canadian races. He had entered the Cabinet only to be defeated at the by-election of Drummond-Arthabaska; had delivered at the age of thirty-six one of the few great speeches of Canadian politics to warn his people and the clergy that religion must not enter politics lest a Catholic party produce its Protestant counterpart and doom the nation to "religious war"; had been elected in Quebec East and now took Blake's place as the Prime Minister's right-hand man. Laurier's arrival was timely. Blake, the great Liberal brain, had finally resigned in such distress that he left Ottawa without saying good-bye to anyone.

Laurier had arrived too late to save the Government, too early by many years to replace the depleted Prime Minister. In any case, though physically beaten already, Mackenzie still expected to win the election. To him as to so many of his successors, defeat was unimaginable.

Like Macdonald six years earlier, he was hurrying from one political platform to another in a nightmare, hiding his sickness behind a torrent of speeches. He could even rise now and then to moments of apparent gaiety, always followed by exhaustion and anger—as when his friends gave him a surprise party on the silver anniversary of his wedding and he ordered his wife to return all their silver presents, "my evening's enjoyment utterly destroyed" by these innocent suggestions of bribery. For the same sort of reasons he and Blake refused titles from the Queen as unworthy of their Liberal creed.

While Mackenzie fretted, foolishly postponed the election until autumn and tried to nominate winning candidates, Macdonald was attracting huge crowds everywhere, talking of the National Policy in glittering, globular phrases and, in Quebec, fighting the campaign to vindicate French Canada's dead idol, Cartier. Though he spoke no French, he was winning Quebec. He was winning Ontario, too. He knew it now for sure and told his wife to prepare for a domestic move to Ottawa.

So came the seventeenth day of September, 1878, and the first secret vote in a general election.

Mackenzie awaited the telegrams that night with confidence. The first returns confirmed it. His Government was holding most of its Maritime seats. Macdonald had been defeated in Kingston—certain augury of his failure. Then the deceptive tide ebbed. Rural Quebec and Ontario were actually voting for the tariff monster, the farmers for the fallacy of protection! Blake and Cartwright had fallen! Mackenzie could win a majority of only 146 votes in what had always seemed to be his pocket borough of Lambton.

This was not defeat. It was debacle. Macdonald had reversed the Liberal majority of 1874.

Stunned and incredulous, Mackenzie prepared to resign not only his office but the party leadership. He was brave in his catastrophe but bitter. The Liberal Party, he wrote to a friend, must find a leader acceptable to the deluded public, a man who had "graduated as a horse thief or at least distinguished himself as having chiseled a municipality or robbed a Railway company." After making way for Macdonald, the most tragic of all ex-Prime Ministers went home and, in Sarnia, settled down to "contemplate with interest the spectacle of a nation lifting itself by the bootstraps out of the mud and increasing its wealth by changing its money from one pocket to the other."

His legacy to his successor was the end of the Great Depression, the unbuilt railway and, all unnoticed, the precedent of honesty. But honesty was not enough. It would never be enough in such a nation. Only Macdonald could supply the missing elements of imagination, bravura, luck and myth. And misfortune was not finished with Mackenzie even now.

4: The Indispensable Man

Now came Macdonald's second and his last chance—the chance to complete the work begun in 1867 and interrupted for five years, as he thought, by the Liberals; the chance to vindicate himself; best of all, the chance to retire and end his days in peace.

All this would not take long. One more term of power should be enough. Then the sweet serenity of twilight as younger men assumed his burden. From the beginning, like Sisyphus, he had pushed the slippery orb of the nation uphill. Escaping his grip, it had nearly crushed him. But from here to the end an easy path led down a gentle slope.

These fond hopes seemed reasonable. The whole climate had changed from storm to sunshine. After the Great Depression, times were suddenly good again when he took office, proving (though he could not admit it) that Liberal policies had not produced bad times and warning him (though he failed to heed the warning) that Conservative policies would have little effect on the state of a nation which must prosper or languish as the world market decreed.

The barometer of politics, too, was set for fair weather. The Liberals were discredited, divided, demoralized, their old schisms reopened. The Canadian people had learned that they could not do without their indispensable man. In 1867 he had been an experiment. In 1878 he was an institution.

For the moment the veteran of good times forgot the tidal flux of his profession, the eternal perversity of politics, the inevitable rise and fall of governments.

Macdonald felt so sure of the future that he permitted himself the relief of a mighty debauch at Halifax, where he awaited the new Governor-General in a prolonged stupor. The secretaries who tried to rouse him from his bed were ordered from the room; and thence issued another legend in his swelling apocrypha.

"If," Macdonald was said to have told one of these trembling messengers, "you come officially, tell the Governor-General to go to hell. If you come unofficially, you can go there yourself."

Pale and shaky, he was at the gangplank to welcome the Marquis of Lorne and his wife, Princess Louise. The Queen had sent her daughter to Canada—an honour to titillate all Canadians—and the befuddled Prime Minister managed to greet her with a fair show of sobriety.

The housekeeping arrangements of the new Government were quickly completed.

Macdonald had chosen to sit for Victoria, a town he had never seen, after being elected there and in Marquette, Manitoba. As their own representative in Parliament he might be able to soothe the discontented British Columbians.

The inner Cabinet was for the most part pre-made—Tupper in Public Works, Tilley back in Finance, Langevin at the Post Office as patronage boss and heavy-handed fixer of Quebec. Macdonald took the Interior Department where he could supervise the settlement of the Prairies, while Tupper built the C.P.R. and Tilley framed the National Policy. A fourth familiar figure had reappeared when Britain reluctantly accepted, in the mercurial Galt, a Canadian High Commissioner at London, the opening wedge of Canada's future independent foreign policy.

The triumvirate around the Prime Minister were all proved masters of their trade, good men and true, but, as Macdonald observed them at the Cabinet table, they seemed surprisingly old. He was old himself—sixty-three now and, after the election campaign, in wretched health. Despite the addition of some younger, untried men, the Treasury benches had the undeniable look of extinct volcanoes. The original firm of Macdonald & Co. was back again with little change of personality or policy, as Mackenzie judged from his place as opposition leader.

Mackenzie was wrong, his judgment warped by bitterness and by an honourable poverty which forced him to buy a mean house in Toronto and, as a harsh humiliation, to sell his fine Ottawa home to Tupper, of all people.

Mackenzie was wrong, in the first place, about his victor. Macdonald's personality had been subtly changed, sharpened and matured by his years in the wilderness. Secondly, he was about to launch two momentous policies that would convert a mere geographic and constitutional expression into a transcontinental state. The railway would be its skeleton. The protective tariff would supply its flesh.

Lubricated by the business boom, both policies moved ahead at astonishing speed.

Tilley "adjusted" the tariff drastically upward—only to increase revenues, of course, and by a happy coincidence, to protect Canadian industry. Macdonald assured the London Government that he had no intention of injuring British exports or indulging in the "economic depravity" of protection; but he had done both.

London was not deceived by his offer of a reciprocal tariff preference, since the free-trade Conservative ministry of Disraeli obviously could not accept it. The protective Canadian tariff was here to stay (for more than eighty years) and Britain was grudgingly reconciled to it. For Macdonald an awkward imperial corner had been turned. It was in a co-operative Britain that he must find the money for his railway.

Where Mackenzie could find no money, it was now increasingly available, coaxed out of hiding by the boom. Offers to build the railway came from many sides, giving Macdonald the opportunity to pick and choose.

Before two busy years were out he had suffered a dangerous attack of cholera, the doctors advising him to make his will; had survived a series of minor illnesses; had fully recovered in a long English holiday; had closed his deal with the new Canadian Pacific Railway Company headed by George Stephen.

The Montreal financier, a bearded, willowy and brooding Scot of extraordinary gifts and frequent fits of black melancholy, had learned the railway business with his cousin, Donald Smith, by leasing a line from St. Paul to Winnipeg against Macdonald's implacable opposition in the days of the Liberal Government. That quarrel was forgotten now; Smith, "the biggest liar I ever met," was kept discreetly in the background of Stephen's syndicate, and the largest, the most risky and unbelievable economic adventure ever attempted in America was under way.

Stephen agreed to join Montreal and the Pacific Coast with steel tracks in ten years or less on the Government's promise of $25 million in cash and 25 million acres of land.

The Liberals said the scheme was immoral because it created the

Frankenstein monster of a railway monopoly, and was impossible as well. Again they were wrong.

Stephen proved better than his word. Under the direction of William Cornelius Van Horne, an American turned rabidly Canadian, a self-made man, a musician, painter, conjurer, gourmet and corpulent giant of Gargantuan appetites and wily, hooded eyes, the tracks of the C.P.R. seemed to roll ahead automatically as from some mysterious machine, often by a mile in a single day, racing a parallel American line, the Northern Pacific, to the western sea.

Van Horne's methods were simple. "Oh, I eat all I can, I drink all I can, I smoke all I can, and I don't give a damn for anything," he said, adding to the London *Times* reporter that his family coat of arms was "A Dinner Horne, Pendant, upon a Kitchen Door." His work was not as easy as it sounded. He crossed and recrossed the continent by canoe, horseback or handcar, driving himself even harder than he drove his crews, and worshipped his railway as a god.

Westward along the bluffs of Lake Superior, across the Prairies, toward the Rockies, and eastward up the black canyon of the Fraser, Van Horne led his army of workmen with a strange mixture of encouragement, threat and bluff. Macdonald watched this prodigy from a distance, amazed and delighted, sure now that his double work was near completion—the railway to articulate the nation's disjointed limbs, the National Policy to provide the traffic and nourish a national organism.

The C.P.R. was moving so fast that by 1881, as he prepared for an election next year, the Prime Minister announced that the tracks should reach the Pacific in five years instead of ten and he hoped to travel it himself "before I am just quite an angel."

Old Tomorrow's vindication had come far sooner than he dared to hope, not only in Canada but in Britain. Disraeli rated him "a considerable man." The Queen admitted him to her Privy Council. His Pacific Scandal expunged at last, he was a recognized imperial statesman, a proconsul of Empire.

These were heady days. Political success, as usual, brought physical recovery. Macdonald was frequently ill with "coats on the stomach," according to Dr. Tupper's personal diagnosis, with nagging colds, bronchitis and sciatica but invariably a few weeks in England, a gay round of theatres, dinner parties and country weekends restored the patient and postponed the retirement which he was always promising himself and never seemed able to execute. High tide and glorious summer—but Indian summer, delusory and brief.

Despite his show of confidence, Van Horne was beginning to

worry. For one thing, the railway route, moved far southward since Mackenzie's time to keep it beside the American border and to monopolize all Canadian traffic, now ran by Calgary and straight west, though no pass had been found through the labyrinth of the Selkirk Range. Perhaps there was none. More alarming was the recent confidential news from Stephen. Under the poisonous propaganda of the Grand Trunk, which wanted no competitor in the East, of the American railways and most of the British press, the C.P.R. found the London money market suddenly hostile.

Macdonald could handle the Opposition in Parliament when it denounced an all-Canadian route as economic madness and proposed to by-pass the badlands of the Great Lakes by a southward American detour. He could forbid the construction of branch lines that would drain future C.P.R. business southward to the United States. But Stephen's latest confession to him was staggering—the C.P.R. had spent far more than it expected and, at the present rate, would soon go broke.

That prospect, jeopardizing not only the railway but the Government and Confederation itself—Macdonald's whole life-work—was in the back of his mind but boldly concealed from the public as he planned the election of 1882. Its result seemed certain but he took no chances.

By gerrymandering the Ontario electoral boundaries he "hived the Grits," concentrating their vote in as few constituencies as possible. They screamed their protests in Parliament and he calmly replied that he had given them what they had always demanded—"Representation by Population." The gerrymander was an exceedingly rough job, perhaps unnecessary, but in the critical game ahead he needed every card he could deal himself from the bottom of the deck.

The Liberals were now reorganized. After the defeat of 1878 Mackenzie had intended to retire and remained in politics mainly at the insistence of Brown who, living comfortably in his palatial Toronto home, urged his sick friend to fight on. Mackenzie led the Liberals until 1880, led them almost single-handed, too proud, too hurt, too suspicious of the younger Blake wing to share his mind with anyone—a lonely figure, erect but broken, a ruin that refused to fall.

When the blow came he took it stoically, comforted by the thought that he was the victim of a cabal. "It is only human nature that a defeated army should seek another general," Laurier was supposed to have told him, with a touch of compassion, at the caucus. Before the young man could finish his sentence Mackenzie cut him short. "Very well then," he said. "If that is so I shall very soon cease to lead the Liberal Party."

In the afternoon he went briskly through the routine of Parliament, asking questions, offering criticism and, at the adjournment hour, rose to say without the slightest tremor in his voice: "I yesterday determined to withdraw from the position as leader of the Opposition and from this time forth I will speak and act for no person but myself."

He had left, by common consent, a failure. Thenceforth he must walk alone to his final agony. The Liberals replaced him immediately with Blake, the man of intellect who could not fail.

In the election of 1882 Blake had his chance and Macdonald waited sceptically to see how he would use it. The spring campaign had not been long under way before Blake threw his chance away. The great mind tired its audiences by long, complicated speeches, bristling with theory, figures and legal argument—excellent for Parliament or a court of law, no good in the back concessions. Moreover, as Macdonald quickly reminded the public, Blake was wobbling on free trade. As an honest man he could hardly attack the National Policy outright any longer since its results, or its apparent results, were known to everybody in these good times.

The poll of June 20 went about as Macdonald expected—139 Conservatives to 71 Liberals. He was elected in Lennox, near Kingston, where he had lived for a time as a boy. The Government had been returned but its victory was no more than a whistle stop on the railway's breakneck journey to the sea.

With a little luck, the C.P.R. should be finished well before another election if it could escape bankruptcy meanwhile. That luck already was planted in the most unlikely place, by the most unlikely hands. At the moment, however, Macdonald heard nothing but bad news and again his health seemed to be collapsing.

The bad news came from all sides.

Oliver Mowat, Macdonald's former law student and now the Premier of Ontario, was defying federal jurisdiction. As the Prime Minister thought, Mowat had assaulted the constitution by a spate of obnoxious provincial liquor and inland-navigation laws. If this went on the centralized State conceived at Confederation would be split into a congeries of sovereign provinces, the constitution unworkable. To Macdonald's consternation, the Imperial Privy Council, by a series of shifting verdicts, supported Ontario.

In the old pre-Confederation Assembly Macdonald had once

lost his head, shaken his fist under Mowat's nose and, calling him "a damned pup," had promised to "slap your chops." Now, with the broad hand of the Empire's highest court, Mowat was slapping the chops of the nation. The "Little Tyrant," as Macdonald named him, had beaten the federal Government, thanks to the legal crotchets of over-washed Englishmen in London.

This was intolerable to Macdonald's pride but soon the news from Nova Scotia looked even more shocking. There Premier W. S. Fielding, in curious overture to his career as a national statesman, was actually asking his province to secede from the union and proposed to call an election on that issue. The ghost of the young Howe walked again.

Quebec was restive, too, in desperate financial straits and threatening to use its local railways to damage the C.P.R., while Manitoba insisted on building superfluous lines to the American border and breaking the C.P.R. monopoly in defiance of the federal Government.

All these troubles were released and compounded by another change in the weather of business. As the boom subsided the return of hard times brought its familiar backwash of local grievance, sectionalism and disintegration. The systole of a federal system pumped power from Ottawa to the provincial capitals until the diastole of good times could reverse the flow. Such problems were never entirely curable and must be lived with somehow. They were dwarfed by the infinitely larger problem of the C.P.R. It tottered on the knife's edge of insolvency.

The thing was peculiarly tantalizing—a line nearly completed across the continent, Roger's Pass through the Selkirks discovered in the nick of time, the long dream almost realized, and yet, on the eve of his triumph, Macdonald looked into the face of catastrophe, catastrophe for him and for the nation.

While he waited, helpless, events moved in sudden landslide.

The last funds in the C.P.R. treasury running out, its stock falling on the market; the London and New York banks refusing to lend another penny in these times of depression; Stephen and Smith pleading for government rescue, mortgaging their private fortunes and determined, if the crash came, that "not a dollar" would be found in their pockets; Van Horne telegraphing in code from the West that he could not pay his crews; the workers at Port Arthur on strike for their wages; the Liberals of Parliament howling with mixed pleasure and indignation that the railway scheme was a fiasco as they had predicted; worst of all, a revolt in the Cabinet against more aid to the C.P.R. and a clear warning that Macdonald might not get it from a frightened Parliament—all these hammer blows had driven him to bed again in his new house of "Earnscliffe," now less a home than a hospital or the headquarters of a besieged army.

If Old Tomorrow could not keep his health, he kept his head and applied his dependable remedy of delay.

The nerves of other men were breaking. Blake wrangled perpetually as if Parliament were a courtroom and the railway Exhibit A, as if the nation were not totally committed to the C.P.R. beyond any chance of withdrawal. Cartwright fulminated. Tupper writhed with impatience, demanding instant attack on the enemy. From London, Stephen, remembering the ancient battle cry of his Scottish clan, telegraphed his imperishable transatlantic shout to Smith: "Stand fast, Craigellachie!" It was noble, it was heroic, just what Macdonald would expect from Stephen but it was of little help now.

Delay was the only possible tactic until Macdonald could be sure that Parliament would approve the all-or-nothing policy which he had framed but dared not reveal yet—a loan of $22,500,000 to the C.P.R. He must push it through against a divided Cabinet, a hostile party, an Opposition sure that he and his railway were perishing together. He must wait and hope, like Mr. Micawber, that something would turn up.

Invisibly his luck already had begun to change. Something was turning up and, of all places, on the Saskatchewan River.

Ignorant of events there, sick in body and mind, Macdonald steeled himself for the hardest parliamentary struggle of his life, the most doubtful and, for Canada, the most dangerous.

It could not be conducted as a lightning raid, his favourite tactic, or as a pitched battle. It must be directed as a war. Tupper would lead the charge in the House at the appointed hour. Macdonald, free of detail and saying little, would direct the grand strategy from headquarters, hold the Cabinet together if he could, suppress an ugly rebellion among the Quebec Conservatives with threat and cajolery, pacify the caucus and, if possible, keep the C.P.R. afloat for a few more days. It had to come to that by the spring of 1884. Within a week at most the railway would be bankrupt, the work stopped, the Government and the nation paralyzed.

A supreme crisis had arrived and one man alone could meet it. But even as Macdonald ordered Tupper to advance, the decisive move had not been made in Ottawa. It had been made by a madman far out in the West.

Tupper advanced frontally in Parliament with eleven resolutions

82

guaranteeing the C.P.R. loan. Macdonald watched him, a picture of serenity, almost of boredom.

The counter-attack from Blake was stronger than the Government anticipated—day after day of orator's eloquence against the vicious C.P.R. monopoly and lawyer's argument on every minor point; night after night of harassment and blockade, the most ferocious scene in Parliament's history.

Yet the counter-attack was plainly failing. It must fail because Blake attacked on the periphery. He could not discern the centre, the single fact that mattered now, the survival of a nation dependent on the survival of the railway. As the days and nights wore on Macdonald knew that he must win, but the victory was larger than he had assumed. The C.P.R. loan passed by overwhelming majority.

He had won in politics but, as never before, he was exhausted in body and fled to England for release. As always, he found health again in London's social whirl and, for good measure, the Grand Cross of the Bath. Health, yes, and honour; but he carried with him a terrible secret. Stephen had told him on shipboard that the railway loan would not be enough. Within a year still more money must be found. The fierce war of Parliament had not been decisive after all. A worse one lay ahead and a second victory seemed impossible.

Perhaps it would have been impossible without the new ally who appeared in the guise of a traitor.

For some months Macdonald had heard vague whispers of trouble from the West. The Métis people, some of them from Red River, had settled on the Saskatchewan, had set up at Batoche a tribal rule under an ignorant but intelligent leader, Gabriel Dumont, and now were complaining about their treatment by the Canadian Government.

They wanted sure title to their squatters' land, they wanted scrip in compensation for supposed losses on Red River, they wanted more money than any government could give. Macdonald understood all that, for he had learned a harsh lesson in the so-called rebellion of 1870. Reluctantly changing his mind, he agreed to an issue of scrip, though he knew the money would be squandered, set up a commission of inquiry and counted on an expensive but peaceful compromise. The "present effervescence" would quickly "subside." His inveterate blind spot still hid the western horizon.

Even the amazing news of Riel's return did not much disturb him. The exile, now a married man with two children—middle-aged, almost patriarchal with his curly brown beard and mild manner—evidently had reformed, had taken the mystical name of David and,

when Dumont summoned him to Saskatchewan, had come quietly
enough with his family, beholding on the way a vision of himself on
a gibbet. Unhappily he did not heed the vision.

At Batoche he behaved peaceably, spoke moderately to the
Métis and the white settlers and uttered no word of violence. But
strange stories were soon coming from Saskatchewan.

Riel had quarreled with the Catholic priests who saw in him the
madness that Macdonald would not see. Refused the sacraments, as
he began to talk of rebellion, Riel declared that "Rome has fallen,"
proclaimed "The Living Catholic Apostolic and Vital Church of the
New World" and presently announced to his dubious communicants
the revelation that they had nothing to fear from heresy since hell
might last for millions of years but not forever.

These were the sure symptoms of the mania which had often
been treated in the asylums of Quebec. In another crafty mood Riel
was offering to sell his people out and leave the country if the
Government paid him a sufficient bribe.

Macdonald heard the reports from Batoche second-hand and
probably garbled. Riel's demands were absurd, of course, his bribe
would not be paid but he could be handled with patience and a little
money for the Métis. Certainly there would be no second rebellion.

Thus, as in 1870, Macdonald totally misjudged the Métis and
their prophet. He was walking blindly into his second error, the
worst, by far, of his life. Paradoxically, it was to be also his greatest
piece of luck. The half-breed adventurer and lunatic, the cool and
calculating Prime Minister, never seeing each other, were bound
together in a kind of weird Götterdämmerung. It would outlast
them both.

Meanwhile the guest of Disraeli's country house and Windsor
Castle comforted himself with the thought that Riel was annoying,
treacherous, venal and harmless. On his return to Canada Macdonald found the crowds of Toronto celebrating his seventieth
birthday with such an outburst of adulation as he had never seen
before, and from the back of a crowded auditorium he heard a single
voice pronounce the common people's myth—"You'll never die,
John A!" In a sense it was true. But it was drowned out in the news
from Saskatchewan.

Dumont and his two hundred sharpshooters hidden on a hill-
side near Duck Lake; a detachment of Mounted Police approaching
on sleighs through a spring blizzard; Riel clutching a two-foot
wooden crucifix in muttered prayer; the crack of rifles, ten police-
men dead on the snow, the rest in retreat; Dumont wounded in the

scalp, blinded by blood but determined to follow and exterminate the enemy; Riel shrieking, "In the name of God let them go, there's been too much bloodshed already!"—such was the news from Saskatchewan.

Throughout Canada a convulsion of anger, in every town volunteers enlisting for a civil war, in Ottawa a Prime Minister who saw rebellion clearly at last and his own mistake, but failed to guess the sequel—so began the curious salvation of the C.P.R.

One man saw it instantly. Van Horne telegraphed the Government that within eleven days he would move troops to Saskatchewan. Impossible as it seemed, the offer was accepted. Macdonald had seen its larger possibility.

Van Horne loaded General Frederick Middleton's little army of amateur soldiers on hay-filled flat-cars, carried them by sleigh across the railway gaps along Lake Superior, laid tracks on the ice of frozen rivers and fulfilled his promise. Within eleven days the troops (including Macdonald's son, Hugh John) were at Qu'Appelle and moving slowly toward Riel's capital of Batoche.

It was a mimic war but deadly. Dumont's victory at Fish Creek, Indian massacre at Frog Lake, siege of Fort Pitt and Battleford, advance on Batoche, a brave, hopeless defence by the Métis from their gun pits, Riel's surrender, Dumont's escape to Montana, the rebel's trial at Regina on charge of treason, his refusal to plead insanity, verdict of guilty from a jury of six white men, his corpse swinging from a gibbet on a cold November morning and then, frozen, carried to its grave at St. Boniface by a C.P.R. train—thus ended the rebellion, thus the value of the railway was demonstrated for all men to see and thus the Government, in its hour of triumph, was wounded fatally.

A French-Canadian Catholic had been hanged at Regina. Quebec would never forgive that affront to its race and religion. The wound had gone so deep that for the moment Macdonald could not estimate its consequences; deep into the nation's vitals, not to be healed for half a century at least, not healable by any English-speaking Conservative physician.

In the meantime, however, there was no doubt that the Government could get the money for the railway which had proved its worth. The Opposition still haggled but after weeks of hesitation and reconnaissance Macdonald could risk a vote in Parliament.

Everything went as he hoped, and faster.

On June 16, he introduced his plan to save the C.P.R. by purchasing $35 million of its bonds. Though Blake still fought the hateful monopoly, Parliament voted the money and now the London banks were willing to lend still more.

On November 7 of the same year Smith, Macdonald's old enemy and new friend, drove the last transcontinental spike at a lonely stopping-place in the Rockies, appropriately called Craigellachie, while the shy Van Horne, who had built the railway, could only mumble that "the work has been well done."

Next summer Macdonald and his wife traveled westward and saw for the first time from the windows of their private car the nation he had created. They rode on the locomotive's cowcatcher through the Rockies and down the Fraser's canyon, where the wheels killed a pig near Yale and hurled it within an inch of Agnes' head. After that narrow escape from death the visitors enjoyed the expensive hospitality of Victoria, thinking themselves outrageously overcharged at the Driard Hotel. Macdonald drove his own last spike on Robert Dunsmuir's newly built Esquimalt and Nanaimo Railway and, escaping the watchful ladies, drank Dunsmuir's whisky in the safe depths of a coal mine.

At last the maker of Confederation held the gorgeous West in fee. It had been almost a fairy-tale of mountain gorges, Indian powwows and cheering processions; but although he could dismiss reality with this medicine, stronger with him than drink, he knew that reality awaited him in Ottawa.

What, he must have asked himself, had been taught by all these events of '85 and '86? Three lessons, clearly and permanently: the Canadian people might quarrel and threaten but in a crisis they would unite as a true people and nation; the office of the Prime Minister, incomparably greater and more powerful than the constitution had foreseen or intended, alone could invoke, lead and deploy the people's energies; and the office, now expanded by its opportunities and its dangers, could be adequately filled by no one but a great man—with luck, one man in each generation.

The contemporary man was nearing the end of his long journey but the holiday seemed to revive him and, as he had hoped, the Government's strength in the West. Macdonald would need this double strength. He had begun to realize, very late, the depth of Quebec's wound.

In life Riel had been a rebel. In death he was a martyr—a French-Canadian and Catholic martyr. His gibbet at Regina had become one of the lasting landmarks in the nation's journey. The Prime Minister need not ask for whom the church bells tolled along the St. Lawrence. They tolled for his Government and party.

Still he did not and would never understand Quebec's spiritual hurt and inward bruise for which there was no sovereign remedy but time.

Riel had been found guilty, as Macdonald reasoned, by an honest court. His appeal had been dismissed by the Privy Council. Then, against his own judgment as a lawyer, Macdonald had sent three doctors to examine the prisoner's mind and determine not whether he was insane at the time of the rebellion—surely the relevant question—but whether he was sane enough to understand the meaning of his trial. The doctors had found him sane, as he himself claimed, within the meaning of the law, though by ordinary standards he was stark mad. By the standards of our age he certainly would not have been executed. By the standards of politics in any age his execution was worse than a judicial murder—it was a blunder, unnecessary and irrevocable.

Despite these dangers, Macdonald was determined from the start to hang Riel, come what might.

"He shall hang," said the Prime Minister, "though every dog in Quebec should bark in his favour."

Macdonald was thinking with his Anglo-Saxon blood but the decision of a distracted Cabinet turned mainly on political calculation—to appease Ontario by a hanging or Quebec by clemency? Riel had given up hope, reconciled himself to God and fearlessly awaited the end while the Cabinet argued until the eve of the day fixed for execution. Weighing the narrow odds, it finally confirmed Riel's death warrant and signed its own, for enforcement later.

Macdonald did not suspect that yet, nor the longer sentence of defeat passed on his party. For the present he held all his French-Canadian ministers, notwithstanding their fear and horror, held all but seventeen of his Quebec Members and even split the Opposition, Mackenzie and twenty-two other English-speaking Liberals voting approval of the execution. And of course Ontario, as in 1870, rejoiced at the just punishment of a Catholic traitor.

All this was good news for a Prime Minister in bed with tortures of sciatica; good, but transitory. For the struggle, as he soon saw, could not be reckoned in parliamentary arithmetic. It had moved to a lower level. Quebec's anger burned like a fire in a coal mine— slow, subterranean, often unseen but never to be quenched by the Prime Minister who had ignited it. The race, the Church, the language, the ancient folk memory of French Canada, which Macdonald had thought he understood, united to indict and detest him as "the hangman."

The first rumbles from Quebec were heard on the night of Riel's death when a Montreal mob burned Macdonald's effigy in Dominion Square. On the following Sunday, before a sullen audience in the Champ de Mars, Laurier unfurled his flag of future victory, a bloody flag and a dangerous one, but inevitably victorious among his own people.

"Had I been born on the banks of the Saskatchewan," he cried later in Parliament, "I would myself have shouldered a musket to fight against the neglect of government and the shameless greed of speculators!"

That was shocking to Macdonald and much of English-speaking Canada, it was vicarious treason, it was also a considered manoeuvre of politics but it came from Laurier's heart. Soon he was condemning Riel's martyrdom in some of his greatest speeches. With a physical and moral courage that surprised the nation, he carried his campaign into Ontario and Ontario listened. The rebellion had killed Riel. It had made Laurier.

Blake, now trying to ride the two racial horses, was able to put the issue in a typically neat syllogism: "Had there been no neglect there would have been no rebellion. If no rebellion, then no arrest. If no arrest, then no trial. If no trial, then no condemnation. If no condemnation, then no execution. They, therefore, who are responsible for the first are responsible for every link in that fatal chain."

This was magnificent oratory but was it political war? Blake, facing an early election, was strained by his double equestrian feat and took refuge in ambiguity. Since he could not afford to quarrel with Ontario while Laurier aroused Quebec, he said only that he did not "propose to construct a political platform out of the Regina scaffold or to create or to cement party ties with the blood of the condemned." Again magnificent but not successful war.

Blake could maintain his judicial logic and necessary balancing act but Blake no longer controlled the future of the Liberal Party. Laurier controlled it; and the nation, for the first time, began to notice him.

What the nation saw was a man of forty-five years—tall, slim, regal, his chiseled and sensitive face crowned by an aureole of dark curls. He was, indeed, when you came to look at him, almost a retouched portrait of a younger Macdonald with the wrinkles removed, the nose remodeled, the English speech deliciously flavoured with French accent. There was more to the resemblance than that. Laurier, denouncing Macdonald, was learning to imitate his methods and would use them to the end.

What the public did not see yet was the spine of hard steel behind the French Canadian's almost womanly charm, the cold streak of cunning concealed by the warm language of chivalry. Laurier was a genuinely great man by any reckoning, one of half a dozen equals in Canadian history, and the people sensed his greatness. He had the imprint and aura of a Prime Minister. He had all the other equipment, too, except luck. *It* would arrive in due time.

The next Liberal leader had emerged, the first French-Canadian Catholic leader in a nation of English-speaking and Protestant majority. Was it possible for him to lead the nation? Only if he was a man of unique gifts, only if the nation was more tolerant and mature than it appeared to be.

On the other hand, Macdonald was firmly established but he had found no durable heir. Frantically seeking young men, he had lured John S. D. Thompson from the Nova Scotia bench to the Justice Department and regarded him as his ablest colleague. There was no one else so far to replace the tired veterans. Old as Macdonald and his Government were—"too old," he wrote Tupper—he still could not quit as he desired, or thought he desired. Out of duty and habit—above all, because he could not trust his unfinished creation, his frail darling, to untried hands—he must stay a little longer, and time was running out.

It flowed fast from the Regina watershed.

Laurier's revolt, carried on by less responsible men against his opposition, was going much further than he intended. He had helped to release from the bottle of Quebec's separatism the jinn which he would try to control for the next quarter century, which would end by overwhelming him. Could the Conservatives outlive this racial upsurge? If not, could the Liberals tame it and make their party viable outside Quebec? At first the answers to both questions were misleading.

The formation of Honoré Mercier's Le Parti National in Quebec, a party of nationalism, racialism and revenge, a revival of the old Canadian nightmare, fed by the memory of Riel and the deepening economic depression; the sharper talk of secession in Nova Scotia; murmurs of the same sort from Manitoba where the farmers' crops were bad and the C.P.R. monopoly hated; renewed quarrel with the United States on the Maritime fisheries after the end of the Washington treaty and the recent seizure of American fishing vessels; Mowat's re-election in Ontario and Quebec's swing to Mercier —step by step Macdonald was driven, on the defensive now, toward the doubtful election of February 22, 1887, in a season of deep snow and a sub-zero climate of politics.

Blake, for all his ambiguity in the Riel affair, was still formidable. If he took a broad, generous and constructive view of the C.P.R. and an economy now committed to the protective tariff, if he accepted the facts as they stood, Blake might be unbeatable when clearly Quebec was against the Government.

As Macdonald soon saw, there was no danger of that. Blake indicted the whole record of the Government, the C.P.R. and the National Policy as madness. His keen, myopic eye unerringly distinguished every single tree of mismanagement, abuse, mistake and scandal but never saw the forest. His orations were flawless, unanswerable and soporific. They offered no comfort to a depressed country.

Blake's last chance had come and he was spoiling it. The Liberals, cocksure of victory, campaigned with the smug literal-mindedness that was their congenital vice, a vice they would indulge again on another disastrous occasion seventy years hence. Macdonald had expected this from Blake but it was astonishing in the spacious Laurier, more astonishing than Macdonald realized. Within a decade Laurier, who now attacked the C.P.R., would be planning superfluous railways of his own.

Despite Blake's assistance, things were not going well for the Government. After the last election Macdonald had seemed unchallenged and unchallangeable, the country prosperous, his work almost finished. Now Government, country and his career were all imperilled. How could all this happen in so short a time? It was beyond belief, unnatural.

Where had he gone wrong? He could not tell. He was not even sure that his wasted body would carry him through the campaign. Yet he must go on and at least he would not imitate Blake's error of talking over the voters' heads.

Tired, sick and fearful, no longer the agile, black-haired Macdonald of old times but a gray and wrinkled actor playing a familiar part by rote, he put on his mask of grin and persiflage, trudged through the Ontario cold and, suddenly galvanized by his mysterious inner force, turned on Blake the lethal weapon of his irony.

The *Globe*, he said, had reported his suicide in 1873, was now predicting his early death and diagnosing his illness as paralysis of the brain, but since he was "enjoying a few lucid moments before an attack of frenzy came on," the voters might like to hear their business discussed.

The voters were amused and Macdonald hardly discussed their business. He ran on his nerve, his record and his myth. Long ago he had proved that the public preferred him drunk to Brown sober. Now it preferred him clowning to Blake reasoning.

His strategy of diversion and human appeal, combined with Blake's lack of both, were just sufficient to save the Government and keep the French Canadian fire underground a little longer. Macdonald came back with a majority of about thirty reliable Conservatives—not much, but it would do.

In politics Blake was a spectacular anticlimax but in the Liberal legend to this day he is a hero, though he never won an election or governed the country, while Mackenzie, who had done both, would be remembered almost apologetically as a failure.

That living relic of early times, still in Parliament and listening intently, had been struck down by nature's final blow. His vocal chords paralyzed, Mackenzie could not speak. Bursting with unutterable protest, he could only croak a hoarse, inaudible objection now and then as Macdonald winced with sympathy, perhaps with a twinge of remorse.

Looking about the House and speaking seldom, Macdonald saw few survivors of his generation. It seemed only yesterday that Cartier had been at his side to share the load. McGee, Rose and Howe were all dead. Even the faithful Tupper was gone, refusing to leave his cosy post as High Commissioner in London. Brown, the old enemy, had been murdered by a printer in the *Globe* office. Blake was sulking in retirement. A new generation stood at the door, led by a better man. Yes, Laurier, Blake's successor, was dangerous.

So was the mood of the country. As the years rolled past at accelerating speed, they gathered, like snowballs, a swelling bulk of trouble. Despite the completed railway, the National Policy and all the splendid achievements of his time, the aging master of an aging Government saw that he could never complete his work after all.

Canada was more divided now than it had ever been since Confederation—a racial, cultural and religious division, the barren harvest of Regina. Soon the subterranean fire of Quebec leaped to the West where it became an anti-French, anti-Catholic fire, the two threatening to join in national conflagration. Manitoba was determined to abolish the separate Catholic schools established in Riel's time. A new provincial law could be stalled off until after the next election but not for long.

The Conservative Party in Parliament was fractured by the same revolt against Catholicism. Macdonald's close friend, Dalton Mc-

Carthy, and his "Noble Thirteen" broke with the Government to oppose its settlement of the shaking Jesuit Estates controversy in Quebec and campaigned everywhere on a nakedly anti-French policy. What Macdonald had most feared, what he had skilfully avoided for thirty years—a collision of the races—looked unavoidable.

Business was bad again after a brief recovery. The National Policy contained no magic.

Langevin, the rapacious boss of Quebec patronage, was involved in a nasty little scandal.

The Americans, still coveting the Maritime fisheries, monopolizing the fur-seal industry of the North Pacific and seizing Canadian vessels, were now in one breath proposing a new tariff deal and, in the next, threatening to cease all commercial intercourse with Canada. Probably President Cleveland's posture of intimidation was no more than an election dodge but it revived Macdonald's lifelong fear of Manifest Destiny.

In all this catalogue of misfortune the old man's eye had detected one hopeful entry.

Having unloaded Blake, a neo-protectionist, the Liberals under Laurier had decided to stake everything on unrestricted reciprocity or "commercial union" with the United States. Macdonald regarded that policy as "a dead duck," a fatal trap for any party, and proposed to let it "blaze, crackle and go out with a stink." But it would not go out. Though it was "sheer insanity," it would continue to smoulder until it consumed Laurier in 1911.

Meanwhile Macdonald must square the old circle of the tariff issue again lest he antagonize an electorate increasingly suspicious of the National Policy in these times of depression. Though he would not repeal it, or basically alter it, he was prepared, he said, to negotiate lower tariffs if the United States would accept reasonable terms. Privately he thought a deal impossible but in his latest version of the old trade issue he kept that chance alive with encouraging gestures to divert the Liberal attack.

As usual, the Conservative tariff policy was well wrapped in equivocation, its sharp edge blunted, while the Liberals, for once, were taking a definite stand. That was always a desperate risk but how could Macdonald exploit Laurier's mistake?

So the Prime Minister pondered and time passed for him with the terrifying speed of his age. Now, incredible as it seemed, the year 1891 had arrived. It was Macdonald's seventy-seventh year when he should have been in comfortable retirement. This hope, postponed so often, was finally lost. He knew it, knew that he would die in harness, and he set about his final campaign with all the enthusiasm and craft of his younger days.

Moreover, he had traveled by a long circle back to his original position as if, in policy, as in the journey of life, he was coming home. The United States, he was now convinced, had determined to impoverish Canada by restricting its trade and then to annex it or, at least, to make it an "independent republic."

As this old Canadian bogey grew in the old man's mind, so did his suspicion of the Liberals and the bitterness of his political speeches. Laurier, he warned, would receive "Yankee money" to "corrupt our people" and support reciprocity, the beginning of annexation. After months of wobbling on the tariff, Macdonald had decided to fight the "veiled treason" of Liberalism in the open, win or lose.

By all the laws of politics he was bound to lose. A disintegrating party, a Cabinet weakened by age, a broken-down political machine held together only by Macdonald's personal magic faced an Opposition united by Laurier, vigorous with youth, carried by a flood tide. There was only one chance for a Government on the defensive —it must attack.

Macdonald called the election for March 5, 1891, and, staking the Government's life on this last fling, announced that the issue was Canada's survival or its annexation. His formal and rather melodramatic address to the electors was built around Baldwin's phrase which he had used so successfully before: "As for myself, my course is clear. A British subject I was born—a British subject I will die. With my utmost effort, with my latest breath, will I oppose the veiled treason which attempts by sordid means and mercenary proffers to lure our people from their allegiance."

This was over-used but still potent medicine. Macdonald's charge against the Liberals lacked nothing except proof. By luck and larceny the proof appeared just in time.

A few weeks earlier, Edward Farrer, one of the *Globe* editors, had met Secretary of State James G. Blaine in Washington as the unofficial agent—or so the Canadian Conservatives affirmed—of the Liberal Opposition. Laurier, it was said, had gone behind the Government's back to conspire with the Americans against his own country.

Such a pitiable canard might have died quickly if Farrer had not committed his private thoughts to print in a pamphlet for secret distribution. As he pleaded afterwards, the pamphlet was intended merely to survey Canadian-American relations from an American point of view and in this dispassionate spirit explained how the United States could coerce Canada in the fishery and trade disputes.

To suppose that Laurier would approve a document certain to discredit him was to underrate not only his morals but his intelligence. Nevertheless, when a friendly printer stole the proofs of the pamphlet and smuggled them to the Conservative bosses, Macdonald knew that a precious accident had delivered the Liberal Party into his hands. With poetic justice, long postponed, the Liberals who had bought the telegrams of the Pacific Scandal were now the victims of identical thievery.

Macdonald used this dirty weapon, as it had been used against him, to prove that "there is a deliberate conspiracy, by force, by fraud, or by both, to force Canada into the American union."

The Conservative counter-conspiracy had been perfectly timed, the roorback introduced too late for a successful answer, Laurier's denials lost in the tumult. But even while Macdonald played this winning game an unseen player intervened.

After a rousing speech near Kingston, he returned late at night to his private car. There his secretary found him sprawled, helpless, across his bed. He spoke no more in the campaign and seemed near death. Not until the day before the election could he be brought back to Ottawa.

He was in bed at "Earnscliffe" when the first returns told him that his last miracle had succeeded. The Government was returned with a loss of seats, a minority of fifteen in Quebec, but still a narrow total majority. The stolen pamphlet had done the business. Farrer had defeated Laurier, his friend. All that was true, but only the presence of Macdonald, well or sick, as a man beloved and an institution respected, could have won brief reprieve for a party marching toward the wilderness.

Mortality, the unseen player, now took over the game. On May 12 Macdonald met the Governor-General, Lord Stanley. Without warning, his voice became thick and blurred as if he had been drinking. Yet he was cold sober. In sudden terror, he remembered that both his parents had died of paralysis.

For a few days his speech seemed to improve. Then, on the night of May 27, as he cried out in his sleep, Agnes found him paralyzed. He could speak in whispers to his physicians, could even discuss the future of the Government with Thompson and warn him against the choice of Abbott as the next Prime Minister, but the flame which

94

had lighted Canada since the day of its birth was flickering out at last.

On the afternoon of May 29, Dr. R. W. Powell watched his patient sink slowly as in sleep. Macdonald never spoke or moved again. Still he could not die. The spirit in the shattered body fought on in silence, the struggle sometimes gleaming in the fearless old eyes.

Day after day the doctors issued their bulletins, the people waited and Parliament was hushed by the prospect of the unthinkable event. Macdonald recovered slightly. Speechless but fully conscious, he answered questions by a feeble pressure of his left hand. What thoughts floated through a mind surviving the useless flesh, what hopes and fears for Canada, what conclusions about a life of prodigious labour, achievement, happiness and heartbreak, what memories of the long road from Scotland, the watchers at the bedside would never know. No one would ever quite know Macdonald, the man lost in the myth.

At a quarter past ten, on the night of June 6, the long road ended.

According to his will, the first and greatest Prime Minister was buried beside his parents, his first wife and infant son in the Cataraqui graveyard at Kingston while across the nation he had made men who had never seen his face paused to talk of him as a lifelong friend. Their grief, their affection, their forgiveness of his frailties were the only monument he needed. No one could ever quite replace him but his myth, a common possession always drawing a divided people together, would prove to be as valuable as his life.

The generation around him was going, too. "Oh, take me home!" Mackenzie cried on his death-bed a few months after Macdonald's departure. Both the old enemies were home now. A new generation must take up the toil, the risks and the unsolved problems of a Canada which might be mortal like its makers.

5: The Long Obsequies

Everyone knew that with Macdonald a Canadian era had ended. The same cliché had been applied to earlier figures and would be applied to all comparable statesmen later on, in all countries and times. For Canada, however, it was more than a cliché.

Not only the man but his era actually had died. The man was buried. The era still wore the semblance of life and would wear it for a little time as the long obsequies of the Conservative régime were conducted by Macdonald's four feeble successors. But even if he had lived and governed for another twenty years his era—not only in politics but in society at large—would have passed. The world was moving from one century to another and Canada with it.

Hence the task of a political machine broken beyond repair by the loss of its essential cog was not only the choice of a new Prime Minister, as the Government supposed, but the transition into a new age now being born far beyond the range of Canada. The first rustle of the twentieth century could be heard by a discerning ear already.

There were few such ears in Ottawa as the Government, without Macdonald, began the wracking organic process of readjustment to conditions that it could not understand, that nobody understood yet. Five years of trial and error were to be spent, and wasted, on this attempt to revive the aged Conservative régime. It had served Canada well but was now worn out.

Meanwhile the old show must go on somehow, lacking its leading actor. A new Cabinet must be formed but who could form it?

The obvious choice was Thompson, by far the ablest of Macdonald's surviving colleagues, or, alternatively, Tupper, who had long been regarded as the natural successor. In both of them the shattered ministry and frightened party bosses saw fatal defects.

Thompson, as a convert to the Church, should have strong Catholic support but he might antagonize Protestants. No Catholic had been considered for the supreme office since Confederation. Such an experiment looked dangerous. Besides, Thompson had offended Quebec by his powerful defence of Riel's execution. Finally, as a Nova Scotian, he came from the periphery of politics. A Prime Minister should come from the centre, Ontario or Quebec.

In any case, as Thompson told the Governor-General, Lord Stanley, he did not consider himself ripe yet for government leadership and recommended Senator J. J. C. Abbott. Tupper had unequalled experience back to pre-Confederation times, a reputation of dogged courage, an almost unbroken record of victory and a thundering rhetoric but he was now seventy years old, comfortably installed as High Commissioner in the best society of London and unwilling to come home. Moreover, he did not get on well with Thompson.

The first chance to install a man of stature was therefore missed. The Cabinet compromised on Abbott as a temporary caretaker. That was the first of many mistakes and typical of any dying government. When a government begins to die (as the future would fully demonstrate) mistakes are about all that it can make.

In his last illness Macdonald had told Thompson that the party must rally around Abbott but he had changed his mind just before the end and decided that Abbott was "too selfish." Yet no man could have been more reluctant to accept the burden of office, few less able to carry it.

Four days before Macdonald's death Abbott, expecting it momentarily, had written to a friend that "I hate politics and what are considered their appropriate methods. I hate notoriety, public meetings, public speeches, caucuses, and everything that I know of what is apparently the necessary incident of politics—except doing public work to the best of my ability. Why should I go where the doing of public work will only make me hated and my ministry unpopular and where I can only gain reputation and credit by practising arts which I detest to acquire popularity?"

This shrill *cri de coeur* from a stern man who rarely showed his feelings was vain, as Abbott must have known. He had no choice. Aware of his prospects as only a stop-gap until a better candidate turned up, he answered the Governor-General's call and settled into hateful office. A tired, grizzled man of shrewd, hooded eyes, grim, downturned mouth and square, massive jaw, he was accepting his last brief when the need of a depressed country was not a lawyer but a leader.

Abbott had proved himself a good lawyer, the trusted family solicitor of the Conservative Party, but he was not cut out to be a Prime Minister and he knew it. In addition to his rigid legal temperament and his age of seventy years, he suffered other disabilities.

As a young man he had signed the notorious Annexation Manifesto of 1849, but he had repented this folly long ago. Since he had been Allan's lawyer and the papers of the Pacific Scandal were stolen from his office, some scent of that affair still clung to him, though his personal honour was unquestioned. As the veteran counsel of the C.P.R. he represented the big-business community of Montreal, that whipping boy of every small-town politician. Also, he sat in the Senate where he would be free of the Commons' brawls and intrigues but in a weak position to control them.

Thompson, undertaking this disagreeable chore as the real manager of the Government, must have guessed that the division of the Prime Minister's powers between two men in separate legislative chambers could not last long. Thompson had responsibility without ultimate power. Abbott had ultimate power, at least in theory, but hated responsibility. The Government was falling between two stools.

These natural difficulties would have been bad enough in the best of times but Abbott had been thrust upon the stage at the worst of times.

After a brief pause, the world depression had descended again and the Government was blamed for conditions far outside its influence, as it had blamed Mackenzie. The false magic of the National Policy had palpably failed. Everything appeared to be going wrong at once and the real magic of Macdonald's spirit was no longer present to cheer a disillusioned people.

Everyone felt this national malaise. Laurier was writing to Blake that "we have come to a period in the history of this country where premature dissolution seems to be at hand. What will be the outcome? How long can the present fabric last? Can it last at all?"

All thoughtful Canadians asked themselves the same question, as it is asked even more urgently in our time.

On top of economic stagnation politics now dumped a fetid load of scandal. Israel Tarte, a deep-dyed Bleu (Quebec Conservative) who masqueraded as a Liberal and was firmly established as Laurier's right-hand man in Quebec, suddenly uncovered Langevin's wholesale plunder, the crooked public-works contracts, the rake-off for Conservative campaign funds, the crude, effective apparatus of graft to be rebuilt, with modern refinements, in the days of Maurice Duplessis.

Canada was accustomed to a strong stench in politics but never had government looked so squalid. Many Canadians were inclined to agree with *The New York World* when it said that their country was easily purchasable, that five or six million dollars "judiciously expended" could assure Canada's annexation to the United States.

All this was made to order for any opposition. The Liberals exploited it with gusto but ineffectively, since they were tainted with the same poison. Premier Mercier, the counterfeit reformer and French-Canadian hero, had recently been dismissed from office by the Lieutenant-Governor for corruption on a scale which even the tolerant people of Quebec could not quite stomach.

Laurier suffered from another wound, a stab in the back delivered by friends.

Before the Liberal Party had absorbed the shock of the last election Blake, long silent among the shadows, uttered without warning a curious death-wish known to history as the West Durham Letter. In it he denounced the Conservatives for wrecking the country, urged commercial union with the United States and, like a Delphic oracle, added this tantalizing postscript: "Political union, though becoming our probable, is by no means our ideal, or as yet our inevitable, future."

The Government joyfully interpreted the oracle as meaning that the Liberal policy of unrestricted reciprocity must lead to annexation. Laurier indignantly repudiated that interpretation of Blake's meaning but as Blake returned to silence the voters believed the Conservative version and defeated many Liberal candidates in the Ontario by-elections of the following year.

As always, Blake had sowed disaster. Lacking his help and Mercier's disgrace, the Conservatives' narrow election majority could hardly have lasted a twelve-month. Now, after its by-election victories, the Government seemed and felt almost as strong as ever. Apparently it could do without its maker after all. That illusion was to end soon. Meanwhile if the Government felt better the nation was sick and motionless. No one, politician or business man, seemed able to get it moving.

Into a dismal mixture of political and economic paralysis the catalyst and first birth pangs of the new age already had entered, though few men had the wit to see them. Oddly enough, they came again from the West, from the seat of Riel's uprising on Red River and directly as a result of his victory over Macdonald there. A newer Canada was moving to shake, and perhaps redress, the balance of the old.

When, in 1890, the Manitoba legislature decided to abolish the provincial system of separate, state-supported Catholic schools that were part of Riel's heritage, a barometer as sensitive as Macdonald possibly measured the potential size and force of a prairie cloud no bigger than a man's hand.

If the veteran of many hurricanes had lived a little longer he might have found a storm cellar for his Government as he had often done before. At least he would have tried to divert the wind and seek an accommodation between the old racial and religious passions which, issuing anew from the Manitoba School Question, had so often threatened the nation's life and now threatened it again. Perhaps the historic conflict between races and religions was too savage, in its latest guise, for even the master's management.

Abbott did not intend to manage it. He was on the way out. Conceivably Thompson, as a Catholic enjoying the full confidence of the Church, might have diverted its anger against the Manitoba government if he had been given enough time. Unfortunately the God of his devout worship could spare him little. So the gale of the School Question, one of the most violent and least understood in Canadian experience, rolled on to transform politics and usher in the new age.

Conflict had been planted in Manitoba from the beginning by the French-Canadian and Catholic enclave of the Métis people who had wrung from the national Government a constitution of their own design. Under it, they supposed, a system of separate Catholic schools was permanently established.

Then came a wave of Protestant, English-speaking settlers from Ontario to change the racial and religious texture of the province. Among them was the Sifton family, whose youngest son, Clifford, had a curious appointment with history. In this young man from Brandon a primal power had emerged out of the prairie earth at a tender age, but there was nothing tender about Sifton.

Canada's public life had never seen before and may never see again the chilled steel and flawless, machinelike competence of his nature. Once he was appointed Attorney-General of Manitoba just after his thirtieth birthday all those qualities were visible in Sifton's athletic body, the taut face, bristling moustache and beach-pebble eyes; also in his smooth, untiring energy, his staccato speech, his hatred of liquor, sloth and human weakness of every sort.

By now he had mastered the professions of law and politics, was on the way to a vast personal fortune in business, had become a champion horseman and dominated the Liberal government of Thomas Greenway. Only with Sifton's muscular hand on the tiller and a secret chart in his head could Manitoba possibly navigate the tempest released by its school legislation. As he had foreseen, the whole Catholic community from coast to coast would probably unite against the government and, since it was Liberal, against his own party in Ottawa.

That danger did not frighten Sifton. Nothing in heaven or earth would ever frighten him. He intended to abolish separate denominational schools supported by the State regardless of consequences to his government, to his career or to Laurier. But he moved so slowly, quietly and remorselessly, this man without nerves, that the federal Government was not seriously alarmed at first. Some kind of solution doubtless could be arranged with time and patience. Only one firm decision was taken at Ottawa—the Manitoba legislation would not be disallowed, as the Church demanded. The Government could not afford to interfere directly at the cost of infuriating the Protestant vote. Far better to leave the whole business to the courts which might happily find the legislation invalid. Anyway, action could be delayed indefinitely in legal argument.

Not, however, by Abbott. He resigned, in sickness and disgust, on December 5, 1892. As it should have done in the first place, the Conservative caucus chose Thompson as the successor, unaware of the sentence already passed on him.

That doomed leader began what looked like a promising Prime Ministry. He brought to it considerable talents and not a little charm. At the age of only forty-eight years, apparently in life's prime after his career on the Nova Scotia bench, Sir John Sparrow David Thompson was a man of pleasant face, rather too plump but unlined and intelligent. His curly hair descended in thick sideburns to exaggerate his heavy jowls. He looked like a judge, had a judge's dignified manners and perhaps was intended by nature to be nothing else, until he caught Macdonald's roving eye.

"The great discovery of my life," Macdonald had written, "was my discovery of Thompson." After further experience, he added: "Thompson has two faults. He is a little too fond of satire and a little too much of a Nova Scotian." An anonymous Conservative boss is recorded as saying: "Thompson will never make a politician. He won't even consider whether a thing is good for the party until he is quite sure it is good for the country."

All in all, he was a superior man who, with even a few years' time before him, might have made a superior Prime Minister.

"I have never shrunk in my calling as a member of the bar," he had said, "from taking any man's case, no matter how desperate it might be, for the purpose of saying for him what he might lawfully say for himself." Now, as leader of the Government, he was taking a very desperate case with every show of confidence and with a humility rare among Prime Ministers.

"I do not know," he once answered a questioner in Parliament. "There are many facts in the history of this country of which I am not aware, and a great many statements of fact in regard to history I find controverted so often that I am not able to state a positive opinion in regard to them." It sounded like a judge's *obiter dictum* from the bench. A Prime Minister should never admit ignorance of anything.

Yet Thompson could be brutally ironic in argument—as when he replied, in the session of 1892, to Cartwright, the terrible old man: "I, as a member of the Liberal-Conservative Party, owe him such a debt of gratitude that if it shall be necessary to retain his services in the party which he does not lead, which would not have him for a leader and which barely tolerates him as a supporter— if it be necessary to retain him in that capacity I for one will propose a subsidy to Parliament to keep him there . . . . he above all others made in the same mould which, thank God, nature broke when she cast him."

Or again, he dismissed Cartwright's latest Liberal attack as "one of those war, famine and pestilence speeches which so often carried the country for the Conservative Government."

The terrible man had found his match in his own congenial sport of knock-down-and-drag-out debate. The retired judge could play rough, too, in Parliament and outside it.

It was on the hustings that Thompson coined his most memorable phrase of denigration. Referring in a bland ornithological aside to Laurier's Quebec lieutenant and to the firebrand of Manitoba Liberalism, he called them "the Black Tarte and the Yellow Martin." Those names stuck.

In more serious vein the new Prime Minister saw more clearly than his colleagues and deplored the dangers of the School Question: "The one calamity above all others which stands before this country is that political divisions should follow the division of race or the division of religion."

As a Maritimer he inherited the Loyalist tradition. "We were taunted," he said, "with waving the old flag. And a lot of traitors, a lot of cowards who have not the courage to be traitors although they have the will, would sneer at the old flag, sneer at the loyalty we inherited from our fathers, sneer at the institutions which our fathers were so proud to leave us." There spoke a Conservative of the old school.

He sometimes showed, too, a puckish sense of humour. Dining at Rideau Hall on a night infested by mosquitoes, he said to Lady Minto who moved to close the windows against them: "Oh, pray do not bother to close the windows. I think they are all in now."

Such a man, urbane or harsh as occasion required and always clear of mind, was well equipped to face the western storm and now it was moving fast eastward.

In 1891 the Catholics of Manitoba had challenged the abolition of state aid to their schools by a lawsuit and the Abbott Government had done nothing. It hoped that the courts would find the provincial law invalid and make federal intervention unnecessary. These hopes were confirmed by the Supreme Court of Canada, which so found. Then, in the summer of 1892, while Thompson was still Minister of Justice, he had read with horror a cable from London announcing that the Privy Council had reversed the Canadian verdict. The Manitoba law was valid.

If the Catholic schools were to be saved the federal Government, soon led by Thompson, must save them. But how? Had the federal Government the right to interfere with the Manitoba policy and alter it by remedial legislation? Buying time, Thompson waited for a weary war of litigation to decide that point. In the end the Privy Council ruled that Ottawa could interfere.

Thompson was now on the spot. A remedial bill preserving the separate-school system, in whole or in part, would bring the Government support—or so it was glibly assumed—from every Catholic in the nation, including the French Canadians of Quebec, but it would probably antagonize even more Protestants.

Here was an issue striking to the double roots of Canadian life when the country was least able to stand the shock. However the lawyers might argue the small print of the Privy Council judgment, the politicians knew what it meant in the large print of an approaching election. It meant that the irresistible force of English-speaking Protestantism was about to collide with the immovable body of French-speaking Catholicism. Any politician or party caught in that collision could hardly hope to survive.

Thompson fully understood his danger and the nation's. How he would have met it, if given more time, we shall never know. He escaped the collision mercifully and instantaneously by attending Queen Victoria in Windsor Castle on December 12, 1894, accepting membership in her Privy Council and dropping dead at luncheon. Next to Macdonald and Cartier, he was the Conservative Party's greatest loss since Confederation. And the Party had no adequate successor.

How it came to choose Mackenzie Bowell is not clear even today. Sir Joseph Pope, Macdonald's trusted secretary and later assistant clerk of the Canadian Privy Council, says in his memoirs that on Thompson's death Tupper, as the logical man, "should have been summoned without delay" but "for some inexplicable reason was passed over by Lord Aberdeen in favour of Mr. Mackenzie Bowell, a worthy, loyal man, but one as little qualified to be Prime Minister as Lord Aberdeen was to be Governor-General."

In choosing the fifth Prime Minister, presumably after he had sounded out the Cabinet, Aberdeen was scraping the bottom of the Conservative barrel.

Bowell had been born in Rickinghall, England, in 1833, had been brought to Canada by his parents at the age of ten and had become a prosperous citizen of Belleville, Ontario, where he published the *Intelligencer*. By the year of Confederation he was the leading Conservative politician of his town, a large frog in a very small puddle.

Elected to the first Parliament in 1867, he began to distinguish himself by an almost manic hatred of Liberals and Catholics. In his own little world of demons he referred to every Liberal opponent as "a most violent Grit," "a violent Rouge Grit" or "a brawling Grit." Doubtless he would have remained a parochial Conservative boss if he had not worked his way up in the powerful Orange Order to be its Grand Master. Once he had reached that office he, or the voters behind him, could be valuable to Macdonald. To manage a diverse coalition of right and left, French and English, Catholic and Protestant, Macdonald brought Bowell into the Cabinet after the victory of 1878.

Though he was a tiny, stupid man, his influence over the extreme lunatic fringe of the Tory vote represented a political asset of sorts. He also had some minor talents as a small-town political fixer, and a certain cunning. Even Catholic votes were not to be despised, if he could get them. Once he helped a Conservative prelate to acquire windows for his church at the cost of the Government. His Protestantism did not prevent him from advising Macdonald to attend a Catholic picnic and make "an anti-Huxley speech, with a slight sprinkling of politics."

104

When he entered the Prime Minister's office and became a knight, Sir Mackenzie Bowell was sixty-one years of age. The crumpled face behind the whitening beard gave him the look of a bitter Santa Claus with crafty eyes. In anything like normal times such a man would have merited no more than a footnote in the history books, but these were not normal times. The forces now flowing had placed in this pitiable personage the future of the Conservative Government, the Liberal Opposition and the nation's fragile unity.

He lacked the wisdom to solve the Manitoba conundrum, the stature to carry through a solution if it could be found and the confidence of his Cabinet as well. Worst of all, he lacked humility.

Watching the Cabinet at first hand as its assistant clerk, Pope was appalled. "Then followed," he wrote, "days which I never recall without a blush, days of weak and incompetent administration by a Cabinet presided over by a man whose sudden and unlooked for elevation had visibly turned his head, a ministry without unity or cohesion of any kind, a prey to internal dissensions until they became a spectacle to the world, to angels and to men."

By the summer of 1895, only six months after taking office, Bowell had lost all control of the Government. "I remember," says Pope, "it was almost impossible to get public business transacted at Ottawa. . . . Weeks passed without a Treasury Board being held. When at last a necessary quorum was obtained, the Governor-General had gone out to his country place in the mountains of British Columbia and the papers had to be sent out after him. The place took fire and the Treasury minutes, while lying there awaiting the vice-regal approval, were consumed. When at length fresh papers were procured, signed, sent to British Columbia and returned to Ottawa, the Auditor General of the day held up many of them by reason of some obscure feud between himself and the Deputy Minister of Finance, with the consequence that public business during that unhappy summer was well-nigh paralyzed."

Unfortunately the School Question could not be paralyzed. Forced to grapple with it, and with Laurier, the tiny Prime Minister began to show no wisdom but at least a snarling courage.

For some months he had hesitated to interfere with Manitoba's legislation, thinking that Sifton might compromise. The provincial government yielded nothing and said nothing. The school law was valid and would be enforced.

Step by step Bowell was being driven toward a paradox almost incredible. To hold his French-Canadian ministers and the essential Quebec vote he must coerce Manitoba in favour of the hated Catholic Church. A Protestant Orangeman must stultify himself. Bowell was prepared to do it if necessary in the hope of placing Laurier in the same, or a worse, position.

A first irrevocable step was taken on March 21, 1895. The Government issued a remedial order instructing Manitoba to restore the rights of its Catholic citizens.

Profound abstract principles were now at stake. About them sincere Catholics and Protestants could peacefully disagree, but on the philosophical issues thus raised the two political parties began to build a political arena in which one or the other must perish.

For Bowell the initiative was essential. The life of Parliament would end with an election in little more than a year. By then, he hoped, the crisis would have passed and passions cooled.

The Government would placate Protestant voters by saying that it had rescued the Manitoba Catholics not of its own free will but because it had been compelled to do so by the Queen's Privy Council. This was not true, of course, since the Privy Council's ruling only permitted and did not even suggest remedial action; but it might wash. Queen Victoria was a name to conjure with. The formula should serve through an election campaign if it were shouted loudly and patriotically enough.

On the other hand, the Government could expect all Catholics to rally around it as the champion of their Church. Between the two conflicting pressures Laurier would be crushed.

This strategy seemed so good that Bowell prepared to take the final step. If the remedial order were not obeyed by Manitoba, he announced, it would be enforced by federal legislation which must be obeyed. At this point, however, the Government was in no condition to do anything while Manitoba still ignored the remedial order and said nothing.

As the parliamentary session dragged to its close two French-Canadian ministers threatened to resign if the remedial legislation were further delayed. Some rebellious Ontario ministers were equally determined to delay it, having lost faith in Bowell's political strategy. This family quarrel was patched up only in time to permit Parliament's adjournment without the passage of the legislation—whereupon, as related by Pope, the Governor-General and the Government disappeared from Ottawa.

Laurier remained the unknown factor in the equation. His bland silence and repeated ambiguities throughout the events of the last two years were baffling and yet, for the Government, encouraging. Bowell concluded that Laurier could not make up his mind on the

School Question. He seemed to be stumbling into the trap already laid for him as if he did not suspect it. Either he must hold Quebec by supporting the coercion of Manitoba and lose Ontario. Or, by opposing coercion, he must lose Quebec, his only sure base, while, as a French Canadian, he could not hope to win much of Ontario. Either way he would be trapped.

Bowell was quite right in assuming that Laurier could not make up his mind. As late as August 5, 1895, the puzzled Liberal leader was writing to a friend that if the Government went ahead with its remedial legislation "it is very much to be feared that all party lines will be broken and chaos will ensue." Again, on November 5, he wrote that the School Question "may break the Opposition or break the Government."

For all his serenity on the platform, Laurier knew that he was facing the second momentous decision of his life, from which there could be no turning back; but actually it was an extension of the first. He had defied the Catholic bishops on the general principles of liberalism and beaten them. Now he must defy them on a concrete policy or, by retreating, must forfeit his stature as a national states-man above race and religion. He might remain the leader of a Quebec rump but he could never be Prime Minister.

At these frightening cross-roads his qualities of decision and courage seemed to falter. He hid his vacillation under smiling plati-tudes and the fatuous hint that the School Question could be solved by his "sunny ways" and mere words. Refusing to commit himself, he was waiting like Wellington, he said, "within the lines of Torres Vedras."

All this meant exactly nothing. For Laurier the complex School Question had resolved itself into a personal question, simple, stark and agonizing: Could he reconcile his Catholicism and his French Canadianism with his duty, and his opportunity, as a national states-man? In short, was Laurier a French Canadian or a Canadian?

He could not make up his mind but another man made it up for him, thus saving his career and his party.

Tarte, the old Bleu who called himself a Liberal, had long been assessing Laurier's position in Quebec with cold-blooded impar-tiality. His verdict was that the French Canadians would vote for their idol on any policy, even a policy denounced as anathema by their Church.

If this assumption was reliable all aspects of the Liberal strategy fell into place. As Tarte outlined it with chilling candour, the Lib-erals in all the English-speaking provinces could say anything about separate schools that seemed necessary to elect them. They could be as anti-Catholic as they pleased. "Make the party policy suit the campaign in other provinces," said Tarte. "Leave Quebec to Laurier and me." Uttered off the cuff, it was a classic dictum of Canadian politics. Though doubtful, Laurier decided to accept it, but it must not be revealed until the last possible moment. The Government would be led into a Liberal trap.

When Laurier's decision was actually made no one ever knew, if he knew himself. Certainly until the end of the year and well into 1896 he was still mouthing his laborious equivocations according to plan and still could not be sure that the strategy would work.

That was natural enough, for the strategy depended absolutely on his personal aura in Quebec and its power had never been tested against the power of the Church in a concrete issue of explosive force. To ask the French Canadians to vote for him and against the Church was asking a lot, more than any French Canadian had ever asked. A modesty which he was soon to lose made Laurier question the result.

But the decision had been made, the die cast, solely on Tarte's assurance. Laurier need not have worried about his lieutenant's judgment. With his flowing beard and noble brow, Tarte rather resembled a saint on a stained-glass window but he was the most subtle, cynical and accurate politician in the business, so long as he remained in opposition. No man knew so well the grass roots of Quebec and its smouldering anger at Riel's martyrdom. He reckoned its votes like an adding machine but he knew that French-Canadian mathematics was different from that of other provinces. So did Laurier, who once wrote to his young friend, Henri Bourassa, that "Quebec has no opinion, only sentiments." On sentiments the future was to be gambled.

Once set, the Liberal strategy was refined in detail, perfectly timed and kept so secret that Bowell never suspected it and, if he had heard the truth, would not have believed it. The notion that Laurier would oppose separate schools and the Church was preposterous.

Thus the first stroke, well prepared between Sifton and Laurier, caught the Government by complete surprise. Without warning the Manitoba government called a snap election, was overwhelmingly returned to power and defied Ottawa to touch its school law.

Even now Bowell could not imagine that Laurier would back Manitoba but as the parliamentary session approached the Government was forced to act at last on the remedial legislation. Bowell took his policy to Cabinet and immediately faced a rebellion. This time rebellion could not be suppressed or postponed. Just before Parliament was to open the Prime Minister heard his sentence of political death, delivered by his friends.

Seven Cabinet ministers, led by George Foster and Charles Hibbert Tupper (son of Sir Charles and a substantial chip off the old block), demanded Bowell's immediate resignation.

"Father," the young Tupper once said to his reproving parent, "you have no idea how I enjoy and cherish my animosities." He was savouring that pleasure now against his helpless leader. Foster, an abler politician with a distinguished career ahead of him, seemed to hope that he would succeed Bowell but the Conservative caucus was not prepared to accept this gifted and waspish orator.

With all the fury of a little man, Bowell denounced the rebellion, screaming that it was "a nest of traitors." Those were the only words from his lips that most future Canadians would remember. If true, they were futile.

Bowell attempted to replace the rebels. They systematically picketed all possible successors on their arrival in Ottawa. It was perhaps the roughest operation ever known to a rough trade but it succeeded. No Conservative politician of consequence cared to break the strike. Bowell perforce capitulated. He would remain as titular Prime Minister for the parliamentary session while Charles Tupper, father of a leading rebel, would be summoned instantly from London, would enter Parliament and lead the Government into a summer election.

The bulldog of Confederation times, now seventy-five years old but still dauntless, rushed home to find the Government in disarray. But then, so was the Opposition. Indeed, Laurier, facing a break with English-speaking Canada or with his own race, might well be *in extremis* despite his look of confidence. Certainly the hour was late but the Conservative trap could still be closed. Thus reasoned Tupper, who would never say die.

His reasoning had more substance than he, or many Liberals, yet realized. Sitting calm and regnant in the opposition benches, often reading the English dictionary, as was his custom, the long, elegant fingers running down the columns of words, Laurier was deeply troubled. He could not quite believe that Tarte's strategy would work. It was almost too good to be true. Whether true or not, it could not be delayed, after Tupper introduced the Remedial Bill amending the Manitoba school law.

As the hour of action neared some of Laurier's confidants lost their nerve. On March 2, the day before he was to speak, they urged a safer course. Let the Liberal Members vote as they pleased on the Remedial Bill, the French Canadians supporting it, the others opposing it. Laurier listened and quietly prepared his speech. His mind was made up.

On March 3 he crossed his Rubicon and, as the Government thought, entered the trap. His motion that the Remedial Bill be read six months hence, or in plain terms, rejected, meant an outright quarrel with the Church. Tupper breathed easily again. He had not read Tarte's arithmetic.

Laurier still doubted the figures, though his career was now staked on Tarte's double assurance that Quebec was safe and Ontario favourable. As late as April 20 Laurier's doubts were written in an extraordinary letter to J. S. Ewart, who was persuading Sir Oliver Mowat to seek election, possibly as the new Liberal leader.

"The interest which I take in the Manitoba School Question," Laurier wrote, "and my desire to see it settled in a way that will give satisfaction to the minority are so great that it would be a pleasure for me to make any sacrifice in order to induce Sir Oliver to enter federal politics. The question of the premiership can be easily settled. I would most gladly make way for Sir Oliver." He even promised that a "syndicate of capitalists" would guarantee Mowat "an annuity for the rest of his life."

The sincerity of Laurier's offer to resign his leadership must be doubted but even at this advanced date he felt compelled to make it. This was a shrewd move. If his generous gesture were refused, as he must have expected, Mowat and others like him would be compelled to support a leader who was ready to throw his career away. So it turned out.

Ignorant of the Opposition's secret misgivings and underestimating his own party's quarrels, Tupper pushed the Remedial Bill toward a vote.

Laurier had no intention of allowing a vote if he could help it. Day after day the debate dragged on. The second reading was finally carried by only eighteen votes, fourteen Liberals supporting the legislation and as many Conservatives opposing it. Party lines, as Laurier had expected, were crumbling, but only at the edges.

In the committee stages the Liberal blockade was resumed while the constitutional life of Parliament ran out. The legislation could not be passed. Tupper must face the electors as a Prime Minister who could not control Parliament. No matter, Laurier must face a hostile Quebec and a Church in arms.

Tupper formally replaced Bowell, took the plunge and called an election for June 23.

Canada's sixth Prime Minister seemed to be better equipped for this crisis than any of his Conservative predecessors, except Macdonald. In a personal sense that was true.

Tupper had been active in politics for two score years. Almost single-handed the "little doctor," as Howe had called him, with premature contempt, had beaten that great tribune of Nova Scotia and brought the province into Confederation. Then, to accommodate Macdonald, he had stood aside when he could have demanded a seat in the first ministry of 1867.

Later, on entering the Cabinet, he had become at once its fighting arm. Macdonald was the brain and Tupper the battering-ram of the Conservative Party. In good days and bad, each could count absolutely on the other. Tupper's rather simple view of politics as a battle between good and evil complemented the sinuous methods of his leader. Tupper's florid oratory and growling declamation lacked Macdonald's wit and whimsy but they fired the Conservative troops and often rallied the Government's flagging majority in the House of Commons.

Sometimes Tupper could coin a telling phrase, too. He had given protective tariffs the name of "the National Policy." He had called the Liberal attack on the C.P.R. "the Pacific Slander." The true-blue Tupper, in short, was no intellectual of politics but he was a man you could safely tie to and Macdonald had presented him publicly as his successor.

All those plans were changed because Macdonald could not bring himself to retirement and Tupper, now a knight, was overcome by the luxury, flattery and nobility of London. By taking the High Commissioner's post there he had deliberately renounced the Prime Minister's office and settled down to the cosy life of an English gentleman while the Government, after Macdonald's death, fell rapidly to pieces.

It was typical of Tupper that when the call came, too late, he answered it without a moment's hesitation. Perhaps as he took over the wreckage left by Bowell he remembered one of his first memorable speeches, in 1860. Even then he had uttered his youthful faith in a future nation: "The human mind naturally adapts itself to the position it occupies. The most gigantic intellect may be dwarfed by being cabind'd, cribbed and confined. It requires a great country and great circumstances to develop great men."

Confederation had developed such men, Tupper among them. Now the challenge of a government which had built Confederation but lacked great men instantly summoned his patriotism and his courage. And fortunately for him Tupper was so built that he could never imagine defeat. The very image of John Bull, with flowing curls, bristling side-whiskers and square, shaven jaw, the old man leaped joyfully into battle with an enemy twenty years younger.

On both sides the campaign of 1896 was ferocious, mendacious and more than usually cynical, but it marked a great turning-point in Canadian history. That the turning had come mainly from world-wide forces was little noted at the time, for no Canadian yet understood the meaning of a new century about to be born. At least all Canadians knew that times were bad in their own country and everywhere else, the climate dangerous to any government; and none could guess that within a year the long depression would suddenly lift as if by magic. If Tupper could have waited even twelve months conceivably he might have been able to save the Government. Bowell having exhausted the life of Parliament, Tupper could not wait. He must confront a country depressed in business and distracted in mind by the School Question.

Under the impact of this racial and religious schism, everything else was forgotten, the old reliable tariff issue muted. Tupper was in no position to extol the National Policy since it seemed to be a patent failure. Laurier quietly dropped the hot potato of unrestricted reciprocity which had burned him five years earlier and now talked vaguely of expanded trade by means unspecified. The country's political future was to hinge on the educational law of an obscure government in its muddy capital of Winnipeg.

Now the opposite qualities of the old man and the young were put to the trial.

Tupper reasoned that English-speaking Canada would not support a French Canadian, even if Laurier supported the coercion of a Catholic minority in Manitoba. On the other hand, it was inconceivable to Tupper that Quebec would support Laurier in defiance of its Church. Logically these assumptions were sound enough but Tupper, with his age and experience, should have known that logic seldom settles elections, that they are settled by prejudice, hunch and personalities.

Anyway, the logic of his own posture in the English-speaking provinces was too thin and fictitious to deceive a majority of intelligent voters. Many doubtless would believe the falsehood that the Government had been compelled by the British Privy Council to rescue Manitoba's separate schools, but not enough to win an election. In Quebec, as Tupper failed to see, the French Canadians would vote for their own native son regardless of logic and religion.

All these facts, the decisive ones, were clear to Laurier because his mind was as subtle and pragmatic as Macdonald's.

Thus the campaign, a classic of confusion, was fought on two separate levels. In ritual it was a test of sacred principles—provincial rights as espoused by Laurier versus the religious rights of minorities as championed by Tupper. In truth it was nothing more than a test of cunning and political power—a dying Government versus a young, vigorous Opposition, both determined to win on any principle or none.

For these purposes all the facts were turned upside-down in the blustering rodomontade of Tupper and the flashing rhetoric of Laurier. Any intelligent voter could see that the political process was standing on its head when an English-speaking Protestant Prime Minister appeared as the rescuer of a French-speaking Catholic minority and a French-speaking Catholic strove to make himself leader of another race by quarreling with his Church.

Never had distortion and paradox been pushed to such lengths. For example, in the *Manitoba Free Press,* which he had not yet purchased, Sifton was accused of "treason." He had raised "the standard of rebellion" because he refused to accept the verdict of the Empire's highest court. Sifton was anti-British.

Nowhere in English-speaking Canada did the Government admit that it was coercing Manitoba solely to win Quebec. There, however, the Conservative Party solemnly presented itself as the only defender of the French race and religion.

The Liberal campaign was equally unscrupulous. In the English-speaking provinces Laurier stood on the hallowed doctrine of provincial rights which he could never violate, while his candidates denounced the excessive demands of the Church. In Quebec he sugared a bitter pill by arguing that the Government had so bungled its business that it was powerless to help the French Canadians of Manitoba. The only hope for that minority was to trust in his "sunny ways" (a phrase worked to death by now) and if they failed to achieve an amicable solution then a Liberal Government still had power to discipline an erring province.

This, of course, was cynicism writ very large even by the standards of politics. Laurier had no intention of touching the Manitoba school law but, unknown to any of his friends, he had certain other intentions that would smash his alliance with Sifton in due time.

The priests in Quebec, Manitoba and elsewhere did their best to defeat a fellow Catholic. The bishops thundered. One of their spokesmen threatened, in a private message to Laurier, that the hierarchy "like one man" would support the Protestant Conservatives "who may have fallen in defending us"; and the Liberal managers promptly leaked this letter to press, knowing that it would antagonize Protestants everywhere.

All the attempts to repel the western storm were bootless. Tarte's double-barreled campaign, conceived in cynicism, was brought forth in victory.

On election day Quebec, voting solely for a man, gave Laurier 48 seats out of 65; Ontario gave him 44 out of 92. Over all, he had a clear majority in Parliament of 23—not a big margin to be sure, but the wonder was that a French Canadian had won a working majority at all. In any case, the victory could not be calculated in figures. It introduced a new age quite incalculable.

The election had been won in Quebec by Laurier's personal appeal, exactly according to Tarte's plan, but that shrewd strategist had not anticipated everything. As if to prove that the Liberal argument was phony, Manitoba, which had split the nation by abolishing state aid to private schools, gave four seats to the Tupper Government, whose policy was to revive that system, and only three to the Liberals who backed the provincial policy.

On election night such details didn't matter. Laurier was in. He had reaped the French-Canadian harvest sown in a Regina jail yard eleven years ago and avenged Riel. Perhaps he and a few others could also see that, apart from his victory, the election had begun to recast the basic party lines of politics.

By allying himself with the Church and the extreme right wing of Quebec, Tupper unknowingly had committed the Conservative Party to allies who would elect it fifteen years hence and then wreck it. Laurier was established permanently as the Quebec moderate, the conciliator of the two Canadian races; but this achievement, though it was his chosen life-work, would be fatal to him.

None of these ironies was understood on the morrow of the election as Tupper prepared to relinquish his office but not his party leadership. One last bark was left in the old bulldog. When he tried to appoint some of his friends to comfortable jobs Governor-General Aberdeen rejected his advice. Huffing and puffing, he resigned. On second thoughts, however (according to his grandson), he told his son that, after all, a change of government was good for the country —a temporary change, as he still hoped.

On July 11, 1896, Laurier took his oath as Prime Minister.

6: The Happy Time

In the contemporary Liberal myth, Laurier's arrival was the ultimate salvation of Canadian life, the end of evil and depression, the
beginning of virtue and prosperity. As that event receded in memory
and was followed by new depressions, new evils and world war, the
myth should have shrunk. Instead, it expanded. Laurier became a
shining hero, a demigod, or at least a knight *sans peur* and almost
sans reproche.

There was something in this, as in all myths, but not nearly as
much as Laurier's worshippers supposed, and they worshipped him
for the least of his achievements, neglecting the greatest. Usually he
has been painted larger than life because his stature was inflated by
a fortunate accident. His fifteen-year term of office happened to be
the happy time of Canada's experience—a long time as it appeared
then but a mere moment in history and ending in the double calamity of man and nation.

The man, indeed, was bigger than his measurable public work.
His supreme achievement was himself—a spirit of moral grandeur
unique in the Canadian breed. Perhaps as a man he was the greatest
ever known in the nation's politics, but not as a Prime Minister. In
intellect and learning he outranked all who came before and after
him. Yet Macdonald had done far more for Canada than Laurier
ever did. King would do more in his time. Borden would succeed
in a harder struggle.

These works are measurable. By the immeasurable dimensions
of character none of our Prime Ministers could equal the serene,
inward nobility of Laurier, his sunny spaciousness of soul, his deli-

cate, feminine touch, his mystical power over other men, his personal charisma. But he had great faults, too. As Dafoe says out of long, intimate knowledge, Laurier had touches of Machiavelli well obscured by the look of Galahad. He was part saint, part autocrat and part actor. In short, a human being.

Here the contrast between our two most admired leaders is especially sharp. Macdonald, with his more constructive, practical and pragmatic mind, was loved as much for his fleshly weaknesses as for his intellectual strength. Laurier was loved, only this side of idolatry, for his spirit. His weaknesses—none of the flesh—were generally ignored.

Macdonald lived in the common world and enjoyed its pleasures. Laurier practised politics, often with scant scruple, according to the rules, but he lived alone in his own world and his exquisite manners were used as an invisible boundary which even the closest friend could never cross. Macdonald was a man among men, above all, a House of Commons man, delighting in its daily drama of human nature. Laurier, though always the leading figure on any stage and jealous of the spotlight, was a spiritual recluse, an intellectual admirer of Parliament but by inclination a remote orator and executive who usually left the parliamentary routine to his lieutenants. Both by imitation and bent of mind, King tried to maintain the same remoteness, when he could.

Another curious fact is usually overlooked. The members of that towering trinity, Macdonald, Laurier and King, were as unlike one another as men could be but all of them succeeded by precisely the same method, the only workable method in their nation. Character, age and chance divided them. They were united by instinct, or necessity.

Of the three, Laurier was probably the worst administrator. Macdonald never seemed to work but he was a master of minutiae with the memory of a modern business machine. King, too, was a systematic executive who fussed about the smallest detail. Laurier disliked detail and thought best only when he was thinking in broad concepts. He could conceive a Commonwealth of Nations. When he attempted to reorganize the Canadian railway system he produced a costly botch. When he undertook a subtle intrigue against his chief colleague he ended in humiliating defeat.

As in no other Prime Minister his oratory revealed the man. The minds of Macdonald and King were both bigger than their speeches. Laurier's speeches may not have been bigger than his mind but they were far bigger than the mind or the means of Canada. The right word came trippingly to his tongue, in French or English. Usually extemporaneous, his major speeches seemed to be built by an architect, stone on stone. They soared into Gothic towers, flying buttresses and intricate groining. They bloomed like stained-glass windows. They rang like cathedral chimes.

Effective as political weapons, they were more important as a mirror of a generous and poetic temperament. Like Macdonald, Laurier was the romantic in politics but much better than Macdonald he could articulate his dream and Canada's.

Laurier reveled in language as an artist might revel in paint. It was his natural medium. But it depended as much on his pipe-organ voice, his delicious accent, gestures and presence as on his words. The orator's appearance and emanation are remembered by a few survivors of his time. The words stand up well in print. Rereading them in old age, Meighen, another romantic and equal master of the art, pronounced Laurier's speeches the best ever delivered in the Canadian Parliament.

The arrival of Laurier seemed to change everything. In fact, the world was changing and he was borne on a rising tide. His look of itself inspired confidence and then reverence. The tall, slender figure, the nimbus of white hair, the truly beautiful face, the gray frock-coat, high collar, flowing cravat, jeweled pin, and gold pince-nez dangling on thread of silk introduced a note of colour and animation into the fusty East Block. A special destiny, almost a divine intervention, seemed to hedge and protect a natural king. So men thought after five bitter years and four disastrous Prime Ministers.

No one could imagine then that Laurier's sorrows would come not as single spies but in battalions, that fortune had designed for its darling a cross of affliction the most harrowing in our politics, supportable only by his religion and a private life of ascetic purity.

Another generation must pass before the dimensions of his success and failure could be measured and another French Canadian could resume his work. In St. Laurent, Laurier was to find his vindication but he must die without foreseeing it among the rubble of his dream.

What was to become the strangest human drama of Canadian government began with no visible portents and precious few advantages.

The Lauriers, using a different name when they first arrived in Canada, had always been good, solid citizens of Quebec, nine generations of them back to an ancestor who had helped Maisonneuve to found Montreal in 1641. Peasants in the beginning—the most durable race that America has ever known—they gradually entered the respectable, undistinguished petty bourgeoisie. They bequeathed to Wilfrid Laurier strains of northern and southern French blood, a mixture of Norman shrewdness and Provençal imagination which was to produce surprising results.

Wilfrid's grandfather had taught himself to survey land and thus graduated from the peasantry. His father, Carolus, had followed the same trade, with rather less success but with an unlikely respect for learning. He married Marcelle Martineau, a woman of strong, loving nature, and settled in the village of St. Lin, not far north from Montreal by modern roads, but then on the fringe of settlement. There Wilfrid was born on November 20, 1841. More than anything else, the influence of the mother shaped the boy but she died when he was only five years old. His only sister had not survived infancy.

The father soon married Adeline Ethier, who became a second mother to Wilfrid and gave him three half-brothers. It was a happy family, all the boys succeeding in their various professions. Through them the Lauriers advanced to the status of the gentry.

At the time of Wilfrid's birth his father was a humble man, his village of St. Lin a dusty cluster of hovels around a mill pond. The modern visitor who cares to inspect the Laurier home (somewhat refurbished and primped as a museum) will see at once that Wilfrid was raised in poverty, as things are reckoned nowadays. The tiny rooms with their hand-made furniture, the dark staircase, the mere closet where the boy slept on a narrow cot were near enough to the log-cabin legend of American presidents for effective political use, though they were never so used. On the contrary, Wilfrid was regarded in the poor society of his time and town as belonging to the more fortunate classes. So, in reality, he did. His father lacked money but he had a sober wisdom without which the boy's later career probably would have been impossible.

After preliminary schooling at St. Lin, Wilfrid was sent to the nearby village of New Glasgow, a Scottish settlement where, as his father had planned, he was placed among English-speaking pupils and quickly learned their language.

The French Canadian also came to understand the mind of the other race. As a boarder in a Presbyterian home he attended its evening prayers. Above all, he was influenced by Sandy Maclean, a remarkable teacher of Scottish descent who seems to have suspected the boy's talent and cultivated it by special instruction outside school hours.

In his thirteenth year Wilfrid was sent to the modest college of

L'Assomption. His father had decided that he must have the best education within the small means available.

Seven years at L'Assomption gave Wilfrid a strictly classical and literary training, together with a stern discipline under Catholic priests. Since he was physically frail and forbidden to join in athletic games, he spent his spare time in books or easy rambles about the countryside. The habit of reading produced a deep and abiding scholarship.

Even at that age his gift of speech had been revealed. He was the school's leading debater until he argued the proposition that Huguenots should have been admitted to early Quebec, whereupon the priests dissolved the debating society.

When he moved to Montreal as a law student in the office of the leading Rouge lawyer, Rodolphe Laflamme, Laurier was a precocious youth of twenty, his character firmly set.

If, like all thoughtful youngsters, he was confused and starry-eyed, there could be no doubt about the transformation of the village boy. Not by the artificial definition of birth but by the sure imprint of nature Laurier had become a gentleman, the supreme Canadian gentleman of his time. Beside him all other politicians were to seem somewhat barbarous.

He had every asset of mind and manner, but the liability of failing health would have extinguished ambition in a lesser man. His doctors diagnosed "lung trouble" which may have been tuberculosis. He suffered from terrifying hemorrhages and his companions did not expect him to live long.

While Laurier was working in a law office by day and taking night courses at McGill University, his friend, L. O. David, described him as "ill, sad, his air grave, indifferent to all the turmoil raised around him; he passed through the midst of it like a shadow and seemed to say to us, 'Brother, we all must die.' " This was hardly the portrait of a long-lived Prime Minister.

Laurier's health had deteriorated so far that his doctors advised him to leave Montreal and live in fresh country air. He moved to the new settlement of Arthabaskaville in the Eastern Townships where he practised law and edited a weekly paper. His *Le Défricheur* antagonized the local priests by its radicalism and collapsed within six months but the law practice throve. At the age of thirty Laurier was elected to the Quebec legislature, three years later to Parliament and, after one by-election defeat, entered Mackenzie's Government.

Meanwhile he had married Zoë Lafontaine, of Montreal, on May 13, 1868. It was to be a perfect though childless marriage, a love affair to the end. From now on the wife ruled his private life by gentle but inflexible pressure and quickly strengthened his health. Unlike Macdonald, he was never to know domestic sorrow.

This long apprenticeship fixed the political slant of his mind unchangeably as a Liberal. In his early struggle with the bishops and in a later struggle to tame the Quebec Rouges, he was established as the leader of the moderate Quebec centre, the one man who could reconcile the extremes of right and left, the natural heir of Lafontaine and Cartier.

His liberalism, as judged by modern standards, was exceedingly mild but in those times it seemed dangerously radical to the Church. His faith in the essential rightness of humanity and the collective wisdom of electors seems somewhat naive at this distance but the world had not yet returned to the jungle of international anarchy, of big government and regulation prevailing in our time.

Another thing had happened to him, little noted by friend or enemy. Though a French Canadian and spokesman of a supposedly conquered race, he had become perhaps the most ardent advocate and interpreter of the British parliamentary system in Canada. Its history, its laws, its lore and inner workings fascinated him. So did power—gentle in his hands, imperceptible if he could keep it so, but power nevertheless. This was necessary equipment for a leader of men. Without his appetite for power he could never have endured the years of disappointment and frustration under Mackenzie and Blake. Without it he could not have undertaken the ghastly election of 1896 or formed his first Cabinet.

The list of colleagues selected by the new Prime Minister was immediately styled the Cabinet of all the Talents and remains in the Liberal legend as the ministerial masterpiece of Canadian politics. Actually it was an able Cabinet, far above average, but not as able as at least two others in later times.

By the unwritten law of all Cabinets, an inner group controlled everything. Under Laurier it consisted of Fielding (the Nova Scotian who had threatened to withdraw his province from Confederation) in Finance; the aged Mowat in Justice; Tarte in Public Works as dispenser-in-chief of patronage; Cartwright in Trade and Commerce; William Mulock, whose intelligence was much larger than his portfolio, in the Post Office; and after a few months' delay, Sifton in the Interior. The remaining ten run-of-the-mill ministers were hardly noticed then and have since been forgotten.

Whatever its talents might be, this Cabinet was Laurier's personal creation. To get the men he wanted he had thrust aside many deserving candidates and imported five colleagues from provincial politics. Even Cartwright, who had counted on the Finance portfolio, was shunted into a comparatively unimportant department where he could not resume his feud with the manufacturers.

Wisely the Prime Minister did not burden himself with any portfolio. He needed all his time to whip the new team into shape. His appointments had demonstrated that he was not a gorgeous dilettante, as many friends and enemies supposed, but a man of ruthless will. He intended to be and already was the boss. In Dafoe's memorable metaphor, the diet of royal jelly had begun to turn an ordinary bee into a queen and an autocrat. Still, it was a harmonious, competent and busy hive that soon set Ottawa buzzing with new purpose.

The fact that the head of the Government was never a liberal in twentieth-century terms but a pretty conservative Whig of the nineteenth, and the other fact that Sifton, the second most powerful minister, was a strong conservative by any modern definition escaped the public on the birthday of the new Liberalism.

Laurier's first task was to make a deal with Manitoba and, if possible, save the Church's face. A provincial government of his own party conveniently agreed to allow religious teaching in the last half hour of the school day "by any Christian clergyman." No child need attend. Laurier said the settlement did not fulfill his own desires but "it was not possible to obtain more."

The Church angrily repudiated these arrangements as betrayal, renewed its war on Laurier and banned various Liberal newspapers. This last-ditch resistance was too violent and too late. Now Rome intervened. In answer to Laurier's private ambassadors and a petition signed by him for forty-four Members of Parlament, a papal intermediary arrived in Canada and the attacks on the Government suddenly ceased. Laurier's long war with the bishops had been won. The School Question was dead, almost.

As the Prime Minister settled down in his large, ugly mansion on Sandy Hill to a quiet domestic routine under his watchful wife, the second act of the new Government, the Fielding budget of 1897, seemed to disclose an impressive courage and a rare devotion to principle. In the legend it was to become an event as important to Canada as the repeal of the Corn Laws had been to Britain. In truth it was a wonderfully smooth and subtle device to extricate the Liberal Party from its youthful tariff whimsies, a superbly executed retreat from free trade dressed up to look like the opposite.

The total tariff fell by about 10% but Fielding's great invention was a preference which reduced the rate on British goods by one-fourth, increased in 1900 to one-third. As Macdonald had done to the Grits on another occasion, Laurier had now hived the Tories. They could not claim that protection had been seriously disturbed and certainly could not condemn a French Canadian's generous gift to Britain when they pretended to be the guardians of Empire.

Canada continued under a firmly protectionist tariff in denial of the legend. Laurier had confirmed Macdonald's National Policy which he and all Liberals had denounced six years earlier as deep damnation. And if Laurier had not retained a nostalgic fragment of free trade in his subconscious for later expression the whole history of Canada would have turned out differently.

For the present he was glad to forget reciprocity and was soon saying complacently that "we are not dependent on the American market now."

The reversal of Liberalism was complete. In 1907 he told the people of Britain, as if he had invented the National Policy, that he was doing everything possible to move Canada's business east and west, where nature intended it to move north and south, thus "forcing trade within the British Empire." This only four years before he was to reverse himself again.

Though the prairie farmers assailed the tariff reductions as quite inadequate, the National Policy was safe for at least sixty years; but only the Government's wonderful break of luck made Fielding's budget successful, his name memorable. For now the long-ebbing tide of the world economy was in flood again. Naturally, the return of good times for external reasons was installed in the legend as Laurier's work. The Fielding budget became a miracle.

No tinkering with the tariff, but Sifton's revolution in the West, represented the Government's real economic achievement. His massive influx of settlers from Britain, Europe and the United States, the hordes of "men in sheepskin coats," whom Sifton called "good quality," the creation of the wheat industry and all its ancillary towns, cities, ports and railways, fleshed the national skeleton.

A price was to be paid for Sifton's revolution. By sinking the nation's revenues and credit into the gamblers' partnership of William Mackenzie and Donald Mann, who guaranteed to build a second transcontinental railway, and then in a third, the Grand Trunk Pacific, the Government assured a top-heavy transportation system certain to collapse later on. So it did, with costs still carried by the taxpayers today. Yet Laurier, the architect of this crazy structure, was the same man who had condemned the original C.P.R. as ruinously expensive. Canada's happy time had gone to everybody's head.

The statesman who would be chiefly celebrated for domestic reform was compelled, on taking office, to divert most of his attention to the concrete problem of Canada's status in the Empire, a problem which he had considered only in abstractions until now.

Facing it, he could see no solution. That was not surprising. Hardly anyone suspected that the Empire, then apparently at its apogee, was already in the first throes of dissolution, much less that it was being reborn in an unprecedented experiment of autonomous states to be called a Commonwealth.

All Laurier knew when he crossed the Atlantic for the first time, to attend Queen Victoria's Diamond Jubilee and the Colonial Conference of 1897, was that any resistance to British imperial policy would be peculiarly dangerous to him as a French Canadian, whom half the country considered lukewarm to the Empire; also that the present status of Canada as a colony could not last much longer.

Those two conflicting factors, slowly clarifying in a mind as gifted as any under the British flag, came to focus at London. Laurier was caught up in an exhausting round of speeches, dinners, theatres, country week-ends and finally a knighthood. The "democrat to the hilt" accepted this honour, lest he offend the Queen, but with the feeling that he had been tricked into an affectation by well-meaning friends.

To the British Government and Establishment he appeared as a creature wellnigh unbelievable if one remembered his origins. The Canadian wilderness and Ottawa's sordid politics had produced, of all things, a gentleman—more than that, a genuine aristocrat who made most British politicians seem a trifle vulgar. His stately look and the charming flow of English, perfected by that faint, musical echo of French accent, fascinated society and set the duchesses aflutter.

Flattery had always been the Establishment's reliable weapon with overseas visitors of importance and now it was laid on with a steam-shovel. At first this familiar treatment seemed to work. The Establishment solemnly approved when Laurier said in a London speech: "If a day were ever to come when England was in danger, let the bugle sound, let the fires be lighted on the hills and in all parts of the colonies. Though we might not be able to do much, whatever we can do shall be done . . . to help her."

Then, abandoning himself to the imperial euphoria of the Jubilee, he actually announced that "it would be the proudest moment of my life if I could see a Canadian of French descent affirming the principles of freedom in the Parliament of Great Britain."

From a Frenchman the words were amazing, but precisely what the Establishment wished to hear since it planned some vague central Cabinet of Empire. Moreover, Laurier's aspirations were obviously sincere. Had he not already given Britain a valuable tariff preference and asked nothing in return? Here was a freak of the mysterious French nature who understood the Empire and the parliamentary system, a man to be educated, lionized and captured. Why, despite his blood, he was authentically British!

The Establishment only pretended an interest in his social charm. It had known and engorged plenty of charmers before now. How would Laurier perform in the council chamber?

Once the doors had closed on the Empire's family conference his whole manner changed alarmingly. Having quickly repented a brief triumph of his public oratory over good sense, he was polite, stubborn, inflexible. As soon as Joseph Chamberlain, the Colonial Secretary, proposed an "Imperial Council" with more than advisory power and certain "to develop into something greater," Laurier rejected it out of hand.

This was a cruel disappointment. The colonial prodigy had been overestimated. He did not realize that the Empire must be revitalized and reorganized under a single foreign policy to complete its God-given labours among lesser breeds without the law. As Chamberlain had said (temporarily forgetting that Laurier was French), the British race belonged to "that proud, persistent, self-asserting and resolute stock which is infallibly destined to be the predominating force in the future history and civilization of the world."

Unfortunately Laurier did not belong to that stock. Lacking its inner light, he would never agree to any dilution of Canada's partial independence. On the contrary, he wanted more of it. And by now he had seen through the Establishment's game.

"One felt," he wrote later, "the incessant and unrelenting organization of an imperialist campaign. We were looked upon not so much as individual men but, abstractly, as colonial statesmen to be impressed and hobbled. . . . In this campaign, which no one could appreciate until he had been in the thick of it, social pressure is the subtlest and most effective force. . . . It is hard to stand up against the flattery of a gracious duchess. Weak men's heads are turned in an evening and there are few who can resist long. We were dined and wined by royalty and aristocracy and plutocracy and always the talk was of empire, empire, empire."

The imperialists, he added, had selected him as "the bell wether" of their campaign, "but I fear they were disappointed." The Establishment had misconstrued him and the Empire also.

To the British Government he was the paradox of a man outwardly loyal and intelligent but somehow unable to comprehend the Empire's mission. In fact, he comprehended it better than his hosts. His dawning concept of independent nations freely associating under a common Crown was no paradox. It was the ultimate logic of the evolving British system and it was a native Canadian product. The seeds of the modern Commonwealth had been planted in Canada by Lord Durham's Report. Harvest time was now approaching with the new century.

The Establishment could not be expected to understand it but in his resistance to a centralized Empire Laurier was being more British than the London Government. His British instinct of freedom made him jealous of Canada's independence. His sure grasp of the illogical, the pragmatic and the workable compromise was the immemorial British method. He could not yet discern the final goal, nobody could, but he was moving forward step by step as Britain had always moved and still moves today. In Laurier, the French Canadian, a new British institution was beginning to emerge, the institution of the future.

At the moment, however, a baffled Establishment saw him only as an obstacle to Chamberlain's grand design. He simply could not be fitted into the imperialists' current ecstasy, the day of Victoria, Kipling and the White Man's Burden. Perhaps he might be tempered by further experience in government or turned out by a sensible electorate, but the Colonial Conference adjourned with the bleak announcement that "the present political relations are generally satisfactory." To the Establishment they were just the opposite.

From then on, through all the subsequent conferences, Laurier smoothly resisted all attempts, under many different guises, to centralize the Empire and diminish the independence of the self-governing colonies. His attitude, perforce, remained entirely negative. He could not yet offer any alternative to Britain's frustrated policy. Canada was not ready by a long way for complete independence.

For the next fourteen years, the polite blockade continued. Laurier would give no subsidy to the British Navy. He would not create a military force for service overseas. In 1911 he would not even join other colonial leaders in asking that the colonies be consulted on British foreign policy. He saw that if they gave advice they must back British policy, no matter what it might be.

By 1907 he had achieved at least a symbolic change in the Empire's arrangements. The Prime Ministers of Britain and the colonies met as equals and called their meeting an Imperial, instead of a Colonial, Conference. Next year his mind was clearer, or he felt strong enough to reveal it more frankly.

"We are reaching," he said in Quebec, "the day when our Parliament will claim co-equal rights with the British Parliament and when the only ties binding us together will be a common flag and a common crown." Two years later he declared that "we are under the suzerainty of the King of England. We are his loyal subjects. We bow the knee to him. But the King of England has no more rights over us than are allowed him by our own Canadian Parliament. If this is not a nation what is a nation?"

A commonplace and established principle today, this doctrine sounded then almost like treason among the Canadian imperialists. Foster denounced these subversive notions as dangerously mischievous. If such statements were "merely for the sake of rhetorical adornment," he said, "they are foolish. If, however, they are studied and serious they are revolutionary."

Of course they were. Laurier was preaching a peaceful revolution in the Empire. But men like Foster failed to see that it was the same revolution preached, within the limitations of his time, by Macdonald, the inevitable revolution. Others must finish what Macdonald had begun and Laurier had carried forward in giant strides. None of their successors, Conservative or Liberal, could follow any other road.

At his last Imperial Conference in 1911, Laurier knew that the effort to consolidate and centralize the Empire had collapsed, for the time being anyway. Even the British Government, now Liberal, had abandoned it.

"We are making," he wrote, "for a harbour which is not the harbour I foresaw twenty-five years ago. It will not be the end. Exactly what the course will be I cannot tell but I think I know the general bearing and I am content."

That was true and prophetic. Laurier's successors must steer into new waters, darkened by world war, Communism and atomic weapons. Perhaps there was no harbour after all but a perpetual voyage ahead. In any case, the major work of Laurier's life—not the work he had planned—was the establishment of a new status for Canada. If younger men must complete it, he had done that work with his own subtlety and style against the deep grain of English-speaking Canada and, as he soon found, against the isolationism of his own race.

7: The Twilight of a God

Throughout these years of lonely struggle, when he could seldom speak his mind aloud, Laurier had grappled not only with the British Government but with its agents in Canada and their friends among the Conservative politicians. The fight at home was much more dangerous, since it involved votes, than the fight in London where no voter could hear him.

Among others, he fought off the Governor-General, Lord Minto, who was appointed to run interference for Chamberlain in Ottawa. There ensued, though no record of them is preserved, a series of unpleasant encounters at Rideau Hall like those between Mackenzie and Dufferin.

Finally Laurier decided to fire Lord Dundonald, the British commander of Canadian military forces, for criticizing the Government. Minto refused to sign the order of dismissal until Laurier threatened to resign and take his case to the people in an election.

Minto was beaten but the Conservative imperialists remained. Some of them sincerely believed that Laurier was undermining the Empire. Some saw a chance to discredit him in the loyal English-speaking provinces. Better still, in 1899, they saw a chance to turn his flank in Quebec. For now, like all Prime Ministers, Laurier encountered his nemesis. Henri Bourassa had arrived.

This extraordinary man, a mixture of genius, scholarship and phantasy, began his career as Laurier's friend and personal mascot. With his black, satanic beard, his splendid profile and dandy's clothes, Bourassa was almost as impressive as his tutor, almost Laurier's equal in eloquence. He seemed quite harmless.

To be sure, he claimed a special place in Quebec society as the grandson of Louis-Joseph Papineau, the rebel, whom he claimed to remember in childhood, whose radicalism he cherished, whose anti-clericalism he deplored. The heritage of rebellion lighted in young Bourassa a bonfire of ambition, a flaming sense of French-Canadian destiny. A similar heritage already was producing the same results in a greater man, but the young King had enough Scottish caution to keep his private conflagration under control. Bourassa could control mobs. He could never control himself. Laurier regarded his mascot at first as naive, later as dangerous and finally as mad.

Such a talented egomaniac, with powers of agitation far beyond his wisdom, needed only a suitable opportunity to launch him into flight. The South African war exactly fitted his needs.

Laurier saw at once that this event, apparently so remote, must touch the racial roots of Quebec if he came to Britain's aid and those of the other provinces if he did not. When the British Government suggested that a Canadian contingent join the fight against the Boers, Laurier confronted, in naked form, the dichotomy of Canadian life. True, Macdonald had refused to take part officially in the Soudan campaign; but that had been a minor episode and now the royalist feelings of the Canadian majority were still ablaze with the glories of the Queen's Jubilee.

Laurier hesitated, knowing that his Government could not live a month if it rejected Britain's call and repudiated his own recent speeches in London. He must have a little time, as he explained later in Toronto, "to guide public opinion in my own province"; but the time was too short. Only ten days after the message from London the Government abandoned its plan to call Parliament and by Order in Council provided a force of one thousand men for service in South Africa. Before the end of the war more than seven thousand Canadians were to serve there.

Bourassa instantly resigned his parliamentary seat in protest against imperial wars, was re-elected without opposition and conferred darkly with his daemon. He continued to denounce the Government but remained in the Liberal Party and still considered himself the friend of a misguided Prime Minister. Though it was too early for his destined work of wreckage, he had made a good beginning—good enough anyway to require Laurier's serious attention.

In one of his Gothic speeches, a *tour de force,* Laurier pictured before an applauding Parliament Canada's pride in the heroism of its soldiers, "the noblest of all pride, the pride of pure patriotism. . . .

Today there are men in South Africa representing the two branches of the Canadian family fighting side by side for the honour of Canada. Already some of them have fallen, giving to the country the last full measure of devotion. Their remains have been laid in the same grave, there to lie to the end of time in that last fraternal embrace. Can we not hope, I ask my honourable friend [Bourassa], that in that grave shall be buried the last vestiges of our former antagonism?"

Eloquence was lost on Bourassa. He had plenty of his own and he was made of rubber that bounced like a ball inflated by windy racialism. From then on he was surging from one Quebec platform to another, addressing crowds of worshippers and arranging, perhaps unintentionally at this time, the materials of his own rebellion.

As Laurier called an election for November 1900, the opposition leaders said, and some may have believed, that the end of a brief aberration was at hand. The second Liberal Government would go the way of the first under Mackenzie, and the Conservatives' hereditary right to rule would be confirmed.

The two Tuppers, equal in their courage and egotism, conducted the campaign as a family affair with their usual noise and gusto, the father now in his eightieth year, the son in his prime. This reversal of nature's order was absurd on the face of it. If the father had quit after his defeat four years earlier the son almost certainly would have succeeded him and in time might well have come to office. By hanging on, the old man had spoiled Hibbert's career.

(Another son of a famous father was to suffer the same eclipse. Resigning the premiership of Manitoba and, for reasons of partisan loyalty, running against Sifton in Brandon, Hugh John Macdonald assured his own defeat and retirement from public life.)

Both Tuppers exuded the confidence of a royal family while they attempted an elephantine manoeuvre.

In Ontario they attacked Laurier for his lukewarm attitude toward the South African war. What would one expect? After all, Laurier was a French Canadian and the tool of that notorious Anglophobe, Israel Tarte, whom the Conservatives would soon be adopting as a hero.

In Quebec the elder Sir Charles announced the amazing discovery that "Sir Wilfrid Laurier is too English for me." Then, hastily squaring the circle to appease his outraged English-speaking supporters, Tupper explained in Toronto that Laurier was "not half British enough."

Even in those days of comparatively slow communication such

double talk could not be entirely concealed from the voters. Nevertheless, Laurier's Ontario strength obviously was falling after the South African incident, and though he appeared stronger than ever in Quebec, Tupper had clumsily laid the cornerstone of a Conservative alliance with the extreme Nationalist elements. On it, if the Conservatives averted their noses, a winning combination perhaps could be built some day.

Few men suspected these possibilities when the Government, campaigning on the nation's abundant prosperity, was easily re-elected. It lost 14 seats in Ontario, a chilling omen, but with 58 of Quebec's 65, and gains in the Maritimes and the West, its majority was increased, its longevity demonstrated beyond doubt. So was its primary dependence on French Canada—an omen still more chilling, in the long run deadly.

Tupper retired and since his son had been engulfed in his two defeats, the Conservative Party turned, rather hopelessly, to a new man. Robert Laird Borden, a Halifax lawyer with only four years' experience in Parliament and a leader who seemed least likely to succeed, reluctantly took over a discouraged Opposition.

He agreed to serve for one year only until a better substitute turned up. This plain, honest man, of rugged face, sprawling hair roughly parted in the middle, bristling moustache, mild eyes and solid Anglo-Saxon look, was the antithesis of Laurier in appearance and mind. Yet he contained larger qualities than any friend or enemy knew—more of intelligence, modesty and vanity, more of dogged perseverance and high achievement. This was fortunate for Canada. Borden must guide it through the most terrible days of its experience.

While he commenced a long and arduous journey, the Government seemed safe (it was good for two more victories) but its troubles had begun. In Bourassa the old French-Canadian mystique was now finding its ablest prophet and one-track mind.

Laurier's vision of Canada had been best painted in a casual election speech at Arichat, Nova Scotia: "As long as I live, as long as I have power to use in the service of my country, I shall repel the idea of changing the nature of different elements. I want the marble to remain marble; I want the granite to remain granite; I want the oak to remain oak; I want the sturdy Scotchman to remain the Scotchman; I want the brainy Englishman to remain the Englishman; I want the warm-hearted Irishman to remain the Irishman."

He wanted them to remain themselves in union, strengthened by diversity. Bourassa wanted his people to remain French Canadian but in separation. There was the quarrel between the two sons of Quebec, the enduring quarrel of Canada's whole future.

A man of powerful eyesight, with a magnifying glass, might already see the first faint cracks in Laurier's coalition of opposites, but the Government's affairs seemed to go swimmingly as the new century dawned.

Only one colleague dared to challenge the Prime Minister. In 1902, while Laurier was in London, gravely ill, Tarte expected his early retirement. The Quebec boss chose himself as the logical successor, moved through Ontario preaching high tariffs and earned the admiration of many Conservatives for his treachery. Laurier came home with the look of a dying man, curtly dismissed Tarte and, after a holiday in the United States, fully recovered his health.

The most notable of the accumulating scalps on the Prime Minister's belt convinced the public that the gentle knight *sans peur et sans reproche* was also without mercy as occasion required. Tarte's attempt to rally his old friends, the Bleus, against the Government failed completely. The Liberal coalition and the tariff of 1897 were left intact.

A much more serious challenge came, next year, from an unexpected quarter. The Yukon gold rush had brought wealth to Canada but it also turned the thoughts of President Theodore Roosevelt to the unsettled line of the Alaska boundary. He decided to fix it immediately and permanently on his own terms.

The submission of this old dispute to a commission of "six impartial jurists of repute," the decision of the British member, Lord Alverstone, to vote with the Americans against the two Canadians, and the loss of the Canadian case is too long a story for telling here. But it was to have long-term effects on Laurier and Canada far beyond the expectation of the American and British Governments.

Sifton, who had managed this affair for Canada, regarded the outcome as the crudest sort of betrayal by Britain. "The British government," he wrote, "deliberately decided to sacrifice our interests at any cost for the sake of pleasing the United States."

That statement, in one of Sifton's favourite phrases, had the added advantage of being true, though certainly the Canadian case was doubtful in law, and in practical international politics Britain wisely regarded friendship with the United States as the first objective of its foreign policy. At any rate, Laurier, smarting under a harsh blow from Roosevelt's celebrated Big Stick, was now convinced that Britain could not be trusted to conduct the foreign policy of Canada.

In a speech shocking to the statesmen of London he mildly criticized the "grasping" habits of the United States but directed his real anger at the British Government.

"I have often regretted," he said, "that we have not in our hands the treaty-making power which would enable us to dispose of our own affairs. . . . It is important that we should ask the British Parliament for more extensive powers so that if we ever have to deal with matters of a similar nature again we shall deal with them in our own way . . . according to the best light we have."

The theory that Canada could ever manage its own foreign policy was wildly heretical in those days and would not be fully implemented by Laurier. By establishing a Canadian External Affairs Department in 1909, however, he created the machinery of future independence. In the same year he ended his quarrel with the United States by agreeing to the creation of the International Joint Commission which thenceforth settled all disputes about rivers crossing the Canadian-American boundary and opened a new era of goodwill between the neighbouring nations.

Meanwhile the Canadian people's sense of betrayal by Britain on the Alaska boundary strengthened Laurier's hand in the struggle for autonomy and dulled the weapons of his imperialist enemies. Canada had lost its chance of access to the Pacific through the Alaskan Panhandle but it had acquired a new will to independence. The gains probably outweighed the losses.

When he called his third election in 1904 Laurier was impregnable. Borden, who had given up his hope of early retirement, saw the future consequences of the Government's reckless railway-building schemes and its insane guarantees to the gamblers' partnership of Mackenzie and Mann but most of the voters would not listen. Laurier came back with a majority of sixty-four seats. Borden himself was defeated in Halifax but quickly found another constituency.

The election result was not as satisfactory to the Government as it looked on the surface. The Liberal Party had won a majority of only fifty thousand votes across the country.

If that fact disturbed Laurier he soon had a more pressing and painful matter to consider. By 1905 he was plotting the first serious blunder of his life.

For the last several years his colleagues had begun to notice the Prime Minister's habit of deciding large questions without consulting the Cabinet and then presenting it with a *fait accompli.* He could rely, up to a point, on his blandishments to soothe the feelings of the offended ministers, but only up to a point. By double-crossing Sifton the genial queen bee went too far.

The break between the two Liberal giants had long origins as it was to have long results.

Once the Government decided to carve Saskatchewan and Alberta out of the Northwest Territories it could not avoid a new version of the Manitoba School Question. Sifton, the victor in that contest, was willing, even at the cost of strict consistency, to be reasonable about the school system of the new provinces. He agreed that they should maintain the arrangements fixed in 1904. Previously the Catholic schools had enjoyed virtual autonomy and full state support under clerical direction. Now they were so hedged about by the latest arrangements of the Territorial Assembly that, from the standpoint of the Church, they were hardly worth preserving. Sifton felt, however, that he was being generous in allowing minor Catholic school privileges abolished in his own province.

On the clear understanding with Laurier that the old separate-school system would not be revived, Sifton went to the United States for a holiday and for treatment of his growing deafness.

He had not been there long before he learned by letter that Laurier had broken the bargain. The Government's legislation establishing the new provinces gave the Catholic schools virtually all the privileges that they had enjoyed in 1875. Never satisfied with the treatment of his Church in Manitoba, Laurier proposed to offer it some recompense in Saskatchewan and Alberta. Sifton, he assumed, would complain but consent.

That assumption was wrong. Sifton hurried to Ottawa and prepared to resign at once. The Prime Minister professed surprise, pleaded an honest misunderstanding of Sifton's attitude, used all his arts of persuasion and, these failing, threatened his own resignation since he had evidently lost the confidence of Protestant Liberals. This ultimate threat had been used before and it had always worked. It did not work with Sifton. Too late, Laurier saw that he had misjudged the man of steel.

If Sifton could not be placated he would not only resign but would take other powerful ministers with him, Fielding among them. The Government would be smashed at the height of its powers, the racial and religious tensions of 1896 revived.

There was nothing for it but retreat, which Laurier executed in humiliating disorder. Sifton was allowed to rewrite the school legislation on its original lines, with a few face-saving devices. Laurier knew that he must face the anger of the Church and his own people in Quebec but he could not face the alternative of a shattered Government and party. The Conservatives, who had hopefully watched this promising family row, were disappointed to find it suddenly healed. Laurier had been bruised, more deeply than he yet realized, but he was still Prime Minister.

Even after his victory, Sifton would not remain in the Cabinet. At the age of forty-four he was established as Laurier's natural successor but this restless man had grown tired of office, was more interested in private business and, with his incurable deafness, could not hope to lead a government.

As a private Liberal Member of Parliament he maintained friendly relations with Laurier, who often consulted him and tried to lure him back into the Cabinet. Negotiations to this end seemed likely to succeed at one time but failed because Sifton insisted on bringing three new colleagues with him and Laurier could not face the trouble of a complete Cabinet reorganization. He wanted no new faces or new ideas. He wanted yes-men. The last chance to arrest the Government's decay had been lost. Sifton was out of office for good. He was not out of politics. His future would include the destruction of one government and the creation of another.

The election of 1908 now approached, and Laurier's Government still looked indestructible. Actually it was dying of dry-rot, the occupational disease which exempts no government.

The visible symptoms of loose administration and quiet graft seemed to give Borden his first real opportunity. He exploited it with surprising skill. The last two sessions of the existing Parliament were spent largely on scandal. Though Laurier's honour was never questioned and he remained a poor man, the Liberal machine was demonstrably corrupt. It could hardly fail to be in its lucrative association with Mackenzie and Mann, who bought minor politicians wholesale.

Borden, however, had overworked his cry of scandal. Its repetition bored the public. Much more effective, in the campaign of 1908, were the Liberals' cry of "Let Laurier finish his work" and his own bland advice to the voters—"Follow my white plume." The country followed it by giving him a solid Quebec, a majority of 4 seats in the English-speaking provinces and a total majority of 135 to 86. The majority had fallen by 15 seats but even so the defeat of such a Government in the next election was unthinkable.

No one discerned the most important results of 1908. A former Deputy Minister of Labour named William Lyon Mackenzie King had been elected in North Waterloo and next year became minister.

Arthur Meighen, a young, unknown Conservative lawyer, had carried the safe Liberal seat of Portage la Prairie. The two men of the future immediately began a personal feud which would continue for the next thirty years.

Borden had been deeply dejected by his second defeat but he hung on to his leadership because there was no adequate candidate to replace him and because his public image of modesty hid a brittle pride. Perhaps he suspected the truth. Whether he did or not, the Government was surely dying.

Laurier already knew the truth and sometimes admitted it to his intimates. After the election and its clear intimations of mortality, he wrote to a defeated Liberal candidate in a rare moment of candour: "What has happened to you in your county will happen to me before long in Canada. Let us submit with good grace to the inevitable." He had no intention of submitting for some time yet. The Government surely could win one more fight.

For two reasons it was far weaker than its architect realized. Most of its original energies had been dissipated, all its original policies completed and its capital of ideas exhausted.

The only formidable survivors from the Cabinet of all the Talents were Laurier and Fielding. Assuredly King had brought to government a bursting enthusiasm and talents potentially superior to those of any man in politics but as he began his boyish social revolution, with various hopeful statutes and much pious bluster, he was too young in the Liberal hierarchy to count for much yet.

Apart from King, whom he regarded only as a kind of promising apprentice and useful chore boy, Laurier refused to seek new capital of men and ideas. He no longer relished adventure, wanted no prickly colleagues around him and preferred the old hands who would do his bidding without question. Sometimes he thought of reforming a Cabinet of yes-men but always he retreated from the prospect of trouble in his official family.

Moreover, he was still deluded by the basic Liberal assumption of inevitable human progress, the relic of another century and now quite obsolete. How could he, or any man, imagine that an age and a familiar world were dying? If his Government was to die, let it die in peace.

For a second reason even that last comfort was denied to him.

After his breach with the Government over the South African war, Bourassa was reassured by Laurier's rejection of imperialism at London. The French-Canadian racialist subsided for a time, was aroused again by Sifton's victory in the school policy of the new provinces and blamed Laurier for the defeat of the Church. Within two years he had finally repudiated the Government and was forming a "sea-green incorruptible" Nationalist Party of his own in Quebec to replace those "syndicates of appetites," the corrupt Liberal and Conservative Parties.

The Bourassa campaign, though chaotic, was based on a clear and primary fact: in voting for Laurier Quebec had not become Liberal. Only its label had changed when Rouge and Bleu united behind the French-Canadian father image. Quebec was still the most conservative and the largest single truly Catholic community in North America. Also, it was Laurier's essential base of power without which his Government could not live.

Laurier must hold Quebec not only for political but for psychic reasons deeper than politics. With him and all future French-Canadian leaders, even the broad-minded St. Laurent, a sense of kinship with his own people was a spiritual necessity, an unsevered umbilical cord. It would remain so after it had become a political liability and the stuff of Laurier's tragedy.

Dazzled and confused by his racial vision and his determination to keep French Canada unique, chaste and separate, Bourassa nevertheless understood the political facts with cold clarity. His Nationalist Party struck at the vitals of the nation-wide Liberal coalition. Bourassa was attempting to replace Laurier as the accepted leader of his race.

For several years the conservative Catholic rebel kept Quebec in a state of excitement unknown since the time of his grandfather, the anti-clerical left-wing rebel.

Bourassa was here, there and everywhere. He was in Parliament. He was out of Parliament. He was sitting in the Quebec legislature as an ally of the Conservative Opposition. He stood for Canadian unity while splitting it single-handed. He stood for the British system, "this admirable political creation with its nerves of steel and its rich blood." He now experienced "the full pride of British citizenship" but that pride must not involve Canada in any aid to Britain. It must be kept in a vacuum, a jewel admired but never paid for with blood or cash. Bourassa was for and against many things in varying combinations. Yet on one thing he never wavered. Bourassa was always for Bourassa.

He carried his farrago of contradiction from town to town like the Grail. He addressed crowds of ten or fifteen thousand people and by his magic of eloquence, wit and invective reduced them to tears, laughter and rage, sometimes to riot. Almost nightly, as a newspaper reporter described it, his voice "swooped and curved and beat upon the walls . . . the scream of a war trumpet or the wail of the north-east wind down an old chimney." Soon he had his own newspaper, *Le Devoir*, of Montreal, wherein his editorials bit like acid.

This man could materialize the racial memory of Quebec and summon up the ghosts of the conquest. He could never replace Laurier. After an emotional purge at Bourassa's latest meeting, the ordinary French Canadian, a shrewd and sceptical citizen by nature, returned rapidly to his senses.

Given the right political circumstances, however, Bourassa might defeat the Laurier Government by allying himself with the Quebec Conservatives. For he had now created a third force in national politics. His nationalism opposed both new-fashioned imperialism and old-fashioned colonialism. It was dedicated solely to Quebec's separatism in Canada, an impossible retreat from the present into the womb of the past. On such a primitive impulse much could be built, if the political circumstances were right.

Laurier knew that Bourassa's exercise in nostalgia and passion would not stand the test of facts for a moment, especially the facts of international power now beginning to assert themselves across the Atlantic. How far dare he push the test? In 1909 he pushed it cautiously but too far.

Once an anxious Britain had decided to beat Germany in a race of naval power Laurier promptly reacted as an overseas British institution. "The supremacy of the British Empire," he said, "is absolutely essential . . . the salvation of England is the salvation of our own country." His plan to build a Canadian Navy was submitted privately to Borden, who approved it without reservation. Naval policy had been lifted completely out of partisan politics. But not for long.

During the summer of 1909 the Conservative Party broke into three factions. The French-Canadian wing was opposed to a Canadian Navy or any aid to the British Navy, Frederick Monk, the Conservative leader in Quebec, openly rebuking Borden for his support of a "costly and useless" experiment. The imperialist wing demanded that the Government abandon the project of a Canadian Navy as too little and too late. Canada, it said, should contribute to a single British fleet. Sir Rodmond Roblin, Manitoba's premier, found a happy phrase of denigration for Laurier's policy. He called it the "tin-pot navy," a name that would outlast his own. The moderate faction of the centre backed Borden but it was now a minority.

Laurier finally introduced the Naval Bill of 1910, providing for five Canadian cruisers and six destroyers at a cost of eleven million dollars. He faced the opposition of many Quebec Liberals but he could control them. Borden had so far lost control of his party that he described its warring factions as "cabals." If he was to reconcile them, if he was even to survive as leader, he must find a colourable reason for repudiating the agreement of the previous year, and an alternative to Laurier's policy. Here was the recurring dilemma of all political leaders. Borden proceeded to manage it with more dexterity and less scruple than Laurier had suspected in this blunt, simple man.

Adroitly shifting his position, Borden announced that the emergency was too grave to allow time for the construction of a Canadian Navy. Later on it could be built, if the people approved, but meanwhile Canada should give Britain the price of three dreadnoughts for the Royal Navy, about thirty-five million dollars. Thus Borden satisfied the imperialist wing of his party. The Quebec wing, though opposed to any naval expenditures, would prefer a gift of cash to a Canadian Navy in which Canadians might fight Britain's distant wars.

Laurier's policy was approved by Parliament but Borden had held the Conservatives together and staked out a flexible position of manoeuvre. All he needed was the right circumstances. Bourassa now provided them.

As he judged it, the hour of his show-down with Laurier had struck and he embraced it eagerly. Soon *Le Devoir* was shouting that Laurier's navy would involve Canada in all Britain's imperial wars "on the shores of the Baltic or the banks of the Black Sea or in the China seas." Before huge crowds in Montreal, Bourassa recounted Britain's more than twenty wars since 1812, none of them in Canada's defence. As an extra barb, tipped with poison, he reminded Quebec again that Laurier had failed to save the separate schools of Manitoba, Saskatchewan and Alberta. The life-and-death struggle of French Canada's two leading sons was now in the open.

Laurier saw his danger but in the complacency of old age underrated it. He could easily overcome Bourassa with sound argument and corrosive sarcasm. He could reprimand "those who constituted themselves the defenders of a religion which no one has attacked; those who handle the holy-water sprinkler as though it were a club; those who have arrogated to themselves the monopoly of orthodoxy; those who excommunicate right and left . . . those who seem to have only hatred and envy for their motive and instinct."

Unfortunately the struggle between Laurier and Bourassa was no longer a trial of oratory. It was a trial of votes. And while Bourassa had rejected Borden's naval policy, he was disrupting the Liberal Party of Quebec.

After the first naval argument, disruption was revealed by the second event in a sequence of three.

Nothing but his waning powers, his ego fed by royal jelly, could explain Laurier's next blunder, the Drummond-Arthabaska by-election. Never doubting his strength in this constituency, once his home, where he had first been elected to the Quebec legislature, he appointed the local Member of Parliament to the Senate. The resulting vacancy, he thought, would be quickly filled by another loyal Liberal. Still, the matter was important enough to require his presence at the party's nominating convention which, with his advice and consent, chose a candidate of excellent qualifications, a man certain to win.

This move was designed to put Bourassa on the defensive, and he knew it. Since the Conservatives did not dare to fight the by-election themselves, Bourassa must nominate a candidate or admit that he dared not fight it either.

The Nationalists' hour, as he judged it on second thoughts, had struck prematurely and in the worst possible place. No one could beat Laurier in his old stamping-ground of Drummond-Arthabaska. Bourassa wrote an editorial to be published after the ballots had been counted, blaming his defeat on "drunkenness, debauchery, tumult," but he must fight or surrender. Even the choice of a candidate representing the half-formed Nationalist Party apparently was mismanaged. A local farmer unknown in politics was nominated.

All the odds against him, Bourassa plunged into battle, with the open support of Monk and the Quebec Conservatives. His campaign was simple, grotesque and diabolical. Laurier's recruiting officers, he said, would soon be "scouring the country and compelling young men to enlist in the navy or in the army to go to foreign lands and fight the battles of Great Britain . . . to maintain, at the price of their blood, the supremacy of the British flag in Asia or Africa."

Thus the overture of the conscription crisis seven years ahead, thus the first act of Laurier's downfall and thus, after two months of racial wrath in Drummond-Arthabaska, while the whole nation watched, the defeat of the Liberal candidate by two hundred votes.

For Laurier it was a double disaster. It had informed Canada that his control of Quebec was in jeopardy. It had enabled the Conservative Party to strike at him in his home ground without publicly admitting its arrangements with Bourassa. But Borden, ostentatiously absent from the by-election, and detesting the Nationalists with all his Anglo-Saxon blood, did not reject their support.

The third event, though Borden misconstrued it in the beginning, soon gave him his chance. The right circumstances, so long delayed, appeared at last. Laurier had lurched into a final blunder.

After the budget of 1897 the Government had made only minor changes in the tariff. Having achieved a tolerable balance of forces between manufacturers and raw producers, and created his reputation as a free trader who could not quite reach his goal for the time being, Laurier buried the tariff issue. Apart from the dismissal of Tarte for threatening the balance and his own leadership, he did no more than discipline other ministers if they favoured any substantial change of policy.

The tariff issue, its practical implications and its potent mythology, would not stay buried.

It was unexpectedly disinterred by a most unlikely agent, President William Howard Taft of the United States. A Republican and a high-tariff man, he had been alarmed by an upsurge of agrarian protest which threatened to split his party. The Taft Government was dying anyway and the Republican Party would be totally split two years hence by Theodore Roosevelt in his latest disguise as a Bull Moose, but Taft could not anticipate that. He saw in a deal with Canada a chance to escape the immediate pressure of the farm vote for reduced tariffs.

His views were conveyed to Laurier by a curiously roundabout route. The Reverend James A. Macdonald, editor of the Toronto *Globe*, met Taft in Washington and found him "almost in a panic." Would Laurier consider a "reciprocity measure"? Macdonald rushed back to Ottawa with this electrifying news.

Laurier was not convinced that Taft meant business but he instructed Fielding to find out. On March 20 the Finance Minister met the President in secret at Albany. The principle of negotiation was accepted on both sides without commitments.

Laurier toured the Prairies in the summer and found the Canadian farmers surprisingly restive. They had never liked the compromise of 1897. Now they were ready to vote against its author, if they could find an alternative.

The old politician perceived at once the value of the opportunity offered by Taft. Reciprocity would hold the farm vote. It would have the added advantage of returning the Liberal Party to its old forgotten faith. Some manufacturers no doubt would object, but surely most of the nation wanted reciprocity and had always wanted it since its collapse after the American Civil War. Even John A. Macdonald had wanted it.

As Dafoe, a leading figure in these events, wrote later, the Government seized on reciprocity not for any reason of principle but to extend its own life if possible for another election.

One wise Liberal realized the fallacy of his party's reasoning. Sifton was convinced from the start that reciprocity would defeat the Government. Though he had called Sifton "the master mind in Parliament" who "could discern the current political tendencies, put his finger on the popular pulse better than any other man of my experience," Laurier was convinced that for once the western sage had erred. Fielding was instructed to close a deal with Taft. This he quickly did in the first days of 1911 and brought a detailed written agreement to Ottawa where, it is said, he absent-mindedly left it in a cab on his way from the railway station.

Recovered and read, the agreement was nothing like free trade as advocated by the young Laurier. Still, it represented a fundamental change in Canadian and American policy. Tariffs on many raw Canadian products sold in the United States were to be reduced or abolished. Canada would reduce its duties on various American manufactures. This was virtually the reciprocity of 1854 over again.

The agreement, as introduced in Parliament, seemed so good that the Conservative Opposition was afraid to attack it. Next day Borden consulted his caucus and found "the deepest dejection. . . . Many of our members were confident that the Government's proposals would appeal to the country and give it another term of office. Foster was greatly impressed by the proposals and said that when they were presented his heart had gone down into his boots. The western members were emphatic in their statements that not one of them would be re-elected in opposition to reciprocity. . . . I stemmed the tide as best I could, although I was under great discouragement. . . . The difference of opinion which had developed seemed in itself to be a forerunner of disaster."

Borden had suffered so many defeats and disappointments that despite the hopeful news from Quebec he instinctively erred on the side of pessimism. His mind was changed for him by the business community of central Canada and by Sifton.

Bankers, industrialists and boards of trade in Ontario and Quebec perceived in reciprocity the end of the National Policy, probably the end of Canada. Van Horne feared the end of his C.P.R. and, condemning Laurier's agreement, announced that he was "out to bust the damn thing." Sifton, backed by sixteen other prominent Liberals, issued a manifesto to the same effect and after secret talks with Borden became an unofficial adviser to the Conservative board of strategy. Borden was elated. Sifton could split the Liberal Party in English-speaking Canada as Bourassa had split it in Quebec.

The elation was short-lived. On hearing that he had conferred with Sifton, some of Borden's followers rebelled. Once in Sifton's pocket, they said, the Conservative Party would never emerge again. Failing to placate the rebels of his caucus, Borden resigned his party leadership but withdrew the resignation in the middle of the night after a delegation of party stalwarts approached him "almost with tears" to guarantee their loyalty. Now, for the first time, he was truly master of his party. He had the backing of big business, ample campaign funds, Sifton's organizing genius and, as an extra dividend, the folly of the American Government.

Thus reinforced, Borden fought reciprocity so ferociously that the Government's legislation had not been passed when Laurier adjourned Parliament in the spring to attend the coronation of King George V. Even then Laurier thought he could ram the agreement through and if that failed he could take it to the people, sure of their verdict. On his return from London the blockade continued. He dissolved Parliament and called an election for September 21. That was the fatal blunder.

The "democrat to the hilt" was entrusting a complex tariff document to voters who would never read or understand it but would vote by hunch and prejudice. The autocrat was overestimating his popularity though he could easily have forced reciprocity through Parliament without an election. The royal jelly had done its work.

Now began a political campaign even more cynical than that of 1896 but with the two parties' roles reversed. However dishonest, it was to prove, from an economic standpoint anyway, the most decisive campaign in Canada's history.

For Borden it was really two campaigns, one denying the other. In a man so upright his strategy seems, at this distance, unbelievable. It must be remembered, however, that he had come to regard reciprocity as ruinous to both Canada and the Empire. He could not stop the Quebec Nationalists supporting him and doubtless thought that he could moderate them in Parliament. Like all successful Prime Ministers, he had a strong power of rationalization. Thus step by step this fine and honest man was dragged by his friends into an alliance most foul, strange and unnatural. Perhaps he knew that it would crack under the first strain but it might elect him and save the country from its immediate peril.

Certainly Borden had no direct contact with Bourassa and says in his memoirs that he disapproved the Nationalists' anti-British propaganda. The Conservative and Nationalist bosses made their arrangements at a lower level, never admitting it, of course, on either side. Borden could not afford Bourassa's kiss of death in the English-speaking provinces. Bourassa could not afford Borden's neo-imperialism in Quebec. The covert deal between the two men's parties worked smoothly just the same.

Monk, the ostensible leader of the Conservative Party in Quebec, had made himself an appendage of Bourassa's campaign by backing him in Drummond-Arthabaska. In the general election the Conservative candidates for the most part were outright Nationalists or Nationalist sympathizers. Their strength depended on Bourassa, as their speeches echoed his. Whatever he might call himself, Bourassa was the real leader of the opposition in French Canada. From him alone Borden could get the votes he needed even if they were votes against his basic policy.

It was a miserable and humiliating strategy but where else could Borden go? The execution of Riel had broken Macdonald's old alliance with the Quebec moderates. Only the extremists were prepared to support Borden, partly in the absurd hope that his mind and character could be changed, mainly because they were determined to destroy Laurier, who basically agreed with Borden on the only issue of importance to Quebec. The issue was Canada's support of Britain.

Laurier's "tin-pot" navy happened to be the current symbol of this support, hence the target of the Quebec Nationalists, who conveniently ignored Borden's demand for a still larger navy and still closer ties with Britain. Accordingly, the navy was represented by the Nationalists as Canada's surrender to imperialism, as the guarantee that French-Canadian boys would be killed in Britain's wars. The other issue of reciprocity, though Bourassa had finally come out against it, after first approving it, was almost forgotten in this racial hysteria.

Outside Quebec the Conservative campaign took the two issues and combined them in a single indictment of Laurier's loyalty both to Britain and to Canada. On the one hand, he was disloyal to Britain because he would not contribute directly to the British Navy and his own was no substitute. On the other, he was disloyal to

Canada because he would surrender its economy to the United States by reciprocity.

Some fancy footwork was required for these contradictory tactics in the two Canadas. With comical gravity the Conservative press of Toronto began to deodorize the party's campaign in Quebec. The *World*, for example, solemnly discovered in Bourassa a man "of stainless reputation, of great moral energy, a sincere admirer of English institutions." The support of Montreal's Conservative business community was even more useful to Borden than that of Bourassa. While holding their noses, the financial interests supplied the Nationalists with campaign funds, no questions asked.

Good-naturedly, because he did not yet sense his danger and could not imagine his defeat, Laurier dismissed the Conservative contradictions as too absurd for serious thought.

"I am branded in Quebec," he said, "as a traitor to the French and in Ontario as a traitor to the English. In Quebec I am branded as a Jingo, and in Ontario as a Separatist. In Quebec I am attacked as an Imperialist, and in Ontario as an anti-Imperialist."

Absurd, yes, false beyond description on both sides and, in politics, murderous. Laurier delivered fifty of his superb speeches in a month but they came too late.

Possibly unaware of his handiwork, certainly unaware of its consequences to him, Borden had hatched a cockatrice. His immediate calculation, however, was clear enough. He could not hope, even with Bourassa's help, to win many Quebec seats but there might be enough to tilt the electoral balance. The balance must be won mainly in English-speaking Canada. There reciprocity became a handy catch-all for practical tariff arguments, for imperialist sentiment, for anti-Americanism, above all for the Canadian people's will to maintain an independent State.

Many Canadians, perhaps a majority, believed, as Borden did, that reciprocity must lead to annexation, that nothing less than Canada's survival was at stake. After more than half a century no one can say for sure whether these opinions were right or wrong.

Sifton, for instance, an original free trader, had no doubt that reciprocity would devastate Canadian business. He feared, moreover, that having integrated Canada into its own economy the United States might change its mind without notice, repudiate the agreement and leave Canada economically defenceless.

His great editor, Dafoe, took just the opposite view. He held that the prosperity resulting from the tariff bargain would nourish Canadian independence. Canada, he argued, had never been interested in annexation except at times of declining trade, as in 1849.

The spectacle of the *Free Press* proprietor crusading against reciprocity while his paper was for it further enlivened a campaign already in a violent flux of imperialism, anti-imperialism, Canadianism, financial greed, agrarian protest and plain buncombe.

Borden's killing ammunition came unexpectedly from the United States. Laurier knew at last that he was in deep trouble when the clumsy Taft said that Canada had reached "the parting of the ways." Then Champ Clark, Speaker of the House of Representatives, promised that the American flag would soon float over "every square foot of the British North American possessions clear to the North Pole" and announced that "we are preparing to annex Canada." Who could doubt these ambitions after the Alaska boundary award, now recalled by every Conservative speaker?

The official American utterances, and others from lesser politicians, descended on Borden's Conservative camp like manna from a just God. They provided the ultimate, unanswerable argument. In its own words the United States was using reciprocity to absorb Canada at leisure.

Overnight the ancient Canadian love of Britain and the hardy native instinct of independence were fused with Quebec's separatism in the hard instrument of Laurier's ruin. Taft, by an unconscious feat of infanticide, was killing his own child. To make doubly sure of it, the Conservatives invoked the authentic voice of Empire, though not in Quebec. On election eve, Rudyard Kipling obligingly cabled from London: "It is her own soul that Canada risks today."

No stone, however slippery, was left unturned. The Canadian railways warned that reciprocity would drain their east-west traffic into the United States and the American railways idiotically confirmed this prophecy. The club women of Montreal organized the "Woman's Branch of the Anti-Reciprocity League" and advised the Government that its policy meant not only annexation but "injury to home life and the marriage tie, a lessening of national religion, morals and patriotism." Robert Rogers, of Manitoba, the hardest-boiled politician in the trade, burst into soft poesy against "the treason that barters our birthright for the gold of the Kings of the South."

This was not a campaign. It was a landslide. On election night the debris buried the indestructible Government with 7 of its ministers, including King and Fielding. While Laurier had held 35 of Quebec's 65 seats, he held only 14 in Ontario against Borden's 72. Bourassa had done his work well, transforming French Canada's Conservatism and some of its Liberalism into Nationalism. The business interests and the genuine patriotism of Ontario had done even better. With gains elsewhere, Borden had a total parliamentary support of 134 seats to Laurier's 87. The position of the two parties had been exactly reversed. Macdonald's National Policy was safe for two generations at least.

So ended the illustrious régime of Wilfrid Laurier. But the issues raised and distorted in the election had not ended. The issue of Canada's place in the Empire was to be settled, three years hence, on the battlefields of Europe. The broad principles behind reciprocity, were to be revived in our time by a foreigner named John F. Kennedy.

Laurier tendered his resignation and like so many defeated Prime Ministers, hoped for revenge, though he had now passed three score years and ten. Defeated by the dishonesty of political strategists, by the honesty of the average voter and by the age of his Government, the old man retired with the dignity expected of him—no bitterness, no excuses, no explanations.

None were needed. Even if he could not resume it, his had been a mighty work—a new status for Canada in the Empire and the world, a peopled West, a truly national economy, a fifteen-year period of prosperity, a reconciliation of Church and State, perhaps a reconciliation of races. The Liberal had faithfully carried forward Macdonald's dream.

Yet Laurier had his private reservations. "It is becoming more and more manifest to me," he wrote, "that it was not reciprocity that was turned down but a Catholic premier." At all events, the twilight of Quebec's god was the world's twilight, too. For him, for the nation, for all mankind, the happy time had ended.

William Notman, courtesy Mrs. C. H. A. Armstrong

JOHN ALEXANDER MACDONALD

Notman Collection,
courtesy McCord Museum, McGill University

Notman & Fraser, courtesy Mrs. C. H. A. Arms

JOSEPH HOWE

EDWARD BLAKE

ALEXANDER MACKENZIE

JOHN J. C. ABBOTT

JOHN S. D. THOMPSON

MACKENZIE BOWELL

CHARLES TUPPER

WILFRID LAURIER

Toronto Star

ROBERT LAIRD BORDEN

ERNEST LAPOINTE

CLIFFORD SIFTON

ARTHUR MEIGHEN

WILLIAM LYON MACKENZIE
KING

RICHARD BEDFORD BENNETT

LOUIS STEPHEN ST. LAURENT

The Telegram, Toronto

JOHN GEORGE DIEFENBAKER

LESTER BOWLES PEARSON

8: The Plain Man

Canadians knew little of their new leader, nothing of the black night through which he must lead them. Sir Robert Borden's stocky figure, his double ruff of dark hair and his bristling moustache were familiar in the news pictures and cartoons but he had never excited the public or challenged the glamour of Laurier. He lacked any talent of self-advertisement, any lovable eccentricities, any gift of speech. Up to now no phrase of his was remembered and none would be remembered, outside the history books, after his departure. The Prime Minister had become no more than a solid fixture of politics, a sound, shaggy man, as the people judged him, but his real talents were hidden from them, perhaps even from himself, at the beginning.

It was typical of Borden, a plain, shy person almost aggressive in his privacy, that, hearing the election results at Halifax, he addressed no words of triumph to the voters nor any rousing promises. Instead, dumbfounded by the scale of his victory when he had expected nothing more than a narrow margin, he slipped away to his boyhood home of Grand Pré. There he secluded himself to ponder a task long sought but now suddenly daunting.

As he could not foresee then, the task was to be by far the hardest yet undertaken by any Prime Minister. All Borden's predecessors had lived in trouble but they had worked in peace. He must live in trouble, too, and work in war, always conscious that he was committing thousands of Canadian boys to certain death. It almost killed him.

That a man of law, business and quiet civilian life had been designated as a man of war in the nation's deepest crisis, that he must be the first Canadian to grapple directly with the statesmen of Europe in the work of carving up the world—these and many other unlikely prospects were outside his imagination on election night.

He was not an imaginative man anyway. He was only an able, orderly, laborious and brave man. Laurier had genius. Borden had common sense. Laurier was a sport of the French-Canadian breed, Borden a normal Anglo-Saxon product with all its virtues and faults. He knew his own limitations, had a rather touching reverence for his great predecessor and always addressed him as "Sir Wilfrid," while the old patriarch wrote to the Prime Minister as "My dear Borden." Meighen, a man of larger mind and smaller common sense, rightly said of Borden that he was not by nature a politician at all and for him Parliament was "a workshop and little more . . . a weighty not a happy warrior."

But perhaps Borden's qualities were exactly what the nation needed in the dark days ahead. If he lacked eloquence, inspiration or any touch of magic, he possessed a staying power of body and spirit quite as strong as Macdonald's and with none of Macdonald's vices. Through his nine years of leadership in war, peace and perpetual alarm Borden was usually on the verge of nervous exhaustion, often gravely ill; but he seldom showed it and worked grimly on despite the warnings of his doctors. Such a man would never lift the nation up. He would never let it down either.

There was another side to him, rarely seen but unconsciously committed to the diary which he wrote every night without fail. Over and over again, as if his ego required these flimsy props, he noted the success of his latest speech in Parliament, the good impression he had made in caucus, the praise of his colleagues, the "tremendous ovation" at some political meeting.

Modesty was the trade mark of his public life. A curious vanity, a rather desperate need of self-justification, flavours a private record monotonously sprinkled with the sincere flattery of self-quotation.

Yet he was a very human person behind the stern front and the stone face. The large fortune earned at the bar he conserved and expanded by rigid thrift. When he could spare the time he liked to go with his wife to the farmers' market in Ottawa and bargain for a fat capon or a mess of spring vegetables. Usually he rode to his office on a bicycle. He was an excellent raconteur among his intimates and enjoyed a rough joke over a drink. He loved the outdoors and the soil and understood them. Tobacco, which he chewed in private, was his only vice. Sometimes he showed flashes of humour unexpected and profane.

In his lawyer's punctilious language he once summed up a highly confidential meeting with his colleagues that was followed by immediate publication of important secrets in the press.

"I have endeavoured with no small expenditure of time and energy," he told one of his cronies, "to trace the origins of this extraordinary circumstance and have at last discovered the person responsible for a betrayal unprecedented in my experience." Then, referring by name to an eminent Canadian statesman, he added: "I am driven reluctantly, sir, to the considered conclusion that this gentleman is a dirty, low-down son of a bitch."

His humour occasionally extended to himself. Addressing the ball on the first tee of an Ottawa golf course, the Prime Minister was heard by a companion to mutter: "Now Borden, God damn you, keep your fool head down."

He seldom lost his temper but when the patient man was pushed too far by fools he exploded with cold violence. An erring colleague, the Governor-General, or the British Government would hear from him in words of brutal reprimand or ponderous sarcasm.

Even less known to the public was his odd streak of subtlety— as when a Conservative cabal attempted to replace him with Richard McBride in 1910 and Borden invited the flamboyant British Columbia premier to speak at a lavish banquet in Ottawa. After that lamentable speech, as Borden undoubtedly expected, no more was heard of McBride.

In short, Borden was a highly successful business manager at the beginning, an Empire statesman at the end, always a man of complete sincerity when anything less would have been ruinous to Canada; a man who, as he once told a gathering of young students, agonized and wrestled with himself; and finally, a conservative not by label but by instinct and absolute conviction. Nevertheless, the conservative perforce became almost a radical in the society of Canada and a revolutionary in its external affairs.

Had Borden always remained the man he was in his fifty-eighth year as he took office, his work would have ended in failure. He made himself a great leader because events changed him—or, at any rate, his views of Canada's future—completely.

More than any other Prime Minister he grew on the nourishment of events but the growth, while rapid and extraordinary, was imperceptible to the public. A whole generation must pass before his drastic impact on the nation and the British Empire would be recognized. At his death few Canadians knew that he had done more than any contemporary to transform the structure of both.

In the meantime the nation thought it could tie to Borden without knowing quite why. As usual, this vague, unspoken verdict on a public figure was right. Probably the nation was more confident than its leader, for he had got off to an unimpressive start.

His people, of mixed English and Scottish blood, had long been in the new world. A great-great-grandfather moved to Nova Scotia from Massachusetts before the Loyalists in 1760. Later he returned to New England but his descendants settled around the Bay of Fundy, establishing themselves eventually on a small farm at Grand Pré.

There Borden was born on June 26, 1854, in a poor but comfortable household. His father, by turns a farmer and a railway-station agent, educated himself by much reading. The mother was a voracious reader also and a woman of strong character. The home was much given to lively talk of literature and politics in the best tradition of the Maritimes.

Borden received the only formal education of his life at the local school, Acadia Villa Seminary, which provided a good grounding in the classics but not much else. The teachers noted in the boy a habit of study and an undoubted precocity. He mastered Latin, French and German in his spare time while working all summer on his father's farm or chopping wood in the winter. His experience of land, weather, nature and basic things would always colour and fortify his sedentary life in Ottawa.

At the improbable age of fourteen he became an assistant school master, turning over his meagre wages to his mother. While still in his teens, he taught for a short time in New Jersey where he was appalled to find himself advertised as a "professor." Never able to attend a university, he entered a Halifax law office as an articled clerk, learned his profession at night and passed his examinations before he could be legally called to the bar. In his early forties he was recognized as one of Nova Scotia's leading lawyers, arguing frequently before the Canadian Supreme Court and the Privy Council in London. His marriage to Laura Bond, of Halifax, was perfectly happy though childless.

The Bordens had always been Liberals. Robert's cousin, Sir Frederick, was Laurier's Minister of Militia. Doubtless Robert, too, would have remained a Liberal but for Fielding's reckless threat to take Nova Scotia out of Confederation. Having played no part in public life until then, Borden was outraged by this folly and became an ardent Conservative in politics as he was in nature. His reputation was so high in Halifax that he headed the poll in 1896, when he agreed to serve no more than one term in Parliament.

On Tupper's retirement four years later the despairing Conservative caucus forced the party leadership on Borden because it could think of no one else. He rejected the offer as preposterous and regarded a permanent career in politics as unthinkable. Moreover, his doctor warned him that his nervous system, always delicate in a muscular body, could not endure such a life; but after two days of resistance he gave in, agreeing to act as the party's caretaker for another year until a better man turned up.

Two things happened to bar this easy escape. In a party rent by repeated rebellions and intrigues Borden was quickly established as an uninspiring but indispensable director, and he began to relish the struggles of Parliament. More important, he soon overcame the insularity of the depressed Maritimes. By 1911 he was a broad Canadian and a robust nationalist (not, of course, in the Quebec meaning of that word).

When Borden reached Ottawa from Grand Pré to form his Cabinet the people expected far more from him than he could possibly deliver. Tired of Laurier's humdrum happy time, they looked forward to an exciting new era, while the Prime Minister was distracted and bitterly discouraged by the familiar riddle of squeezing the square pegs into the round holes.

After nineteen days of chopping and changing, the new Cabinet was Borden's own. He had rejected many insistent and deserving candidates to reward others who had long been his enemies. He had remembered Macdonald's dictum that personal likes and dislikes must never influence a political leader.

The Cabinet roughly represented the geography and conflicting interests of the nation but it was a mediocre Cabinet, as Borden well knew, since the long years of opposition had attracted few promising recruits to the Conservative Party.

Borden himself had no experience in government. Foster, the only formidable survivor of the old Conservative administration, had been damaged by certain charges against his integrity in private business, charges unproved but not forgotten. Besides, though Foster was a national power and a famous orator of stately, bearded presence, he was old and Borden did not altogether trust his judgment. In any case, Foster's ambition to regain his former portfolio of Finance must be disappointed because Borden had already chosen Thomas White, an apostate Liberal who would hold the support of the anti-reciprocity section of the Liberal Party and the big business community of Toronto. No abler man could have been found.

So, having refused a lucrative non-political job on the Tariff Commission, Foster grudgingly accepted a compromise and was stowed away, like Cartwright before him, in Trade and Commerce where his diary recorded gnawing doubts about the Prime Minister's wisdom.

The Foster diary is significant mainly as showing how wrong the contemporary opinion of Borden could be. "The interests," Foster wrote, "seem to be dominant and Borden doesn't know his mind from day to day . . . seems helpless on the surf . . . irresolute and fearful . . . an odd man." What Foster and other disappointed Conservatives failed to see was that Borden had done precisely as he pleased.

The outstanding member of the Cabinet—outstanding for an eccentricity verging at times on madness—was Sam Hughes, the editor from Lindsay. He took over the Militia Department and proceeded to turn it upside down. Borden had appointed him with grave misgivings after making Hughes promise to change his erratic, violent ways. The promise was solemnly given but if Borden could believe that he could believe anything.

Hardly less of a liability was Robert Rogers, of Manitoba, Minister of the Interior, a notorious back-room politician, a skilled fixer and chief custodian of government patronage.

Borden's closest friend, George Halsey Perley, entered the Cabinet without portfolio but exerted an unequalled influence on the Prime Minister. Charles Joseph Doherty, Minister of Justice, representing the English-speaking Catholics of Quebec, provided a leavening of quiet good sense.

Not only was the Cabinet mediocre; it was divided by the unnatural alliance of the election.

In the vain and rather humiliating hope of cementing his deal with the Nationalists and building a sane Conservative Party in Quebec, Borden sent Monk to offer Bourassa a portfolio. The new master of French Canada, as he regarded himself, refused to join the Government. His hands would not be tied. He wanted them free to reach for Borden's jugular if that became necessary.

Despite the angry protests of his Ontario supporters, Borden therefore appointed Monk to Public Works and two Nationalist nonentities to minor departments. This trio, Bourassa's ambassadors, represented a Quebec conservatism ranging all the way from the extreme Nationalist position to that of the old-fashioned Bleus.

Such a Cabinet, failing to bridge the racial schism and not even disguising it, was ill prepared for the shock of any serious crisis, a war for example.

Within a year the Borden Government received its first shock. The long boom of Laurier's happy time petered out and the Prime Minister, who had nothing to do with them, was blamed for bad times in accordance with the ancient fiction.

His mind, however, was concentrated on a graver problem. As the armament race of Europe accelerated he must frame a definite policy to replace Laurier's "tin-pot navy," but any policy must threaten the spurious *entente* with the Nationalists. Already Bourassa had boasted that "we have destroyed one government and we shall destroy yet another unless our principles are respected," those principles absolutely excluding any naval expenditures.

No one understood Borden's dilemma as well as the new leader of the Opposition. Laurier had offered to resign his party leadership as a matter of form, had remained at the unanimous demand of his followers and, confessing that "I don't feel ripe for heaven and at all events I want another tussle with the Tories," undertook to precipitate an early election.

He regarded the verdict of 1911 as only an aberration which could be quickly reversed now that Borden was impaled on the horns of an unknown naval policy and the veto of his Quebec allies. The happy time, the diet of royal jelly and his own legend convinced Laurier that the nation already wanted him back in office. Divinity that hedges the kings of politics also isolates them from their subjects.

As soon as Parliament opened Laurier politely requested a statement of the Government's plans for aiding the British Navy. Borden could not answer. The long duel between the old leader and the new had begun. For five tumultuous years it would continue to its appointed end of triumph on one side, tragedy on the other, but it differed from all the duels of the past and future, both in the gravity of its issue and the temperaments of its antagonists.

The issue soon became the survival of the nation. But whereas Macdonald had pursued his blood feud with Brown, Mackenzie and Blake in a spirit of hatred and contempt on both sides, and King would fight Meighen for twenty years in mutual loathing, Borden and Laurier always fought cleanly with no word of personal insult because each respected and liked the other.

Borden recognized in his adversary a man greater by nature than himself. Laurier recognized in Borden a man of high abilities and unquestioned honour. Hence in their historic struggle—the old master against the apprentice, the glowing myth against the plain man—Canadian democracy was to see its finest hour; also its paramount test.

For the moment Borden's naval policy was paralyzed. He knew what he wanted to do, what he had promised to do, but the Nationalists already had asserted their veto on any contribution to the British Navy. Monk revealed the falsity of the alliance by telling Parliament in his leader's presence that Quebec would tolerate no naval policy of any sort without a plebiscite. Six months after an overwhelming victory the alliance was showing the first cracks.

Its uneasy maker went to London in the summer of 1912 and there found an interesting new friend in young Winston Churchill, First Lord of the Admiralty, who was to flit through Canada's affairs for the next forty years in blunder and in glory.

Borden agreed to contribute $35 million to the British Navy, the price of three dreadnoughts, until a permanent naval policy could be devised. Churchill agreed to support the Canadian Government by a series of urgent messages and speeches. Hearing this news, Monk instantly resigned. Bourassa cheered. The alliance was breaking up.

When Borden introduced his naval plans into Parliament it was perhaps symbolic, in a ridiculous fashion, that he pushed his chair aside as he rose to speak and then, interrupted on a point of order, sat down again in a vacant space, fell to the floor and broke his glasses. Fortunately he had brought another pair with him and, getting to his feet, was able to read the notes of a lengthy, well-reasoned speech.

It was what Laurier had expected. He denounced Borden's policy as "a cross between Jingoism and Nationalism." By a money gift to Britain, he jeered, "you are ready to do anything except the fighting."

Parliament now beheld in the leader of the Opposition the full fury of a Prime Minister spurned. Laurier intended to force a quick election on defence policy and he expected to win it, now that the alliance was crumbling. The great naval debate and Borden's long misery were under way as only an overture to the misery of the nation.

Never had Canada witnessed anything like the length and rancour of the blockade against Borden's Naval Bill, a Liberal riposte to the Conservative blockade against reciprocity. The villainy taught by the alliance, as he saw it, Laurier intended to repay and it would go hard but he would better the instruction. Having declared a siege, he settled down to await the garrison's surrender. From then on

Parliament ceased to be a deliberative body. It became a suburb of Bedlam.

Messages in stirring English prose from Churchill to prove that Canada could not build or man a warship; Liberal outrage at this interference in Canadian affairs, the worst exhibit of British arrogance "since the days of Lord North"; anti-imperialist oratory from Bourassa, the fair-weather friend and now the outright enemy of Borden; the House in session twenty-four hours a day for two successive weeks; Members sitting in regular eight-hour shifts and sleeping in their offices, constantly under the eyes of the party whips; the Liberals obstructing every clause in the Naval Bill, wasting time by quotations from old speeches, bluebooks, the Bible or any handy document; endless wrangling on points of order, clanging of division bells, pounding of desks, cries of "Shame!", the Speaker's voice drowned in the clamour, physical exhaustion on both sides; Laurier calm but vibrant in his old age and the rousing scent of victory, sure now that the Government would be driven into an election; Borden, the younger man by thirteen years, sick with painful carbuncles and sick in heart, confined to bed, appearing in the House with neck heavily bandaged, a doctor at his side—this was the new Prime Minister's baptism of fire, the first fruits of the unnatural alliance, the spectacle of a feverish nation on the eve of Armageddon.

Had the election really settled anything? The depleted Borden must have wondered as winter dragged into spring and the Liberal blockade dragged on without a day's interruption. How long could Laurier maintain it? How long could the Government take such a pounding? Could a naval or any other basic policy be enforced since the Government had evidently lost the support of French Canada and Laurier seemed to have lost his head? If Churchill was right and war might break out at any moment could Canada fight it at all?

So Borden pondered in those awful days of spring, 1913, and finally reached a decision—bold, tricky, repulsive to the plain man but unavoidable.

For weeks the abrasive private Member for Portage had been demonstrating a tactical talent amazing to the Prime Minister in one so young. Meighen's formula as presented secretly to Borden looked too complex and hazardous. It depended on perfect timing and, with the slightest slip, might be disastrous. Borden accepted it doubtfully because he could think of nothing better.

He prepared his followers for the show-down by telling their caucus only that they must remain silent next day while a certain strategy was executed. Without warning, at the appointed hour, as

Laurier rose in committee of the whole House, a chosen Conservative member rose also, the Speaker recognized him and by a complicated use of the rules a division was forced. The Government won it, the Opposition was trapped and the debate closed. Thus the iron law of closure, invented in the cold mind of Meighen, was applied over the screams of the Opposition and the first known outburst of temper from a flushed Laurier.

The deed had been done. The Naval Bill was pushed through at last. It was dead nevertheless.

In a Senate dominated by Laurier's appointees, Sir George Ross, the Liberal leader (who had privately sought an accommodation with the Government), called Borden's plans "as empty as an exploded cartridge, soulless as its plated sides." The Naval Bill was rejected on Laurier's instructions.

Borden had made the worst possible start as Prime Minister but that was the least consequence of the naval fiasco. While Britain and the rest of the Empire armed for imminent war, Canada was impotent, humiliated and divided. Borden could never enforce his policy and, though he could not anticipate it yet, the policy was doomed by events in any case. So was the original structure of the Government. Though all but five Quebec Conservatives had voted for the Naval Bill, the Nationalist Party had disintegrated. The French-Canadian voters, repenting their desertion of Quebec's great son, were returning *en masse* to Laurier. The alliance was in ruins.

On the other hand, Laurier had failed to force an election and by his brutal tactics had antagonized most of the English-speaking vote. Surveying the debacle, only Bourassa was happy. He boasted of "a moral triumph without precedent." Perhaps it was, for him. But only for the moment. His party had been killed by Laurier. And after little more than a year everything said in Parliament, all the pretences of 1911, the whole political balance of the nation and its brave hopes of half a century became irrelevant overnight.

In the summer of 1914, prostrated by a hard parliamentary session, sick again with carbuncles and yearning for retirement, Borden went to a Muskoka lake resort on holiday. He knew that Europe was troubled but from the British Government he had heard less news than he read in the daily press. Rumours of war did not seriously disturb him.

His colleagues were scattered all over Canada in this holiday season. The Governor-General, the Duke of Connaught, was enjoying a western vacation. Laurier, in a fit of blindness and pique, had recently told Parliament that there was no possibility of war, that the Government's concern with naval policy was only political sham.

A telegram from his secretary reached Borden in the last week of July. He boarded a fast motorboat, caught the train to Ottawa and, arriving there on August 1, assembled his few available colleagues. They cabled to London Canada's offer of military aid. Then, as Borden wrote later, they passed a long series of Orders in Council, all without legal authority, to prepare Canada for war. Parliament was summoned for August 18 to validate these decisions.

After all the months of indecision and failure, the day of August 4 found in Borden a leader prepared for anything, a new Borden, calm, determined and now master of the nation. At five minutes to nine that night a cable was brought to him in the Cabinet chamber. Britain had declared war on Germany and automatically Canada was at war also.

White turned to Borden and said that this was "the suicide of civilization." Borden refused to believe it but admitted, in his diary, that "it was difficult to retain one's balance." In the next five dreadful years he never lost it for a moment.

The response of Canada to this news was naive, ignorant and magnificent. How its young men fought through the war as bravely as any men had ever fought anywhere in any age, how the war was financed by White's bonds, "temporary wartime" income taxes and outright inflation, how Canadian society was permanently altered by the massive interventions of the State, and how the nation truly felt its nationhood for the first time cannot be told in this book.

War was also a political as well as a military, social and spiritual fact. Here we are concerned only with the political fact. It necessarily centred around the Prime Minister and he proved strong enough to bear it.

At the beginning Borden found in Parliament the accurate image of a nation suddenly united by foreign catastrophe—gone the squalor of the naval debate, forgotten the reciprocity quarrel, hushed in political truce the duel with Laurier. Even Bourassa, who had attacked Britain's remote wars, escaped on foot from Germany where he was holidaying and rushed home to declare that "I have not written and will not write one line, one word, to condemn the sending of Canadian troops to Europe."

In the excitement of the day few Canadians noted Bourassa's next sentence—Canada must take "an exact account of what can and what cannot be done and ensure her own domestic security before beginning or following up an effort which she will perhaps not be able to sustain to the end." There was the tiny seed of domestic tumult, the unseen issue sure to split the nation as it had never been split before. Meanwhile Parliament gave the Government dictatorial powers, agreed to vote unlimited military appropriations and vowed, perhaps even believed, that party politics must cease until the day of victory.

Borden made a plain, businesslike speech, impressive for its lack of ornament. Laurier's oration in reply was one of his greatest, as if he repented his words of complacent folly a few months earlier. Yet this superb credo of patriotism, if one read between the lines, was seen to contain a divisive doctrine not clear even to the orator.

Laurier assumed that Canada was contributing and must contribute without stint to a British war. Britain was a principal in the war, Canada a contributor, not of necessity but only of sentiment. That doctrine, if carried to a logical conclusion, must break Laurier, his party and the nation's unity.

Borden regarded it as Canada's war in which it was not a contributor but a principal, fighting primarily for itself. If he saw the hidden division of principle between himself and the old opponent who was now a friend, this was no time to argue it.

As the nation's first war leader the Prime Minister had undertaken work and assumed powers unknown to any predecessor. He went about it quietly, systematically, doggedly, his health restored by the sense of a clear and single purpose. Nothing mattered to him now but victory and he wrote to Laurier that the future of politicians and parties could look after itself. Some Conservative managers suggested that he call an immediate election and cash in on the nation's ardour but he rejected the advice with contempt. Borden was making war.

So, in his own way, was Laurier. The old orator's recruiting speeches took on a ring of passion that no other Canadian could hope to equal. After collapsing from his exertions in Ontario, he told an audience of fifteen thousand in Montreal that "for my part I want to fight for England and also for France. To those who do not want to fight either for England or for France I say: Will you fight for yourselves?" The theory of Britain and France as principals and Canada as a contributor was temporarily set aside in the excitement of the moment but not for long.

Now began the splendid, often comical and sometimes mad epic of Sam Hughes. He had seen some action in the South African war, he had persistently claimed but did not receive two Victoria Crosses for his heroism and he regarded himself not only as Minister of War but as commander-in-chief, almost as a separate, one-man government.

For all his *gaucherie,* his insults to colleagues and soldiers alike, his raging profanity mixed with outbursts of tears, his queer notion that Borden was "a most lovely fellow, gentle-hearted as a girl," Hughes achieved his own prodigy.

Though he had found, on taking office, a permanent military force of only three thousand and a militia of fifty thousand, he mobilized and trained thirty thousand men at Valcartier and embarked the immortal First Contingent for England a month after the declaration of war.

Borden was incredulous and delighted, the nation moved as it had never been moved before. If only Hughes could control his strain of megalomania, if only the politicians could maintain the truce of politics, if only the spirit of autumn, 1914, could endure, then Borden's task, while heavy, would be simple. That was asking too much of human nature. Already men and events were conspiring to make the task, as then planned, impossible.

The war had not been under way a year before Meighen, now Solicitor-General and ablest of Borden's colleagues, realized that the whole political organization of Canada must be changed to win the war. In proposing a non-party union government during those early days, Meighen was right but no one would listen to him.

Borden had no time to think of politics. His only interest was the war in Europe but he soon found himself fighting another war at home.

It was easy to reject Rogers' cynical demand for a general election before the Liberal Party could be rebuilt. The horror of Ypres made an election unthinkable to Borden and would outrage a proud and mourning nation. It was not easy, it was almost impossible to deal with the swarm of old Conservative friends who wanted army commissions, titles and, most of all, graft.

To the plain man this sordid side of war was sickening. He set up a huge apparatus of control to enforce honesty and thrift in the Government's purchases of military supplies; but those lush times made graft inevitable and graft soon produced a series of scandals.

The Liberals in Parliament exploited them with skill, always supporting appropriations for the war, attacking the undoubted waste of money, condemning the grafters, paying out the rope which would hang the Government.

Then there was Hughes. Borden could manage and fully trust his other ministers but Hughes baffled and, at times, seemed to terrify him.

Hughes was parading as a major-general in his Canadian camps, promoting or demoting other generals wholesale, affronting the whole French-Canadian race, suddenly taking off for London, visiting the trenches of France, making fiery speeches everywhere.

He was also letting outrageous contracts to his friends, though he remained strictly honest himself. Worst of all, he was stubbornly defending his chosen weapon, the Ross rifle, after impartial experts had condemned it and Canadian soldiers had often lost their lives because its mechanism jammed in battle.

Hughes, in fact, seemed to think he was fighting a private war about which he told the Government little. Why should he? His civilian colleagues would not understand war anyway and the Prime Minister, "gentle-hearted as a girl," would never dare to interfere with him.

Like so many others, Hughes was wrong about his leader. Borden treated him with infinite patience, far too much patience, but with a cold judgment of political possibilities. For the moment Hughes, a public idol, could not be fired without grave risk to the Government.

As Borden admitted candidly in his memoirs, "I knew that Hughes had a considerable following . . . and while I felt that his continued presence in the Government was a handicap rather than a support, I determined to let him continue until I was perfectly sure that his dismissal would not entail any serious danger to my Administration."

It took Borden two years to make perfectly sure.

First he moved in on Hughes's closest friend, "guide and counselor," J. Wesley Allison, whose war contracts were scandalous beyond any possible justification. While a commission investigated them, Borden temporarily took over the Defence Department from Hughes, who "wept at one time and laughed at another." Hughes's personal honour was vindicated but the Allison case, as condemned by the commission, and many other cases, convinced the nation that the war was being managed with widespread inefficiency and corruption.

Borden, too, was shocked, angry and determined to cleanse his Administration. Suddenly he rose in the House of Commons and read two corrupt Members out of the Conservative Party. This had a salutary effect but Laurier was persuaded that a reeling Government could never win another election. Unfortunately for the Liberal Party but fortunately for Canada, the people still trusted Borden.

The show-down with Hughes came in the autumn of 1916.

Unable to get any adequate information from his colleague or from the British Government, Borden sent Perley to London as Minister of Overseas Forces. Hughes regarded the appointment of this personal enemy as a public repudiation. He threatened and bluffed but found that the Prime Minister was not as gentle as a girl after all.

In a series of childish letters to Borden from London, Hughes blamed White and Foster for conspiring against him "but I know you are capable of seeing through them." Borden had seen through Hughes at any rate. Satisfied at last that the risk could be taken, he asked the War Minister to resign.

After Hughes had fumed and wept in Borden's office his resignation was written on November 11, 1916, a day on the calendar to be notable two years hence. Hughe's last letter was a jumble of abuse, self-praise and pity for Borden's "soft mannerisms." Borden merely recorded in his diary the opinion that Hughes had become "most mercurial." The phrase was too generous. Hughes began at once to intrigue against the Government and told his friends he would wreck it along with his successor, Edward Kemp.

At last Hughes was gone but he had been only the most notorious, not the most serious, of Borden's almost insoluble problems. Far more difficult to deal with was the imminent bankruptcy of the Canadian Northern Railway. As usual, Sir William Mackenzie ("that old man of the sea," Borden called him) was clamouring for money and as usual seemed able to hypnotize any Canadian government.

The Liberals, having assured this dilemma by their prodigal railway policies, now attacked Borden's attempt to cure it. He spent many anxious days with Mackenzie and with financiers in New York trying to devise a solution short of expropriating the Canadian Northern, and finally turned the whole mess over to Meighen who, in his first major trial, proved to be the Conservative Party's clearest intellect.

With infuriating calm, language of classic symmetry and frequent sand-blasts of irony, the young man from Portage la Prairie persuaded Parliament to bail out the Canadian Northern once again by giving it more loans of public money. This was a formidable job. As Borden watched in a mixture of alarm and amusement, another promising Conservative apprentice, Richard Bedford Bennett, of Calgary, condemned the Government's policy in speeches of burbling invective and called Meighen "the gramophone of Mackenzie and Mann," a phrase as lasting as it was slanderous.

The first struggle of two youngsters, both to be Prime Ministers and both failures for all their great gifts—the plump and wordy Bennett venting his jealousy on the lean, almost spectral and impassive Meighen—delighted the Opposition but Borden knew that the Conservative quarrel was not dangerous. What worried him was the permanent future of the Canadian Northern and, a little later, the threatened collapse of the Grand Trunk Pacific. In the end he was compelled to take them both over in a state system called the Canadian National Railways.

Its attention focused on the war, the public failed to observe that Borden, the philosophical Conservative, had given Canada its first gigantic experiment in socialism. Secretly he would have preferred to take over the Canadian Pacific as well, holding that government management could be as effective as competition in the railway business—a heresy not disclosed to Parliament.

All the scandals, the rise and fall of Hughes, the railway problem, the public quarrel of Meighen and Bennett, the customary private quarrels of any Cabinet, were manageable and Borden managed them, not brilliantly but effectively. Through the competent White he achieved something like a financial and economic revolution in which Canada became a lender instead of a borrower and a huge contributor of food and materials to the Allies. Before the war was finished Canada had recruited 628,000 men for the armed services and sent 425,000 overseas from a population of about eight million.

This was management on a tremendous scale—often bungled in detail, sometimes enforced with unnecessary damage to civil liberties when harmless cranks were jailed and questionable publications suppressed, but the total result was stupendous in the end for a people of Canada's numbers.

Those achievements lay ahead. For the present Borden was dissatisfied with Canada's efforts and less satisfied with the attitude of the British Government. On one of his visits to London he told Prime Minister Asquith that he could not ask Canadians to carry their present load unless he was convinced that Britain "takes the war seriously, realizes the necessity of the task, is making preparations accordingly and there is no more cry of 'Business as Usual.' "

While Borden knew that the British Government was making a botch of the war, he had come to realize that his own problem, the crisis of his career, lay elsewhere. It lay in Quebec. And like every Conservative Prime Minister except Macdonald Borden could never manage Quebec.

All things considered, Dafoe, who had watched six of his predecessors, decided that Borden was "a well meaning incompetent." As a new phase opened, the western sage and many other qualified judges were compelled to reverse their verdict.

9: The Old Nightmare

The split between the Government and Quebec widened so slowly and quietly that Borden hardly saw the gulf before it became unbridgeable. For this he had to blame both Hughes and himself.

Hughes, a rabid Orangeman and imperialist, had treated Quebec with undisguised contempt, made English the sole language of the army, refused at the beginning to form Quebec regiments and appointed few Quebec officers to important commands. Still worse, with inspired stupidity he had chosen English-speaking officers, even Protestant clergymen, to recruit French Canadians, who suspected an attempt to undermine their religion. Hughes had committed these blunders but Borden had failed to stop him.

Even if all such problems had been reasonably managed, the basic problem remained—Borden had encountered the ancient riddle of all Prime Ministers, deeper than any mistake of management or any calculation of politics. Under the worst possible circumstances of war, circumstances aggravated by Borden's alliance with the Nationalists and his failure to penetrate the French-Canadian mind, he had stumbled into Canada's racial chasm.

His trouble began in 1915, when he mistook it for a chance of reconciliation with Quebec.

After a little cagey bargaining, Laurier had agreed that the nation could not afford an early election and consented to the extension of Parliament's life for a year after its normal expiry in 1916. Borden had hoped, in his friendly correspondence with the opposition leader, to keep Parliament alive until the war was won but a one-year extension might be enough. No one expected the war to

164

last long. In any case, Laurier would go no further for he was already meditating his own grand strategy.

It was first intimated to a puzzled Prime Minister in 1916 as Laurier suddenly took his first step toward ruin, a step generally misunderstood at the time and comprehensible only to those who knew Laurier's inner soul. Not many men understood it and they did not include Borden. To his dying day he would never understand his great and respected adversary.

Laurier's decision to intervene in the Ontario school controversy seemed irrational to Borden. Certainly it was disruptive for Canada and for the Liberal Party, as Borden saw at once, but it was not irrational. It was essential to Laurier's strategy and the strategy was essential to his soul.

The Ontario government, by its famous Regulation Seventeen, had compelled the use of English in many schools attended only by French Canadians and formerly using French.

Even before the war began Bourassa had grasped at this opportunity to make himself the sole champion of his race. As the war went on he began to denounce the provincial school policy, calling it the work of Canadian "Prussians," and his eloquence was used to arouse Quebec's sympathy for "the wounded of Ontario."

Why did Laurier bring this dispute into Parliament, which had no jurisdiction over the school of any province? Why did he instruct his young lieutenant, Ernest Lapointe, to introduce a resolution asking Ontario to allow its French-Canadian pupils the use of their "mother tongue"? How could Laurier inject this wounding wedge of racial discord and, in the same speech, urge Quebec's young men to enlist despite the grievances of their Ontario compatriots?

The answer eluded Borden but, given the nature of his opponent, was quite simple.

Towards its end Laurier's life had been reduced to three ambitions, or obsessions. As a statesman he was sincerely convinced that if Quebec fell into Bourassa's hands it would finally reject the war and precipitate a clash of races fatal to Canada. Therefore, he must unhorse Bourassa and hold Quebec for the nation's sake. As a human being he hoped to be Prime Minister again but that was secondary to his highest purpose. Above all, for reasons that no Anglo-Saxon like Borden could comprehend, he was determined to remain the hero of French Canada, the father of his people. To assure that place in history, he would sacrifice office, power, policy, national reputation and life, too.

The intervention in the school question was only the first deliberate act of Laurier's self-chosen tragedy, as it seemed to Anglo-Saxons, or his triumph as it seemed to him. By supporting the cause of the French-Canadian pupils in Ontario he had told Quebec that he would never desert it, and immediately Quebec began to desert Bourassa. The price to be paid in old friendships for this manoeuvre of politics was even higher than Laurier had expected. His English-speaking supporters began to desert him.

Sifton, now living in London, wrote that Laurier had disqualified himself for office. Only a coalition government of Conservatives and Liberals, said Sifton, could carry Canada through the war. And what Sifton decided usually came to pass. In Ottawa a group of English-speaking Liberals told Laurier they must vote against his school motion. His threat of resignation did not deter them.

The old man then began to suspect the possible depth of his isolation, the end of his life-work as the bridge between the two races, but still he trusted his stars. If Quebec returned solidly to him and he could win only a few extra seats in other provinces he would beat a Government discredited by bungle and scandal. Some Liberals might leave him on the school motion which, he said, was not a matter of party policy, but they would come back.

Not since his last brush with Sifton had he calculated so erroneously. The dissident Liberals might come back but for the first time their faith in Laurier's omniscience had been shaken. On a greater issue than schools they might not come back.

Borden knew nothing of the Liberal cleavage when he applied Anglo-Saxon logic to the school motion. As he said in an unanswerable lawyer's speech, Parliament had no jurisdiction over schools and no one had ever stood so firmly as Laurier for the constitutional rights of the provinces.

But Borden was facing difficulties unknown to Laurier. Three ministers, T. Chase Casgrain, P. E. Blondin and E. L. Patenaude were driven by their French-Canadian feelings to suggest a preposterous solution. The school dispute, they said in a long, tortured letter to Borden, should be submitted to the King and his Privy Council for arbitration. Borden politely rejected this "abdication of our self-governing powers." The rebellious ministers, Patenaude in tears, agreed not to resign; but after defeating the Lapointe resolution, with the support of a dozen western Liberals, the Government was riven on racial lines beyond all possible repair.

Meanwhile the war was going badly in Europe. Nothing was going well in Canada, except the enlistment of soldiers and the production of military supplies. As the grim year of 1916 advanced,

Borden felt himself drowning in a sea of troubles, political and personal.

Sick with sciatica, neuritis and lumbago, he had somehow risen from his bed, staggered to Parliament and declared in one of his best speeches that the war would weld the Canadian races in "a more perfect and splendid unity."

As if to illuminate the falsity of that assurance by a blazing symbol, the Parliament Building took fire on a night of bitter cold and burned to the ground. Borden ran from his office, hatless and coatless, but, by a remarkable feat of organization, opened the House next day in the National Museum.

These physical arrangements were easy. What worried Borden and kept him half ill was growing disunity of the nation, the almost total failure of recruitment in Quebec and the evident mismanagement of the war in Europe.

Over and over again, in private talks with its leaders and in speeches to its people, Borden tried to convince Quebec that Canada was fighting its own war, not Britain's. Unlike many of his colleagues, he did not regard the French Canadians as an inferior or a cowardly race. On the contrary, he considered them, as he wrote, "a fighting and heroic race." It was impossible for him, however, or any man of either race, to persuade Quebec that its own interests, even its survival, depended on victory in a remote war.

As Laurier's first speeches had indicated, if anyone had paused to analyze them, Quebec still regarded Britain as a principal in the war, Canada only as a contributor out of gratitude and friendship. On that premise how could the Government expect from Quebec the same contribution freely offered by English-speaking Canadians who held for Britain sentiments of history, blood and language unknown to French Canadians? It simply was not in nature for the two races to feel the meaning of the war equally—the conquerors of 1759 and the conquered.

Borden was a man big enough to grasp these facts of history better than most English-speaking Canadians but the necessities of the war came first. Already he could see that Canada's resources were over-strained, or inefficiently distributed, and his national registration of manpower was designed to assure a wiser distribution. He knew that the registration was taken in Quebec as meaning the eventual conscription of soldiers, though he still intended to avoid it, as he had often promised, if he could. Nevertheless, if it were necessary, he was prepared to take that final step regardless of consequences.

Even more alarming at present was the news from London where the British Government, eagerly seeking aid from Canada, refused to deal with it as a principal, took all its efforts for granted and told it almost nothing. Infuriated by this treatment, the quiet man at last exploded in a letter of cold violence to his friend Perley in London.

For months, he wrote, he had received from Britain only the information "gleaned from the daily press and no more . . . It can hardly be expected that we shall put 400,000 or 500,000 men in the field and willingly accept the position of having no more voice and receiving no more consideration than if we were toy automata. Any person cherishing such an expectation harbours an unfortunate and even dangerous illusion. If there is no available method [of consultation] and if we are expected to continue in the role of automata the whole situation must be reconsidered. Procrastination, indecision, inertia, doubt, hesitation and many other undesirable qualities have made themselves entirely too conspicuous in this war."

Perley must have showed this unprecedented ultimatum to Andrew Bonar Law, a Canadian who had become a powerful member of the British Cabinet. Results followed fast. Law collected a bag of the most secret war documents, weighted them with lead in case of an accident at sea and requested that Borden alone should read and then burn them. The bag was carried on the bridge of a British liner, under the captain's eyes. Its contents mollified Borden somewhat but he still was not satisfied with affairs in Britain or at home.

"No description," he wrote in his memoirs, "could make the reader adequately realize the anxiety and strain" of those times. He seemed to live in a shifting "political kaleidoscope."

There was trouble even with that eminent British field marshal, the Governor-General. The Duke of Connaught had been warned by Borden early in the war that he was wrong to consider himself Canadian commander-in-chief except in name. Now he was proposing that Canada recruit soldiers in the United States.

Borden permitted himself another outburst but couched it in language of dead-pan sarcasm which the Duke may not have understood. While respecting the Governor-General's long army experience, the Prime Minister had the honour to observe that "the matters under consideration do not call so much for the exercise of military skill or the application of military experience as the consideration of international law and the exercise of the commonplace quality of common sense."

No Governor-General had ever been slapped down so roughly, and by a Prime Minister generally suspected of toadying to Britain. Connaught took the rebuke in good spirit and remained one of Borden's closest friends.

Then there were the labour unions. They descended on Ottawa to demand a promise from Borden that he would never impose conscription since they abhorred it as strongly as did the Quebec Nationalists. Borden said he hoped to avoid this extreme measure but flatly refused to give a pledge against it.

How could he? Recruitment was still inadequate, had almost ceased in Quebec and was falling elsewhere. The nation's resources were stretched as they would never be in the Second World War. Something had to be done. Sick again with a throat infection and weakened by insomnia, Borden set out in the depth of winter to address recruiting rallies from coast to coast. His reception was warm everywhere, even in Quebec, but produced few recruits. "How tired and sick," he wrote, "I am of this infernal life."

Certainly neither Prime Minister nor nation could go on like this. Borden had almost decided to form a coalition, as increasingly urged by conscriptionist Liberals but bitterly opposed by most of the Conservative Party, which saw it as only a plot to dislodge the best of all possible governments and redistribute the rewards of office. On the other hand, Laurier had recently written to N. W. Rowell, the Liberal leader in Ontario, that the project of a union government was only a conspiracy to prevent a French Canadian becoming Prime Minister.

It was ironical, as Borden must have reflected in this winter of his discontent, that all his troubles stemmed from the Quebec Nationalists, the allies whom he had courted in 1911, whom Laurier had always fought. It was useless now to lament this muddy water over the dam. Somehow Borden must regalvanize the Government and, through it, the nation.

To be sure, the Canadian people as a whole had never behaved so well in their entire history and never before, in all their frontier wars, had they undergone anything like the present blood-letting among their sons, sixty thousand of whom would soon be dead in Europe. Yet the existing state of the political system, with an election unavoidable in 1917, since Laurier evidently would not agree to prolong Parliament's life again, was neither worthy of the nation nor adequate for the trials ahead.

Moreover, though the Liberals were divided, the Government could not be sure even of its re-election. Laurier, a shrewd judge, was convinced that the Government would be defeated by its ugly record of scandal, the obvious corruption among its hangers-on, its mismanagement of the war program. After all, if he could hold his existing strength in the English-speaking provinces a solid Quebec would give him a total majority. This seemed, at the time, a reasonable calculation, and to Liberals who criticized his strategy as unpatriotic Laurier always made the same wistful but chilling reply. Perhaps, he would say, it had been a mistake in the first place for the Liberal Party to choose a French-Canadian leader. If so, he had no thought of repealing the mistake.

Unaware of these growing quarrels in the Liberal camp, and physically depleted, Borden had sunk into a mood of black pessimism by the end of 1916. While he hid his thoughts from the Cabinet, a note in his diary pictures a man near the end of his resources.

On a winter afternoon, his nerves frayed by the Cabinet's daily wrangle, he had gone home and grimly shoveled snow. The exercise, perhaps reminding him of happier boyhood days at Grand Pré, seemed to bring relief. Thus comforted, he wrote in his diary a revelation of feelings never known to the public: "Falling snow in light of park lamps almost fairylike. The flakes seem like flowers from heaven strewing the bosom of mother earth, fast asleep until spring." The farm boy had never lost touch with nature. In the man there was more than his closest friends suspected. There had to be if he was to survive the unexpected, unexampled crisis of 1917.

As Borden was thus pondering the most important work of his life, his prospects were suddenly changed by a cable from London. After replacing Herbert Asquith as Prime Minister of Britain, David Lloyd George had decided to consult the Dominions at last. Borden was invited to sit as a full member of the British War Cabinet. He accepted eagerly, little realizing where this adventure would lead.

At London he encountered Jan Christiaan Smuts, of South Africa, and the two men instantly became friends. Together they drafted a momentous resolution which they hardly expected the British Government to approve.

It demanded for the Dominions the preservation of "all existing powers of self-government . . . complete control of domestic affairs . . . full recognition of the Dominions as autonomous nations . . . an adequate voice in foreign policy . . . continuous consultation in all matters of common Imperial concern . . . such necessary concerted action, founded on consultation, as the several governments might determine."

170

Borden moved the resolution, Smuts seconded it and the Lloyd George Government accepted it without a word of demur. How this concept of a common, agreed Empire foreign policy could be implemented Borden did not know and would never be able to discover, for in fact it was irreconcilable with the autonomy of the Dominions. Once autonomous, each of them would make its own foreign policy and those policies were sure, in such a diverse Empire, to differ in emphasis at least, if not in fundamentals.

The future would not follow Borden's vague and hopeful blueprint but he and Smuts had written one of the decisive state documents of British history, on which the Declaration of 1926 and the Statute of Westminster five years later would be founded.

As the South African said to the Canadian: "You and I have transformed the structure of the British Empire." That was true, though their work could not have succeeded then without the general transformation of the war. And true also that Borden, starting life as a narrow imperialist, had become a Canadian nationalist building boldly on the foundation laid by Macdonald and Laurier.

He had much more building to do yet and when the Allied cause slid into the almost fatal disasters of 1917 the Canadian people took little note of the work already accomplished at London.

Borden toured the trenches of France, talked with the Canadian soldiers and visited half a hundred hospitals. After seeing the wounded, many of them near death, he confessed in his diary that he could hardly restrain his tears. The sense of his own responsibility for the misery of other men was devastating, but it only strengthened his final resolve.

That experience had settled the future of Canadian politics. From then on Borden would see war not as the paper work of government, not as a debate of Parliament or a compromise of political parties but as a physical, human struggle of men, and beside his duty to them nothing else mattered.

He was certain now that only conscription could adequately reinforce the dwindling Canadian army. He was determined to get reinforcements if it were the last thing he did. Whatever happened to him, his Government or his party, he would not let the army down. In politics, Borden had burned his boats.

Immediately on returning to Ottawa he informed the Cabinet and then Parliament of his decision. He knew, of course, that the decision was grave but hardly that it was the gravest in Canada's life of fifty years. He knew it would split the Canadian races but not that it would split the Liberal Party and wreck his own. He knew that it would cause a brief convulsion but not that it would imperil the Canadian State.

His first intimation of these consequences was the revolt of many Quebec Nationalist members who had stood with him up to now. Then came Bourassa's veiled incitement to violence: "Conscription would soon transform the most peaceable, perhaps the most orderly population of the two Americas into a revolutionary people."

This sounded like treason. It meant, at any rate, that no government of a single party could enforce conscription. Borden had traveled by a long detour of alternating failure and success to find himself dependent on Liberal allies against his lost friends in Quebec.

His mind made up to this necessity, he moved fast. Meighen was ordered to write a Military Service Act while the Prime Minister undertook to form a coalition with the Liberals. Thus opened the supreme trial of Borden's life.

His liabilities, by any practical assessment, were frightening— hostility to conscription not only in Quebec but in the farm and labour organizations of other provinces; almost certain opposition from Laurier; dubious support in the Liberal Party; sharp division in the Conservative.

What were his assets? He had two—the nation's will to win the war somehow, anyhow, and its trust in him. Without the first asset, if he could deploy it in policy, nothing could be accomplished. Without trust in Borden all the events of 1917 would have been impossible. With all his lack of magnetism and crowd appeal, he had become Canada's indispensable man.

A third asset now appeared. Sifton was back in Canada to drive, persuade or wheedle the Liberal Party into a coalition. As in 1911, he made himself the general manager of Borden's affairs, the co-architect of a Union Government.

The Prime Minister's methods in this latest crisis were typically blunt. First he told his Cabinet that he intended to approach Laurier directly. The Cabinet dividing about evenly on this proposal, he quickly ended the argument by saying that he would settle it himself. Those who would not follow him were free to resign.

On the morning of May 25 Laurier appeared by arrangement at Borden's old-fashioned house on Sandy Hill. The two men had been fighting one another for nearly a score of years but they were still friends, their friendship in this emergency being another precious national asset. Unlike Macdonald and Brown at the Quebec conference that launched Confederation, Borden and Laurier did not have to disguise a personal hatred. They liked and admired each other. Their long quarrel was one of abstract principle only.

Borden came to the point at once. His offer to Laurier was candid and astoundingly generous. He would construct a conscriptionist Cabinet composed equally of Conservatives and Liberals apart from his own office as Prime Minister. What, asked Laurier, if the Conservative ministers and caucus would not agree? Then, said Borden, he would resign.

This proposition must have shaken Laurier but he answered cautiously, knowing better than Borden the consequences of conscription in Quebec, certainly knowing better its consequences to himself. Conscription, Laurier said (according to Borden's diary), would be dangerous under any conditions, more dangerous without a referendum or an election. Quebec might obey a conscription law passed by a newly elected Parliament but not otherwise. In a gentle rebuke he added that he was not invited to consider a policy, only to accept a decision already made.

Borden countered with the warning that the upheaval of an election might paralyze the whole military program.

At the end of an extraordinary conversation Laurier promised to consider these questions. He consulted his friends at the Rideau Club next day and found them divided. None favoured coalition with Borden. Some would accept it under another leader.

The youngest and ablest of them, Mackenzie King, urged the conscription of soldiers, workers and capital as well as the postponement of an election until after the war. A wartime election fought on conscription, King told his chief, might "annihilate" the Liberal Party.

Little suspecting that he would face precisely the same issue as Prime Minister twenty-seven years hence, King had given sound advice but Laurier rejected it. He was still convinced that he could beat the Government and improve the management of the war. Actually his decision was not based on these calculations. He was hearing advice only to mollify his conscriptionist friends. He would not urge conscription but he would accept it if the people approved it by a national vote.

On May 29 Laurier returned to Borden's house. The Liberal Party, he admitted frankly, was divided. He himself could not consent to conscription without a referendum or an election.

To the old man's amazement, Borden instantly agreed. A conscription law should be passed but not enforced until a coalition government had been elected, and if it were defeated "we shall have done our best and the responsibility will rest with others."

As Borden remembered the second interview, Laurier "seemed impressed with this proposal, took out his notebook and asked me to repeat it while he set it down in writing. I had strong hope that he would accept."

The high drama of that moment, and its futility also, escaped Borden—the plain man making a business proposition, the devious patriarch solemnly recording it in his little notebook while in his mind he had rejected it already. For both men the outcome must be decisive to the end of their lives. For the nation it must mean unity or disunity in the crisis of war and long afterwards.

Even at this late date the Anglo-Saxon still did not understand the French Canadian. Laurier never had any thought of accepting Borden's terms. The three original factors in Laurier's mind absolutely barred acceptance—his fear of driving Quebec into the hands of the Nationalists and perhaps into civil strife, his ambition to be Prime Minister again and, failing that, his determination to remain Quebec's father image.

On the other hand, Borden had opened a new schism in his own party. Hearing of his talks with Laurier, some of the Conservative ministers said the coalition plan would end by destroying the Government. Borden replied that "the country was entitled to a new government if it so desired and I was quite ready to be relieved." The threat of resignation silenced but did not change the opinion of his rebellious colleagues.

Laurier was playing for time, striving to unite his party and preparing for an election. On June 4 he met Borden for the third time and asked what Conservative ministers would be included in a coalition Cabinet.

Then Borden played his last card. Laurier, he said, could appoint the Liberal ministers and approve or veto Borden's nomination of the Conservatives. The new proposition was almost unbelievable. Borden had virtually offered Laurier the highest prerogative of a Prime Minister. In effect, the opposition leader would choose the ministry.

"This," Borden wrote in a queer understatement, "was going very far . . . . however, I felt it my duty to go to that length and I was determined that the negotiations should not be broken on the minor issue of personnel."

Laurier left to think over the latest proposal. Both he and Borden were now nearing their points of no return. Later events would make it appear that Borden already was triumphant, Laurier defeated. In those June days of 1917 nothing was settled. And neither man yet knew the forces operating to change everything.

By June 6 Laurier believed, quite wrongly, that he could control his party. He called on Borden again to say finally that he could not join a conscriptionist coalition but if conscription became law he would urge all Canadians to obey it.

"He feared," Borden wrote, "the effects of Bourassa's influence and propaganda and he felt that his own position would be stronger in opposition."

That was true but less than half of Laurier's mind. Reconsidering his rival after the lapse of a decade, Borden wrote that "Sir Wilfrid Laurier was then in his seventy-eighth year. If he had been ten or fifteen years younger I am confident he would have entered the proposed coalition. . . . I am convinced that he underrated his influence and that Quebec would have followed where he led."

There Borden conceivably may have been right about Quebec. He was still wrong about Laurier who would never risk a breach with his own folk. The umbilical cord of the spirit uniting mother and son could not be severed or even strained. Morever, as Laurier told King (according to that tortured young man's diary), "if Premier, he cld. raise an army in Quebec by voluntary enlistment." A strange flux of idealism and egotism had persuaded the old man who had only twenty months of life before him that he could become Prime Minister, reunite the nation and preside over its victory in the war.

To Borden, Laurier's inner thoughts would have appeared irrational. So, in view of the currents now running, they were, but the currents were still hidden from both men and from the nation which rode on them. Borden, the factual man, recorded his verdict with a fine generosity: "An instinct of patriotism led Sir Wilfrid Laurier to believe that . . . his duty was to stand apart from the coalition."

Patriotism, yes, but mixed with it a conflict of emotions, an immemorial feeling of race, family and ancient loyalties that the mind of Borden, or any Anglo-Saxon mind, could never grasp. The toil of three hundred years on the St. Lawrence, the Indian wars, the long marches, the British Conquest, the stubborn will to survive —all these memories of victory and defeat, all these wounds, hopes, passions and prejudices now issued in Laurier's tragedy, the tragedy of a man and a race joined in mystical union. Through all future time man and race would remain inseparable. For Laurier, if all else failed, that was enough.

In June, 1917 he still could not believe in the possibility of failure but his sensitive seismograph had detected the first tremors of an earthquake. Sifton, in constant touch with Borden, was openly organizing a conscriptionist revolt in the Liberal Party. Dafoe was publicly pleading in the *Free Press* for a coalition government and pleading privately with Laurier, who would listen but would not change.

As his cool judgment began to falter, Laurier concluded that the conscriptionist drive was the work of the old imperial centralizers. "Ontario," he wrote to a friend, "is no longer Ontario; it is again the old province of Upper Canada and again governed from London."

He was wrong. Borden had been fighting the centralizers as hard as Laurier had ever fought them and with more success.

Laurier felt sure also that conscription would not produce significant reinforcements. "How many men," he asked, "will conscription bring in? Just a few slackers, exactly the same as in England . . . conscription will take in a few farmers and school boys." There, for all practical purposes, he was right.

At the moment Borden knew only that his break with Laurier was final. By agreement they exchanged and published letters explaining their disagreement. The nation now realized for the first time that a grave crisis was at hand, much graver than it could yet guess.

Borden apparently had failed in his paramount objective but while most of his party rejoiced at the failure he went ahead with conscription anyway, hoping, from Sifton's assurances, that some Liberals would join him later. Meighen, the Cabinet's indefatigable man of all work, already had drafted a Military Service Act. On June 11 Borden introduced it in Parliament with a speech of lawyer's logic and undisguised emotion.

He denied that his policy was dictated by the British Government, which he had never consulted. Conscription, he said, had been embodied in Canadian law for half a century but its method of selecting soldiers by ballot was "unwise, even disastrous" when men must be chosen according to "the country's needs." Hopefully he argued that no "disunion, discord and strife" should follow the enforcement of conscription on a sensible, selective basis.

The concluding words came straight from his experience at the war front. With the first revelation of his true feelings, he warned Parliament not to betray the Canadian soldiers in France lest they come home "with fierce resentment and even rage in their hearts . . . I am not so much concerned for the day when this Bill becomes law as for the day when these men return, if it is rejected."

That warning struck deep into the Liberal Party. Borden thought Laurier looked "pale and wan." The old man might maintain a front of confidence but he knew by now that he had passed his point of no return. The road ahead led into the dark. Nevertheless, he must follow it. For him there was no other road. So he fought the Military Service Bill with all his old skill and eloquence, said it was dangerous and ineffective and proposed that it be delayed until the electorate had approved it by referendum.

Having cast his own die, Borden left the management of the debate to Meighen who met all Laurier's arguments with self-destroying brilliance. This was the hour of Meighen's highest triumph and his certain ruin. As a *tour de force* conducted in icy logic Parliament had seldom seen the equal of Meighen's performance but it was ruinous just the same. By making himself the executor and the symbol of conscription, he had permanently alienated French Canada and, in his temporary success, had assured the failure of his career.

Yet in these electric moments Meighen saw only the success. Laurier saw only his own tragedy and his people's. It could be denied no longer. Some of his leading colleagues already were supporting Meighen's Bill. Others were prepared to follow.

While Laurier watched, his head resting wearily on his hand, Frank Carvell of New Brunswick—"Fighting Frank," one of his closest friends—announced in a moving speech that he must vote for conscription. As he sat down Laurier scribbled a note to him. Carvell read it through his tears. "Dear Frank," Laurier had written, "that was a noble speech." Friends could desert Laurier. His own nobility remained.

One by one his oldest comrades were slipping from him—Fielding, George Graham, F. F. Pardee, "as dear to me as my own brothers."

"Oh," he wrote, "what a wrench at all my heart's strings! . . . Do not, however, think hard of them, for I do not. . . . The pain is not less acute even on their side than on mine and I know only too well the difficulties which face them. . . . How it will all end I venture not to predict. I still hope, perhaps against all hope, that when this nightmare is over we may still maintain the party together."

The nightmare was not his alone. It was the nation's. It was Durham's old nightmare of two races warring in the bosom of a single State.

For Laurier it was peculiarly harrowing. He saw his friends go one by one and he saw all his long labours going with them. He had worked since youth to reconcile the races. Now they were divided as never before since the nation's birth. Had his life-work failed? And where had he gone wrong? A secretary found him standing alone by his office window as if he could see outside it a map fractured on the line of the Ottawa River. "I have lived too long!" he whispered.

On June 24 a broken Liberal Party was driven within the walls of French Canada. Parliament passed the Military Service Bill by 102 votes to 44. The eighteen Liberals voting for it included all but four of those from Ontario and the West. In the greatest shift of political power ever known, Borden held English-speaking Canada and Laurier held Quebec. Even the Conservative Nationalist voters, even Bourassa himself, had returned to the Liberal Party. The Liberals who abandoned Laurier thus had rescued Borden from the alliance of 1911, for without them he could not hope to carry through his policy. The Conservative Party had lost Quebec for two score years at least, but the war would go on as planned.

When he rose to make his final speech on conscription Laurier knew that his career, the happy time, and all his hopes were finished but his own people were with him to the end. They would be with him, in racial memory, forever. The son and father of Quebec was coming home.

In his loneliness and heartbreak he had never looked more serene, had never been more respectd by the victor in the long duel.

He made only one complaint against the Government. It had framed a policy without consulting him, drafted a statute and only then asked him to accept a *fait accompli*—"as in the play of children they asked me: close your eyes and open your mouth and swallow. I refused."

To the friends now turned against him he said only that "I have my conscience and they have theirs." Then he added a final prophecy: "We are face to face with a cleavage which, unless it is checked, may rend and tear this Canada of ours to the very roots. But what is the use of lamenting? We must face the situation like men. Sir, all my life I have fought coercion; all my life I have promoted union; and the inspiration which led me to that course shall be my guide at all times, so long as there is breath in my body."

Laurier had been beaten in Parliament, no doubt he would be beaten in the country, but Borden took no chances. The second product of Meighen's handiwork was now produced—a wartime election law disenfranchising conscientious objectors to military service and immigrants from enemy countries who had been in Canada less than fifteen years, all people who might vote Liberal. Women who were next of kin to soldiers were enfranchised for the first time to swell the Conservative vote. By a still cruder device the votes of overseas soldiers could be applied to the constituencies where the Government might need them most.

Even in those times, and even by the normal standards of politics, the statute was exceedingly rough, a far-flung net to catch every possible government ballot, but Borden and Meighen defended it vigorously against Laurier's attack and it was passed under closure. The end justified any means.

All this time Parliament had been only one theatre of events.

In a second, while he pushed through his conscription law, the Prime Minister saw the results of the one great failure of his public life, the failure to reach any durable agreement with French Canada.

Mobs marched through the streets of Montreal shouting "*A bas Borden!*" and "*Vive la révolution!*" The house of Lord Atholstan, who published the conscriptionist *Montreal Star*, was dynamited. One of the dynamiters confessed that he and his friends were plotting to kill Borden and other Conservative leaders. This first outburst soon passed but Borden suspected that it would not be the last.

In the third theatre he had been quietly building his Union Government. Before completing it, however, he decided to offer Laurier one more chance to avoid the turmoil of a wartime election. He would propose another extension of Parliament's life. Unless his motion received virtually unanimous support he would abandon it.

Most of his Cabinet and caucus, fearing an election, insisted that it must be postponed even if Parliament's vote were narrow. Again Borden overruled his colleagues and when his motion was opposed by sixty-two Liberals he prepared to take his case to the people.

It was a terrifying decision for the Conservative managers who knew only half of Borden's strategy. They could not expect a single seat in Quebec. Hostility to conscription was widespread in the English-speaking labour unions and farm organizations. The Opposition had broken in Parliament but it would unite in the election. Liberal conscriptionists probably would double-cross the Government.

What the managers had failed to grasp was that the politicians of Parliament, apparently in control of events, were only their agents. The Canadian people, with characteristic lack of outward emotion, had taken over. They might disagree about the details of policy, they might distrust the Government, but they were determined to finish the job in Europe. And throughout this period of political tumult they had increasingly come to trust Borden.

Though they knew nothing of it yet, he had lately pushed that trust to the limit.

Appealing privately to Liberals inside and outside of Parliament, he found none who would enter the Government. For the last time he appealed to Laurier at a conference called secretly in Rideau Hall by the Governor-General, the Duke of Devonshire. Laurier again refused. Borden was growing desperate.

His plodding prose, always in understatement, indicated his desperation: "A more difficult and even tragic situation for a party leader could hardly be imagined."

Then the outer rim of the Opposition began to melt. C. C. Ballantyne, a more or less Liberal business man from Montreal, and Hugh Guthrie, a Liberal leader of secondary rank from Ontario, joined the Cabinet. They alone could not provide even the pretence of a coalition. Borden's real hope rested, as in 1911, with Sifton.

That incomparable organizer had been at work for months delivering conscriptionist speeches, persuading western Liberals, thundering in the *Free Press* and telling Borden not to despair.

At first Sifton, who had never known failure, seemed to fail. Newton Wesley Rowell, the provincial Liberal leader in Ontario, half decided to join Borden but hesitated until Sifton could guarantee support from the West. Despite all Dafoe's efforts behind the scenes, a convention of western Liberals in Winnipeg voted to reject coalition and support Laurier. Apparently the chance of a Union Government had been lost.

Sifton refused to accept failure. He was satisfied that the politics of Ottawa no longer represented the nation's will. Most elected politicians in both parties opposed a coalition only because it would disturb their vested personal interests. The nation, careless of their convenience, demanded a coalition as essential to victory. If Borden's Union Government was to emerge at all it must emerge from the grass roots far beyond Ottawa.

Sifton's strategy was pressed ahead on two levels.

Publicly he attacked Laurier outright in language more brutal than any ever used by Borden. Laurier, said Sifton, "does not lead the people of the province of Quebec; he submits that they shall lead him—and lead him to the rear instead of to the front. It is nothing less than a tragedy that this venerable statesman, after a lifetime of loyal service during which he has striven to reconcile the two races . . . should find himself, at seventy-five years of age, in the position in which he is placed today." He added that victory for Laurier would take Canada out of the war.

While Laurier indignantly repudiated this charge from his former friend, Sifton's words and Sifton's influence were fatal to the unity of the Liberal Party. All that Borden needed now was a group of western Liberals willing to serve with him and break Laurier's blockade. And Sifton now promised to produce them.

The exhausted Borden had gone to the Laurentians for a few days' rest when he learned from Sifton that three strong western Liberals outside Parliament were ready to join the Government, but only if the Prime Minister retired.

"Two of my colleagues who were with me," Borden wrote, "declared vehemently that we would not accept them and must reject their offer. It had that appearance at first but after the most careful consideration I came to a different conclusion. . . . I fully realized that there was fierce resentment in my party against these official Liberals because of their proposal to replace me as leader. But I was sure that I could control that feeling. The situation was grave, the decision difficult. I gradually came to the conclusion that we must resume negotiations with these gentlemen upon their renewed offer."

Sifton had refused to enter the Government himself, as Borden urged, since his deafness barred him and his estrangement from the Liberal Party would only assure future trouble. However, he had found three powerful candidates in the western grass roots—his own brother, Arthur, premier of Alberta; James A. Calder, a member of the Saskatchewan government, and T. A. Crerar, a young Manitoba farm leader with a long and surprising future before him.

In coded telegrams to Ottawa these three demanded, first, that Rogers be fired. Borden agreed at once, glad to get rid of a serious liability. They demanded, second, that the Union Government be led by Mr. Justice Lyman Duff of the Supreme Court, or alternatively by Foster, Sir William Mulock, Sir Adam Beck or Carvell—almost anyone but Borden, whom they still distrusted as a Conservative and whom none of them knew well.

Again Borden agreed. He would happily step aside, he said, even at this crescendo of the war, if another man could form a Union Government. No more generous offer had ever been made in Canadian politics but Borden found that his party would not allow it for a moment. If he went, there would be no coalition. It was Borden or nothing.

Again, stalemate and apparent failure. Borden despaired. He

still underestimated the influence of Sifton and that unseen factor of public opinion which had decided on a coalition and would not be denied.

On October 11 Arthur Sifton, Calder and Crerar, accompanied by A. B. Hudson, Attorney-General of Manitoba, as their adviser, met with Rowell at the Chateau Laurier in Ottawa. After an evening's consultation they decided to obey the nation's conscience and their own. It was midnight when Rowell and Calder walked up Parliament Hill to the Prime Minister's office and told Borden that they and other Liberals would serve under him. The deadlock was broken, a Union Government assured.

Where a more exciting and ambitious leader would certainly have failed, the plain, patient man had succeeded because his trustworthiness was better in these times than any talent. In Borden the new chemical combination of politics had found its slow catalyst.

Next day the Union Government was formed. It included nine Liberal ministers: Arthur Sifton, Calder and Crerar from the West; Guthrie, Rowell and S. C. Mewburn from Ontario; Ballantyne from Quebec; Carvell and A. K. Maclean from the Maritimes. With its twelve Conservatives it was a strong Cabinet but it contained, as Borden knew, a dangerous, perhaps a deadly, flaw. For the first time since Confederation the French-Canadian race had no role in the Government of Canada.

That final public admission of the racial breach must shake or smash the political balance first established by Macdonald; it might well have much more serious consequences in the immediate future; but for most Canadians these risks were drowned in the fury of a wartime election.

Sure of victory at home, Borden fought the campaign on the simple plea for victory in the war. He made no personal attack on Laurier. He was still trying to heal the breach. Almost everywhere he was still received with enthusiasm, though the voters of Kitchener, most of them German by descent, howled him from the platform.

Realizing that defeat was certain, Laurier fought the election as if he expected to win; and he hoped at least to prevent a Liberal collapse.

Outside Quebec everything was against him—the press, the Protestant Church, the whole Conservative organization and a large part of the Liberal. Even his friends in Quebec were undermining him. The Liberal candidates there generally embraced the anti-war program of the Nationalists—a last ironic turn of the wheel built by Borden in 1911—and thus helped to convince the other provinces that Laurier's victory would take Canada out of the war, as Sifton had warned.

It was all hopeless but Laurier had never appeared more magnificent than at this hour of catastrophe—a figure pathetic in his destruction, heroic in his courage. Though a majority of the people outside Quebec would not vote for him, they listened with respect and watched almost with awe the last march of a wounded warrior to the wilderness of politics and the Valhalla of his race. The cheap jibes of the Conservative machine, the posters declaring that "A vote for Laurier is a vote for the Kaiser" could win votes. They could not touch the old man's honour or tarnish his myth.

On election night, December 17, the figures were decisive and yet misleading.

Borden's Union Government had won 153 seats out of 235. Laurier had won 82 but 62 were in Quebec, 10 in the Maritimes, 8 in eastern Ontario and only 2 between the Great Lakes and the Pacific. His party had been hived in French Canada. Could it ever burst out of its prison?

Among those tormented by this question was the defeated Liberal candidate in North York. Mackenzie King, on his forty-third birthday, appeared as the least likely among all politicians to contrive his party's escape.

Nevertheless, the Liberal defeat was not the rout that a triumphant Union Government supposed. Laurier had actually won 42% of the popular vote. While few stopped to consider it then, this was amazing under the circumstances of war and national passion. Laurier had left a foundation for his successor to build on and now, with a tired tranquility, he awaited the end.

His last public testament, given to a group of university students, summed up his verdict on the past, his vision for the future: "You have a safe guide, an unfailing light, if you remember that faith is better than doubt and love is better than hate." Laurier had been defeated in politics. In life he was the victor.

A conscriptionist Union Government had been safely installed but conscription remained, so far, only a statute on paper. Once the Government's tribunals began to enforce it in the spring of 1918 thousands of men in Quebec and all the other provinces applied for exemption wholesale. Though exemptions were freely granted, especially to farm boys, they failed to satisfy French Canadians, who detested conscription not so much as a call to military service but as a symbol of English coercion. The combustibles of history only awaited a match.

A French-Canadian Catholic hierarchy which had generally

supported the war now denounced conscription for endangering the rights of the Church. "We are nearing racial and religious war," said Archbishop Bruchesi, of Montreal. Armand Lavergne, Bourassa's chief lieutenant and a colonel of militia, declared that he would go to jail or be shot before he was conscripted to fight outside Canada. These threats alarmed even Bourassa, who protested against "sterile violence." His warning came too late.

On March 29 a screaming mob burned the federal police station and the office of the conscription registrar in Quebec City. The Government suspended habeas corpus and ordered a battalion from Toronto to suppress the riots and to shoot if necessary. English-speaking soldiers dispersed the mobs with bayonets. Next day a cavalry charge drove the rioters from the streets but they perched on housetops and hid behind snowbanks to shoot at the troops. Their fire was returned with rifles and machine-guns. When order was restored five soldiers had been wounded and four civilians killed.

For a few days the fabric of Confederation seemed torn as Laurier had feared. With the best motives, for the best reasons, Borden had materialized the old nightmare that all his predecessors had dreaded and avoided.

Now came the old Canadian reaction. Laurier, the Church, the Quebec press and Bourassa appealed to French Canada's good sense and the appeal was instantly heeded. The riots ceased. No part of Canada had been more horrified than Quebec itself by this brief paroxysm among a quiet people long schooled to obey the law. They settled down to a peaceful, sullen anger which Borden could not cure with his more lenient enforcement of the conscription law, which must dog all his Conservative successors from that day to this.

In Confederation's most wrenching trial Quebec had decided that it belonged to Canada. Borden's career had surmounted its watershed. How much he owed to Laurier's work of conciliation in their prolonged duel of public enmity and private friendship will never be known but the nation's debt to the son and father of Quebec is larger than it realizes even now.

What had Borden actually gained by conscription, at high cost to his party and greater cost to national unity? Not much, as Laurier had predicted. Enlistments in Quebec and elsewhere improved quickly as Canada saw the Allied line rolled back by the last German offensive but only 83,355 Canadians were conscripted, of whom 47,509 went overseas. Altogether 35,000 French Canadians served in the armed forces and fought with the peculiar dash and valour of their race.

As Borden knew, the deep emotional experience of 1918 could

not be reckoned in figures or extinguished by victory.

On the one hand, the nation had faced and mastered the gravest decision of its life so far, Borden's decision primarily, and was permanently strengthened by that achievement. As never before, it felt like a nation. On the other hand, the ancient work of uniting its races had been set back for at least a generation and then it must be tested, by the same means, again. Macdonald's political balance would be distorted even longer.

An armistice silenced the guns of Europe on November 11, 1918. Canada had paid its full price for victory and its nationhood had been smelted in the fire of war.

Borden had paid a full price, too. He had governed his people for more than seven years, the hardest and most momentous in its life. No Prime Minister had made a worse beginning. None had carried his task more bravely to the end. Physically, mentally and spiritually the man was gutted by these labours but still he could not quit. A final task awaited him.

Summoned by Lloyd George to London, Borden called his Cabinet together immediately on a Sunday night and told it that Canada must be separately represented at the approaching peace conference. Membership in the British delegation, he said, would not be enough. If the great powers refused to accept an independent Canadian delegate Canada would not be represented at all.

Some of the older Conservative ministers protested that Borden's venture would imperil the unity of the Empire but he refused to change his mind and a majority of the Cabinet backed him. He was embarked on the last struggle, and not the least important, of his public career.

With Foster, Doherty, and Arthur Sifton, and with his admiring friend, Dafoe, as a personal press adviser, Borden set out for London where he told Lloyd George that Canada expected to take a full part in the negotiation of a peace treaty and then to sign it as an independent State.

After only a little demur Lloyd George accepted Borden's terms and pressed them on President Woodrow Wilson, of the United States, and Prime Minister Georges Clemenceau of France. The American and French leaders found this proposition baffling, probably sinister. Was not Canada part of a single Empire? Why should it seek or require a separate voice in the peace? If that concession were granted, the Empire would have too much influence over Wilson's brave new world or the old, impossible world which Clemenceau intended to revive.

They could not understand, but Borden understood thoroughly, that the separate Canadian voice was needed to prove in action what had been set down in theory at the London conference of 1917—the dominions, Canada chief among them, were autonomous nations.

For Borden the peace conference offered the first clear test of this constitutional advance. It was unthinkable, he told Lloyd George, that Canada, after all its sacrifices, its casualties and its huge contributions of economic aid to the great allies, should have no more standing than some minor state, or even some neutral state which had done no fighting and contributed nothing. As Borden said to Prime Minister Botha of South Africa, "We must hold our own against Patagonia."

Finally the Council of Ten, representing the five great allies, agreed that the larger British dominions should each have two independent plenipotentiaries at the peace conference.

Borden had not been long in Paris when he learned that the political enemy who, more than any friend, had influenced his life, was gone.

On Sunday, February 16, while he was dressing for church, Laurier suffered a paralytic stroke. Stricken again next day, he feebly pressed his wife's hand and murmured, *"C'est fini."* Those were the last words of the orator whose eloquence had inspired the nation as long as most men could remember.

Borden, though he had never understood his opponent, was deeply grieved. Mackenzie King, understanding Laurier better, looked at the face of his dead friend and confided in his diary a secret never suspected by the Canadian people: "I could not but wish that Sir Wilfrid had had more of faith in his life. I believe he was an agnostic. . . . He had a great love for humanity but it was not a belief in God or immortality. . . . His greatness was that he remained true to the humble people and that he could stand against the world for a conviction. This will give him his place in the chivalry of God."

Such was the opinion of King, the spiritualist. According to another, and even closer friend of Laurier, he had always been a believer, had read his Bible daily and prayed for patience under the attacks of his enemies.

The fire of Bourassa, long fueled by a love-hate complex, died with his rival. Though he had thirty-three more years to live, the Nationalist leader would never be a serious force in politics again. His lamentation was genuine but, as usual, contradictory: "The last letter Laurier wrote in his own hand he wrote to me and the answer I wrote came to him two days before his death. He knows now that although I fought him because of differences in principle, I loved him all my life; and he knew it then." This from Bourassa, who had called Laurier "the most nefarious man in Canada."

Meighen's tribute was delayed but in his old age he concluded that Laurier had been the greatest of all Canadians.

Borden had no time for such reflections. He had won his first point at Paris and now must pursue a second. Attending the plenary sessions as an independent Canadian delegate, he also sat with the Empire delegation and often presided over it—a unique precedent —in framing a collective imperial policy. He acted for the Empire in a vain attempt to restore order in Bolshevik Russia and also in the disposition of former German colonies. Above all, he insisted that Canada must sign the peace treaty to demonstrate its autonomy.

After long and sometimes angry argument among the Big Three who controlled the entire world for the moment, an ingenious compromise was at last invented. The British delegates signed for "the British Empire" and the dominions signed separately under this heading.

Borden's theory of a common foreign policy for the Empire, devised by its members in consultation, was to prove unworkable but he had won for his nation a status of independence almost unthinkable five years earlier. That, perhaps, was his most important work, long outlasting the discord of the war years and establishing him as one of the few decisive figures in Canadian history.

He had accomplished probably much more than any predecessor except Macdonald, and the strain of perpetual crisis at home and abroad had destroyed his health. His Government was near destruction, too, the great coalition already dissolving.

In a last desperate effort to save it and erect a new alliance with the moderates of French Canada, Borden asked Lomer Gouin, Premier of Quebec, Rodolphe Lemieux, and Lapointe, three of Laurier's lieutenants, to join the Government. They were polite, and the first two shared Borden's general philosophy of conservatism under their Liberal label, but they all refused. The schism of 1917 could not be repaired then or for many years to come.

All these superficial manoeuvres of politics, though Borden could hardly understand them yet, reflected the deeper changes within the nation. A new society, pregnant with strange possibilities, was emerging from the war.

Borden was too old, too tired and too sick to deal with them. Warned by his doctors, he decided to retire at once but under the pressure of his Cabinet agreed to take a long holiday in the Southern

States. Even when his health improved, he realized that his work was finished and he resigned on July 10, 1920.

Seventeen years of life remained to him, years of quiet usefulness as Canada's elder statesman, of much reading, writing and lecturing, of contented old age as Ottawa's leading citizen, a constant borrower of books from the parliamentary library, a keen bargainer for fresh poultry and vegetables at the public market.

He died peacefully at home on June 10, 1937, respected by all, appreciated by very few. In the general opinion he had been a good enough Prime Minister, no more. The plain, shy man had never caught the imagination of his people and never tried to. That he was a great Prime Minister and his work crucial for Canada, only the sadder and perhaps the somewhat wiser generation of our time has begun to realize.

10: The Heroic Failure

After listening to a speech by the newly elected member for Portage-Neepawa in 1908, Laurier turned to a colleague and uttered a prophetic judgment: "Well, Borden has found a man."

That man succeeded Borden on July 10, 1920. Arthur Meighen was then forty-six years old, the youngest of Canadian Prime Ministers, perhaps the most brilliant in mind, certainly the most unfortunate in politics.

Already his lavish talents, his insatiable ambition and the plans so systematically perfected since youth were doomed by the backwash of the war, by an infallible instinct of self-destruction and by a blow of fortune unprecedented and irrational.

His current liabilities and a final accident of the future were mercifully hidden from Meighen and his friends when he took office. His enemies could not imagine their own good luck. Indeed, no one except King, and he only vaguely, had begun to comprehend the true state of Canada after a war which had seemed to restore the normal order of things but, in fact, had buried the pre-war world. All the calculations of Meighen, of larger and lesser men throughout the world, were now irrelevant. He, and humanity, were bobbing corks on a torrent that they pretended to control, a torrent flowing on, uncontrollable, into the vortex of our time.

Yet Meighen, who, like everyone else, misunderstood everything, Meighen who could never build a viable government, was building his own myth, the most remarkable and fictitious in Canadian politics.

Or it may be fairer to say that others were building it for him.

Meighen's worshippers, the few truly knowing him and the many dazzled by his cold iridescence, have fully persuaded themselves, in our time, that he who accomplished virtually nothing in government was a bigger man than his rival, King, who accomplished, among other things, the management of a war and a social revolution.

Nevertheless, the worshippers were convinced and still continue to preach that Meighen was struck down at the pinnacle of his powers by nothing less than an unforgivable lapse of Providence. Without a monstrous freak of nature Meighen, we are asked to believe, would probably have been the greatest Canadian of all time. He is the tragic hero defeated by the erring gods. The art of myth-making can go no further.

Meighen, to be sure, was a great man, but not a great statesman. Success in statecraft was forbidden by his times. It was forbidden by his brief moments of office. It was forbidden by his luck. It was forbidden by his own character. It was forbidden, above all, by King.

In calling King "the most contemptible charlatan ever to darken the annals of Canadian politics," Meighen not only was wrong but showed a capacity for misjudgment and self-delusion absolutely fatal to his own career. It is hardly too much to say that no one could beat Meighen except Meighen himself.

In almost any profession except politics he was certain to succeed, as he proved later on. In politics he was certain to fail. With him success always hung by a frayed thread which invariably broke. Even his choice as Borden's successor was a touch-and-go decision in the Conservative Party.

The sick Borden had anxiously polled his Cabinet and, to his disappointment, found strong opposition to Meighen, whose superior ability and wounding arrogance had antagonized smaller men. Doherty, Calder and Ballantyne said flatly that they would not serve under him, but they did. Putting his finger on Meighen's central liability, the wily Calder wrote that he was "absolutely out of the question as far as Quebec is concerned."

In the caucus a narrow majority seemed to favour Meighen but the issue was now irrelevant, since for personal domestic reasons White, who had about equal support, had already decided to abandon politics. The Governor-General then called the young man from Portage la Prairie, who had every asset but luck and comprehension of the public mind.

One remembers the Meighen of those days as an arresting, alarming, almost melodramatic figure—the massive bald dome of his head, the lean, wedge-shaped face and hard, piercing eyes, the upright, skeletal body with arms akimbo or hands tightly clasped, the voice with no music in it but the language flowing and glittering like a mountain river.

"While language," he once said, "is the vehicle of thought, it is a great deal more. It is part of the texture. It is inseparable from thought itself." In his case it certainly was. He used language as a tool of construction and a weapon of demolition. He worshipped it for its own sake. He had a musician's ear for its tone and melody. With him a major speech was a work of laborious orchestration, sedulously committed to memory and uttered with convincing spontaneity.

Noble speech, however, though a useful tool or weapon, is no substitute in politics for the ignoble work of manipulation, cajolery, compromise, healing and bluff that must carry the daily round of democratic government. So Meighen learned—too late.

Perhaps his greatest speech, delivered in his old age, was advertised in advance under the title, "The Greatest Englishman of History." The audience came to hear him discuss some political figure of the past but heard instead a tribute to William Shakespeare. It was worthy of the subject, was delivered without a note and yet contained 150 lines of quotation from a dozen different plays without a single slip.

If a man's idols are a reliable index to his mind, Meighen's choice of Shakespeare above all other Englishmen was significant. This speech showed that Meighen's mind had recovered from the bitterness of failure, but it was never changed.

"You and I," he said, doubtless thinking of himself, "have mused a hundred times on a tendency of the masses to turn on their heroes, to cheer for the latest victor just because he is a victor"; but after a journey with Shakespeare "you may come back a mystic; you certainly will not come back a cynic. . . . We find our interest in our fellow being quickened. We find it growing broader and deeper and more wholesome. Out of it all we emerge without any particular explanations advanced or special ideas established, but we do feel surer than we ever did that it is worth while to live, that there is always at hand an eternal common sense ready for the using, which will see us through, and that everywhere there is a right and a wrong, a good and a bad, and that the good is to be loved and the bad to be avoided and deplored."

Here was the credo and philosophy of his later life. Those mellow conclusions lay far ahead however, when Meighen formed his first of two fly-by-night ministries. As a young man his manner appeared hard and brittle. His speech was shaped in the stark logic of a Euclidean theorem, illuminated by lightning flashes of sarcasm and sometimes enriched by unbidden passages of poetry in prose.

No man heard Meighen without recognizing his genius. The whirring wheels of his mind were almost visible as he spoke, the machinery always working rapidly and smoothly, with a sure sense of direction, but the direction was often wrong. This flawless engine was half of Meighen. Only a small coterie of intimates saw the other half, the tender human being beneath the outer layer of supercilious perfection.

The same was even truer of his rival; but Meighen was too honest to mask his political thoughts, while King, though also full of hatreds, wore an amiable disguise so long that it became a part of him.

Yet Meighen's icy image and incurable shyness hid a warm, sensitive nature, easily hurt, always quick to help a friend. The Shakespearian scholar, the laughing story-teller, the happy companion and indulgent father—that second Meighen the public was never allowed to see.

If it had been invented in his salad days the politician's modern method of hiring public-relations experts, image builders and keyhole-peepers would have disgusted Meighen. Now and then some human incident trickled into the press—as when he absentmindedly entered the House of Commons wearing his bedroom slippers, or when his friends stole his worn-out overcoat and threw it from a train, only to find it returned by a well-meaning railway section hand and worn several years longer. But Meighen never exploited his appealing eccentricities. He appealed only to the mind of the electorate, supposing, as his excellent biographer, Mr. Roger Graham, explains, that voters were a jury of reasonable beings influenced only by the evidence. This assumption being as untrue as it was naive, all the labours built on it were bound to fail.

Meighen's lifelong loneliness and secret fire seem to have been born in him and were nourished by a harsh upbringing.

His grandfather was a school-teacher from Ulster who emigrated to Canada in 1843; his father a small farmer near the village of St. Mary's. Arthur (his only given name) was born in a typical Ontario farm-house on June 16, 1874.

There were two brothers and three sisters but from childhood Arthur was set apart by his solitary habits, his aversion to sports, his incessant reading of the classics, especially Shakespeare or Carlyle, and, as he grew older, by his skill in school debates. These he rehearsed, with speech and gesture, in the woods. His memory was photographic. He could read a long chapter once and recite it almost word for word, as in mature life his apparently extemporaneous speeches showed no sign of their minute preparation.

The Meighens were poor, Presbyterian, God-fearing and thrifty. For them, and for their gifted son, even when he was old and rich, life remained a struggle under a stern moral code and a jealous God.

Arthur's first business venture was the sale of subscriptions to a magazine, for which he received an imitation gold watch. The discovery that the watch would not work was an odd, unnoted symbol of his whole life. The highest honours would come to him but they were always empty. The watches would never work.

His father, though himself uneducated, and his mother, a woman of strong character, were determined that the son, since he displayed obvious promise, must have his chance. Somehow they managed to pay for his arts course at Toronto University, where the lean and lonely farm boy encountered a plump extrovert named William Lyon Mackenzie King but paid little attention to him. In the occasional rivalry of college debate the longest and most bitter contest of Canadian politics had begun.

After graduating in 1896 with first-class honours in mathematics (an indication of his mind's real bent) Meighen taught school briefly and resigned in an honourable quarrel with the local school trustees (a portent of other honourable, lifelong quarrels). Then, borrowing six hundred dollars and investing it in a new-fangled machine for cleaning dried fruit (an augury of his weakness for losing gambles) he went west on a harvest excursion train and, having lost his investment, returned to teaching in Winnipeg, repaid his debt and articled himself to a law firm. Before he was called to the bar he moved to Portage la Prairie in 1902 and took over a legal practice so profitless that he lived in a single room with no furniture except a bed and little food except a barrel of apples.

The rest followed in neat, mathematical progression—instant success at the bar; marriage in 1904 to Isabel Cox, his first sweetheart; the birth of a son christened Theodore Roosevelt as if to indicate the father's notion of political leadership, then another son and a daughter; profitable speculation in real estate; a deepening interest in politics; and, in 1908, Meighen's astonishing election to Parliament in the usually safe Liberal seat of Portage-Neepawa.

The farmers hearing, in grubby schoolhouses, the nation's second orator did not realize, as Laurier instantly realized in Parliament, that Meighen was a man to watch. The breakneck speed of his climb to power in Borden's Cabinet and his succession to the Prime Ministry were unprecedented; but as always the gold watch now in his grasp would not work. His first Government, seemingly invulnerable before a shattered Opposition, had no life in it.

The fiction of a Conservative-Liberal coalition was preserved by the presence of Calder, Ballantyne and Guthrie. A frail bridge to French Canada was maintained in the person of P. E. Blondin, who had stood by Borden throughout the conscription crisis. With Foster still at his right hand and a new recruit, Henry Drayton, in Finance, Meighen both by name and philosophy had formed a Conservative Government.

It could not be anything else under his leadership, for of all contemporary politicians Meighen was the most dedicated Conservative, not merely by label but by the unalterable grain of his mind. Hence the paradox of a right-wing, high-tariff leader arriving from the radical, free-trade West, a vagary and sport of politics; hence, in the existing circumstances of Canada, his Government's assured dissolution. From Borden he had inherited an estate already bankrupt.

Everything was against Meighen, five things in particular that must separate him from the basic currents of his time. By sponsoring the Military Service Act and making himself the fact of conscription incarnate, Meighen had quarreled beyond any chance of reconciliation with Quebec, whose return to the collective life of Canada was the first priority of politics, the nation's most urgent need. Even in this sensitive area a slip of his facile tongue had betrayed him. The French Canadians did not forget that at the climax of the conscription debate he had called them a "backward" people.

By sponsoring futile aid to Mackenzie and Mann he had made himself their "gramophone," according to Bennett's gross slander, and in any case the friend of Big Business, according to the labour unions. Then, in the Winnipeg general strike of 1919, he had smelled a Bolshevik conspiracy, had arrived on the scene as Borden's invariable handyman and had in a secret telegram to the Government approved the arrest of the chief strike leaders.

"Notwithstanding any doubt I have as to the technical legality of the arrests . . . I feel," he said, "that rapid deportation is the best course now that the arrests are made, and later we can consider ratification."

Fortunately for the Government this message and its dangerous doctrine of illegality were not disclosed for some years but the prosecution of James S. Woodsworth had launched a career much more important to Canadian history than Meighen's and antagonized the whole labour movement.

The paralysis of Winnipeg, with its overtones of class war and Canada's first faint whiff of Marxism, was the immediate symptom of those social forces that Meighen resisted throughout his life. Labour was not going Communist, or even socialist. It was determined only to win a better place in the society of the brave new world. The strike also expressed labour's hatred of wartime conscription, of Big Business and of the Government. Meighen's part in suppressing the strike identified him, in labour's mind, as the enemy of the poor, the tool of "the interests." This was slander but it stuck.

More serious for Meighen in terms of votes, and totally demoralizing to national politics, was a new force gathering momentum in the West like a prairie fire and burning eastward into Ontario. A farmer's party had been conceived in the defeat of reciprocity and was brought forth in the post-war depression.

Crerar (who later became one of Meighen's closest personal friends) had been the first minister to leave the wartime coalition in protest against its high tariffs and in complete ignorance of his own unlikely future.

He knew, of course, that the western farmers, whose ambassador he was in Borden's Government, were inflamed as never before against their treatment in the nation's economic policies as represented now by their swollen wartime mortgage debt and a ruinous post-war fall in the price of their wheat.

Crerar knew also that his friend Dafoe was scheming to liberalize the Liberal Party and reduce the tariff. Neither Crerar, the destined agent, nor Dafoe, the philosopher of agrarian protest, foresaw the full effects, or the later schism of the farmers' movement, once it entered directly into politics.

It was now deep in politics as the Progressive Party and well advanced under Crerar's quiet leadership when Meighen took office. If it could capture some fifty seats the Meighen Government could not be re-elected and the Liberal Party could not win a majority. That target satisfied Crerar and Dafoe. It seemed impossible to Meighen.

A fourth factor against the Government was all too clear. In the autumn of 1920 the world suffered what then was judged the worst business depression of modern times. It would quickly pass but not soon enough to help the luckless Meighen. He must face the electors under the worst possible conditions, for which, by the unwritten law of politics, he would be blamed.

The fifth factor, embracing all the others, was decisive in Meighen's career though he could not comprehend or would not admit it, at least until his old age. Canada's society had felt the first touch of a world revolution. Meighen, refusing to accept the new social facts of life, the world-wide swing from the sovereign individual to the collective group, stood against a tide certain to engulf him and all uncompromising conservatives.

For these many reasons the life of the Meighen Government must be dismal, barren and short.

Meanwhile the invisible tide carried a waterproof passenger who, in time, would learn to ride it. Looking across the House in 1919, Meighen had beheld, with something like nausea, the presence of King, recently elected by a doubtful convention to the leadership of the Liberal Party.

In college days King had appeared to Meighen as a preposterous prig, an ingratiating puppy. Later he had seemed a mere mascot and simpering errand boy to Laurier. Yet here he was bouncing up in Parliament, offered sickly congratulations to his boyhood friend as the new Prime Minister and promising to govern himself in debate "by its amenities and never by its animosities."

The distended speech, the corpulent figure, the round, soft face and the tortuous mind of King were almost physically repulsive in Meighen's eyes. King was not a man, as Meighen judged men. By now he had turned into a windy dumpling.

Totally misconceiving the power of his enemy, Meighen was unable to contain himself. He replied to King's compliments with his best double-distilled irony and barbed wit. That was a mistake in the manners of any Prime Minister against any opponent. With King it was worse than useless; it was suicidal. And it suited King exactly when he was drawing his own crude caricature of Meighen as an arrogant autocrat.

"It is too good to be true," King had written in his diary on hearing that Meighen was Prime Minister. "I can fight him naturally, the issues will come clear and distinct." Now, by his manners, Meighen was helping King to make the major issue. It was Meighen himself.

The mutual detestation of these two men has no parallel in Canadian politics. Borden and Laurier had fought but liked each other. Even the lifelong quarrel between Macdonald and Brown lacked the personal loathing which, in Meighen's case, had been honed to a razor's edge and, in the case of King, took the form of a subtle guile, a constant fear and a comic sense of moral outrage. Both were young, King untested, Meighen confident that he had passed his test. The energies and abilities of both, though quite different, were sufficient to maintain their blood feud for more than two decades and keep politics in repeated convulsion.

After his first brush with King, Meighen left him lecturing the public on his ideals of government and, in the summer of 1921, attended an Imperial Conference in London. There and there alone did Meighen ever accomplish anything of importance as Prime Minister.

He went as an honest broker between the United States and Britain, the traditional Canadian role, to negotiate a delicate deal. Britain, he argued, must abandon its alliance with Japan because the United States objected to it and already feared Japanese aggression.

To Meighen the unwritten alliance between the British Empire and the United States was far more important than the written alliance with Japan but at London he found the British, Australian and New Zealand Governments strongly opposed to his work of brokerage. Rebuffed at first, Meighen quickly dominated the conference and persuaded it to reorient the Empire's foreign policy. The Japanese treaty was to be canceled while another conference of interested powers would meet at Washington and try to devise a general agreement on the affairs of the Pacific.

In one sense Meighen had thus carried forward Borden's theory of a common Empire policy. In another sense he had forced a Canadian policy on the Empire to satisfy the United States. However the conference of 1921 was interpreted, it left unsolved the riddle of the Empire's future family relationships. They were to be tested in the Dardanelles, of all places, a year later.

Canada, obsessed with its own domestic problems, forgot foreign policy as Meighen called a December election. He was still unaware that the nation already had made up its mind and only awaited the chance to dismiss him.

The campaign of 1921 was typically confused but unique in Canadian experience. For the first time three major parties were in the field.

Meighen led the remains of the wartime coalition, now the Conservative Party with insignificant Liberal trimmings. King led the Liberal Party, centred, as a result of the conscription struggle, in Quebec. Crerar, to his surprise, found himself leading not merely a local movement of agrarian grievance but a party which obviously controlled the entire Prairie region and much of rural Ontario as well.

These three men, a new generation of political leadership, were as unlike as men could be—Meighen, the machine of intellect with his gaunt look of superiority; King, the beamish boy of politics with his moon face, his false look of flabbiness and his concealed iron; Crerar, the rangy giant of reddish hair and handsome ruddy face imprinted with the authentic look of the western farm land.

Yet the antagonism between this trio held strange nuances of feeling. Meighen detested King, not only as a politician but as a man, and never muted his sentiments. King hated Meighen as a man but treated him respectfully as a politician. Each absurdly underestimated the other. Crerar, a man of more generous spirit, hated neither of his rivals and regarded himself as a Liberal, temporarily in revolt, who must eventually return to his party; but later on he would learn to abhor King and love Meighen. No one could anticipate that personal drama when Canada entered its first post-war election and no politician, except King, saw in it the beginning of a new era, political, social and economic.

Meighen's campaign had been miscalculated on three separate counts.

It was Conservative in policy, while the nation was sick of a wartime Government dominated by Conservatives and now suffered from a depression under Conservative management.

It was also conservative, in the philosophical definition of the term, while a changing society demanded liberal policies, by the same definition.

Finally the campaign was based on the personality of Meighen though his record had antagonized most of the nation and his real character was largely unknown.

"Canada Needs Meighen" was the slogan plastered on every billboard, and the figure of Meighen, five times life size, was pictured in garish colour leading a shipwrecked Canada safely to shore. What the public saw, however, was not a constructive statesman seeking to conciliate a fractured nation but a sour, negative critic abusing his enemies, almost a cranky schoolmaster bullying a class of retarded children.

Meighen's policy was only the maintenance of existing policies, especially high tariffs built "brick for brick" against the United States. Free trade, the sacred desideratum of the farmers, had "depopulated rural England . . . filled the emigrant ships with fugitives from her shores" and would impoverish Canada.

As for the upsurge of mildly radical ideas then stirring among the misguided Canadian voters, the lecturer declared that "the public mind is confused with a veritable babel of uninformed tongues. A great many people seem to have lost all sense of values, of proportion and of numbers. Extravagance in thought is as great as the undoubted extravagance in living. Thousands of people are mentally chasing rainbows, striving for the unattainable, anxious to better their lot, but seemingly unwilling to do it in the old-fashioned way by hard, honest, intelligent effort."

If this was sound, sincere conservative doctrine (the very doctrine of which Crerar would later become the strongest advocate) it could win few votes in those times of hope and frustration. Canute-like, Meighen bade the social tide to recede. Canada was moving. He would not.

If his eyes had not been sealed by contempt, Meighen would have realized at once that in King he faced not a pudgy youth and mere accident but Canada's third master of politics, his sure intuition equalled only by that of Macdonald and Laurier, perhaps exceeding theirs.

It was the true measure of King, in his first trial, that he knew what not to say, a lesson which Meighen never learned.

Thus in King's long, pious and oily speeches the listener could detect little substance, precisely as the speaker intended. He blandly disregarded the platform laid down by his party, he disregarded his own book of left-wing social theory as meat too strong for the electorate, he disregarded the wartime Liberal schism, he disregarded any concrete issue except one, and it was lethal.

Knowing that attack was the best defence, he declared that the only vital question before the people was the restoration of Parliament's ancient rights. They had been usurped, he said, by an autocratic Government which, elected only for war purposes, had no mandate to govern in peacetime and had become only the servant of Big Business. Somehow, though he never explained the method, Canada must be rescued from rapacious capitalists, from depression, from burdensome taxes, from the high cost of living. Of all these evils Meighen was the architect and the executor.

By urging "freer" trade in the West and the Maritimes, by assuring Ontario and Quebec business that it must have adequate protection and that "free" trade was a libel on his party, King straddled everything.

Meighen considered that straddle clumsy and cowardly. It was neither. No smoother balancing act had ever been seen in Canada and it required high courage when an amateur leader must reject the advice of the party professionals, risk everything on his own methods and invest his whole future in this election.

King's capacity was best revealed by his welcome to the Liberals who had deserted Laurier on the conscription issue. As probably no one else could have done, he was healing overnight a Liberalism apparently shattered for years to come.

The symbolic act of this healing process was also the work of political inspiration, of a showmanship so subtle and innocent-looking that it appeared accidental.

Wherever King went in the campaign—on the platform, in the committee rooms, in editorial offices or Pullman cars—he had with him a towering, swarthy man of square potent face, a tangle of black curls and a musical voice pleasantly flavoured with French accent. King had found in Ernest Lapointe his *alter ego,* his manager of French Canada, the true successor to Laurier.

These partners—the tiny, plump and deceptively feminine King, the huge, articulate and masculine Lapointe—were amusing in their contrast. They looked rather like a team of comedians on a vaude-ville tour. In them nevertheless, a nation split by war was achieving its reunion. Together, if it could win the election, the partnership of King and Lapointe, like that of Baldwin and Lafontaine, of Mac-donald and Cartier, of Laurier and Fielding, would control the future.

The election was not easy to win. King understood that from the start. He understood as well that his real obstacle was not Meighen but Crerar.

The prairie fire of the Progressive Party was a danger. Skilfully contained, it was an opportunity, too. When Ontario had elected a farmers' government in the autumn of 1919, King confided in his diary that "it means as sure as I am writing that I shall be called on to form a government at the next general election if no serious mistakes are made in the interval."

The problem in 1921 was to prevent those mistakes, to avoid an outright collision with the Progressives now and engorge them later. Meighen lectured the farmers on the old-fashioned virtues of thrift. King, once he realized that they would sweep the Prairies at least, treated them as only Liberals in a hurry, as sheep of the finest quality who had briefly strayed from the flock but would be received with tears of joy by a loving shepherd if they returned home.

There he had hit, with unerring aim, on the truth of the Pro-gressive Party. It was for the most part only a temporary revolt within the Liberal Party against high tariffs, high freight rates and the dominance of central Canadian big business. Dafoe, the Pro-gressive philosopher, and Crerar, the public leader, were engaged in a circular strategy designed not to create a permanent third party but to rescue Liberalism from its reactionary eastern elements, to purge it of protectionist sin.

Neither of them yet appreciated the ability of King to hold all the elements, east and west, free-trade and protectionist, good and bad, in an amalgam of no fixed principle but of durable life.

Neither of them yet realized that their base of power, a large and cohesive agricultural vote, was sure to dissolve as new farm machinery drove men from the land to the cities.

Probably neither realized that, in the context of the social revolution now under way, they were conservatives, since they intended to conserve a *status quo* now dying; that their Jeffersonian democracy of the frontier could not long survive. And their philosophy was the antithesis of King's private Liberalism, which issues in our day as a doctrine of central economic planning abhorrent to Crerar and Dafoe.

On election night, December 6, they and the whole nation began to see in King a figure more formidable than they had supposed.

As the leader of a party smashed by the war only four years earlier, as a young man who had spent the war years comfortably in the United States, as an unattractive man with no ray of personal magnetism, as a speaker who made almost an art of boredom, King won 116 seats, only two short of a majority in Parliament. Considering all his handicaps and the presence of three parties, this was a miracle. Miraculous, too, the Progressives' capture of 65 seats in the west and Ontario. But quite natural, considering Meighen's burdens, especially the burden of his personality and record, was the Conservatives' return to Parliament with only 50 seats.

Meighen and nine of his ministers were defeated. He could quickly find a seat for himself, he was still young and he refused, even amid this carnage, to believe that his career as Prime Minister was ended. It was ended just the same.

With King's help, he had made sure of that. With the help of an irrational accident now five years off, the sentence pronounced on December 6, 1921, would prove to be final. Thus, as Meighen's worshippers believed, blind chance and the trickery of "the most contemptible charlatan ever to darken the annals of Canadian politics" had conspired to rob Canada's government of its greatest mind.

11: The Unseen Hand

The man who formed a Liberal Government on December 29, 1921, was little known to the Canadian people. So he would remain until his death and long afterwards. For the next twenty-seven years, with a five-year interruption, William Lyon Mackenzie King dominated the nation's government and penetrated its entire life; but the nation could never penetrate the life of its leader.

Politics produced in him its most complicated and mysterious figure; also, as a politician only, its greatest and least understood. King's look, speech, manner, habits and methods of thought deceived everybody. This was inevitable when he perpetually deceived himself.

But concerning the new Prime Minister at his age of forty-seven one thing was said everywhere with assurance—he would not last long. All Conservative politicians like Meighen, and not a few Liberals, agreed that King's arrival had been an accident from which a sensible country would soon recover. How came it, then, that this unattractive, unliked and unlikely man held office longer than any political leader in the history of the English-speaking peoples?

Many books have been written to explore the enigma of King, with indifferent success. Many myths have been built around him with the help of his famous diaries. Many of his closest colleagues remember him with bitter animosity and curious disagreement on the facts. The contemporary public accepts as reality a man who never lived.

While the professional historians, with all their accuracy of detail, have failed to excavate King from the real monuments of his life and the spurious monuments of Kingsmere, an amateur once summed up the riddle in a phrase of vivid inspiration.

As Governor-General in King's latter years, the Earl of Athlone observed him with neutral English eyes and a shrewd common sense little known outside Rideau Hall. After King's death and his own return to London, Athlone delivered a judgment in his jerky, soldier's idiom.

"Your man King," he said to me. "Knew him well, actually. Bit of a puzzle, what? H'm—King. Great man and all that. And you know, he just missed being quite a decent feller."

A great man who just missed being quite a decent fellow—that was King to the life.

His greatness is recorded in the unification of the Canadian people after the quarrel during the First World War; in the management of the Second, when he avoided another quarrel by the most desperate gamble of bluff and fiction ever known to our politics; in a revolution of Canadian society so slow, subtle and deceptive that it was established beyond repeal before the people began to perceive it and is still the central force in our affairs today.

Behind this public success King's failures were all inside himself. With his ceaseless itch for power, an egotism unique and ruthless because he conceived himself as God's chosen instrument, and an unequalled ability to manipulate men who disliked and distrusted him, King could become an invulnerable leader. He could build an irresistible juggernaut of government. He could never be a successful or even, in the end, a happy human being.

There is the inscrutable paradox of King, or rather the several Kings forever at war with one another, forever grasping greedily the practical rewards of this world and forever seeking the spiritual joys of the next.

Along these parallel paths, mundane and supernatural, the several Kings marched and counter-marched in many combinations and disguises—a hermit, mystic and spiritualist communicating daily with the dead; a Cabinet tyrant and caucus boss feeding mentally on royal jelly and physically on a gourmet's choice foods; a meticulous host, sentimental friend and merciless destroyer by turns; a rich man terrified of poverty; a dedicated social reformer and Victorian snob; an international statesman and incurable isolationist; a pious Christian and practitioner of jungle superstition; a devout Presbyterian singing loudly in church and, in the privacy of his office, often refusing to make a decision or sign a document until the hands of the clock were directly opposite each other to promise good fortune.

These rivals always dividing a single soul wrote a record of political achievement without equal in twentieth-century Canada. Athlone was right just the same. King never came to terms with his fellows in this life because, to him, it was a passing incident in his frightened search for the life eternal; above all, because he could never be the ordinary, normal man of his public act and saw himself as the special agent of divinity, an "Unseen Hand" constantly on his shoulder.

He was a contradiction inside himself and even more contradictory in his queer outward compact with the people. They never loved him but they needed him. The man whose private seismograph registered their slightest tremor was less typical of the Canadian breed than any contemporary and yet he could synthesize its diverse elements into a policy seldom strong but generally acceptable. Though he never knew Canadians as a comrade and participant in their humble concerns, he knew, by a purely instinctive and osmotic process, what they wanted, what they would tolerate, what the political traffic would bear.

Having measured friend and enemy alike, the man who seemed to move so leisurely could strike like a cobra. The man who seemed so cautious could risk everything on a gambler's throw. The man who seemed so timid and effeminate could show, when necessary, a wild and reckless courage.

Besides all these assets he enjoyed two more—a constitution of iron under his flabby exterior and, at critical moments of his adventure, an unfailing luck which he accepted as the special design of God.

All these assets, human and divine, could not quite heal his inferiority complex. He knew, with gnawing certainty, that he remained far smaller as a man than his work as a statesman. He could be Prime Minister. He could not afford to be quite himself.

If King's nature was too complex for dissection, his method was almost absurdly simple, though carefully misrepresented. As he put it to this writer: "An issue exists for me by intuition or not at all. I either see it at once or it means nothing to me. I decide my policy right away. I may spend much time planning how to defend it but I know from the start what I want to do and how to do it."

The weary, overstuffed speeches apparently designed to build a case, or to conceal a vacuum, were in reality the supporting evidence of a decision taken long before in a flash of intuitive impulse.

But the mature King known to all Canadians now beyond middle age was not the King who grappled, at the beginning of 1922, with an insoluble problem, as it seemed then.

Our generation remembers an aging, shrunken little man, of lean, wrinkled face, bald head, artificial smile, mincing manner and ponderous speech. The King who took over a quarreling nation after the first war was a rough preliminary sketch, a bulbous caricature, of the future chieftain.

In his soft war years he had grown so corpulent that his doctors were ordering him to reduce some of his two hundred pounds if he wished to live long. A wisp of hair, last remains of a boyish mop, was plastered across a shiny skull. The face was round, unlined and spiritless. The tiny hand nervously tapped the stub of a pencil on the desk whenever Meighen spoke to Parliament. Then a flush of alarm and fury slowly flooded King's bulging neck, his scalp and cheeks. As he rose to reply his windy language and sprawling syntax were pitiable after Meighen's clean rapier thrusts. Evidently the nation had chosen a Prime Minister certain to fail.

Only a few intimates, who were never his real friends, realized that King's equipment for office was better than it looked and had been conveyed to him almost at birth, along with a frantic need to use it.

The boy born at Kitchener, Ontario (then called Berlin) on December 17, 1874, knew, as soon as he was old enough to know anything, that he had inherited a sacred mission. For his family's honour he must vindicate the treason of his rebel grandfather, William Lyon Mackenzie, whose name he had been given as a burden and a goad.

His mother, the child of the rebel's American exile, saw in her son the avenger of Mackenzie's comic tragedy at the barricades of York. As if the Unseen Hand had arranged a synthesis of the two elements in Canadian life, King's father belonged to the Loyalist tradition. John King was the son of a professional Scots soldier who had fought against the Rebellion of 1837.

The future Prime Minister grew up in a comfortable, genteel home. His parents were fluent in abstract political argument but incompetent in the management of their financial affairs.

John King was a pleasant sort of Micawber vainly waiting for something to turn up, practising as a lawyer with indifferent success and constantly short of cash. His wife was made of sterner stuff. Under her air of tender Victorian womanhood she hid a fierce ambition, all concentrated—since the husband could not satisfy it—in her son. To the mother, as to no other woman in his life, King gave his whole devotion and the nobler side of his character. Her influence over him was greater than that of any man. In return she loved and preyed on him.

Two daughters, Isabel and Janet, and a younger son, Macdougall, completed the family circle but the mother had set all her hopes on "Billy," seeing in him qualities undetected by anyone else.

The quiet rhythm of a small town, the sports of school and woods, the years at the University of Toronto revealed nothing remarkable in the young King except his maternal fixation, his sense of destiny, his opinion of himself as another rebel like his grandfather.

To Meighen, struggling through college in poverty and loneliness, the chubby, priggish extrovert from Berlin appeared objectionable but unimportant. Neither youth could suppose that their occasional meetings had opened a contest of forty years for the control of Canada.

Meighen went about his solitary search for knowledge. King was a campus orator, agitator and social climber, known to his companions as Rex, but he was also a systematic student and, like Meighen, a voracious reader. At night King would hang the notes of the day's lectures on his bedpost, read them as he dressed in the morning and recite them on his walk to class.

What he learned from lectures and books was less important than his first disturbing lessons in the life of Canada. Seen at first hand, Toronto's poverty disgusted him. Canadian society was quite different from its innocent version in Berlin. The economic system failed to operate as in the textbooks of pure liberalism. Somehow the whole system must be reformed.

In his first efforts to reform it he organized a newsboys' club to which he lectured learnedly on Saturday nights, and on Sundays he told stories to the patients of the Sick Children's Hospital. His career of rebellion had begun—honestly, harmlessly, comically but with a vehement flame never to be extinguished until his last years brought him quiet despair.

The boyish fire grew in heat and protest during his year at Jane Addams' Hull House Social Settlement in Chicago, where King lived in the slums and realized with a shock that the liberal theory of laissez-faire and the omniscient Market had not produced the good society but, instead, what he called the "Law of Competing Standards," the debasement of human beings.

Filled with this heresy, he returned to Toronto in 1897 and

there, as a reporter for the *Mail and Empire,* investigated the working conditions of the garment industry. His reports of women making postmen's uniforms at a wage of three cents an hour caught the
attention of William Mulock, Postmaster General, who promptly
inserted a fair-wage clause in all government clothing contracts.
King had been discovered by the Laurier Government.

The next steps were easy. As Deputy Minister in the new Department of Labour, then Minister, and family friend of Laurier,
King established himself as a coming man in the Liberal Party. The
nation's first anti-combine laws and the pioneer Industrial Disputes
Investigation Act were his work. He argued with employers and
labour unions to settle a series of strikes. He negotiated an immigration agreement with Japan.

As an eligible bachelor he became a constant diner-out in the
best society of Ottawa. With his first savings he bought a dilapidated
farm in the Gatineau district which, by pleasant coincidence, was
called Kingsmere. He rode his horse in the summer (frequently
explaining his hopes and fears aloud to this discreet confidant),
skated in the winter, paid suit to several heiresses and suffered his
first sorrow in the gallant death of his closest friend, Henry Albert
Harper, about whom he wrote his first book, *The Secret of Heroism.*

The other side of the young bachelor's life remained unknown.
Apparently prosperous on his minister's salary, he was actually
poor. Most of his earnings were sent regularly to his parents.

Already he was showing a shrewd political judgment surprising
at his age. The reciprocity agreement of 1911, he wrote in his diary,
exposed the Laurier Government to "great dangers" and "well
enough had better be left alone." It was not "left alone" and the
Government perished. In his thirty-eighth year King found himself
without a seat in Parliament, a job, or money to support his family.
The father was going blind, the mother gravely ill, the brother in
the first stages of tuberculosis.

The next three years were largely wasted. King pleaded vainly
with Laurier to find him a parliamentary seat, concluded that the
old man was indifferent to his misfortune and "I sort of despised him
in my feelings." As his small savings ran out King knew "the sting
of the absence of position with income, the privation of not being
able to invite others to a meal or to offer readily a carriage to a
guest," but as his diary records, "somehow I believe God has a great
work for me in this Dominion, maybe at some time to be its Prime
Minister."

Meanwhile he was growing desperate. Only a rich English lady,

Violet Markham, seemed to recognize his talent and gave him three hundred pounds a year. On this allowance and fees for lectures now and then he managed to live in Ottawa and maintain his family in Toronto.

He was nagged not only by his poverty but by the horror of loneliness. He must have a wife and children. "To go into politics without marrying wd. be folly," he wrote in his diary. "I cannot live that cruel life without a home & someone to love and be loved by. . . . . Marry I must."

Accordingly, he set about the quest for a mate as if he were organizing an election campaign but none of his candidates for bed and board could satisfy his specifications. Either the object of his pursuit was beautiful but lacked money, or she was rich and lacked beauty, or, if she had all the necessary assets of purse and appearance, her spirit disappointed him.

When at last he met, at Rideau Hall, a lady who satisfied all his requirements she rejected him. Again, when he fell genuinely in love with a poor woman his affectionate but predatory and snobbish parents vetoed the match. For their son they demanded a stylish mate, for themselves financial security. Still he hoped "to find someone of pure soul and noble purpose. . . . God grant I may & may He guide me in the choice." Over and over again the guidance failed. King must have been the most ardent and rejected suitor in Ottawa.

From the wilderness of politics, unrequited love and poverty he was suddenly rescued by an intervention which he regarded as divine.

God's improbable agency, the Rockefeller Foundation of New York, had heard of the young Labour Minister and conciliator of industrial disputes. Now locked in an endless strike with their Colorado miners, the Rockefellers asked King's advice. His first interview with John D. Rockefeller Jr. led to a lifelong friendship, a lucrative salary and King's worldwide reputation as an expert on labour problems.

While Canada underwent the blood-letting of the Great War, King earned twenty thousand dollars a year (a huge income then) as Rockefeller's closest adviser, and saved most of his earnings. His financial problem had been solved, his family was secure but all his brief love affairs came to nothing. In one of these many suits he actually found the perfect mate and planned a leisurely conquest. Waiting too long to present his proposal, he learned that the lady had engaged herself to another man. "I felt," says the diary, "I would never forgive myself for my delay."

More serious for an ambitious politician was his absence from Canada in wartime. Though he maintained his small Ottawa apartment, he had dropped out of sight. He would have been useless as a soldier, he was doing important work and exploring the economic system of America as no Canadian had ever explored it; but his reputation as a prosperous slacker appeared fatal to his political career.

The election of 1917 confirmed that handicap. King returned to Canada, surveyed his chances, privately favoured conscription if it applied to wealth as well as manpower and, after agonies of doubt, decided to run for Parliament as a Laurier Liberal in North York. Oddly enough, this canny judge of public opinion informed his diary that "Sir Wilfrid will sweep the country"; but a few days later he was writing that his own candidature meant "political suicide." So it seemed to turn out.

Defeated along with most of the English-speaking Liberals, King reached the nadir of his life. His mother dead in the Ottawa apartment, his brother dying in Colorado, his political career spoiled, his matrimonial pursuits all failing, King lost faith in his own destiny.

Like a rotund Hamlet, he brooded on the futility of human affairs. "Last night I wandered about . . . in Toronto alone for a while in Queen's Park, realizing for the first time in life I had no home to go to." That melancholy pedestrian, if the Toronto crowds had paused to observe him, would have appeared as the least likely of Canadians to inherit their Government. King was alone now. He would be alone to the end.

Alarmed by his physical and mental condition, King's secretary and most faithful friend, F. A. McGregor, persuaded him to enter Johns Hopkins Hospital in Baltimore for treatment. His strong constitution and naturally optimistic spirit rallied quickly. He felt again the "command clearly to carry on the tradition and the work Grandfather commenced, the welfare of the great mass of the people."

His book must be the next stage in this work. *Industry and Humanity,* composed in a minute handwriting decipherable only by McGregor, was a chaotic mixture of cliché and heresy, little read then and almost forgotten now. Yet no one can understand King's subsequent career without studying his credo.

Its thesis holds, in brief, that the economic system belongs by right to capitalists, workers and the public, all of whom must be represented in its management and profits by means not specifically explained. Instead, the system enriches the few, impoverishes the many, debases society by the Law of Competing Standards and drives nations inevitably to war.

Competition, the very root of liberalism, is responsible for all these evils. They cannot be cured by the crude device of socialism but competition must be curbed by the wise interventions of the State, which must establish a minimum standard of life for the whole community.

Though the book was badly written, since King had no sense of words or the structure of sentences, and though its notions seem mild and commonplace in our age of revolution, it was revolutionary then. It attacked the whole existing structure of capitalism. It repudiated the fundamentals of liberalism. It presented King as a rebel like his grandfather.

Now that his book was published at last King possessed two vital assets unrecognized by his party. By accepting certain defeat as Laurier's anti-conscription candidate he had made himself something of a hero among the people of Quebec. By educating himself in the economic and social process, as no other Canadian politician was educated, he was better prepared than any contemporary for government in the new age that must follow the war.

A third necessary ingredient of luck was not lacking either. The conservative managers of the Liberal Party did not read the book or, if they read it, refused to take its doctrines seriously. Had they known it, *Industry and Humanity* was a delayed explosion waiting to be detonated at a convenient moment.

For the present King's course was set. He had recognized "the call of the blood," and was resolved "to throw in my whole life with Canada and to give up forever, if the Fates permit, all thought of future association with the States . . . to give up thoughts of pleasure I had been cherishing & follow Duty, to go into the fight as a Sir Galahad" but to make sure nevertheless that "my livelihood for the next year or two remains secured." For "it would be hell itself . . . to be dependent on politics for a livelihood."

The Rockefellers could not hold him in New York. He rejected the offer of the Carnegie Corporation to appoint him its director at an annual salary of twenty-five thousand dollars because "the primrose path does not make for greatness in any true sense." No, he must be Prime Minister.

With Laurier's death the door of opportunity was opened, but King paused listlessly on the threshold. Instead of campaigning for the Liberal leadership he decided to visit England and study labour problems there on the eve of the party convention.

As McGregor tells the story of this interlude in his excellent book, *The Fall and Rise of Mackenzie King*, the aspiring politician refused to lift a finger for his own advancement. The Unseen Hand must settle everything.

While rival candidates were drumming up convention delegates, King idled through the summer of 1919 in England but McGregor was not idle. Against his chief's instructions, he booked return passage on two different ships and persuaded King to take the first. The second was delayed for a fortnight by a longshoremen's strike. If King had waited for it to sail he would have arrived in Canada too late for the convention. The Unseen Hand of McGregor delivered him at Ottawa in the nick of time.

His prospects were still dubious. Even when he had aroused the convention's shouts and tears by his dramatic tribute to Laurier and his melodramatic bow before the dead leader's portrait on the wall, King had to face a rival better known than he, more experienced, certainly more respected. The great Fielding had entered the contest but he was now seventy-one years old and, by supporting conscription, had antagonized not only French Canada but most of Laurier's worshippers.

The other candidates, George P. Graham, a lightweight of irresistible charm, D. D. McKenzie, the temporary Liberal House leader, and Alexander Smith, Laurier's political organizer, counted for little unless they could swing their delegates to King or Fielding.

On the day of balloting King awakened to read, as usual, his book of *Daily Strength for Daily Needs*. His eye caught the text, "Nothing shall be impossible unto you" and he knew at once how the vote would go. After the others had dropped out, a third ballot gave King the leadership by 476 votes to Fielding's 438. As the diary was informed that night, the victory had "come from God . . . It is to His work I am called and to it I dedicate my life."

Only one Daily Need was still unfulfilled—"I need a wife. God will send the right woman." But He did not.

King's electoral victory in 1921 was far greater than the figures suggested. To be sure, most of the people had voted negatively against the Meighen Government but the Liberal Party elected 117 members though it had been split and hived in Quebec only four years earlier. King had reunited it, east of the Great Lakes, by his first important stroke of statesmanship. All his future success flowed from the decision to disregard the wartime schism and welcome home the conscriptionist Liberals.

Though he had thus proved himself a new and surprisingly potent force in politics, Liberalism was still split in the West. Crerar's 64 Progressives, controlling the Prairies and even a few Ontario seats, were for the most part Liberals in revolt against their party. King's first priority, therefore, was to make peace, if he could, with the embattled farmers.

The chances looked good. King's ambassador, Andrew Haydon, arrived in Winnipeg and found Crerar willing to discuss the possibility of a coalition. The secret negotiations went well until Haydon's messages to King leaked from a local telegraph office.

Newspaper reports suggesting that King planned a deal with the western radicals outraged his eastern supporters. Crerar was embarrassed by the report that he intended to betray the farmers. The Winnipeg negotiations collapsed, were resumed in Ottawa and discovered by an eavesdropper who listened at the door of a Chateau Laurier bedroom.

This second leak prohibited the coalition. The Progressives were not ready for it anyway. As King realized, his seduction of the agrarian rebels, while certain in the end, would take time. His minority government must be purely Liberal at the beginning but a lamp of invitation would be kept burning in the western window.

The first and least distinguished of King's six ministries took office on December 29, 1921. It reflected a lack of adequate material, the attempt to reunite the Liberal Party in the East, the divided state of the nation and, above all, the patient work of the cabinet-maker.

King had abandoned the radical dream of his book in favour of reality. He had talked vaguely of reform in his election speeches but his Cabinet had one purpose only—to survive until a quarreling nation was ready for new policies that could not be safely broached or even considered now.

In its maker's mind (though of course he publicly maintained the usual pretence of perfection) the Cabinet was a temporary makeshift, a union of opposites, an instrument of transition. Given reasonable luck, it might begin to usher Canada into a new and better age.

King retained the vestiges of Laurier's times by appointing Fielding to Finance, Graham to Defence, Charles Murphy to the Post Office and Raoul Dandurand to the Senate leadership. Then, to satisfy French Canada and the Liberal Party's right wing, he gave

Justice to Sir Lomer Gouin, Premier and strong man of Quebec who, as King expected, was an immediate failure in national politics.

Already King had chosen Lapointe as his permanent French-Canadian partner and now stowed him away in Fisheries, pending Gouin's retirement. The King-Lapointe coalition, like that of Baldwin and Lafontaine, of Macdonald and Cartier, Laurier and Fielding, was destined to be long and fruitful.

Unable to understand French Canada's mind or speak its language (his French speeches being written by others and read with a ghastly accent), King left Quebec to Lapointe's management. The relations between the two men were as intimate as King's nature permitted. Alone among his colleagues, Lapointe called the Prime Minister "Rex." King addressed Lapointe by his Christian name of Ernest but all the other ministers by their surnames.

Apart from Lapointe, the only important new discovery was James A. Robb, in Trade and Commerce, who represented the English-speaking elements and the business community of Quebec. W. R. Motherwell, a free trader of the old school and one of the three Liberals elected on the Prairies, accepted the portfolio of Agriculture and the inevitable conflict with his protectionist colleagues from the East.

As Meighen and his forty-nine supporters viewed it, this lack-lustre and divided Cabinet must be short-lived. If Meighen could have anticipated certain events only four years away, he would have been even more optimistic. But he failed to detect, in his hatred of King, the solid craftsmanship behind the façade of the Treasury benches.

King, the supreme artist of the possible, knew precisely what he was doing in politics if not in policy. Before he could do anything of importance he must arrange the marriage of the Liberal and Progressive Parties to create a national majority.

The banns were announced when Crerar refused to accept the leadership of the parliamentary Opposition and handed it to Meighen. With Crerar's early withdrawal from public life, for personal and business reasons, his successor, Robert Forke, at first rejected King's advances with contempt but finally entered the Government. The Progressives, except for their "Ginger Group" of western radicalism, were soon returning to the Liberal fold.

For their return a price must be paid. King reduced the tariff just far enough to secure the Progressives' grudging support without seriously disturbing the eastern manufacturers. Even these minor concessions to the farmers required courage since most nations were retreating to the storm cellars of protectionism and launching the economic war which guaranteed a military war later on.

The Government built branch-line railways in the West, encouraged immigration, economized in its budgets and produced, by 1924, the first revenue surplus since 1913. These policies seemed to succeed. The post-war slump lifted overnight.

As a routine housekeeper and meticulous administrator, King had few if any equals. Though he gave his ministers wide latitude in their departments so long as their decisions did not infringe on his central policies, he watched every detail with the eye of a trained bureaucrat, made all important appointments himself and, summing up "the sense of the Cabinet," interpreted it to suit himself, often against a clear majority.

All this was mere routine, managed by the Prime Minister's left hand. His larger objective—too large for public disclosure—was a basic redivision of politics under a personal machine of power.

This project must take time. Never doubting that he would be Prime Minister for many years to come, King settled down comfortably in Sir Wilfrid's spacious old house (the bequest of Lady Laurier), refurnished it in hideous plush with gifts of money from his rich friends, added a tiny elevator, made his cluttered third-floor study the command post of government, enlarged his estate at Kingsmere, began to erect his preposterous ruins there and gradually placed himself, as oracle, philosopher and genial despot, above the daily din of battle.

In this period he made a discovery that changed his entire life. He discovered the proof of life everlasting. The experience of a senator's widow who traced her husband's lost will with the aid of a medium first attracted King to spiritualism. Soon he was conferring regularly with his parents through mediums in Canada and England. The presence of the Unseen Hand had been established beyond doubt.

Only one of his secretaries and none of his colleagues knew that he had become a practising spiritualist. He guarded his secret with elaborate precautions lest the scoffing voters conclude that the Government was dominated by spooks or frauds. After his death, when the facts came out, his mediums agreed that his public policies had never been discussed with the dead but his early sense of guidance by eternal forces was fully corroborated. Even if he had to use trickery and in some cases brutality, he acted always as God's deputy.

His divided nature was stranger in his private than in his public life. He would write innumerable notes of condolence to the bereaved, maintain secret charities, dote on Pat, his Irish terrier, meet some poor boy on the street and take him home to dinner, but he continually plotted the downfall of his rivals, grudged his house servants a decent wage and overworked his secretaries to the point of breakdown.

The loyal McGregor could endure his hectoring no longer and, throwing a pile of documents into the air, ran screaming from the room. King promoted him to a high post in the civil service. A chauffeur was dismissed for smoking a cigarette while waiting for the Prime Minister and was promptly rehired.

King used no tobacco, drank little alcohol and regarded himself as a model of temperance (even if he and Meighen were once seen, after a convivial banquet, standing together on a table and singing "My Old Kentucky Home" in tuneless duet). Food was another matter. King loved it like a glutton and savoured it like an epicure.

As part of his public act he cultivated the notion that he was a rather dull man. Actually his charm, whenever he cared to use it, was irresistible and he had a bubbling sense of humour. His eyes would twinkle with mischief, his artificial dentures glisten in a broad grin as he mocked his colleagues behind their backs. Sometimes he deliberately encouraged their quarrels because a divided Cabinet must be dependent on him.

He could be cold and overbearing in his office but in his home the humblest guest was treated as a superior from whom the Prime Minister deferentially sought expert advice, which he weighed gravely and disregarded.

Generally, however, he followed the rule (as explained to me on one occasion) that "I can deal best with men if I don't see too much of them." He could afford few friends and none, except perhaps Lapointe, was in the Cabinet.

Thus managed, King's first Government was competent, pedestrian and unimaginative. It seemed to lack any basic direction; but this, too, was according to plan. As King said to me in those days, he would not make the mistake of declaring specific objectives and giving "the other fellow a target to shoot at."

Nevertheless, back of the round generalities and sleek platitudes of the speeches that were written and rewritten in half a dozen drafts, King had a target.

The nation, as he saw it then, was deeply sundered by the war. The Maritimes were depressed and angry; Quebec remained in isolation, the West in revolt, Confederation under dangerous strain.

Until Canada regained a feeling of confidence and unity no new and divisive experiments could be risked. Besides, for all his youthful preaching and all the hazy doctrines of his book, King had no clear long-term plans, only the immediate target of unity. To achieve it he would do anything, however contradictory. For the present he kept the nation's mind off controversial issues by directing it to safer arguments on the tariff, financial economy and good government, whatever that might mean.

All this was humdrum work but essential. Indeed, though it is now forgotten, King's patient treatment of a disjointed nation, as a physician treats a convalescent, was his first important achievement when it seemed to be only irresolution and timidity.

Evidently the treatment was succeeding. The post-war depression had ended and the Government, as usual, claimed credit for the recovery. Industrial peace followed the Winnipeg strike. French Canada was quiescent, trusting its ambassador, Lapointe. The western revolt was petering out as the Progressives returned to their Liberal home. The whole nation felt better and showed little interest in politics. That was precisely what King intended. He could take his time now and live his own life.

Except for Parliament, which he attended scrupulously, his habits ignored the convenience of everyone. Rising late, he read his Bible, fussed with his diary or dictated endless notes to unknown correspondents all over the country. About noon he reached his East Block office, summoned his colleagues at one o'clock, usually giving them no time for lunch, and bounced into the House of Commons at half-past two with a schoolboy's shining morning face.

The master of Cabinet, caucus and party appeared as the modest servant of Parliament, obedient to its smallest command, pathetically eager for its approval, repentant at its slightest rebuke. King always treated Parliament as an instrument of national harmony, an organ which, played by a competent musician, must ultimately emit its lost chord.

Two contradictory Kings were now firmly established—the lonely hermit and the gregarious politician. A third surprised Ottawa and the nation. If necessary, King could fight with every available weapon, clean or dirty. Meighen's mistake had been to dismiss his enemy as a coward. In fact, King was naturally belligerent and often merciless, a pacificator or a killer as occasion required.

When, for example, I wrote in another book that King cut the throats of friends and enemies alike, the Opposition solemnly asked in Parliament whether this awful charge could be true. With equal solemnity and a gleam of relish, the Prime Minister replied that throat-cutting was "the only way to treat certain classes of enemies."

His razor, in these early days, was aimed exclusively at Meighen, the only enemy of his life who seriously alarmed him. Their ceaseless life-and-death struggle filled Hansard and the headlines but obscured the actual course of politics that King understood and Meighen did not.

King was patiently building a nation-wide coalition loosely called Liberal, a personal dynasty and a flexible, pragmatic policy for the new age foreseen in *Industry and Humanity*. Meighen, for all his brilliance, was trying to restore an age still lingering but actually dead. King preached a return to "normalcy," as President Harding was calling it in the United States, but knew that the good old days would never come back. Meighen, awaiting their return, considered King, his policies and his Government quite abnormal.

What actually emerged from King's first administration? Only three overt events seemed to give it any historical significance. To King, however, they were hardly more than detours and distractions from his larger plans.

At midnight, September 15, 1922, a coded cable from Lloyd George asked Canada's military aid to repel the Turkish advance against Britain's outnumbered forces defending the straits at Chanak. King, absent from Ottawa at a political picnic, was annoyed to read this news in the press before he saw the cable but the British Prime Minister's bad manners were of small account. As King knew instantly, he now faced the recurring test of all Canadian leaders.

Was Canada obligated to follow a common Empire policy laid down, without consultation, in London? King's reply to Lloyd George answered that old question blandly and decisively—the Canadian Government could not consider the commitment of troops to the Turkish war without consulting Parliament and doubted that the crisis would justify a parliamentary session.

In King's view the British Government's policy was mad. While Meighen, echoing Laurier's words before the Great War, demanded that Canada's answer to Britain should be "Ready, aye, ready, we stand by you," King said and did nothing.

As he expected, the Chanak incident was soon settled peacefully but it had profound consequences for Canada, the Empire and King. He had been compelled to decide a controversial issue, to quarrel with the nation's Loyalist traditions, to reject a common Empire policy. He had started down a road from which there could be no turning back. By thus solidifying the base of Canadian independence, as laid down by Macdonald, Laurier and Borden, he had rightly construed the Empire's future but totally misconstrued the nature of the world. King, in short, was becoming an isolationist when isolation for Canada was becoming impossible.

The second overt act of this period was committed by Lapointe who arrived in Washington in 1923 and proceeded to sign for Canada a fishery treaty with the United States. An uneasy British Government realized that a momentous precedent had been set. For the first time an overseas dominion was conducting its foreign relations independently.

King's work of establishing a new status for Canada was carried forward at the Imperial Conference of the same year.

He went to London convinced that Meighen had tacitly agreed, at the conference of 1921, to a common Empire foreign policy and had confirmed his real intentions by the "Ready, aye, ready" speech. Moreover, British statesmen and newspapers were calling the latest Empire meeting an "Imperial Cabinet" with "executive authority."

In a private conflict of wills and policies that deserve book-length treatment King rejected any attempt, however modest, to centralize the Empire. He quarreled directly with the British Government, the angry Lord Curzon calling him "obstinate and stupid," and even the moderate South African, Smuts, pronouncing him, only half in fun, "a very terrible person."

King knew that he had gone very far in this imperial confrontation. As his diary reports it, "I was very outspoken and perhaps too much so." But Dafoe, who accompanied him as an adviser, was jubilant.

The foundation of the Balfour Declaration of 1926, establishing the dominions as equal and independent partners of Britain, had been laid by Borden and King, to be finally codified by the Statute of Westminster in 1931. The fight for Canada's new status had been won, the theory of a common Empire foreign policy rejected, and in those peaceful days few Canadians observed that King had no foreign policy of his own. For his theory of "no commitments," his promise that Parliament alone would decide issues of war and peace, was meaningless. He had solemnly defined the League of Nations as a debating society without teeth, he had tried to isolate Canada from the quarrels of Europe but events there were about to decide otherwise.

Having won a great constitutional victory in London, digested most of the Progressive Party, given the nation reasonable prosperity, reduced taxes and healed the racial wounds of wartime, King prepared for the election of October 29, 1925, sure that he could not lose it. He promised further tax reductions, a lower tariff without the "chimera" of free trade, larger immigration and generally "the moderate course, the middle of the road."

Meighen's prospects appeared depressing after the rout of 1921 and still worse, in the Government's judgment, when he decided to fight the campaign on a candid policy of high tariffs built "brick for brick" against the new Republican tariffs of the United States to save Canada from "disaster."

There being no real issue in the election, it became a second duel on the hustings between these two opposite personalities. As a duel it was won by Meighen. To everyone's amazement and King's utter incredulity, the Conservative Party carried 116 seats, sweeping most of Canada outside Quebec. King's following was cut to 99. A splinter of 24 Progressives would control the next Parliament.

With his single-handed miracle, Meighen had reached the peak of his career and expected to form a government. King's plight was even graver than Meighen knew. The Liberal Party managers were convinced that King was a failure, that his choice as leader had been a mistake from the start. They now began to groom his successor, Premier Charles Dunning, of Saskatchewan.

Defeated in his own seat of North York and morally repudiated by the nation, King thought at first of resigning. This moment of despair quickly passed. Instead, playing for time and hoping for a Conservative blunder, which soon appeared, he told the Governor-General, Baron Byng, that he proposed to meet Parliament as Prime Minister and win its confidence. Byng, a soldier equally ignorant of politics and of King, agreed. By this agreement he changed the whole course of Canadian history and, as he concluded later, permitted his own betrayal.

According to Byng's version of this celebrated interview, King had promised that if he could not govern with the support of the Progressives, he would hand the Government over to Meighen without another election. According to King's version, he had been given the Prime Minister's normal right to call another election at any time, once he had received a vote of confidence in Parliament. So opened, without either man anticipating its many consequences, the historic quarrel of Byng and King.

Impatiently awaiting King's fall and his own call to office, Meighen obligingly committed the folly of the Hamilton Speech in a desperate bid for a by-election victory in Bagot. To reconcile himself with Quebec, the author of the wartime conscription law now proposed a constitutional monstrosity. In the event of war, he said, the government's decision to enter it should be submitted to the voters at a general election. This plan for a sort of leisurely plebiscite while the enemy advanced not only reversed the "Ready, aye, ready" doctrine of Chanak; it not only made nonsense of Meighen's common Empire foreign policy, immune to local politics; it not only antagonized the Loyalist vote of Canada; it failed to win the by-election.

King knew how to take full advantage at the proper time of Meighen's astounding blunder. For the present his hands were full. He reorganized the Cabinet, introduced the powerful figure of Dunning (whose ambitions for the party leadership must be risked) and arranged a seat for himself in Prince Albert, where a young man named Diefenbaker was as yet unknown to the nation. And unknown also to it, though not to Meighen, was King's appalling discovery of wholesale graft in the Customs Department.

12: The Baited Trap

When the new Parliament opened on January 7, 1926, King's career, by any rational calculation, was finished. Thus thought Meighen. Thus thought many Liberals. They had not glimpsed, even yet, the ultimate irrationality of politics, nor King's luck, his Unseen Hand.

Awaiting his own election in Prince Albert, the Prime Minister sat in the gallery like a prisoner or exile. The huge, rumpled figure of Lapointe dominated the Treasury benches, and with him appeared the newly arrived figure of Dunning, neat and flashy as an advertisement for gent's superior clothing, complete with handsome, angular face and aggressive black moustache.

The tiny man in the gallery looked down anxiously on Lapointe as his loyal lieutenant and saviour, on Dunning as an even abler politician but a rival. If Lapointe failed now and the Government fell, Dunning would become Liberal leader. The necessary arrangements already were complete in the back room of the party. King knew that, as he knew everything. Meighen also knew it and certain even more disagreeable things.

Until he was a Member of Parliament again, King's strategy was to postpone a vote of confidence. Lapointe executed it with a good pretence of cheerful lethargy. He managed to extend the opening debate on the Throne Speech for two months while King was elected and the Liberal managers went to work on the Progressives.

Next to them sat one of Canada's greatest men, in whom King had high hopes. J. S. Woodsworth, a Christian minister, longshoreman, victim of the Winnipeg strike and hardly less than a saint, had come to Parliament as a rather confused socialist distrusting all parties and Meighen more than King. The vote and moral influence of Woodsworth were vital to the Government. His future work would be vital to the nation. King set out to deserve this strange man's friendship.

Meanwhile the expected blow fell on February 2 when Harry Stevens, a Vancouver grocer who had become Meighen's chief lieutenant, rose to inform Mr. Speaker Lemieux of a serious matter. The long-simmering Customs Scandal had broken wide open.

Stevens' speech proved by indisputable evidence that the Customs Department was rotten with graft, its officials in league with a nation-wide smugglers' ring, its minister, Jacques Bureau, guilty of incompetence or worse. And as a reward for debauching the public service, Bureau had lately been promoted by King to the Senate.

All this King had foreseen and knew by now that he faced something worse than Macdonald's Pacific Scandal. In a fine show of moral indignation, he moved for a select committee to study the Opposition's evidence. While the committee examined witnesses for nearly five months and confirmed the whole indictment, he pressed his suit for the support of Woodsworth and the Progressives.

To win a vote of confidence he offered a high price. It was paid in Robb's "Sunshine Budget" of tax and tariff reductions; then, to satisfy Woodsworth, in a scheme of old-age pensions which a Conservative Senate promptly rejected, thus insuring Woodsworth's hostility to Meighen.

After softening up the cross-benches, King, the defendant, suddenly turned to the attack and denounced Meighen's Hamilton Speech for the constitutional absurdity it was. Meighen could not answer. King reduced him to quibbles, later to self-contradictions and finally to impotent rage.

So far, so good. To the delight of his followers King had made himself the friend of tax reduction for the benefit of the business community, the enemy of tariffs for the reassurance of the Progressives and the leader of social reform for the support of Woodsworth.

These were all deadly weapons. On March 3 King carried a vote of confidence 111 to 102 and soon had survived sixteen separate divisions. He had fulfilled, as he thought, his obligation to Byng. He had proved he could govern and was entitled to call an election whenever he pleased.

But as he well knew, these successful parliamentary skirmishes were fought on the outside perimeter of the approaching battle. Nothing mattered now except the Customs Committee. It reported on June 18, unanimously finding the Government guilty as charged. The battle was joined. Its outcome might not greatly affect the future of the nation. For King's career it meant survival or, more likely, downfall.

The Progressives were nauseated by the reeking stench of corruption. Even Woodsworth had wavered, feeling, as he said, like a man in a mud bath. Only the Unseen Hand could save King now. It remained unseen for two terrible weeks but it was still there.

Motions, counter-motions, days of wrangle on some minute point of order; nights of irrelevant procedural argument; questions of privilege; clanging of division bells; appeals to common sense, to the constitution and to God; another battering-ram attack from Stevens "with all the sympathy that one human heart can have for another"; a maiden speech of sheer havoc from Dunning; pleas for mercy from Mr. Speaker Lemieux after nine unbroken hours in his chair—all were heard by King and Meighen in silence. They were saving their energies for the ultimate confrontation.

It came on Stevens' amendment to the Customs Committee report. If the amendment passed, it would be a straight no-confidence vote and would defeat the Government. In these agonizing moments the Unseen Hand began to appear. Woodsworth, not loving King much but Meighen less, proposed, by a sub-amendment, that a royal commission continue the Customs investigation. This was not a no-confidence motion and King grasped it instantly as the only straw available in his shipwreck.

Considering that his Government was convicted of wholesale graft, that he had no case to argue, that his own party distrusted him, King's speech was one of the most notable ever delivered in Parliament.

He argued that the Government had learned of the Customs Scandal long before the Opposition and was cleansing its Augean stables when the Conservatives stole secret official reports and contrived their cheap political trick. Who was guilty—the Government which had already reformed the Customs Department, or the Opposition which sought to profit by the nation's calamity?

His face convulsed, his wisp of hair hanging damply across his forehead, his plump fists waving, his voice shouting above the hubbub, King had escaped from the prisoner's box to make himself the prosecutor. Now he launched the final indictment—Meighen was using the Customs Scandal to seize power, to fasten high tariffs on the nation and sell it to big business.

Meighen listened, unmoved, to this wild irrelevance but he must have realized it was an inspiration. For with the Progressives the tariff issue was still magical and with Woodsworth big business was evil incarnate. Yet the case against the Government was unanswerable and Meighen summed it up with icy logic. Besides, he had just learned that he had the necessary Progressive supporters.

At midnight, June 25, the division bells rang for a vote on the Woodsworth motion. As King watched, breathless, 115 members rose to approve it and 117 to oppose it. The Government had not been defeated in a technical sense but it had lost control of the House and it could not hope to outvote the Stevens motion of direct censure.

Ten minutes later, the House overruled Lemieux on a point of order. In the darkest night of King's life he found himself unable to carry even a motion to adjourn. It was 5 a.m. when a House exhausted, unshaven and bleary-eyed at last agreed to adjourn by a single vote.

King went home in the dawn, apparently undone, at the end of his career. Where was his infallible Guide? The Unseen Hand reappeared briefly on Sunday, directing King to dissolve Parliament. By entering an election still as Prime Minister he could escape from the prison of a hostile House and carry his appeal to the people.

It would be difficult to prove the Government's virginity after the rape of the Customs Department, more difficult to divert the public mind from that glaring issue and raise the pallid banner of economic reform. Nevertheless, it was his only chance. At noon Monday, he took it and drove to Rideau Hall.

There Byng crushed all his hopes by refusing him a dissolution. To the blunt soldier King's request seemed not only absurd but dishonest. Meighen was ready to govern if King could not. And King had promised last autumn that if he could not he would make way for Meighen.

In vain King pleaded that he had governed for nearly seven months, had carried many confidence motions and had never been actually defeated in Parliament. Byng considered this argument unsound in constitution and impractical in the nation's business. Coming from King, it was also the repudiation of a gentlemen's agreement. No, if King wished to resign Meighen must be called. Utterly broken, King resigned at once. The Unseen Hand had disappeared again.

As soon as the House, still ignorant of these events, assembled for business that afternoon King rose, tears oozing from his eyes, to say in a weak voice that he was no longer Prime Minister, only a private Member of Parliament. He therefore respectfully moved an adjournment—but not before he had uttered a lethal sentence whose meaning no one grasped. The Governor-General, he said, had "declined to accept my advice to grant a dissolution to which I believe under the British practice I am entitled."

Meighen sprang to his feet, dizzy with success. King cut him short. A motion to adjourn, he said, was not debatable. Meighen interrupted to propose a conference between himself and King for the dispatch of essential business. King ignored this reasonable request and his reply, though the House failed to understand it, opened a new field of dangerous possibilities: "Someone must assume, as His Excellency's adviser, the responsibility for His Excellency's refusal to grant a dissolution."

Would Meighen assume that responsibility? As the House adjourned King was afraid Meighen would refuse. A trap had been baited. King hardly dared to hope that Meighen would enter it. But the Unseen Hand was still at work. Byng summoned Meighen and asked him to form a government.

The Liberal myth, in one of its largest distortions, holds that Meighen did not see the trap, that, ravenous for power, he eagerly accepted Byng's invitation. The facts are quite different, as proved by the correspondence of the late Grant Dexter, a reliable reporter who enjoyed the trust of both Meighen and King.

Events were moving fast now, and in curious places.

Arthur Beauchesne, Clerk of the Commons, an accepted authority on the constitution and a passionate Conservative, immediately realized Meighen's danger. Beauchesne could hardly approach a party leader but he warned his friend, R. B. Hanson, the pleasant, bumbling Conservative boss of New Brunswick.

Having got the constitutional facts roughly in his mind, Hanson hurried to Meighen and found him conferring in his office with Borden. The two ex-Prime Ministers listened patiently to Hanson's advice. It was unnecessary.

Yes, they understood King's stratagem. They knew Meighen's danger. If Meighen accepted office King would argue that the Governor-General had violated the constitution by refusing a Liberal Prime Minister's advice to dissolve Parliament.

Meighen preferred to fight the election as leader of the Opposition against a Government totally discredited and certain of defeat. Yet how could he reject Byng's invitation? If he did, the Governor-General could not reappoint King, could find no Prime Minister and would be himself discredited. The Crown itself, said Meighen, would be humiliated and that, to a loyal British subject, was unthinkable.

While Meighen honestly felt his responsibility to the Crown, he wanted office also. He was aware of his risk but confident that he would overcome it. For surely no electorate would be stupid enough to think that King, after losing control of Parliament and being found guilty in the Customs Scandal, was entitled to govern? That, too, was unthinkable.

King, unaware of the argument in the enemy camp, waited on tenterhooks to see whether Meighen would enter the trap.

Contrary to the Liberal myth, King had not invented the trap. He had tried desperately to retain office. He had beseeched Byng, at three separate interviews, to grant him a dissolution. He had even asked Byng to seek instructions from London—this in comic contradiction of his whole record as the champion of Canadian autonomy.

If he had succeeded in these pleas then his Government un-doubtedly would have lost the ensuing election since it would appear only as the convicted defendant in the Customs Scandal. Luck and Byng saved King from this disaster and built the trap for Meighen.

All that his friends can truthfully say for King's wisdom—and it is a lot—is that after his resignation he saw the trap clearly, realized its full possibilities and sprang it skilfully. Most of his colleagues were doubtful. Like Meighen, the hard-boiled Liberal Party managers thought that the public would be little interested in the fine-spun constitutional issue which King was preparing to raise. The election would turn on the Customs Scandal and the Conservatives were bound to win it.

If so, King was finished. After his electoral defeat he would be replaced by Dunning. He did not know all the details of the Dunning movement (they were still locked in certain private files) but he knew that Dunning, though ambitious, would loyally support him through the present crisis and he knew that the crisis would settle his own fate. The immediate question was whether Meighen would enter the trap.

On Monday night the good news was flashed to Laurier House. Meighen had been appointed Prime Minister.

King went to work with a subtle artistry unprecedented in Canadian politics. He must not move too fast. He must not appear too eager. Above all, he must not offend the Progressives who still held the blue chips in the dubious poker game now opening. If they gave the Meighen Government a vote of confidence, King had no case. The refusal of a dissolution to him would be fully justified if Meighen could prove his ability to govern. At all costs, therefore, a vote of confidence must be prevented. Some of the wavering Progressives

226

must be persuaded that Meighen had usurped office, violated the constitution and imperilled the sacred rights of Parliament.

To arouse the Progressives on an abstract constitutional issue and make them forget the concrete facts of the Customs Scandal would be an almost impossible task but it was the only hope left.

On the other hand, Meighen faced greater difficulties than he yet understood. By accepting the Prime Ministership he had lost his seat in Parliament under the law of those days. He could not lead his Government in the House where all his genius of debate would be needed. He could not even appoint a normal Cabinet since ministers accepting Crown salaries must lose their seats also and their absence would dissipate the Government's last hope of a majority.

Meighen was thus driven to a device as strange as Macdonald's Double Shuffle. All the Cabinet members except himself were appointed as acting ministers who, in receipt of no salary, could retain their seats.

This egregious Government, a band of brief phantoms, occupied the Treasury benches on Tuesday afternoon, led by Sir Henry Drayton. King looked across the aisle from the Opposition with a frozen face. The Prime Minister stood behind a curtain and watched, seatless and speechless, but undaunted. What, after all, could King do now? His "constitutional froth," as Meighen called it, had evaporated. The Conservative ministry was securely in office.

Within minutes Meighen began to see from behind the curtain that King could do much. His first manoeuvre was to move that all censure in the Stevens motion, still unpassed, be stricken out and that a royal commission complete a study of the Customs Department under both Liberal and Conservative Governments.

The hapless Drayton lurched into his first mistake by arguing that the Liberal motion was out of order. King called for a division. On a vote of 115 to 114 the House ruled the motion in order. One hour after its arrival, the phantom Government had lost control of Parliament—for the moment only. The House promptly rejected the Liberal motion by 119 to 107 and then passed Stevens' motion of censure by 119 to 109.

The issue had been decided, the old Government found guilty, the new Government confirmed in office. The man behind the curtain felt safe at last. King's anger against the Progressives was almost uncontrollable but he hid it and prepared another gambit.

Next day he launched a transparent appeal for Progressive support by asking the House to declare that the Government's high tariffs were "detrimental to the country's prosperity."

The Progressives wanted tariffs much lower than King's but they also wanted a viable government and Meighen's looked better than the alternative of chaos. The tariff motion was rejected by 108 votes to 101.

Again King had been thwarted by his low-tariff allies. He said nothing. Lapointe exploded in bitter protest. Dunning's voice rose above the tumult to ask what sinister bargain the Government had made with his fellow Westerners.

At this ludicrous rift in the Opposition the man behind the curtain could afford a grim smile. He did not suspect that King's motions were only preliminary feints to test the ground for a final attack. It came on Wednesday night—came so blandly and stealthily that poor Drayton saw in it no more than an irrelevant point of order.

King had risen, with a look of boredom, to ask a routine question. All he wished to know was whether the gentlemen in the Treasury benches had "complied with constitutional practice in the matter of assuming office." Had Drayton taken any oath of office? The question seemed innocent, inconsequential, a waste of time. Actually it was the cutting edge of the trap. The second between King's question and Drayton's reply decided Meighen's doom.

Drayton said he had taken no oath but being a veteran Privy Councillor was naturally entitled to act as a Cabinet minister and sit in the House, provided he took no salary.

King, his face blank, repeated the question to the other acting ministers, as if he were examining a Sunday school class of small boys on their catechism. One by one Perley, R. J. Manion, Stevens and Guthrie bobbed up to repeat Drayton's answer. The constitutional trap had closed, but so silently that the Government suspected nothing.

A moment later King's face and manner changed. He pointed his finger at the acting ministers and accused them of usurping the Government of Canada. Having taken no oath of office, they had no right to govern. Either they must take their oath and resign their seats in Parliament, as Meighen had done, or they could not legally administer their departments. This shadow Government was illegal, a farce, a travesty of the constitutional system. By constructing it illegally, Meighen had mocked a thousand years of British practice. And if the crime succeeded, "what guarantee have we of future liberty and freedom in this country?"

Drayton and the shadows beside him protested feebly that everything was in order. Meighen fumed behind the curtain, knowing that if he could speak he would drown King in his constitutional froth. It was too late. The Progressives, pouring into the House from the smoke rooms, had begun to comprehend an issue far larger than the Customs Scandal. "Keep cool, boys," Lapointe cried across the aisle. "It's only beginning."

King's energies had been drained by a week of private torture, he was depleted, sick and desperate but now he felt the Unseen Hand again. It lifted him suddenly to the highest moment of his life. All his toil, his triumphs and defeats, all the memories of his mother and the legends of his grandfather issued in a torrent of clumsy eloquence, the words gushing out above the taunts and laughter of the Conservative benches. They saw the Rebel incarnate in his grandson and jeered to hide their alarm.

"You're thinking of '37!" screamed a Conservative voice.

That slur was all King needed to build his climax.

"Yes!" he shouted back. "Yes, I am thinking of '37 and I tell my honourable friend that I was never prouder in my life than to have the privilege of standing in this Parliament tonight on behalf of British parliamentary institutions. . . . Do the honourable gentlemen opposite advocate that we go back to a condition of affairs in Canada worse than anything that existed in 1837? . . . We have reached a condition in this country that threatens constitutional liberty, freedom and right in all parts of the world!"

At this hyperbole the Conservatives laughed again but uneasily. They could see that the Progressives were listening to King with stern and eager faces.

Now he brought his second indictment. It was contradictory in logic, killing in politics, and it raised an issue which constitutionalists are still arguing in our time.

Though he later took just the opposite position, King admitted that Byng had been entitled to refuse his request for a dissolution if Meighen could govern. For the Governor-General, King hastily added, he had "the greatest affection possible," but he was indicting Byng just the same.

In the next breath, contradicting his earlier statement, he declared that no British monarch had refused his Prime Minister's advice for a hundred years and if a Governor-General could do so then he "reduces this Dominion of Canada from the status of a self-governing Dominion to the status of a Crown Colony."

The Constitutional Crisis, as it was to be fought before the voters, was thus defined and from its conflicting elements King had fashioned the best of all possible worlds. On the one hand, he was the nationalist fighting for Canada's sovereignty. On the other, he was defending the Crown from Meighen who would impair it by his bad advice and lust for power. More than that, he was defending the British Empire which rested "upon the cornerstone of responsible self-government" and without it could not endure.

This, whatever the constitutionalists might say, was a flash of sheer political genius. The tiny man shouting his awkward sentences through the tumult had summoned up the rival ghosts of the Canadian memory as his allies and, with them, had ambushed Meighen from two sides.

It was midnight, the last moment of June, as King sank into his chair, breathless but triumphant. The nation was asleep and had not heard him. Most of his arguments, and fortunately their radical contradiction, would be forgotten in the dawn but a residue would remain. King had defied an Englishman to govern Canada with the aid of an ambitious Conservative adviser. He had identified himself with the nation's independence, Meighen with its old subservience to Britain. Equally miraculous, he had buried the Customs Scandal beyond resurrection.

The man behind the curtain had listened more in contempt than in anxiety. King's speech was worse than constitutional froth. It was plain factual nonsense. Who would understand, much less follow, such paltry hair-splitting?

Meighen went to bed satisfied that he could govern and, if necessary, win an election. But far beyond the curtain and the hill of Parliament the whole political balance was shifting in the first hours of the strangest Dominion Day since Confederation.

On July 1 Meighen felt his first misgivings. The Conservative whips reported at noon that many of the Progressives were returning to King. In the division to be called that night the Government's life seemed to hang on one or two doubtful votes.

Meighen ordered an attack on King to reverse the damage of his latest speech and meanwhile the whips worked on the undecided Progressives. All day and all evening Conservative speakers, hastily crammed with constitutional precedents, tried desperately to substitute for Meighen's missing eloquence and blunt King's double-edged weapon of nationalism and imperialism.

King replied briefly that Meighen had lost control of the House. His advice to Byng had been proved wrong and he should resign. While King still entertained the chance of a recall to office, it probably would have assured his defeat since he must then fight the election on the defensive. Fortunately for him there was no chance of that.

Meighen would not resign and force Byng to humiliate himself by summoning King again. Instead, if defeated in the House, Meighen would be given the dissolution refused to King who had never been formally defeated. Both Governor-General and Prime Minister would be convicted of violating the constitution, infringing Canada's independence and undermining the foundations of the Empire.

The mixture of Canadian passions thus released was perfect for King's strategy but without the defeat of the Government his trap and all his hopes would collapse. If Meighen survived this night's vote he was safe. By King's own admission, Meighen had a right to govern and secure a dissolution at his own pleasure.

The chimes of the Victory Tower were clanging midnight when King called for a show-down. His colleague, Robb, moved a motion declaring that the shadow Cabinet, if legal, had no right to sit in the House and, if illegal, no right to transact business.

Two more hours of wrangle followed while whips on both sides pleaded with the Progressives. The clamour of personal argument and soul-searching in the lobbies drowned the debate in the House. Mr. Speaker protested that he could not hear the proceedings. No one was concerned with them anyway. King, the man of the past or of the future, sat silent in his chair, awaiting the verdict. Where was the Unseen Hand? Not far away as it turned out.

At 2 A.M., July 2, the division bells rang. The Members filed into the House. As the clerk counted the Opposition votes the Government saw that something had gone terribly wrong. Instead of 95, those votes totaled 96. And when the Conservatives stood up they numbered only 95. The Meighen Government had been defeated as no government had ever been defeated in Parliament before.

Defeated by one vote, but where had it come from? In the sudden silence T. W. Bird, Progressive of Nelson, rose to offer a shamefaced explanation. As a supporter of the Opposition he had been paired with an absent supporter of the Government and, by the rules of parliamentary honour, had been bound not to vote. Nevertheless, to his "extreme regret," he had cast his vote "inadvertently."

King leaped up, almost ill with success, but still able to hurl a last dagger at the man behind the curtain. "I shall assume," he said coolly, "that the Prime Minister will immediately advise His Excellency that this House has declared that his Government has no right to be in existence and that he has found it impossible to carry on."

The Prime Minister had no doubt that he could carry on and win an election. Next morning, on his advice, Byng dissolved Parliament.

A dissolution refused to the technically undefeated King had been granted to the formally defeated Meighen. That was all King asked. Thanks to a broken parliamentary pair, his Constitutional Issue had been exactly shaped for him. It had been shaped by the Unseen Hand.

The game, however, was far from won. King had passed the latest of many watersheds but in terms of political possibility, and the apparent impossibility of his own situation, the barrier now ahead towered like the Rockies. He led a party convicted of graft and deep damnation. He had nothing to offer except his abstract Constitutional Issue and the public could hardly be expected to understand it. The Liberal bosses must help him through one more election, since there was no alternative, but were preparing to appoint his successor as soon as he had failed.

Aware of all this, King set out with his papers in a black wooden box, which his secretary mislaid. Happily the man who thought of everything had taken the precaution to load a duplicate box on the train. Among its contents was Meighen's political death sentence.

From city to city, from hamlet to hamlet, often speaking from the rear platform of the train, King delivered a rousing message. As all practical politicians agreed, it was far above the public's head and, as Meighen thought, beneath its contempt.

At first the argument was complex, twisted and, to the ordinary citizen, incomprehensible. After laying down the record or, as Meighen believed, distorting it outrageously, King began to concentrate on the single proposition that a British Governor-General had rejected the advice of his Canadian Prime Minister, had refused dissolution to an undefeated Government and given it to the defeated successor. Thus Byng and Meighen (" a self-appointed dictator") had reduced Canada to the level of a British colony and subverted the liberties of its people.

Then, having invoked one of the strongest Canadian instincts, King invoked its opposite. In subverting the nation's independence, he said, Meighen had threatened its ancient links with Britain by subverting British parliamentary principles. Proclaiming himself at once the only defender of Canadian autonomy and the British connection, King bestrode both worlds. He had contrived a feat of constitutional jugglery superior even to Macdonald's Double Shuffle.

Would the people accept it? Could they be moved by such a combination of fine-spun legal reasoning, sentiment and prejudice?

Meighen thought not and declined to debate these irrelevancies. Instead, he dismissed King as a man who had clung to office like "a lobster with the lockjaw," who was suffering from "constitutional fleabitis" and now had the effrontery to practise a sordid sea-lawyer's trick at the expense of the Crown.

Never had Meighen spoken more eloquently or less effectively. Even in his mood of scorn and confidence he began to see that the Constitutional Issue, phony as he deemed it, had cut straight to the bone of Canada. The people might not understand it but their ambivalent emotions of geography and history were deeply stirred. Those old ghosts of Canadian independence and British nostalgia were flying to King's rescue.

It was maddening. Worse, a new and unfamiliar King had emerged, to the amazement of friend and foe alike. No longer the obese prig of his earlier days but a mature fighting man now raged and thundered across the land. Still more incredible, King had achieved real eloquence at last and a glint of passion because he believed passionately in his own case.

As he had never been before and would never be again, he was, in his own mind anyway, the true reincarnation of his grandfather, challenging a new Family Compact. While his secretaries wilted, he thrived on a few hours' sleep nightly, delivered half a dozen speeches daily and never doubted the result. This he would always remember as his finest hour. He had made it, and now lived it, alone.

Too late, Meighen watched the tide of constitutional froth rising to drown him. He argued with all his cold logic, his cleanly prose and flashing invective until his voice failed and his strength was spent. The facts of record should be clear enough to the intelligent jury of the electorate; but the political facts seemed unbelievable. The jury was actually deceived by a bogus case and a tawdry charlatan. King was winning. And in Rideau Hall, where he could say nothing, Byng saw himself betrayed, the Crown dishonoured. To his dying day he would never forgive King.

Considering the odds against him, King's victory on the night of September 14 has no Canadian equivalent. He won 128 parliamentary seats to the Government's 91 and he could count on the support of a total of 26 Liberal Progressives, Alberta farm candidates, and surviving Progressives. He controlled Parliament. Like no leader except Laurier, he controlled the Liberal Party; and he would control it without challenge for the next two decades. Byng and Meighen, both honourable men but ignorant of the Canadian mind, had united to save their enemy. In King's mind, however, there was more to it than that. His victory must be the work of God.

Whatever its source, it was a mighty work. In seven years King had taken the Liberal ruins left by Laurier and built of them the most durable party that Canada had ever known or was likely to know. He had engorged the Progressives and permanently destroyed Meighen. He had all but completed the structure of Canadian autonomy as half built by Macdonald, Laurier and Borden. Best of all—an indescribable sweetness in his soul—he had vindicated his mother, his grandfather and himself.

At this very hour of vindication, as if success had intoxicated him, he began to squander his assets.

The four years of anticlimax after the triumph of 1926 must baffle the student of King's mentality. What went wrong with the reincarnated Rebel? What turned him into a social reactionary? Whence came a sudden blindness to isolate him from events and deny all his youthful prophecy?

None of these questions occurred to anybody, least of all to King himself, as he settled down to govern in comfort at last without threat in Parliament or party.

The Cabinet, with the addition of James Layton Ralston and later on of Crerar (who thus interred the Progressive revolt) was competent and, for the time being, free of serious quarrel. The country was prosperous, its finances flourishing, its people happily bemused by the pleasant preliminary tremors of the bull market. The world was at peace. Evidently the Good Society of King's book was arriving under its own steam and required little help from him.

For the first time the Prime Minister could take things easy. He expanded his Kingsmere estate, his several houses and his fake ruins. He withdrew more and more into solitude as a tweedy squire but never for a moment did he relax his grip on all the distant levers of the Liberal machine. Occasionally he appeared in public as the oracle of Liberalism which, he announced, was the future struggling against the past. And in these diversions he lost all touch with the present.

It was a simple business, at the Imperial Conference of 1926, to confirm the autonomy of the overseas dominions in the Balfour Declaration, since that fight had been won already.

It was exhilarating, soul-warming and fatuous to sign the Briand-Kellogg Pact, a sure guarantee, as he reported on his return from Paris, that there were "no more wars to be averted, or rumours of war to be quieted."

It was inspiring to hear, and almost unanimous lunacy to believe, his assurance of perpetual human progress. "How mighty," he cried, "has become the power which now holds the peace of the world as the most sacred of all moral and national obligations! . . . What the world chiefly needs today, in my judgment, is to cast aside suspicion and distrust between nation and nation and not merely to feel greater confidence in each other but to display it."

It was gratifying in the spring of 1929 for King to inform Parliament that "we have the prosperity at which we aimed and we intend to maintain it and, if possible to increase it" with more reductions of tariffs and taxes.

Meanwhile it was of little consequence that the Conservative Party had chosen a new leader, R. B. Bennett, who had once attacked Meighen as the gramophone of Mackenzie and Mann, and now replaced him with a more gaudy rhetoric and, as King thought, an absurd revival of protectionism.

All was well in King's little world. In the world at large he misconstrued everything.

His illusions were pierced by the news of October 29, 1929. Even then the great economist could not understand the meaning of the Wall Street crash, could not see that it had instantly fulfilled his own youthful predictions and revealed the flaws in capitalism which he had temporarily forgotten. The predicted catastrophe was here but he simply could not believe it.

Persuading himself that the technical stock-market adjustment would soon pass, he refused to consider any serious economic reform. He refused to admit that the growing unemployment problem was any responsibility of the national Government. The social revolution of his own preaching had begun but, coming so soon, caught him unprepared. His leisurely timetable had lapsed and he could not readjust himself to the new tempo of events.

Instinctively he reverted to the classic Liberalism of *laissez-faire,* held down public spending, though the nation's most urgent need was additional purchasing power, and waited for a brief storm to blow itself out. Then, while the depression deepened in 1930 and Bennett's campaign for the infallible cure-all of high tariffs caught fire, King momentarily lost his head.

He was tired that day by over-work, infuriated by Bennett and frightened by the political prospects when, in a single sentence, he assured the Liberal Party's defeat.

The provinces, he informed Parliament, were asking for federal money to relieve the unemployed but many of them were governed provincially by Conservatives and "I would not give a single cent to any Tory government!"

The Liberals gasped. The rejoicing Conservatives shouted

"Shame!" Now quite beside himself, King lunged deeper into the quicksand as if he were driven by a death wish: "May I repeat what I have said? With regard to giving moneys out of the federal treasury to any Tory government in this country for these alleged unemployment purposes while those governments situated as they are today with policies diametrically opposed to those of this Government, I would not give them a five-cent piece!"

All the perfumes of Arabia and all King's laborious explanations could not sweeten the five-cent speech. Not only had he failed to understand the nation's dilemma but he had played party politics with the misery of the poor.

The people could not forgive him in the election of 1930. Would they ever forgive him? That seemed improbable on the night of July 28. Bennett had elected 137 members against King's 91 and 17 independents.

The Conservative Party was back in office. King secluded himself at Kingsmere and cultivated the legend that he had deliberately sought opposition while his successor perished in bad times. The legend was false. King had tried desperately to win the election and had expected to win it.

Afterwards, he perceived the Unseen Hand in his defeat, reread his neglected *Industry and Humanity,* returned to the economic heresies of his young days and, with growing reverence for God's wisdom, watched Bennett's first acts of suicide.

But King had failed to note one flaw in these satisfactory arrangements. A second scandal, worse than the first, was about to explode within the Liberal Party.

13: The Great Man

"That solitary figure toiling up the heights," wrote Bob Edwards in his disreputable and glorious *Calgary Eye Opener*, "is R. B. Bennett." Now the toiler was at the pinnacle. Since he could share power with no one, he must hold it alone or fall like Lucifer.

As he took office after what King was candid enough to call the greatest personal victory in Canadian politics, the fall of Bennett seemed remote. Certainly King could not precipitate it. But King had an ally, not yet recognized, and Bennett an immeasurable vanity which must erode a talent of equal dimensions and end in bottomless regret. The most fascinating story of success and failure that Canada has ever witnessed, the ultimate drama of hubris and nemesis, was under way.

It had been in systematic preparation for sixty years. Almost from his birth Richard Bedford Bennett had discerned his own genius. Like King, he understood in boyhood that he was to be a man of destiny. The judgment, in both cases, was accurate. Two boys, born within four years of each other and in pretty similar circumstances, held between them the destiny of Canada at the opening of our current age.

The Bennetts were of English stock, had moved with the New England Loyalists to New Brunswick and had lived in America for nine generations before the future Prime Minister's triumphant and unhappy life began at the village of Hopewell, on July 3, 1870.

His father, Henry J. Bennett, once a prosperous sea captain and builder of sailing ships but now impoverished by the new day of steam, wrung a scant livelihood from a small farm at Hopewell

Cape. Still, his family of three sons and two daughters never knew real poverty.

They were superior folk by the standards of their neighbours. The mother, Henrietta, who had been a school-teacher, gave the children a flavour of learning and refinement in the comfortable home.

Richard was her favourite and he adored her. Even in later years, when he was overwhelmed with work, he spent Christmas Day with her so long as she lived. Here the lifelong parallel between Bennett and King first appeared. Neither son could ever give himself wholly to any woman except his mother.

Those parallel lines, later meeting in collision, continued throughout the years of youth. Bennett milked the cows, mowed the fields and chopped the trees of the little seaside farm but, like King's, his mind was on books and filled with youth's long, long thoughts.

By the time he had passed through the public school at Hope-well and won a teaching certificate at Fredericton, Bennett was telling his friends that he would become Prime Minister and then sit in the British Parliament. Both predictions would be fulfilled.

The savings from his first teacher's salary of $160 a year at Irishtown and later of $500 at Douglastown, took Bennett, aged nineteen, to Dalhousie University where he eked out his small resources as librarian of the law school. Like King, he kept a meticulous record of his expenses to the last nickel, as he would do after he became rich, and he devoted himself, without the distraction of athletics, hobbies, drink, tobacco or any pleasure, to his legal studies. He proved to be such a clumsy soldier, in the summer militia camp, that he was made paymaster, a job he would perform as perfectly as he dealt, later on, in billions. After graduation he entered a law office at Chatham.

Already, on a Miramichi River steamboat, he had met a boy of ten named William Maxwell Aitken and formed a friendship which would alter both their lives and deeply affect the life of Canada.

The future Lord Beaverbrook recalls, in his moving little book, *Friends,* that Bennett was then "tall, austere, forbidding, conscious of coming greatness" but "self-deprecating to a degree." He wore a bowler hat, several sizes too large, over a lean, freckled face. His manners were elaborate, his speech an uninterrupted monologue, as it would always be.

Sometimes, says Beaverbrook, Bennett would display "a streak of egotism" and a habit of "dramatising himself." Self-drama and egotism were to be his trade marks to the end. At any fancied affront his temper was uncontrollable, "his face would turn pale and his eyes would change in colour. His neck visibly swelled." He used flattery on others, and enjoyed it in return.

This early portrait is not particularly attractive but Beaverbrook worshipped Bennett then and until death parted them sixty years later.

Theirs was the inseparable friendship of opposites—Bennett the stern, teetotal Methodist Sunday school teacher, reading his Bible daily, quoting it constantly and denouncing sin at temperance meetings; Aitken, a minister's son, questioning orthodox beliefs, playful, practical and determined to enjoy all the worldly satisfactions. The two youths were alike only in their ambition, their appetite for wealth and their lofty vision of the British Empire.

Aitken, delivering leaflets on his bicycle, helped Bennett's election to the Chatham town council, the first rung of a tall ladder, and followed him when, in 1896, he moved to Calgary and the law office of Senator James Lougheed.

Bennett was soon a rising figure in the prosperous little cow town but never shared its gambling, hard-drinking western life. He occupied a single room in the Alberta Hotel and ate heavily in its dingy restaurant to put weight on his slight frame and make himself look more imposing to legal clients. This effort succeeded rapidly and produced the rotund, impressive portrait of his mature years.

Bennett was overjoyed to have Aitken with him again but lectured the younger man on his careless ways and was shocked to learn that he had opened a bowling alley and was himself setting up the pins for customers. The humble foundation of a mighty fortune had been laid. To Bennett, however, Aitken's first business venture was a grievous sin. For several days the friends did not speak to each other. This, like larger quarrels still far distant, was soon healed.

Aitken moved east again and on to England. Bennett remained in Calgary, built up an affluent legal practice, invested his profits shrewdly and, in his thirties, was a millionaire.

Another youthful friendship multiplied his wealth. Jennie Shirreff, a playmate of his childhood, had married E. B. Eddy and, at her death, willed Bennett control of a huge match factory in Hull; concerning which his eminent fellow townsman and sardonic orator, Leonard Brockington, said in a banquet speech that "there is a tide in the affairs of men which, taken at the Eddy, leads on to fortune." We have it from Beaverbrook that there was no more than platonic friendship between Bennett and his benefactress.

Though he had told Beaverbrook, at the age of thirty-four, that he was "almost an old man" and would never marry, Bennett courted several ladies, actually proposed to one of them but failed to find a wife. Here, also, the parallel to King's strange love life is arresting.

Bennett enjoyed more than his rival, and pursued with greater success, the society of women, whose favours were not withheld. His reputation as a gallant was to produce, years later, King's most famous jest as Prime Minister. Asked by an indignant Member of Parliament from the Doukhobor district of British Columbia what he would do if he confronted a parade of nude women, King grinned slyly across at Bennett in the Conservative benches and replied: "I'd send for the leader of the Opposition."

A sharper wit, Bob Edwards, long conducted in his *Eye Opener* a campaign of searing ribaldry against Bennett as the western solicitor of the Canadian Pacific Railway. After publishing photographs of every railway accident in the country, Edwards printed a picture of Bennett under the heading, "Another C.P.R. Wreck." This lively feud ended on a Sunday morning. The upright Methodist and the town's brilliant drunkard met by chance at a church service and became friends. For all his scowling austerity, Bennett could turn charm on and off at will. At times he was loved, at times hated.

Wealth he now had in plenty but it did not satisfy him. As he had predicted to his first friend in Chatham, politics were to be his career. He was driven to public life by a boundless ego, a devout sense of duty, a natural aptitude, an unfailing courage and an unlimited faith in Canada as the future hub of the Empire. From 1898 to 1905 he sat as a Conservative in the Northwest Territories Assembly, was elected to the new Alberta Legislature in 1909 and to Parliament in 1911.

His legend had preceded him to Ottawa. "Bonfire Bennett," as he was called in the West for his fiery style of speech, could utter 220 words a minute, as registered by a stopwatch, never missing a syllable or misplacing a predicate. Without a note to guide him, his language flowed like a purling brook, a swelling stream and, as he gathered momentum, like a prairie river in muddy spring freshet, while the Hansard reporters despaired. In public or private, only sleep could interrupt that burble of elegant English.

Even if he had only one listener he seemed to address a public meeting, always in three-piled hyperbole. It was good talk, for he seemed to know everything. From law, business and books he had picked up an inexhaustible smattering of information which he expounded compulsively in Parliament, in conversation and in massive correspondence. His knowledge for the most part was thin but amazingly diverse, as if he had ravened through the encyclopedia. During my only long talk with him, after he had passed his prime, Bennett leaped from the Canadian tariff to the wars of Caesar, the china of the Ming dynasty, the American Revolution, the cavalry tactics of Oliver Cromwell and the problems of Quebec, ending on the prophetic note of a beaten man. "You will live," he said, "to see Canada split along the Ottawa River."

Such was the arresting, almost overpowering personality who rode into Ottawa from the West like young Lochinvar with the victory of Borden's Conservatives. Bennett immediately broached his railway quarrel with Meighen. Then, denied a Cabinet post, he quickly tired of the Commons and sought a seat in the Senate where he would be free of party ties to advocate his philosophy of a united Empire.

Borden refused him a senatorship and Bennett sulked until the First World War gave him scope for his extraordinary administrative talents as Director General of National Service, or chief recruiting officer. In the election of 1917 he retired from politics, apparently for good, convinced by now, as he wrote to Beaverbrook, that Canada probably would be part of the United States within a generation.

The retirement, naturally, was brief. Their parliamentary quarrel ended, Meighen gave Bennett the portfolio of Justice in the fly-by-night Government of 1921. The new minister was defeated by sixteen ballots in Calgary, only because his confident friends thought it unnecessary to vote. He was elected in 1925, entered the phantom Cabinet of 1926 as Minister of Finance but was absent in Calgary, to fulfil a speaking engagement, as the Government fell. Afterwards he always believed that if he had been in Ottawa during those hectic hours he could have saved Meighen from his blundering lieutenants and King's constitutional trap.

Meighen's contest with King was finished, or seemed to be. Bennett's had begun. When Meighen retired at the convention of 1927 the succession was unquestioned. By his success in law and business, by his wealth and oratory, by his bravura and nimbus of piety, Bennett had earned the Conservative leadership and quickly justified the convention's choice.

He admitted to the delegates that he was a rich man but looked upon his fortune "as a solemn trust in my hands to enable me to serve my country without fear or regard for the future. . . No man may serve you as he should if he has over his shoulder always the shadow of pecuniary obligations. . . . Such as I have I consecrate with myself to this service in which I am."

Canada now surveyed the first truly rich man to lead a political party. Wealth was not, perhaps, a serious liability in the days of the bull market. Nor did it seem to damage its owner even after the crash of 1929. The nation, Bennett and King all regarded the crash as a temporary readjustment in a permanent economic system. Surely a man who understood the system as well as Bennett was best qualified to fix it.

Besides, Bennett wore a convincing air of authority. He was Success incarnate. His tall, stout figure, his round, unwrinkled face, as if made of ruddy porcelain, the shining dome of his forehead, the golden glint of his pince-nez, the invariable wing collar, flowing cravat and pearl pin, the superbly cut tail coats of varied colours which he usually changed twice a day, all conveyed an impression of power, knowledge and virtue. In his presence King appeared tiny, hesitant and weak.

Ponderous and unruffled, Bennett strode through the election campaign of 1930 rather like a magnificently caparisoned elephant in a durbar. His manner was at once lofty and sympathetic. His radiant smile encouraged the weak and humble. As he lowered his massive head and glared over his glasses the strong quailed. Before a vast audience or a small group he struck a pose of natural sublimity. No more than King could he ever be one of the boys but he seemed to symbolize and promise that age of abundance which, briefly lost, would quickly return under his guidance.

His speeches lacked the light, human touch of Macdonald and Laurier, they could never achieve Meighen's cutting edge; but whereas King's platitudes were oozing and oleaginous, Bennett's had the ring of Scripture. Ranging through the whole diapason, his musical voice could supply, as needed, the liquid notes of the flute or the tympanic thunder of the drums.

While it listened to this mighty orchestration, a hopeful public failed to note that Bennett had said nothing new, that all his ideas were as old as Canada, that his cure for the depression would only worsen it. Given his premise, his policies were unanswerable. Unfortunately the premise was wrong, as he would discover for himself within five years. He held all the passports of success, save one. Bennett completely misunderstood the situation of Canada and the world.

Briefly, his program called for the economic reintegration of the Empire in a prosperous trading bloc immune to the world's distress.

"I am for the British Empire next to Canada," he said, "the only difference being that some [Liberal] gentlemen are for the United States before Canada. I am for the British Empire after Canada"— a long way after, as it turned out.

His Canadian nationalism, sincere, crude and obsolete, assumed that the depression could be cured almost overnight if imports—an economic folly and a moral iniquity—were sufficiently restricted. Nothing that could be made in Canada, almost regardless of cost, should be bought from foreigners or even from Britain. High tariffs, in short, tariffs carrying the National Policy to its logical conclusion, were the simple, unfailing answer to the nation's dilemma.

At Winnipeg, on June 9, he proclaimed his faith to the free-trade prairie farmers: "You say our tariffs are only for the manufacturers. I will make them fight for you as well. I will use them to blast a way into the markets that have been closed to you." And then he uttered the phrase that must doom his career. He would end unemployment "or perish in the attempt."

The attempt began on August 7, 1930, when Bennett formed a Cabinet, most of whose original members are now forgotten. Only five of them—Stevens, Manion, Guthrie, Perley and E. N. Rhodes —have any interest for historians and they not much. A wiser colleague was added, eighteen months later, by Meighen's appointment as government leader in the Senate.

Even with Meighen beside him, Bennett remained his own one-man government to the end. As Prime Minister, Minister of Finance, Minister of External Affairs, and Grand Panjandrum, he erected a personal dictatorship—benign, strictly honest, industrious, competent but entirely dependent on its boss. What was to be called, in our time, the cult of personality had arrived.

The Prime Minister, who had never owned a home of his own, now occupied a huge suite in the Chateau Laurier, rose at 7:30 A.M., dressed himself with foppish care (he did not employ a valet), and resplendent in top hat or bowler, cut-away coat, cane and gloves, walked up the Hill to his office (his only exercise) before nine o'clock.

Then he worked steadily for fifteen or sixteen hours, with a brief interruption for lunch and a leisurely dinner in his suite, where he usually consumed a pound of chocolates every night and occasionally, if he had guests, would stretch his principles to drink a thimble-ful of *crème de menthe* since he considered it non-alcoholic. Several times a week expert massage would substitute for exercise. The Chateau barbers grew prosperous on his tips.

Radiant health and unquestioned faith in himself supported

enough daily work to occupy the whole Cabinet, which he treated as a staff of servants.

Bennett was everywhere, in person or by telephone, doing everything. He brought into government the direct methods and mechanical efficiency of big business. His booming voice on the wire would by-pass a Cabinet minister and issue instructions to some minor official. A corps of stenographers strove desperately to keep up with his flood of letters and memoranda. The House of Commons heard him, often several times a day, with amazement. He discussed every detail of government business, from some post office in Kamloops to a wharf in Lunenberg, from high finance to the cost of binder twine.

Yet he never became lost in this forest of minutiae. He always knew what he was doing in great or small affairs, never doubted that he was right, never in his whole parliamentary life admitted a mistake. Better than King, if a mistake had been made, Bennett would wriggle out of it by lawyer's sophistry or sweep it away with a gust of moral indignation against those too blind or stupid to understand his larger purposes.

He could be big or small, generous or mean, ruthless or sentimental. His gifts of money to the Conservative Party and to public charities were enormous. He helped many unknown boys through college and made a lifelong allowance to a woman whose son he had sent to prison. Like King, however, he grudged adequate wages to his domestics, he flew into frequent rages, poured praise on some quivering secretary and wept over the novels of Robert Louis Stevenson.

Such an august person was never called, even behind his back, by his Christian or any nickname. Respectful initials identified the brooding presence of Chateau and East Block. Too remote for familiarity, Bennett became "R. B."

As he had promised, and never questioning the results, he raised the tariff to a new peak, contrived ingenious regulations to restrict imports where the tariff failed and, at an Imperial Conference, persuaded or bullied the British Government into a plan of Empire consolidation. This historic departure was scheduled for the summer of 1932. Meanwhile he signed the Statute of Westminster, completing the work of Canadian autonomy.

The public mind, however, had been diverted from this constitutional landmark and the Government's basic policy by the explosion of a new scandal.

The facts disinterred by a parliamentary committee were horrifying and undeniable. To secure invaluable concessions on the St. Lawrence, a gang of piratical promoters, called the Beauharnois Power Company, had contributed between $600,000 and $700,000 to the Liberal Party before the election of 1930.

An evident sell-out of public resources for campaign funds was bad enough but not unfamiliar. What seemed to ruin King was the discovery that his hotel bill of $283.53, on a Bermuda holiday, had been paid by Senator Wilfrid Laurier McDougald, the front man of the promotion, who had been recouped by the Beauharnois treasury. For the first and last time in his life, King's financial honour had been questioned.

The Customs Scandal had not touched him personally. Could he survive a second scandal which not only touched him but suggested the corruption of his entire Government? Survival would have been impossible in normal times. Happily for King, the times were not normal.

He did not attempt to defend his campaign-fund collectors; admitted, in words of genuine remorse, that the Liberal Party was in "the valley of humiliation"; but Bennett evidently believed him when he said that he had been amazed to discover that his hotel bill had been paid by the Beauharnois Company and not, as he had supposed, by a personal friend.

Left there, King's defence would have been impressive and manly—the upright party leader betrayed, the honest man in a den of thieves. Even Bennett nodded sympathetically across the House. But then King went on, with repulsive holiness, to deny that he had ever known anything about campaign funds or been influenced by them in his public policies. Bennett, on the other hand, had rejected Beauharnois money, after learning that his Party had accepted thirty thousand dollars, and thus said King, must have been fully aware of these sinister arrangements. Perhaps Bennett also knew of contributions to the Conservative Party from other corporations that benefited from his high tariffs?

This brazen attempt by the guilty to indict the innocent was more than Bennett could stomach. "Outrageous!" he shouted. And when King asked him meekly whether a party leader could be expected to keep account of political finances, Bennett retorted: "I have always held that the receiver of stolen goods was a criminal."

King had used candour, repentance and innuendo to make the best of an impossible situation. Next day Bennett's reply demolished all these flimsy pretences. The great courtroom prosecutor, who had sent so many criminals to jail, turned on King a torrent of invective, sarcasm and evidence such as Parliament had never heard since the days of Blake and the Pacific Scandal. That speech, uncanny in its grasp of detail, its clarity and its damning logic, lifted Bennett to the apex of his career. Apparently he had crushed his enemy and his Government was invulnerable.

Alas, he could not see it yet but from this summit the path could lead only to an abyss. For now the fetor of Beauharnois was forgotten in the human stench of poverty. No man or government could survive the nation's travail. The Constitutional Crisis had rescued King from the Customs Scandal, the first mild impact of the depression had unhorsed him but now it turned on Bennett and obliterated all other business from the public mind.

Drought on the Prairies year after year, fields naked and blowing away, wheat prices at sixty cents a bushel and little wheat to sell; most farmers living, half-starved, on government relief; thousands of men and boys riding the freight trains from coast to coast in vain search of employment or charity; provinces virtually, and municipalities literally, bankrupt; the nation dumb and apathetic under a shock unbelievable, inexplicable, unlike anything in its experience—this was the Great Depression, King's only useful friend and Bennett's implacable enemy.

With time to meditate his own blunders in the quietude of Kingsmere, to re-study his *Industry and Humanity*, to consult wiser economists and begin to frame a policy, King was soon ready to strike. He struck on June 16, 1931.

His customary sprawling speech was not a success, it merely irritated Bennett and brought the usual sulphurous reply, but King had finally realized that the depression could not be cured by either Bennett's methods or his own. It was not an aberration, as he had thought in office. It was the symptom of the revolution that he had predicted in his youth and had failed to recognize in his age. Certainly, he said, the restriction of trade would not cure it. Bennett's tariffs would only compound it by throttling the national economy.

There followed a significant phrase which Bennett dismissed as more of his opponent's usual claptrap. The capitalist system, said King, "is under fire, it is on trial, it is being investigated and I hope, indeed, I believe, it is being modified." Bennett merely snorted, unaware that in less than four years he would be saying the same thing with more sombre warning.

For the moment the contest between these two men missed the central point of the depression altogether. Their months of argument were almost irrelevant and, in retrospect, seem almost laughable.

On the one hand, Bennett thought he could use the tariff as a magic wand in the domestic market and blast open foreign markets, though the world economy was withering, and the makers of war were emerging from the strangulation of international commerce.

On the other hand, while King understood this process clearly, he was still blind to the second side of the depression. That it was caused basically by a lack of purchasing power throughout the world, that it could be at least ameliorated by public spending, that ample goods in the warehouses could be conveyed to the Canadian people through the mechanism of money—these were plain facts but intolerable heresies to King's old Liberalism.

With what appears now as economic idiocy, King denounced even Bennett's niggardly budgets as extravagant and ruinous—"the Government's promises of yesterday are the taxes of today." When President Roosevelt arrived in Washington a little later with his promise to balance the American budget, and undertook the opposite spending policies of the New Deal, King regarded them as the work of an economic illiterate.

In justice to Bennett it must be remembered that his trade restrictions were duplicated by all countries. In justice to both Bennett and King it must be remembered that they had been born in the age of *laissez-faire* and now lived in the age of the world's higher lunacy, whose harvest we are still reaping.

The state of Canada then, within the worldwide madness, is believable only to those who saw it at first hand—its numb misery, its dull hopelessness, its total misconception of its own problem. Truly, the wonder is not that Bennett failed to solve the problem, for no leader or nation could solve it alone, but that Canada survived the almost unendurable strains of the nineteen-thirties.

Bennett survived them, and all his personal strains, because he had equal faith in himself and the system he represented.

"I have not seen," he wrote to a puzzled citizen, "any suggested changes that could replace our existing system without entirely eliminating one of the factors in our civilization that has contributed greatly to the progress of the world—that is, individual initiative, coupled with the desire to achieve and succeed."

In the same vein he hushed the Commons and drew applause from the Opposition with his superb defence of that eternal verity, the gold standard. Unfortunately he did not see that it was already in the throes of death. He proved the need of sound money when the national economy was unsound to the point of decay.

The rich man in the Chateau, unchallenged, pious, sublimely

sure of the system and himself; the homeless boys riding the rails through blizzard and drought; the prairie farmers hungry in a nation of food surplus; the unemployed living on doles insufficient to feed or clothe them—here was a parable so grotesque that few Canadians grasped its irony.

Less than anyone could Bennett grasp it. He was triple-armoured by courage, ignorance and self-righteousness. As if to underline the parable and insult its victims, he reintroduced titles of nobility, which King had abolished, and could not understand why they should be resented by Canadians who were losing the titles of their farms and homes.

The insulation of the Chateau and its Bourbon inmate was now complete, but Bennett had the answer to the whole riddle if Britain and the Commonwealth would only listen to him. So far the British Government had listened sceptically to his plan for an Empire trading bloc, J. H. Thomas, the Colonial Secretary, calling it "humbug."

In the summer of 1932 Bennett assembled the Empire at Ottawa. Two British delegates, Stanley Baldwin and Neville Chamberlain, were reluctant, distrustful and quarrelsome. Bennett presided over, dominated and lectured the conference as his own. By reputation at least he was now the Empire's leading statesman. His imperial dream, as long nourished by Beaverbrook, appeared within his reach.

Beaverbrook's horrendous campaign had split the British Conservative Party and finally drove Baldwin into the acceptance of a new Empire system, or a revival of the system repealed by free trade a hundred years earlier.

Britain would tax foreign materials and foodstuffs while admitting those of the overseas dominions and colonies without duty. In return, they would freely import British manufactures and tax those from foreign nations. Baldwin agreed but, according to Beaverbrook, immediately broke his word, betrayed his followers and refused to impose a "stomach tax" on Britain's food supply.

In Beaverbrook's version the Ottawa conference failed through Baldwin's treachery and Bennett's fatal mistake of quarreling bitterly with Chamberlain, the brains of the British delegation. That version is naiveté on Beaverbrook's part, or mere rationalization. For Bennett had no intention of admitting British goods free of duty. He was absolutely committed, by sincere belief and practical politics, to the opposite proposition that Canada must not import anything which could be made at home. His protectionism and his

248

impossible vision of autarchy cut straight across the theory of Empire free trade.

Already he had broken with Beaverbrook and would not even answer his pathetic letters of reconciliation. This personal quarrel, caused by Beaverbrook's neutral attitude in the 1930 election, could not explain and only disguised the real breach of principle between the friends. Beaverbrook wanted all tariffs between the Empire members removed and high tariffs imposed against foreigners. Bennett intended to protect Canadian industry from all competition, British or foreign. And Baldwin (an inveterate liar according to Beaverbrook) had no intention of taxing Britain's food.

Thus instead of blasting his way into external markets, Bennett succeeded only in blasting the Ottawa conference. It adjourned at last, after a summer's sweltering work, far short of its target. Various tariffs throughout the Empire were to be raised against foreigners but reduced little between the member nations. Baldwin went home blaming Bennett and his "brainstorms." Chamberlain reported that "most of our difficulties centred round the personality of Bennett. . . . . He has strained our patience to the limit." Bennett, in reply, accused the British delegates of concealing facts.

In any case, the Ottawa conference had not united, it had divided, the Canadian and British Governments. Bennett called the summer's work successful but, according to Beaverbrook, never ceased to grieve over its failure, for which he held himself largely responsible.

The net result was to increase the Empire's trade somewhat, to restrict trade outside it and to tighten the tourniquet on the arteries of the world economy as King had foreseen, with mixed alarm and relish, while watching the conference from the gallery.

So the depression deepened in the ghastly year of 1933 as Roosevelt came to office and promptly torpedoed a world economic conference that might have prevented worse havoc.

In Canada the formation of the Co-operative Commonwealth Federation, Woodsworth's first effective tool of reform, introduced a new force into politics and, though Bennett could not imagine it then, began to move him toward his own apostasy.

Other strange things were under way, still unknown to the Canadian people. Beaverbrook, possessing Bennett's private papers, said later that they disclosed "drastic, astonishing, even incredible measures for maintaining stability in the Dominion-wide financial crisis." When they were published, Bennett would "be exalted."

Even if this proves to be true, the fact of public record is that

Canada had reached the lowest economic and spiritual depths in its history, that Bennett's promise to cure unemployment had become a grim joke, and that he at last was entertaining the first doubts of his life.

They were nourished in the beginning by Stevens who, playing Iago to Bennett's Othello, whispered disturbing rumours about the chaste matron, Capitalism. Bennett angrily rejected these slanders on the woman he loved but after Stevens revealed them publicly in a sensational speech at Toronto, the Government could no longer resist his Cabinet revolt.

A committee of Parliament and then a royal commission pried open the ledgers of private enterprise and revealed a nauseating mess—watered stock, gamblers' profits, starvation wages and unconscionable price spreads between producer and consumer.

The facts were supposed to be secret. Naturally, the proceedings of Stevens' price-spreads committee, as it was called, leaked at once into the newspapers. They leaked because the committee's evidence was deposited every morning by a nameless messenger in the overcoat of Bob Lipsett, the *Toronto Star*'s press-gallery correspondent. The voice of the Prime Minister, on the telephone, shouting "betrayal!" alarmed the committee's secretary but he, though still young and inexperienced, was abler than Bennett or Stevens. His name was Lester Bowles Pearson.

Bennett had appointed the secretary, had unconsciously launched a greater career than his own and now realized that the appointment had been wise. Pearson ordered all the committee's papers to be sent, within the hour, to the Prime Minister's office and when some did not appear he knew the source of the leak.

Bennett and Stevens were now locked in a quarrel which must disrupt the Government and, with the aid of the depression, must finally destroy both of them.

Stevens, with his square jaw and cannon-ball head, his reckless daring, high ambition and infinite resource, was not a man to be controlled, even by Bennett. His private speech to a group of Conservative politicians on the evils disclosed by his inquiry was circulated in a private pamphlet and then, of course, printed in the press. A nation-wide explosion followed. Bennett dispatched a special messenger to his colleague with a letter demanding public apology for the slander of respectable business firms. Stevens sent back his resignation and announced the establishment of his own Reconstruction Party to reform capitalism. The disintegration of the Bennett Government had begun. It was far less serious, however, than the disintegration of Canadian society.

King's ally, the depression, now hurried Bennett's career to its predictable climax by an unpredictable route.

In ordinary times Bennett would have been a successful, perhaps a great Prime Minister. But the times were out of joint, in Canada as everywhere, and Bennett's cardinal mistake was to suppose that, by bootstrap economics, he could exempt his nation from mankind's catastrophe.

The depression already had expunged the Customs and Beauharnois Scandals. The five-cent speech was no longer remembered. Bennett had become the accepted scapegoat and whipping boy. King blamed him mercilessly for everything, as if a Liberal government, by mere change of label, could alter the basic forces of the world. The depression must overwhelm any man in office, as it did everywhere, and Bennett happened to be its immediate Canadian prey. He was doomed by the bad times, double-doomed by his promise to transform them, triple-doomed by his preposterous notions of autarchy and international dog-eat-dog. Though all nations followed this policy of *sauve qui peut*, nothing could save Bennett.

Nevertheless, as late as 1934, he considered himself safe, his negative policy sound.

A million and a half Canadians, in a population of ten million, were on relief. The western plains remained a dustbowl, their precious topsoil blowing across the nation. Thousands of farmers had hitched horses to their engineless automobiles and called them "Bennett buggies." The Communist Party, its leader, Tim Buck, now released from jail to receive a triumphant welcome from his followers, was fomenting strikes among desperate workers. Social Credit, leaping the Atlantic from Britain, had appeared in Alberta under an Old Testament prophet named William Aberhart. Woodsworth's socialistic C.C.F. had taken firm root in Saskatchewan and British Columbia. A social system was dying.

Yet Bennett, with courage as admirable as it was misguided, continued to preach confidence. "Sound a note of confidence in all your contacts," he advised a meeting of commercial travelers. "One of the greatest assets any man or woman can have on entering life's struggle is poverty," he assured a group of Toronto students. And in Calgary he complained that the business men of his home town walked the streets unnecessarily "morose and solemn."

From London he cabled an astounding Thanksgiving message. It declared that "Canadians should be especially thankful for the manifold blessings that Providence has bestowed upon them" and quaintly urged all good citizens to help their country by lending money at reduced interest rates. Even at this late date he still warned against "embarking upon enterprises calling for expenditures of huge sums of public money" lest credit be undermined and, with it, the nation.

Already the Bennett Government had been fatally undermined and, by the end of 1934, was *in extremis*. The Government of Britain thought so anyway and expected King's early return to power. It therefore sought his approval before appointing a successor to the Governor-General, Lord Bessborough.

Sure of electoral victory, King replied to King George's intermediaries with arrogance and pedantry. He told Bessborough that he would not approve a new appointment in advance of the next election. If pressed far enough, he would publish his refusal, and if an objectionable appointment were made he would feel free to re-open it on taking office. The aged monarch in London was alarmed at the prospect of a second Constitutional Crisis in Canada.

Bennett, though outraged, behaved with good sense and dignity, almost as if he knew that King would soon replace him. Out of respect for the Throne, he actually called on the opposition leader and at this weird interview of February 21, 1935, the two men agreed that John Buchan, as Baron Tweedsmuir, should be the next Governor-General.

Meanwhile the born romantic was coming to the end of his dream. A discerning eye might have perceived Bennett's awakening when he founded the central Bank of Canada and appointed Graham Towers, the nation's greatest financial brain, as governor. The bank was a semi-private institution and, as such, was promptly denounced by King as "fascist"; but the engine of an economic revolution had been installed. Even the public's eyes, dulled by four years of torment, suspected the change in Bennett as he suddenly discovered the need of "a sane and regulated capitalistic system and a wise regulation of undesirable practices."

The grand apostasy soon followed. W. D. Herridge, Canadian Minister to Washington and husband of Bennett's beloved sister Mildred, was at the bottom of it. Through long argument he had convinced the Prime Minister that nothing less than a new economic system would serve the distracted country. Once convinced, Bennett did not dawdle. Early in 1935 he amazed himself and the public by five shattering radio speeches that proclaimed a new society.

"The old order is gone. It will not return. . . . I am for reform! And in my mind reform means government intervention. It means government control and regulation. . . . If we cannot abolish the dole we should abolish the system."

The barking, staccato voice on the air was familiar and unmistakable but surely the words could not be Bennett's? Electrified or cynical, the listeners were not left in doubt for long. Night after night the Prime Minister elaborated his revolutionary theme while insisting that there had been no real change in his principles. On the contrary, he had foreseen everything, and planned everything, from the start. Perhaps he even believed that absurdity. Like King, he could convince himself of anything.

"For more than three years we have supported the economic system of this country vigorously and effectively. We averted chaos. We defended your institutions. We saved you from national bankruptcy. It was hard work. At the end of that time it was the right and proper time to introduce reforms in our capitalistic system."

The Government had given "its heart's blood in your service," had thus laid the essential basis of reform but wisely had postponed its long-cherished policies since it could "only save the ship from sinking." Conditions would have been worse if premature action had been taken, though "the temptation was great." Now the day of deliverance had come, as planned. The yawning gulf of philosophy between a progressive Conservatism and a reactionary Liberalism had been revealed for all men to see.

While the Liberal Party of *laissez-faire* would leave the social system unreformed, Bennett saw that "when capitalism controlled the modern state the result was fascism." King would "carry you right back to the gay old days of coaches and sailing ships and crinolines."

Every constructive step taken by the Government, especially its central bank and its new marketing laws, had been opposed by King, who "is forever against intervention by the State . . . is committed for all time as a Liberal leader and a believer in the doctrine of *laissez-faire* to do nothing." Amid "the crash and thunder of toppling capitalism" (which Bennett had not perceived at the time) King had done nothing in office, "had seemed to hear nothing" and "was asleep at the switch." Still, Bennett was no longer interested in partisan politics and had "most assuredly no intention or desire to say anything offensive about Liberalism."

The circle of his life, the most unlikely and heretical in Canadian politics, was complete. It would have baffled King if he had taken the *volte-face* seriously, and frightened him if he had thought it would work. These pious preachments, as King knew, were the setting of an election. Having contemptuously rejected Roosevelt's New Deal, Bennett was introducing it in Canada and hoped, by a death-bed confession, to appear as the only true prophet of the Good Society, to turn the tables on the Liberal Party, to out-reform King, the apostate reformer, and to win another term of office.

The Government's program, with the oratory stripped from it, appears pretty pallid in the retrospect of our time when most of it has long since become established and commonplace. There would be, said Bennett, unemployment insurance, regulation of wages and working hours, control of prices, marketing, mortgage foreclosures and banking.

Some of these plans being outside ordinary federal jurisdiction, Bennett tried to get around that difficulty by the ingenious device of implementing Canada's agreements under the International Labour Organization. His legal gimmick was unconstitutional, as the courts later found.

The invisible contents of Bennett's transformation were more important and lasting than the visible. All unknown to King or the public, the Prime Minister who had attempted to isolate the Canadian and the Empire economy from the world was secretly negotiating reduced tariffs with the United States. In his broadcasts he had wrung from his soul the admission that all nations have "no real economic independence of the rest." But the promising American trade deal was too great a reversal for disclosure before an election.

Opening with Bennett's conversion to reform, the year of 1935 moved forward like a steamroller. While no reasonable man could doubt his pledge that "with all my heart I want to serve you," and his doctors knew that his heart was gravely impaired by his labours, the gods had no pity for him.

The climax came fast. After three or four years in Bennett's western relief camps, with pay of twenty cents a day and forty cents for their entire keep, the inmates began, under Communist supervision, a march on Ottawa. Moving by freight train from British Columbia, some two thousand men gathered at Regina and there Bennett ordered the Mounted Police to stop them. In the inevitable riot of four hours, two men were killed, a hundred injured. The depression had drawn blood. The New Deal, though it had not yet been tried, seemed to be a failure. As nearly everyone but Bennett saw, the Government's confession had come indeed from its death-bed.

He, incredibly enough, remained hopeful, called an election on October 14, cabled Beaverbrook that the prospects were good, "the goose honks high" and now faced, fearless as always, his crucifixion.

For King the campaign was easy. He had only to await, like a death-watch beetle, the certain end of the Government, to summon that ever reliable witness, hard times, to denounce all Bennett's remedies, though he had few of his own, to say that the New Deal was composed either of illegal measures, of reforms stolen from Liberal policy or of dangerous "fascist" schemes like a private central bank. His ally, the depression, would do the rest.

Still, King took no chances. He had used the years of leisure to fortify his own health and redefine the meaning of Liberalism. The voters found a startling change in the man and the policy. Strict diet had slimmed down the stout little figure. In his sixty-first year King's face had taken on the wrinkles and angles of strength. His eye was clear, his smile friendly. The contrast between his evident vigour, as he gained a second wind, and Bennett's exhaustion was as clear as the contrast between their theories of government.

King found a happy phrase to illuminate both these contrasts: "What the country needs is not the fist of the pugilist but the hand of the physician." Pugilist and physician now grappled in combat which must be the end of one or the other.

Bennett had planned to resign, or so he wrote Beaverbrook, on the advice of his doctors but Stevens' rebellion had compelled him to fight to the last. His campaign, considering the state of his health and Government, was perhaps the bravest and most spectacular on record, his finest and his vainest hour. Though sick and depleted, he rode through the election like the fourth horseman of the Apocalypse.

When he reached the Pacific Coast, Communist organizers took control of his meetings but his cold contempt, his chalk-white face, his mighty voice and rolling rhetoric of defiance hushed the hecklers until they heard him in silence and admiration. If he was a reeling pugilist he was still a champion.

While the Liberal managers ignored the fine points of policy and presented the election as a choice between "King or Chaos," the physician presented an elaborate prescription for an ailing society. To give it the nostalgic flavour of Woodrow Wilson's New Liberalism, King stretched his program into Fourteen Points, this ponderous agenda containing the usual clichés of human welfare and two points of substance.

A Liberal government would end Bennett's mad theory of economic self-containment by reducing tariffs, enforcing competition (with undisclosed restraints on business abuses) and expanding trade. It would place the central bank under state control and manage money "in terms of public need." King thus proposed to seize the central lever of the economic system, though he had never seen that necessity in his years of office and did not recognize its results even now.

He was still demanding a balanced budget and he flatly opposed large government spending because "once these expenditures cease the last stage may be worse than the first." He had returned, after a long detour, to the vague radicalism of his youth; he was the rebel again and dismissed Bennett's New Deal as "a pretty cheap order"; but his confusion remained. Neither pugilist nor physician yet understood the sickness of the nation. Neither had a cure for it.

The political sickness of the Government, however, was incurable, its death more violent than King had expected. He won 173 seats to Bennett's pitiable remnant of 40. Social Credit appeared for the first time in Parliament with 17, the C.C.F. with 7 and the Reconstruction Party with Stevens alone.

Victory so overwhelming (in terms of parliamentary seats but not of votes) quite intoxicated the victor. King announced on election night that "a new era dawns. . . . Poverty and adversity, want and misery, are the enemies which Liberalism will seek to banish from our land." It would need more than King to banish them. It would need a world war.

Bennett remained briefly as opposition leader but his health, his spirit and his faith in Canada were broken. Retreating to a rather chilly welcome in the heart of Empire, he bought a country mansion beside Beaverbrook's and lived the desolate life of an exile at the end of the long road from New Brunswick. His belated title of nobility, procured from a reluctant British Government by Beaverbrook, was less an honour to a faithful public servant than a badge of defeat. At the age of seventy-seven years the exile died in his bathtub, almost forgotten by Canadians, as Viscount Bennett of Mickleham, Calgary and Hopewell. His burial in an English village churchyard ended, for the time being at least, the theory of government by a Great Man. Bennett's era had been buried, without benefit of clergy, long before then.

14: The Fighting Man

The supposed era of the physician was inaugurated on October 23. King took office again and constructed a Government which, under two leaders, would last for twenty-two years. No greater ministry had ever governed Canada. None that followed has equalled its achievements. Yet it began in total blindness to the facts of national and international life—no member of it so blind as King himself because he could evade any unpleasant fact at will.

Only in his own day-dream was it the era of physicians. In the practical world it was the era of pugilists far more dangerous to King and Canada than the patriotic Bennett had ever been. It was the era of Hitler and Mussolini. King failed to recognize their meaning or their power and, in his ignorance, immediately committed his first folly.

When Mussolini invaded Ethiopia the Canadian Government approved minor sanctions, by the League of Nations, against Italy; but when effective sanctions were considered, the courageous Canadian representative at Geneva, Walter A. Riddell, received no instructions from Ottawa in response to his anxious cables.

King was holidaying in Georgia. Lapointe, in charge of the Government, was hearing from an isolationist Quebec and elsewhere that Canada had gone quite far enough in opposing Mussolini by warlike gestures. The British and French Governments were preparing to sell out Ethiopia by the cold-blooded Hoare-Laval Deal, already under secret incubation.

Lacking instructions, but taking King's earlier statements seriously, Riddell proposed the imposition of sanctions on oil, coal, iron

257

and steel which would have stopped Mussolini in his tracks, as he later admitted. The League's working committee agreed unanimously and for three days the Canadian Government stood behind its delegate. Then, without warning, it repudiated him.

His views, said a sleazy official statement, were his own "and not the views of the Government of Canada." There followed, with accelerating momentum, the collapse of all sanctions, the conquest of Ethiopia, the death of the League and the assurance of a world war.

It is oversimplifying the ugly Riddell affair, however, to say that King acted insincerely. He had never been more sincere than in this double error—the belief that sanctions would produce war and that, without them, war could be avoided.

He was not cynical. He was merely terrified and profoundly wrong. He could not have saved the League, since Britain and France were hatching the fatal policy of appeasement; and if, perhaps, he could have saved Canada's honour, he acted nevertheless precisely as his people wished. For they were as isolationist, blind and terrified as their leader.

Even in the following year, when he went to Geneva and sanctimoniously construed the League as a toothless instrument of peaceful conciliation, not "an international war office," even when he boasted that but for his repudiation of Riddell "the whole of Europe might be aflame today," few Canadians objected, just three years before Hitler struck down King's world of phantasy.

His new beginning had been cowardly, humiliating and disastrous abroad but at home things went well, mainly because King had around him now the ablest Cabinet of modern times.

Of the older generation only Lapointe, Dunning, Crerar, Cardin and Raoul Dandurand remained. The younger generation included Clarence Decatur Howe, an American by birth and Canada's greatest administrator since Sifton; James Garfield Gardiner, a tiny man of huge ambition, who quickly set out to demolish Dunning, his former Saskatchewan chief, in a blood feud which King observed with Olympian detachment; Norman Rogers, King's brilliant young heir-apparent, who soon died in an airplane accident; Charles Gavan Power, a gallant war veteran of Irish descent whom the French-Canadian people trusted as one of their own sons; and the granitic James Lorimer Ilsley, who abhorred King but served him and the nation faithfully.

Among men of such stature King found strength but scented danger. Both expectations were to be confirmed before long.

The Government's first step in domestic policy was simple and quick. King signed with the United States the tariff-reducing agreement secretly negotiated by Bennett. This was only the opening installment of a much wider plan.

Two years later King received from Roosevelt a handwritten note addressed, "Dear Mackenzie" (a name which no one else ventured to use) and, hastening to the White House, established a queer personal friendship of momentous consequence for the free world.

After the Washington conference—its meaning little suspected at the time—King attended the coronation of King George VI and the Imperial Conference of London as Roosevelt's unofficial delegate to the Commonwealth, the broker between the New World and the Old.

His brokerage was completely successful. A three-way agreement, signed in 1938, reduced tariffs between Canada, Britain and the United States. Canada's trade, by now, was twice its volume in 1932. Bennett's policy of unlimited protection had been reversed, the blasting powder safely removed.

Yet the depression had not been removed or even seriously alleviated. The prairie drought continued and unemployment was not significantly reduced. The Bank of Canada was nationalized to provide money "in terms of public need" but little was provided. King still regarded Keynesian spending as an economic hallucination, and Roosevelt, the great spender, as a well-meaning economic illiterate.

Why had King so suddenly retreated from the New Liberalism of his *Industry and Humanity* which he had preached so ardently in the days of Bennett's New Deal? Mainly because his entire mind, and the nation's, had been diverted from the depression by a worse horror. The world had started its descent into war. And from now to their end the several Kings would never be at peace again.

With all the passion of a pacifist and old-time liberal, this many-sided man hated war and denied its possibility. With the knowledge of a historian he began to suspect that war was inevitable. The struggle between hope and reality, though never admitted in public or even in Cabinet, produced mental agony, physical illness and a paralysis of action. It also produced the worst mistake in King's life.

After the Imperial Conference he had found time to consult his spiritualistic mediums in London and then to visit the mystic now ruling Germany. His conference with Hitler distorted his whole judgment of events.

As he assured me in the third-storey sanctum of Laurier House,

Hitler was only "a simple sort of peasant," with rather low intelligence, who wanted to repossess some naturally German territories but would not risk war to get them. A few days later King informed the Canadian people that Europe could adjust its differences "without adding widespread international conflict to the difficulties all have to face"—this though the Spanish Civil War already was under way as a planned experiment in modern weapons.

Undoubtedly, in half his mind, King believed his own words because disbelief was intolerable and because he understood, feared and exaggerated a special danger for Canada. War, he thought, would finally split the two Canadian races, perhaps end the nation.

Nevertheless, he was taking any warlike precautions that he considered politically possible. He had fought through his reluctant Cabinet a pitiable defence budget of $33 million. He had rejected the Conservative policy (which reversed Meighen's Hamilton Speech) of consolidated Empire defence, since it involved political consolidation; but he had started secret continental military planning with Roosevelt. The two leaders, meeting ceremoniously in Canada, had proclaimed, in disarming generalities, what was actually a binding North American alliance.

All these measures, of course, did not make a policy. King was simply unable to make it. He could not bring himself to face the prospect of war or the resulting division of Canada.

He could not even trust the Cabinet with his real thoughts as Chamberlain flew to the surrender of Munich but, sick in bed with sciatica, read the telegrams from London alone. He told me that he had personally decoded these messages, lest anyone else should see them; and if this was pure fancy—for King knew nothing of codes—it is true the Cabinet did not discuss the European crisis.

Canada still had no policy, only the negation of all policy in King's repeated, fatuous assurance that Parliament would decide everything, without any advance commitments, at the proper time.

King was numb with his shattered ideals, with mental and physical pain. The nation was numb with bewilderment. But so, it must be remembered, were the greater nations of Britain, France, Russia and the United States that alone could hope to arrest the cataclysm.

Then came the false dawn of Munich. King greeted it with gushing rapture, cabled his "unbounded admiration" to Chamberlain and hoped that the danger had passed.

What explains King's alternating fits of optimism and pessimism, his refusal, even in the spring of 1939, to make any commitments, the guarded warning to Parliament that Canada must stand with

Britain and yet, in possibly his greatest speech—because it was wrung with torment from his soul—the prediction that "war would settle nothing, prove nothing, help nothing"? Was this merely the confusion, the stupidity or the cowardice of a pacifist who could not face war?

All those factors were at work in his tortured mind but the people did not see its larger content.

They saw a quivering old civilian, apparently the last man in Canada to lead a nation at war. King, seeing much farther, knew that if other men must do the fighting, only he could manage the political process which alone would save the nation from racial fracture and impotence.

This large and arrogant assumption happened to be true. By its own curious arrangements Providence had installed in one unlikely Canadian the exact qualities required for the task at hand now.

All King's training had been in the ways of peace, his faith in God's mercy and mankind's intelligence. His genius in politics had been proved but what use was it in war? As the people had yet to guess, and would never quite understand, that combination of talent and experience had been perfectly blended for King's ultimate work. He had never foreseen it, had always denied it to himslf and now approached it with loathing.

He must take Canada into war united. He must succeed, where Borden and Laurier failed, in preventing a schism, perhaps the final schism of the races. And since he was the only statesman trusted, if not loved, by both of them, he alone could hope to succeed.

By the spring of 1939 he had reconciled himself to his hateful mission and, after these years of blindness, had begun to perform it with his own peculiar methods. All his contradictory and tangled speeches in this period had a deliberate and double purpose—he must convince Quebec on the one hand that Canada could not contract out of a world war and the rest of Canada, on the other, that any attempt to coerce Quebec would first immobilize and then dismember the nation.

Hence, for Quebec, his increasing emphasis on the peril to man's freedom everywhere. Hence, as a warning to the English-speaking provinces, his absolute commitment against military conscription under any circumstances. In short, he was trying desperately to construct the rough, illogical but working compromise that Borden and Laurier had been unable to achieve. Their failure had produced the calamity of 1917.

So he reeled, or seemed to reel, through the spring and summer while in fact he was preparing for the only kind of war within Canada's means, as he judged them.

The people were little impressed by his speeches, his brief hour of glory as the companion of the King and Queen on their bitter-sweet tour through Canada, his frantic cables of personal warning to the simple peasant of Berlin, or his continual promises that Parliament would meet, in an emergency, and make a decision. How could the people understand King? He hardly understood himself or the monstrous irony of Providence now suddenly reversing all the plans and hopes of his sixty-five years.

If the latest touch of the Unseen Hand was inexplicable, he did not doubt the wisdom of the universal Mind or his selection as its servant. Already he was serving it better than the people knew. Though he had shamefully neglected the nation's outward military defences, he had erected the inner defences for its divided nature and his own. When the blow fell he was ready for it.

His secretaries, watching the cables all night, telephoned him at Kingsmere, at six o'clock on the morning of September 1, to say that the German armies had crossed the boundary of Poland. King thanked them, ate a leisurely breakfast, read his Bible, scribbled in his diary and reached his office at nine o'clock as if he faced a day of routine business.

The world was convulsed. He could not afford convulsion. The war, he knew, would be long and terrible, as only one spasm in a human revolution, its outcome far beyond his control, and he would not live long enough to see its larger consequences. All his resources, therefore, must be husbanded, none distracted from the unwanted and supreme trial of his life. The worst had happened but after the tortures of uncertainty it had come as a relief.

Decision at last brought an instant flow of health, energy and confidence to the civilian who, as his enemies usually forgot, had always been a fighter. From that day onward he set aside all minor concerns and, with a new peace of mind, made war. No other living man, in Canada's situation, could have made it so well.

The nation which he could never inspire but certainly could manage seemed to rally around him without question. After his limping, pedestrian speech to Parliament—a lamentable collection of documents, quotations and clichés thrown together at the last minute—the Conservative Party, now led by the honest, light-weight Manion, offered the Government its full support. Only two Quebec Members, from motives of fear, hate and isolation, and the saintly Woodsworth, from the highest motives of Christian conscience, voted nay as Parliament advised King George to declare that Canada, of its own independent will, was at war.

King could not be deceived by this flush of unity. He knew that the old racial crisis would erupt again to threaten him, the Government and the nation until the end of the war, or longer.

The first installment of the crisis appeared within a fortnight. Premier Maurice Duplessis called a provincial election on the vague issue of Quebec's "autonomy." Everyone knew his meaning. The Quebec government proposed to veto and dislocate Canada's war policy before it could get under way. "If Duplessis wins," Power told King," the war is over, so far as Quebec is concerned."

What, asked King, were the chances of defeating Duplessis? They were, said Power, no better than fifty-fifty but that gamble must be risked, the alternative being national havoc. While King hesitated the decision was made by Lapointe. The Quebec leader realized at once that his own hour had come. There could be no delay, no evasion, no compromise, and no one else could hope to convince his race. He must win now or lose everything.

No more important election had ever been called in Canada. No greater triumvirate than Lapointe, Power and Cardin had ever fought for Canada together. The oratory of the two French Canadians brought the Quebec crowds to tears. Power organized the campaign with the quiet passion of a man who had seen war at first hand and carried its scars. The work of these three and the defeat of Duplessis was Canada's first war victory and of itself made possible all those to follow.

But the margin had been close. The triumvirate had won by giving Quebec an absolute guarantee against conscription. If that promise were questioned in the future the crisis would arise again, probably uncontrollable in its next installment.

King had no time to waste on these reflections. After the easy years he was working as he had never worked before, always on a strict daily schedule arranged to conserve his health as a precious national asset.

Overnight he reorganized the whole Government and civil service and built a machine of administration with virtually unlimited powers, quite unlike that of the first war in its ability, its cohesion, its complete freedom from graft. To the end it carried a load and performed a prodigy outside all past experience.

As finally constructed, the machine was always under King's hand but he rarely interfered with his ministers. The Army was left to Colonel James Layton Ralston, a war veteran, a wealthy lawyer and the most selfless public servant of his time; the Navy to Angus L. Macdonald, who was drafted from the premiership of Nova Scotia, bringing with him a strange combination of practical common sense and Celtic poetry; the Air Force to Power, who had been warned by the experts that his Commonwealth air training scheme was impossible and made it perhaps Canada's largest single contribution to allied victory.

The unsinkable Howe, having survived a submarine attack and shipwreck on the North Atlantic, undertook to manage the economy by his own methods of daring, imagination and sheer will-power. Before he was finished this rough-and-ready genius had doubled Canada's production and changed its economic direction forever. An American had become one of the greatest among all Canadians.

When illness forced Dunning's resignation, Ilsley succeeded him and shattered his own health in mastering the almost insoluble problems of wartime finance. He, too, must be numbered among the great.

Crerar, as the only survivor of Borden's Government, became a kind of watchdog in the all-powerful War Committee of the Cabinet where he watched both the war and King with increasing anxiety.

Lapointe remained as the Prime Minister's closest colleague for a short time only. After fighting his last fight the giant was dying.

Ottawa had never seen and may never see again a comparable aggregate of ability. The Government seemed to grow with its burden; but its record in the overseas military war, and the heroism of Canada's fighting men, cannot be discussed in a book concerned only with the Prime Minister and his war of politics at home.

King now had power, constitutional and personal, such as no predecessor had ever been given. He controlled the Government, and the Government had been given virtually a blank cheque by Parliament. The War Measures Act, the National Resources Mobilization Act and the thousands of Orders in Council implementing them began to tax all the nation's economic resources, though the war brought no real hardship to any Canadians except the fighting men and the overworked administrators in Ottawa. Quebec accepted the conscription of a separate army for home defence—the so-called Zombies—and the rest of the country tolerated this costly racial compromise.

While King treated Parliament with outward reverence and felt safest when it was in session and he could use it as a sounding-board to reach the people, he had established something very like a legal dictatorship, with full public consent. By the end of 1939, however, he had decided that he must have the nation's formal vote of confidence to fight the war. Since he had no intention of extending Parliament's five-year term, as Borden had done, he needed an excuse for an early election, which the nation did not want. As usual, his luck held.

Mitchell Hepburn, the ambitious Liberal Premier of Ontario, rammed through the provincial legislature a resolution condemning the management of the war as lacking in vigour. King instantly grasped both his danger and his opportunity—Hepburn intended to replace him, if possible, or at least to create a coalition government. Therefore Hepburn, like Duplessis, must be eliminated. The last challenge to King's authority would then be removed.

The process of elimination was quick, brutal and almost ludicrous.

King assembled Parliament at the end of January, 1940, for its promised session, solemnly introduced the newly elected Members, wished them a long life in politics and, after this weird masquerade, announced that he could not govern under the threat of the Ontario legislature's resolution. If the great province of Ontario distrusted him, he might be compelled to dissolve Parliament before it could do any business.

Hepburn's outburst had furnished only the shadow of an excuse for dissolution, since King had promised to conduct another parliamentary session. As King hoped, Manion immediately furnished the substance. Leaping to his feet, scarlet with anger, the opposition leader denounced King for gagging Parliament, subverting the constitution and proving himself "unfit to govern."

That was enough for King's purposes. If, he said blandly, the Opposition had no confidence in the Government, the people must decide between them. In this unexpected situation (which he had fully expected) he would have to reconsider his duty. The Members went to dinner, wondering what would happen. King went to Rideau Hall and secured a dissolution.

In retrospect it is easy to see that he could hardly lose the election, but he was by no means sure. The country resented the slaughter of Parliament. Manion might even make inroads into Quebec where he pledged himself against conscription and, surrendering the ancient Conservative label, now called himself the leader of the National Government Party. It would fight the war and forget partisan politics.

All these fears were groundless. The nation liked but did not trust Manion. It disliked but trusted King. On March 26 the Government won 181 seats, 8 more than in 1935, the largest majority since Confederation, and a solid Quebec. King had his mandate, and just in time. For now the phony war of the winter turned into the spring blitzkrieg.

The events beginning in 1940 changed all human prospects. They also changed King from a national politician into a major international statesman, by far the most influential Canadian of our history. Into Howe's industrial revolution, Power's air training scheme, Ralston's Army, Macdonald's Navy and the Government's management of the whole economy King crammed the work of several lifetimes. Still larger work lay outside Canada, in the United States and Britain.

An afternoon and evening with Roosevelt, in his railway car at Ogdensburg, New York, produced the first binding defence agreement between the United States and Canada, as scribbled by the President on the back of an envelope. Lacking any approval by Congress, Roosevelt had actually ended the fiction of American neutrality and linked his nation to the uncertain fate of the Commonwealth. Lacking approval by Parliament, King had committed Canada to permanent military partnership with the United States. The affairs of North America had been totally transformed.

As always, when a great constructive act came from King, Meighen misunderstood it. He contemptuously damned the Ogdensburg Agreement, called it mere "twilight twitterings" (one of his fatally facile phrases) and sincerely believed that his enemy had sold out Canada and Britain to the Yankees. There was no limit to Meighen's intelligence, none to his perversity, or to a last ambition, now dawning.

In fact, the agreement had brought the United States and Britain into a new and enduring relationship by a secret deal which King could not disclose under Meighen's reckless attack.

At Ogdensburg Roosevelt had used King as his intermediary with Churchill to give Britain fifty desperately needed American destroyers in return for military bases in Newfoundland and the West Indies. The exchange was the germ of a transatlantic alliance that would expand into the contemporary alliance of the free world.

As King told me a year later, the destroyer deal had not been easy and for a time looked impossible. Britain had balked at the transfer of the bases. Roosevelt and Churchill, almost strangers to each other then, had wrangled nearly to the point of a quarrel. In the end an honest Canadian broker had reconciled them by calming the impatience of both. That seemed a fanciful claim but, to prove it, King took from his wallet Churchill's cable of almost tearful thanks. An extraordinary transatlantic triumvirate had begun to take shape.

Unable at the time to answer Meighen's slander, King could tell Parliament only that "Canada, in liaison between the British Commonwealth and the United States, is fulfilling a manifest destiny." While no one understood the meaning of those words, with their cryptic reversal of a century-old American slogan, King had made a reality of Canada's mythical role as the hinge of the English-speaking world. Or so he thought.

His youthful acquaintance with Roosevelt now ripened into a strange, unshakable friendship of opposites. Roosevelt told "Mackenzie" his most secret thoughts, often withheld from his Cabinet. King, addressing the American as "Mr. President," opened his mind in the White House as it was seldom opened in the East Block of Ottawa.

This friendship soon paid, in the spring of 1941, a huge dividend. The Hyde Park Agreement, invented by King and scrawled by Roosevelt at his family home, was to save Canada from imminent bankruptcy by assuring it American dollars for Canadian goods supplied to Britain under the United States' lend-lease program.

Probably Roosevelt had not understood King's lesson in economics, as the two drove about Hyde Park in the crippled President's hand-manipulated car. He understood at least that Canada's new war industries were essential to Britain, and its goodwill to the United States. Light-heartedly confirming the wartime integration of the American and Canadian economies, Roosevelt added a typical postscript to the contract: "Done by Mackenzie and F.D.R. on a grand Sunday in April." Where the experts of Washington and Ottawa had been baffled for months by a problem of finance, two politicians had settled it in half a day, only because Roosevelt trusted King as a friend.

With Churchill, King's relationship was equally close, but quite different. The two men had heartily disliked each other in their youth and in middle age had quarreled openly on the issue of Empire consolidation. Now, after his first airplane flight, in an unheated bomber, King reached Britain to make a friend of Churchill, to feel, as a personal wound, the ravage of the London blitz and to salute, in a moving speech, those ruins "whose very name reverberates around the world like the sound waves of a great bell, calling together all those who love and cherish freedom."

Even Churchill was touched by this unexpected eloquence from the mousy Canadian and thenceforth, not venturing to use King's Christian name, always called him "Dear Friend." Perhaps he never liked King and certainly rejected his whole political philosophy but he knew him as Britain's loyal ally and publicly described him as the "link which, spanning the oceans, brings the continents into their true relation."

No greater tribute was ever paid to King by a greater man. Though the leader of a small nation must be dwarfed by the British and American giants, the Canadian's influence on the growing partnership of Churchill and Roosevelt was profound, his position unique, yet his people have never understood it, even to this day.

King's overseas visit was marred by an incident which humiliated him and delighted his enemies at home. Having come to consider himself the real commander-in-chief of Canada's military forces, a reformed pacifist aflame with martial spirit, the Prime Minister set out eagerly to visit the Canadian troops in southern Britain. He was late for the appointment and the soldiers, who had stood for an hour in cold rain, booed and laughed at him.

King pretended to take the rebuff lightly. He did not believe, as Conservative politicians were happy to conclude, that the troops had been angered by his no-conscription policy, since Canada already had recruited more manpower than it could use. He blamed his own tardiness, the rain and the impatience of fighting men who had no chance to fight. Nevertheless, this absurd *contretemps* announced the first faint prelude to the largest crisis of his life.

If any soldiers supposed that King felt lukewarm toward the war they were wrong. Now that Canada's independence was fully accepted, the old autonomist had become an ardent admirer of Britain, an intimate of its royal family, an unofficial colleague of its Prime Minister.

At the end of the sentimental journey to London two men could hardly lift King's valise. He had filled it with stones from the bombed House of Commons for incorporation in those synthetic ruins of Kingsmere that proclaimed his deepest worldly faith. A still deeper faith in the other world to come had been renewed by the spiritualistic mediums of London. But two pieces of bad news awaited him at home.

Lapointe, his essential partner in Quebec, died on November 19 at the worst possible moment. On Power's advice, and more in despair than confidence, King replaced French Canada's tribune with Louis Stephen St. Laurent, an eminent lawyer whom he hardly knew. St. Laurent, knowing little of politics and less of King, agreed against his will to serve as Minister of Justice for the duration of the war only. This appointment was the luckiest of King's many gambles.

A second development revealed the Government's desperate need of French-Canadian support.

In a final bid for power and revenge, Meighen resigned from the Senate, became leader of the Conservative Party by a vote of its caucus and sought election to the House of Commons in the apparently safe seat of South York. His demand that a national government enforce conscription for overseas service immediately meant for King that the ultimate crisis, so long feared and skilfully postponed, was upon him.

If Meighen were elected to lead the Opposition, King told me, life would be "insupportable," the nation split, the whole war program demoralized. Then, pacing up and down his office in something close to hysteria, he declared that Meighen's return to politics was the beginning of Canadian fascism and added, his fist clenched above his head: "The people, mark my words, will have their rights!"

The meaning of these words, if they had any, was not clear but King did not permit his hysteria to mar his strategy. As no Liberal could win in South York, he instructed his party to support a C.C.F. candidate. Even this mortifying arrangement might not stop Meighen, who personified conscription, and now, as if King's cup were not full enough of trouble, he returned from Washington at the end of November convinced that Japan would spread the war throughout Asia and further tax Canada's resources.

A few hours after the attack on Pearl Harbor, the Canadian Government declared war on Japan without waiting to consult Parliament. Japanese aggression was not King's real concern (though he yielded to British Columbia's pressure and moved all Japanese residents from the Pacific coast). He had no time for anything except the conscription issue now driven into the open by Meighen with unanimous Conservative and not a little Liberal support. Some members of the Cabinet were wavering and King told them bluntly that if they wanted conscription they must find a new Prime Minister.

The threat of his own resignation served for the moment. King knew, however, that only some drastic overt act could suppress the crisis, defeat Meighen, save the Government and avoid a repetition of 1917.

Brooding in Laurier House, King hit at last on the most adroit and least understood of all his many inventions. The Government, he announced, had pledged itself against overseas conscription and while he had no intention of imposing it, because it was quite unnecessary under present conditions, he must be released from the pledge and given a free hand to meet unknown contingencies. Since the people alone could give him that release, he would ask for it in a national plebiscite.

Here was another big gamble. On the one hand, the plan for a plebiscite should damage Meighen's candidature by persuading the conscriptionist voters of South York that the Government's policy, in King's most famous phrase, (as stolen from an editorial in the *Toronto Star*) was "not necessarily conscription but conscription if necessary." On the other hand, Quebec would probably regard the plebiscite as a sure step toward the one measure that it would never willingly accept. The risk must be taken, with the help of St. Laurent, for at this time, and for nearly three more years, King had no intention of imposing conscription under any conditions.

While Parliament debated the plebiscite, the Conservatives dismissed it as a cowardly ruse and the Quebec Liberals supported it reluctantly under St. Laurent's persuasion, the voters of South York went to the polls, elected the C.C.F. candidate by 16,408 votes to Meighen's 11,952, and ended Meighen's career. Delirious with joy, King realized anew that the Unseen Hand was still guiding him.

Still, its guidance remained mysterious. King had bought time by announcing the plebiscite but he needed a respectable affirmative vote from Quebec. The gorgeous oratory of Cardin, backed by St. Laurent's quiet argument, seemed to assure a favourable result. Instead, to King's horror, Quebec rejected any possibility of conscription by 993,663 votes against 376,188. Together the English-speaking provinces registered an affirmative majority of 2,569,326 to 649,343. The reopening racial gulf had been measured mathematically.

Though more determined than ever that he would never conscript a single soldier for overseas service, King asked for the power to do so under Bill 80, an amendment to the National Resources Mobilization Act. Its introduction, as a sop to conscriptionist sentiment, brought the crisis into the Cabinet chamber. Cardin immediately resigned because, he said, this legislation contained the principle of conscription and violated the Government's pledges to Quebec. In vain King pleaded with Cardin to reconsider. He politely refused.

If Cardin's retirement was a grave blow, the Government's real danger lay outside Quebec. Not because he favoured immediate conscription but because he doubted his leader's promise to impose it "if necessary," Ralston threatened to resign and split the Liberal Party.

The crisis had taken on a new, and to King a totally unexpected, dimension. Sooner or later it must engulf him or Ralston. King could not yet foresee his means of survival, much less his brutal destruction of Ralston, but he did not propose to be engulfed when he regarded conscription, quite sincerely, as sheer madness and himself as indispensable. Besides, Ralston's case against him appeared far too technical and insignificant to justify the joint ruin of Prime Minister, Government and nation.

As Ralston understood it, the new legislation meant that if conscription were ever needed it would be enforced automatically by the Cabinet without further debate in Parliament. King insisted that Parliament must approve conscription by a definite vote before it was enforced.

All his suspicions confirmed, Ralston wrote his resignation and King realized that half his English-speaking colleagues would go with the Defence Minister. The Government would fall over a lawyer's quibble. Actually it was not a quibble. It was the first confrontation of the two most powerful men in Canada and, through them, the confrontation of two historic forces.

Ralston, whose lean eagle's face reflected a character of simplicity, competence and deep religious faith, had never plumbed the subtleties of King and now lost faith in him altogether. King had never grasped the strength of Ralston's simplicity but suddenly saw it now as a rock on which Government and nation might founder. For Ralston had only to crook his finger and most of English-speaking Canada, including the whole Conservative Party, would make him Prime Minister of a conscriptionist, anti-Quebec government. Happily for King, Ralston, unique among politicians, had no personal ambition and no interest in anything but the overseas war.

The public heard nothing of the other war in the Cabinet when King ended it by a typical compromise. He promised Ralston that conscription would be enforced, if necessary, by Order in Council and afterwards the Government would ask a parliamentary vote of confidence. Ralston reluctantly accepted this formula as better than a political smash-up which could only disrupt the war program. King considered the formula irrelevant, since he did not intend to enforce conscription at any time. With his usual prescience, however, he laid Ralston's letter of resignation away for possible future use.

So passed the crisis in its first version but not before forty-five Quebec Liberals, led by Cardin, abandoned the Government to vote against its permissive conscription bill.

This party split did not seriously alarm King. The French Canadians, having registered their protest, must return to him because they had nowhere else to go. Moreover, St. Laurent, who had become French Canada's real leader—a man strangely like Ralston in his simple integrity—had never wavered for a moment. On him more than anyone else, as King began to understand, everything now depended.

There is space here only for a catalogue of the other shaking events that filled the dismal years 1942 and 1943—the gallant Canadian disaster of Hong Kong and George Drew's rise to prominence as the critic of the Government's mismanagement there; the choice (on Meighen's unhappy inspiration) of John Bracken, a lifelong Progressive and virtually a Liberal, as the new leader of the renamed Progressive Conservative Party; the astounding collapse of the Government's popularity, until a Gallup poll indicated that it could not win an election; the upsurge of the C.C.F. under M. J. Coldwell who looked for the moment remarkably like a potential Prime Minister and an able one; the formation of the Bloc Populaire as the latest organ of French-Canadian protest; King's sudden realization of his danger, his bulging package of legislation establishing the apparatus of a post-war welfare State; and on the basis of this revolutionary New Liberalism, as laid down in King's youth and implemented in old age, his decision to call an election in 1944 after the expected victory in Europe and Asia.

The spring of 1944 was filled with false promises and King with false hopes. In a premature mood of confidence he indignantly repudiated the theory of a consolidated Commonwealth, enforcing a common foreign policy, in a world of "Titans," as advocated in Toronto by Lord Halifax, British ambassador to Washington. After crushing this revival of an old theory, King went to London and, speaking to the British Parliament, eloquently portrayed the Commonwealth as strong and permanent because all its members were free to frame their own policies in a brave new world, cleansed of rivalry between the great powers. Then he added in pathetic innocence: "The glory and the dream—are they not being realized at this very hour?"

The brief glory and the hopeless dream were confirmed in King's mind by his tea-party with Field Marshal Montgomery, who was about to cross the Channel, and left his visitor convinced that the war would be won within three months. Montgomery's purpose in meeting King was to tell him why the British high command had insisted on the removal of General A. G. L. McNaughton as commander of the overseas Canadian Army some months earlier and to warn the Prime Minister that McNaughton's successor, General H. D. G. Crerar, would be removed, too, if he failed in the European invasion.

To Montgomery's surprise, his guest took this warning calmly and it turned out to be irrelevant anyway, because Crerar did not fail; but that tea-party on the Channel coast was almost fatal to King's future.

He left for home convinced that, despite its anticipated casualties, the Canadian Army could be fully reinforced without conscription or any risk of another Cabinet crisis. The Government would be easily re-elected, soon after the day of victory, against a helpless Conservative Party led by Bracken, who had not even dared to enter the House of Commons.

Unknown to King, Ralston already had shattered the neat schedule of the glory and the dream.

Since I have fully described in *The Incredible Canadian* the cataract of events now released they will be drastically condensed here.

While King was welcoming Churchill and Roosevelt to their conference at Quebec City and, in a reckless speech, assuring French Canada that he would never enforce overseas conscription, Ralston had flown, with acute alarm, to Europe. There he learned that the reassuring figures given to him by his military advisers in Ottawa were wrong. As a result of this statistical error, the Army was gravely short of men even before the grand assault on Germany had begun.

Dumbfounded and outraged by this mistake, Ralston instantly resolved to correct it by conscripting for overseas service some of the seventy thousand "Zombies" already conscripted for home defence. If King refused to agree, Ralston would resign.

When Ralston reached Ottawa on October 18 and reported his conclusions to the Cabinet King saw at once that the crisis of 1942 had returned, without warning, in a second version likely to sunder the Government and, as he believed, the nation. By its promise of quick victory and its miscalculation of reinforcements, the military mind had betrayed him, the glory and the dream.

Ralston's verdict was quite incredible all the same. Only fifteen thousand additional men were required overseas by the year's end and in Canada and Britain the Army had two-hundred thousand ready to fight anywhere. There was no need, King argued, to conscript the "Zombies," convulse the nation, wreck the Government and re-enact the tragedy of 1917. In any case, if the Cabinet decided on conscription it would be enforced by another Prime Minister.

Beginning on October 19, the Government of Canada was split as it had never been split since 1867. This greatest crisis of the nation's political history differed from all others, however, in the spirit of its antagonists. Though the lines of cleavage were clear and apparently irreconcilable, the crisis had risen above partisan politics in most of the contenders, above personal ambition or private quarrel. Big men on either side, half a dozen of them well qualified for the Prime Minister's office, had realized that the crisis was bigger than any of them or the fate of any government.

On one side stood Ralston, backed by Crerar, Macdonald, Ilsley and Colin Gibson. The powerful Howe would certainly join them in the pinch but was ready to back any policy that would settle the dispute and let the nation get on with its war. On the other side stood King, with St. Laurent, Power, Gardiner, Ian Mackenzie and the promising young recruit, Brooke Claxton.

To say of these anti-conscriptionists, as was commonly said afterwards, that they put politics above war was manifestly untrue. Power had been terribly wounded as a soldier of the First World War and his son was now a prisoner of the Japanese in the Second. Mackenzie and Claxton were both veterans. St. Laurent, a key figure as the representative of Quebec, was prepared to make any sacrifice, including his own career, for the best available policy. Like King, these men simply could not believe, on the basis of military figures, that a disruptive conscription policy was needed or would do any possible good.

To Ralston and his friends the figures offered no alternative to conscription. Unbelievable as it appeared to King, a minor contingent of fifteen thousand men could not be found among two-hundred thousand volunteers because few of them were physically qualified for combat or trained as infantry.

Ralston's calculations went far beyond the figures. This man of facts knew that the required reinforcements would have little effect on the war but for him they were a final test of the nation's integrity. If it failed the test its failure and humiliation would divide, haunt and demoralize it for generations to come, leaving a fatal legacy of hate between its races.

As this issue clarified there followed thirty-four uninterrupted days of anguish in the Cabinet chamber—King's repeated warning that he would never invoke conscription because it was unnecessary and might well smash Confederation; his solemn farce of polling the conscriptionist ministers and asking them, one by one, if they were ready to replace him as Prime Minister; their refusal, as he had expected, to undertake this responsibility; Ralston's patient, polite, unyielding insistence on conscription without which he must resign, presumably taking most of the English-speaking ministers with him and destroying the Government; the clear prospect that Ralston would then be compelled, against his will, to form a conscriptionist government of Liberals and Conservatives against a united Quebec, as in 1917; King's final despair, plainly written on his haggard face at the head table; and yet, through all these days of tension, no word of anger, no raised voice, no syllable of accusation from either side.

"Why blame me for the mess?" King burst out in his misery. He could not be fairly blamed; but by October 31, the military figures unchanged after two weeks of technical study, he knew that the mess could last no longer. The Cabinet must reunite or explode. Either he or Ralston must go.

For motives of egotism and patriotism, of ambition and idealism, of honour and of greed for power all mixed beyond analysis, King did not intend to go and thus expose the nation, as he believed, to catastrophe.

Ralston, therefore, must go. He must go peaceably or he might take half the Cabinet with him. And now, with sudden flash of intuition, King saw an exit from his imprisonment. It was a narrow and dangerous exit to be sure, it involved an act of unspeakable brutality and it depended on Ralston's honour, but there was no other way.

On the night of October 31 King secretly summoned to Laurier House the fallen idol of the Canadian Army who still smarted from his dismissal. General McNaughton, now a gaunt, grizzled yet still wonderfully magnetic figure, was ushered into the upstairs study and there agreed to become Minister of Defence in Ralston's place.

The bargain reached between these two men, and unknown to any other, guaranteed that McNaughton would get the necessary reinforcements without conscription. Assuredly the magic of his name, the compelling portrait of his rough-hewn face and the mystique of his leadership would make the "Zombies" volunteer for overseas service.

When the Cabinet met next day its dilemma apparently was unchanged. No one observing King's calm expression could suspect that he had changed everything. No one except McNaughton shared the secret of Laurier House.

While Ralston renewed his argument for immediate conscription and agreed, as a final compromise, to a voluntary recruiting campaign of two or three more weeks, King listened politely. Only the stub of a pencil in his fingers, tapping gently on the table, suggested the strain of this electric moment and King's nervous habit was too familiar to alert his colleagues. But the tiny hand also held an invisible axe and now, without warning, it fell.

Still speaking in his usual matter-of-fact tone, the Prime Minister reminded the Cabinet that two years ago Ralston had submitted his resignation. Agreement on policy being impossible, the resignation would be accepted immediately, McNaughton would become Minister of Defence and there would be no conscription.

The cold ferocity of that blow struck the Cabinet dumb. All eyes turned on Ralston. Would he accept the murder of his career or, by saving it, end King's? No man at the Cabinet table knew better than King that, by summoning his friends, Ralston could make himself leader of a Liberal-Conservative coalition and master of English-speaking Canada before the day was out. The Government's future, and the nation's, hung on Ralston's next words.

As King waited through an eternity of half a minute for an answer which must rescue or ruin him, Ralston rose slowly from his chair. With no change of expression or voice, he said quietly that he would submit a formal resignation next day. Too shocked to move or speak, his friends watched him walk to the head of the table, silently shake King's hand and, after shaking the hands of all the ministers in turn, leave the room. No one followed him.

By gambling on Ralston's patriotism King evidently had won. Had the crisis actually been solved by the departure of perhaps the finest character in Canadian politics? King thought so and, remarking that he deeply regretted this unfortunate occasion, adjourned the meeting. He knew, though, that Ralston could still overthrow the Government if he changed his mind and asked his friends to resign.

Before King went to bed that night the immediate danger passed. Ralston had urged the conscriptionist ministers to remain in the Cabinet. They must make sure that McNaughton got the volunteers and, if he failed, must force conscription on King or another Prime Minister. Dubiously, and half ashamed of themselves for not leaving with their friend, Crerar, Macdonald, Ilsley, Howe and the others agreed. But the crisis was not solved.

Only because the British war office had demanded it, Ralston had ended McNaughton's long military career. By his arrangement with King, and doubtless with the highest patriotic motives, McNaughton had ended the political career of Ralston. Now Mc-

Naughton proceeded to end his own and came within an inch of ending King's as well.

The agreement of Laurier House, which promised so much, was a failure from the start. For the next three weeks McNaughton used all his energy as an organizer and all his reputation as a soldier to make the "Zombies" volunteer for overseas service. His speeches, and King's appeal on the radio, were greeted with derision. Only 549 "Zombies" volunteered between November 1 and 19.

Having summoned Parliament to approve the success of his policy, King had to admit instead that McNaughton's failure had turned into fiasco and the fiasco could be hidden no longer from the people. On November 20 King told the Cabinet that he would ask Parliament for a vote of confidence anyway, continue the recruiting campaign for two weeks only and, if it still failed, would resign in favour of some conscriptionist minister.

That, in all its chaos, its worthless plans and broken careers, was the situation on the morning of November 22. Even yet McNaughton hoped to get the volunteers somehow. He had written a speech defending his policy and, by the consent of the Opposition—since he was not an elected Member—would read it to Parliament next day.

Full of apparent confidence, he summoned the Army Council to give him its latest recruiting figures. Instead, he received from the commanders of the defence services a written memorandum which, as he saw at first glance, left him, King and the Government defenceless. The recruiting campaign, said the memorandum, had finally failed. Only conscription could provide the needed recruits. And verbally the members of the Council added that if their recommendation were not approved they must resign.

McNaughton knew then that the jig was up. No minister, no government could survive the resignation of the Army Council. Shaken as he had never been shaken in the fighting of two wars, McNaughton telephoned the Prime Minister's office. As King recalled the story later, McNaughton whispered in a voice hoarse with shock: "I have terrible news for you, Chief! What I must tell you will come as a body blow."

On hearing the news King realized that the blow could be fatal. Yet even as his mind reeled at the thought of a revolt in the military high command and the spectre of national disorder, his infinite ingenuity was devising a new plan of escape. Skilfully handled, the crisis in its ultimate form might yet be changed from disaster into victory.

Everything hung on the word of St. Laurent. He must persuade Quebec to accept conscription. That was unlikely but it might just be possible if St. Laurent were as big a man as Ralston.

Summoned by telephone to King's office, St. Laurent found his leader in a state of excitement close to collapse. The French Canadian heard the news impassively and replied without hesitation that Canada was not a South American republic where the military could subvert the civil power. The Government, he said, must fight the Army Council revolt.

"Fight!" cried King. "Fight with what? Our bare hands?"

No, the Government must surrender, impose conscription or condemn Canada to "anarchy."

St. Laurent fell silent for a moment decisive in his life, in King's and in the nation's. Then he said that he had always been ready for conscription if it could not be avoided; and, only because the alternative was evidently unthinkable, he would stand beside King and face the consequences.

Canada at last had found the first Quebec statesman prepared to defy the deepest French-Canadian emotion, to accept the most hated symbol of the conquest, to put the whole nation above its parts. With a dozen words St. Laurent had saved King, the Government and, as King thought, the Canadian experiment. With no such intention, he had made himself the next Prime Minister.

When King met Parliament and the Liberal caucus that afternoon the secret of the Army Council's threatened resignation was known only to its members and to King, St. Laurent and McNaughton. It would not be revealed for nine years yet and then by a curious set of chances which will appear for the first time in this book.

Parliament and caucus were hastily adjourned in order, said King, that the Cabinet might consider "important new developments." What developments? Ottawa writhed in speculation, all of it far from the truth. The conscriptionist ministers, still ignorant of the facts, decided to resign that night.

King knew they would not resign after he had told them just enough of the facts to justify the Government's impending somersault. He was worried about one man only. Could he prevent the resignation of the anti-conscriptionist Power?

Knowing the stern code of honour and political morals behind Power's air of raillery, King doubted that he would be dissuaded from his duty. Still, it was worth a try. By a freak of irony, this politician of Irish descent, with no drop of French blood in his veins, had become Quebec's only significant opponent of conscription in the Government. If he supported St. Laurent the impact of King's intended reversal would be greatly moderated in French Canada.

Power, just out of hospital after an emergency operation, and unaware of the day's events, was summoned to the Prime Minister's office at a quarter to eight. "Chubby," said King, "I don't know what I'd do without you!" It was no use. Even when King had explained that McNaughton could not recruit the promised volunteers (but never hinted at any trouble in the military command) Power refused to consider conscription.

It was unnecessary, he said, would do nothing for the nation's war effort and would destroy its unity. Moreover, he had given his word that he would never accept conscription and that promise must be kept. St. Laurent's position was quite different. He had never made such a promise. Rejecting King's arguments of policy, his pleas of old friendship and his tears, Power concluded this harrowing interview by saying that he would resign next morning.

The Cabinet met immediately in a scene of queer anticlimax. As McNaughton began to speak, the conscriptionist ministers expected his usual assurances of success in the recruiting campaign and were resolved to end the wrangle by resignation. Instead, McNaughton said briefly that the campaign had failed and he recommended that sixteen thousand of the Home Army be conscripted forthwith. King and St. Laurent agreed. With hardly another word (what was there to say now?) the Cabinet approved the conscription Order in Council and went home to bed—all except McNaughton who sat up until dawn rewriting and reversing the speech to be delivered in Parliament that day. And still the great secret of the Army Council was untold.

One danger remained. Ralston could pull the Government down and make himself Prime Minister if he refused to accept the Order in Council as adequate. Ralston was too big for that.

His polite and chilling lawyer's cross-examination of the exhausted McNaughton in Parliament; the Opposition's last hopeless attempt to upset the Government; King's threat of resignation to frighten the wavering Liberals but never any explanation of his *volte-face*; his mysterious warning, which no one understood then and most colleagues regarded as absurd, that if Parliament could not unite "we shall have to face the possibility of anarchy while our men are fighting overseas" and "the pillars of the temple of our Canadian life might be drawn out from under and the structure come down, bringing disaster to the whole nation"; then the final threat that if he resigned he would not call an election but would hand the Government over to a conscriptionist Prime Minister who might have little sympathy with French Canada; Power's resignation "in sorrow, not in anger" because he would not "tear this country asunder" and accept from McNaughton the policy rejected when it came from "my old comrade and tried associate, Layton Ralston"; a long-awaited verdict from Ralston in favour of the Government's policy and against himself as a man unfit for "the dizzy heights of leadership"; a vote by two-thirds of the Quebec members against conscription but their quick return to King as preferable to any other leader—these events ended the crisis on December 7.

There was a sequel which can be told now.

Though King constantly muttered about trouble in the Army, promised to disclose it in his autobiography, and spoke darkly of a military "uprising," no colleague except St. Laurent and McNaughton believed him.

Following King's death, I mentioned in my biography of him his mysterious insinuations, but did not attempt to judge their validity because the key fact was known only to St. Laurent, McNaughton and the members of the Army Council and they had guarded it well. Even the book's suggestion of possible discord among the Army commanders was laughingly construed by King's other ex-colleagues as a horrendous tale invented by him to justify his reversal on the issue of conscription.

For more than eight years no one broke the pact of silence. As soon as *The Incredible Canadian* was published in the autumn of 1952, however, I was informed by a highly placed personage that St. Laurent had been embarrassed by it. Lacking the fact of the Army Council's threat to resign, St. Laurent had been made to appear as a dupe of King's wild invention when, of course, he had yielded to conscription in the face of an unthinkable alternative. Now the whole truth should be disclosed at last in justice to King's successor.

Accordingly, all the facts were conveyed, in a telephone conversation, by a military figure previously unknown to me even by name and were published in *Maclean's* magazine. The best kept secret of our political history was received with a notable public hush. Already the great crisis and most of the men who made it belonged to the ages. And the moral of an odd historical footnote is that politicians and soldiers of the better sort know how to keep their lips sealed in the nation's interest.

After the conscription ordeal King's last years look anticlimactic but only in comparison with his earlier work. Few of his predecessors had accomplished, through their entire terms of office, as much as he now added, almost like a postscript, to his lavish record. Here his final acts will be merely listed, for in truth the King era was ending and the era of St. Laurent had begun.

The high hopes and dreams of King's youth were briefly rekindled at the United Nations' founding conference in San Francisco but after watching the Russian delegation for only a week he decided that humanity was not ready for a rule of law. A Communist conspiracy, he concluded, would attempt to dominate the world and probably would launch a third war. While making all the appropriate public obeisances to the ideal of world government, he considered the second League no more effective than the first and spent most of his time at San Francisco writing election speeches with the aid of an obscure, indispensable assistant, J. W. Pickersgill, who had become more influential than most Cabinet ministers.

By all rational assessment a Government ten years old, its energies depleted by the war, its party rent by the crisis, its English-speaking and French-Canadian segments angry for opposite reasons, must be doomed. Besides, as all the economists seemed to agree, the arrival of peace would be followed by a world depression fatal to all democratic governments.

King was unmoved by these counsels of despair. Even when the voters of Grey North defeated McNaughton in a by-election and the jubilant Bracken expected to form the next government, King was sure that Quebec would not desert him, that the other provinces would not support a party leader who had not dared to enter Parliament.

The electorate had seldom seen King in the last five years. Now, as the election campaign opened, it saw a man deeply changed in look and manner—an old man, of nearly seventy-one years, wrinkled, lean, tired yet surprisingly vigorous, bubbling with confidence and for the first time with mischievous humour at Bracken's expense. The nation did not love him, much of it did not respect him. Yet, after all, he had managed the war, somehow prevented an upheaval of races and, by means little understood then or now, had revolutionized Canadian society with his many-sided reforms, which he now promised to expand. There was no practical alternative to King. He had become Canada's Great Man.

A French-Canadian isolationist movement, led by Cardin, collapsed overnight. King (clad at the moment in his underclothes) was reconciled to Power and embraced his old friend in a hotel suite at Quebec City. Since French Canada would not vote for the Conservative Party of conscription, Bracken depended on the support of various "independent" Quebec candidates. These straw men only damaged him in the rest of the country. On the night of June 11 King won the last of his six election victories—125 seats against Bracken's 67 and Coldwell's 28. The majority was narrow but under all the circumstances astounding. Only King could have gained it.

For the next three years he remained the master of the nation in peace as he had been in war. The smooth transition from a military to a civilian economy, with the brief interruption of a dollar crisis in 1947 and the inevitable inflation postponed by wartime price controls, was miraculous and little noted at the time. Howe's historic White Paper committing the State to provide full employment and perpetual prosperity—a commitment still haunting all subsequent governments and forming the core of our current politics—was almost overlooked in the surging Canadian boom for which, of course, King took full and undeserved credit.

His familiar touch seemed as sure as ever when he completed Macdonald's Confederation by persuading Newfoundland to enter it without any appearance of pressure; but King's age at last was telling on his judgment, his energies and his faith in mankind.

He could work for only two or three hours a day, was often cranky, and though he had made all the able men around him and was proud of such colleagues as St. Laurent, Howe, Ilsley, Claxton, Paul Martin and Douglas Abbott, the able new Minister of Finance, he resented their slightest interference and grew increasingly jealous of his own power. The Cabinet knew that he was unfit for office and should retire but no one dared to bell that formidable cat.

A younger King would not have bungled the Communist espionage plot exposed by Igor Gouzenko or pretended that the Russian Government knew nothing about it. Happily St. Laurent managed this first revelation of Russia's true intentions and, by rough, secret methods, shocking to his leader, smashed the spy ring in Ottawa.

A younger King would not have explored a free-trade deal with the United States, announced a plan of "real reciprocity" and suddenly canceled it without notice or explanation, because he remembered Laurier's defeat in 1911 and could not bear even the appearance of injury to Britain.

A younger King would not have risked two outright quarrels with St. Laurent and Pearson (to be described in their chapters of this book), deplored India's admission to the Commonwealth as a non-white republic and then reversed himself completely to make a close friend of Prime Minister Nehru.

The old King who once boasted of his rebel blood had turned into a nostalgic royalist, a crony of the King and Queen, almost an uncle to their daughters and, in human affairs, a profound pessimist. All the glory and the dream had faded out. An incorrigible world would not fit the design of *Industry and Humanity*. The United Nations could not enforce peace and in the system of naked power which he had perceived at San Francisco King now saw the certainty of the ultimate nuclear war, perhaps only a few years or months away.

This world, the very opposite of his boyhood vision, must pay the price of its folly. King was interested only in the world to come. For his pending arrival there, he prepared himself by constant communication with the spirits of his parents, Roosevelt and his dead Irish terrier, Pat.

All that remained for him in this world was the disposition of his estate (worth nearly a million dollars, though he was still haunted by the fear of poverty) and the choice of his political heir.

He approached the problem of successorship with something of his early talent. Having first chosen Pearson and been rebuffed, he settled on St. Laurent, who at first declined and then consented for no other reason than public duty. His consent, since he towered above all other contenders, made the Liberal convention of 1948 a purely ritual exercise. St. Laurent emerged as party leader and King found himself walking alone and unnoticed from the Ottawa auditorium.

He would always be alone now until he joined his dead friends but he could not bear to give up his office until, on the pretext of a Commonwealth conference, he had paid a farewell visit to Britain. In London his health broke, his doctors put him to bed without indicating the gravity of his illness and the leaders of the Commonwealth consulted him in the sickroom as the longest office holder in the history of the English-speaking peoples, the acknowledged sage and oracle.

King George was among those visitors and knew that he would never see his Canadian Prime Minister again. Churchill came, too, and as he rose to leave was surprised by the patient's last request. In this final moment of parting Britain's old warrior did not hesitate. Churchill leaned over the bed and kissed King's cheek.

Already St. Laurent had been summoned to the Commonwealth

conference, was now Prime Minister in all but name and formally succeeded King on November 15.

The feeble and solitary man wandering about Kingsmere and leaning on a heavy cane could observe his fake ruins against the gleam of Champlain's river. Beyond them, he could survey a life of achievement equalled by no other Canadian except Macdonald and perhaps not even by him—a social revolution, the successful conduct of Canada's greatest war, the smooth transition to peace and prosperity, above all (as he supposed), the reconciliation of the two races, the new unity of the Canadian people.

King had made many mistakes, clung to many illusions and, like most liberals, misjudged the momentum of human progress. He had committed some despicable outrages and ruined several better men. He had also done many acts of secret kindness, he had always considered himself the faithful instrument of the Unseen Hand, he had understood the Canadian people as they had never understood themselves and given them more than any other public servant could give. The mystery of this strange and contradictory creature would long outlive him. Somehow his nature's limited resources had fused in a lifework incomparably greater than the sum of its parts. A little man had ended as a giant.

When King departed from Kingsmere and this world, quite peacefully, on the night of July 22, 1950, most of the nation felt little sorrow but it knew, in mute Canadian fashion, that it would never look on his exact like again.

15: The Amateur in Politics

When Louis Stephen St. Laurent became Canada's twelfth Prime Minister on November 15, 1948, many candid Liberals wryly agreed that he had the perfect equipment for his task. Like a dignified mortician of the better sort, he would conduct the approaching obsequies of the ancient régime with impressive ritual. Meanwhile he would serve well enough as the caretaker of this dying relic.

That St. Laurent possessed the best intellectual apparatus in contemporary politics, a mind for facts as resourceful as Meighen's and far superior to King's, his colleagues already knew. That he had any instinct for those non-facts which govern the art of government, or any rapport with ordinary men, which is the secret of leadership, was generally doubted. Or that this rather aloof, old-fashioned person, at the age of sixty-six, would finally take Canada across the line dividing the nineteenth from the twentieth century no one could suspect.

In hindsight it is easy to see that everyone misunderstood St. Laurent at the beginning because he misunderstood himself. Trained in the law of the statute books, he did not discover the law of politics until he had been in office for at least a year, and the further discovery that he was a politician by nature more than a lawyer came to him as a total surprise.

After the personal wound and the parliamentary blunder that caused his fall in 1957, St. Laurent was the last man to claim that he had been one of the nation's five great Prime Ministers. Yet his public work and his private life place him among the great. He stands with Macdonald, Laurier, Borden and King.

No doubt history will rank him below these four but certainly above all others. St. Laurent lacked Macdonald's genius, his trials, his unique achievements and also his roguery. He had none of Laurier's mystical impulses and none of his vanity either. He had all of Borden's integrity and a larger mind. If he wanted King's sensitive touch, he was free of King's intellectual dishonesty and selfishness. One thing is certain at any rate—no finer human being ever governed Canada and none has been so thoroughly misunderstood as St. Laurent.

It is a complete misjudgment of him and his times to assume, for example, as many Canadians do, that St. Laurent was merely a conservative businessman and corporation counsel dressed up, for partisan purposes, as a Liberal; or a chilly recluse masquerading as the genial Uncle Louis (that final caricature imprinted on him by well-meaning admirers, to his own amusement).

Between the extremes of idolatry and scorn marking his career our generation cannot judge St. Laurent in perspective because it forgets his zenith and remembers his nadir too well. Another generation will see that he entirely altered Canada's position in the world and, for his time, the relations of the two races within the Canadian State. Perhaps the best measurement of his stature is the reviving quarrel of the races which so quickly followed his exit and, at this writing, seems to threaten his major work.

The first Canadian to sense the meaning of his arrival may have been a nameless elevator attendant in the East Block.

After taking his oath of office, St. Laurent had worked until nearly eight o'clock and, when he started for home, was astonished to find this humble functionary awaiting his departure, as he had been instructed to await King's. The unfairness of such arrangements outraged the new Prime Minister. "From now on," he said, "you'll leave with the others at the regular time. I can walk downstairs."

Elevator man, Cabinet, House of Commons and nation soon began to feel a new presence and a new conception of government, apparently fitting no label but seeming to promise a deep change not so much of policy as of atmosphere and style.

The change was deeper than anyone realized at the beginning. It was more than a change of men in office. It was a change of spirit.

Though St. Laurent had been born in the nineteenth century, among the most conservative stock of North America, and looked like a *grand seigneur* of the eighteenth, he was the first Prime Minister to feel the true motion of the twentieth or Canada's respons-ibility to it. Still more remarkable, he was almost sixty years old before he understood or took any serious interest in this process. As he had said, on entering King's Government, "I know nothing of politics and never had anything to do with politicians."

In outward mien he was now too old to learn. The lean terrier face, unwrinkled and ruddy; the bristle of white hair and moustache; the black, sparkling eyes, usually warm and gentle but suddenly turning hard and cold to freeze a presumptuous questioner; the courtly, disarming manner and simple idiom; the immaculate Eng-lish with no trace of French but occasional flecks of Irish accent—all these familiar appearances seemed to define a gentleman of the old British school and to deny the Anglo-Saxon's notion of Quebec.

On the other hand, his own people did not recognize in the second Prime Minister of their race any of the qualities long asso-ciated with French-Canadian leaders from Lafontaine to Lapointe.

Both impressions overlooked the cardinal fact that St. Laurent was neither French nor Anglo-Saxon in temperament. He was Canadian, the most truly Canadian of all our Prime Ministers up to his time. He felt no nostalgia for the old lands of Europe nor any sense of isolation from the rest of his country in Quebec.

Canada was the centre and workshop of his mind, as natural to him as his breath. The emotional claims of other countries that always tugged at his predecessors, even King, never touched St. Laurent. Yet he knew better than they that Canada was totally in-volved in the common situation of mankind.

He understood this involvement because the world of war, and post-war revolution, was the only world within his experience as a leader of men. He approached it fresh in outlook, eager to learn, without commitment to the past. It has been said, quite correctly, that he lived as a French Canadian and thought as an Anglo-Saxon but this cliché does not begin to explain him.

On both sides of politics, and in both races, the people's first judgment of an unknown Prime Minister was tentative, sceptical and wrong. It could not be otherwise. For until now St. Laurent, yearning only for private life, had never exposed his thoughts to the public. Moreover, he had not fully understood and had gravely underestimated himself.

Even his capture of office had been accidental and repugnant. While all his predecessors, except the brief Abbott, had hungered for power, St. Laurent had accepted it against his will and ap-parently against all the rules of the game. An invisible logic, nevertheless, had led straight to this unwelcome goal and the preparations for it had started, as if by deliberate design, at his birth.

A French-Canadian father, Moise St. Laurent, whose people had lived in Canada since 1653, and a strong-minded mother of Irish descent, Mary Broderick, had mingled two bloodstreams in their son, the eldest of six children, and given him two languages.

"I thought," he used to say in later years, "that everybody spoke to his father in French and his mother in English." Hence came our only Prime Minister who spoke both languages in their spontaneous accents, and hence from the mother a flavour of Irish brogue.

Complete bilingualism was the lesser part of a heritage unique among Canadian statesmen. St Laurent was at home, from childhood, not only in the languages but in the feelings of the two races. Even more important, as events would prove, he grew up with no prejudice against any race and loathed all forms of racial discrimination as unnatural and wicked.

His father kept a general store at Compton, Quebec, near the Vermont border, and there St. Laurent was born on February 1, 1882. By local standards the family was prosperous, in a small way. It was hardworking and devoutly Catholic. The boy was taught at home by his mother, who had been a school-teacher. He worked in the store, was soon sorting the letters of its post office and, in a village of mixed French and English speech, had little consciousness of race.

No one noticed anything unusual in young St. Laurent until he went to St. Charles College, in Sherbrooke, to be prepared for the priesthood. His teacher, an elderly priest, was amused and then annoyed by the boy's perpetual questions. Instructed to present them only in Latin, by way of discouragement, St. Laurent quickly added a third language to his vocabulary. It soon became clear to the teachers that they had something of a prodigy on their hands. This modest, polite but insatiably inquisitive lad was cut out for the law, not for the Church.

A legal career followed fast. After being graduated from Laval University, St. Laurent refused a Rhodes scholarship because it would delay his practice and went to work at a salary of fifty dollars a month in a Quebec City law firm; fell in love at first sight with Jeanne Renault, a beauty of nineteen who had many suitors; married her and, in his thirties, was the father of two sons and three daughters.

He had established himself by now as one of Canada's leading lawyers, appearing frequently before the Canadian Supreme Court and the Privy Council in London. Eminent in the law, he was unknown to politicians. He had shaken hands once or twice with Laurier, had met King but had taken so little interest in the Liberal Party that Meighen even tried to introduce him into the Conservative Cabinet of 1920.

St. Laurent had no thought of entering politics and, in middle age, little knowledge of public affairs, outside their strictly legal aspect. His life was successful, comfortable and, as he thought, unchangeable—an opulent income from his profession, a handsome house, a perfect marriage, five children who worshipped him, leisure for his country resort, for golf, fishing and a nightly game of bridge. He was a wealthy, happy, normal, rather conventional man with deep faith in his Church, no vices except the occasional cigarette and no interests but his family and his work.

This tranquil routine collapsed with Lapointe's death and Power's advice to a desperate Prime Minister. When an excited servant heard King's voice on the telephone and summoned St. Laurent from the dinner table, the die of his future, and Canada's, was cast.

Next day St. Laurent went to Ottawa, agreed to accept the Justice portfolio for the duration of the war, but no longer, and telephoned his wife. The assurance that his appointment was temporary could not deceive Madame St. Laurent. A woman's instinct told her that there could be no escape from Ottawa. She burst into tears.

The capital was too distracted by the war to notice the lonely couple in a mean apartment of two rooms. The husband walked to his office. The wife cooked his meals (storing her preserves and pickles under the bed) and awaited him with a hot supper after the long night sessions of Parliament.

If the nation seldom heard St. Laurent's name, which it could not yet pronounce, the Cabinet quickly agreed that its elderly recruit had a mind far abler than Lapointe's and a judgment in council more blunt and often more practical than King's.

St. Laurent spoke seldom, regarding himself as a makeshift minister on his way home, but whenever he addressed the Cabinet or the House of Commons it was refreshing for them to hear, after King's tiresome prolixity, a short, crisp statement reading in Hansard like a considered state paper—no eloquence, no ornament, no wasted word, simply a lawyer's summary of the facts, so clear that any layman could understand it.

As his officials saw him, St. Laurent worked without effort, grasped the meaning of a document at one glance, dictated a reply in smooth English or French, occasionally lost his temper for a moment (the heritage of his Irish mother) and, without trying, produced in the tedious Justice Department a mood of respect, then of adoration. But even the new minister's closest associates failed to observe, as he probably failed himself, the inner transformation now remoulding a legal into a political mind.

St. Laurent had come late to politics, so late that surely he could not be expected to master them and, in any case, sought only a return to his normal life from the wartime bivouac in Ottawa. That delayed start, contradicting all the rules of the political trade, was the sure passport of his future.

Where all the professional politicians around him were twisted or imprisoned by their early loyalties, prejudices and ambitions, St. Laurent's ignorance of the game, his complete indifference to power, his ability to look at any problem without prior judgment or bias, enabled him to see it plain and whole.

He was not a Liberal. He was not a Conservative. He was only a man of immense intellectual talent, natural generosity and delicate honour who had suddenly beheld, like some new argument of law, the baffling riddle of Canada to which no written law applied. The riddle fascinated him, and though its solution must be left to younger men, he was studying it with all his well-known resources of mind and an imagination known to few.

The conscription crisis of 1944 found King shattered but St. Laurent unruffled because he approached it not as a mystical clash of absolutes, but as a practical proposition. Once satisfied that conscription was necessary to avoid worse consequences, he accepted it without a moment's hesitation and, having nothing to lose personally, persuaded his own people to accept it also.

His decision, on the morning of McNaughton's debacle, had several meanings. It meant that a French-Canadian statesman had risen above the deepest instincts of his race. It meant that he had quietly mastered Quebec and prevented another racial convulsion where even the magic of Laurier had failed. It meant that a French Canadian as big as St. Laurent might go on to master the English-speaking provinces, if he chose to try. The conscription crisis meant, in fact, that St. Laurent must be the next Prime Minister.

For the present he did not want or expect to suceed King. On the contrary, he was increasingly repelled by his work in government and lately by frictions with his leader.

The talents of the two men were complementary. King brought to politics his almost feminine intuition, his groping idealism, his sense of inferiority and his lust for power. St. Laurent brought a better factual mind, a pragmatic attitude to all issues and a complete disinterestedness.

Together the King-St. Laurent coalition (for such the government had become) was probably the most harmonious and efficient, in a business sense, that Canada had yet seen but by disposition its partners were incompatible.

As King once told me, St. Laurent was the most gifted colleague he had ever recruited and he doubted that any French Canadian, living or dead, was St. Laurent's intellectual peer.

The partners were incompatible all the same. A mystic and despot like King found it difficult to divide his power with a companion who did not seek it but must share it. A recluse who lived increasingly with the dead was spiritually separated from a man of the world. The mind of a dreamer could not merge itself with the mind of a doer. Thus when King at last recognized his inevitable heir by giving St. Laurent his darling, the Department of External Affairs, he had become a little jealous of a rival.

St. Laurent discovered an absorbing interest in his new portfolio and quietly began to revolutionize Canada's foreign policy. King supported his lieutenant but did not always understand or agree with him. He stood by St. Laurent in the suppression of the Russian spy ring but believed that the secret commission of inquiry, with twenty-six persons held incommunicado and denied counsel or bail, was scandalous, though perhaps unavoidable.

The two men had fallen out briefly over the admission of the Indian Republic to the Commonwealth. St. Laurent welcomed it. Less liberal in the pinch than his colleague, King recoiled with horror from the thought of domination by non-white peoples, but he soon realized that St. Laurent was right. A real quarrel followed in the next year and seemed likely to end St.Laurent's public life.

During King's absence from Ottawa on holiday, J. L. Ilsley, as Canada's representative at the United Nations, agreed that a Canadian should be appointed to its commission in Korea. St. Laurent ratified this undertaking. On hearing of it King flew into an old man's tantrum, warned the Cabinet that the Korean dispute might precipitate a world war at any moment and vainly asked President Truman to release Canada from its commitment.

Since St. Laurent and Ilsley accepted this rebuke without protest in Cabinet, King mistook their silence for weakness. Learning that they both intended to resign, he was panic-stricken. Perhaps Ilsley could be spared but if St. Laurent went the Government would lose its heir-apparent and the Liberal Party might well lose the next election. At all costs, St. Laurent must be dissuaded.

King invited him to dinner at Laurier House and, resorting to charm where bluster had failed, said he had not appreciated how strongly St. Laurent felt about Korea. Of course there could be no thoughts of resignation. St. Laurent replied that of course he would resign immediately if the Korean commitment were repudiated.

In this first serious confrontation between the man of the past and the man of the future, King was beaten and he knew it. St. Laurent's Korean policy stood and he remained in the Government.

King, though never losing his horror of Korea two years before war broke out there, concluded that a man strong enough to defy him was strong enough to carry on his work. On second thoughts, after refusing to consider it, St. Laurent decided to accept that responsibility but not without an aching regret, and his wife's consternation, at the prospect of abandoning his well-earned retreat to the comforts of private life.

It was by no means certain, however, that a party convention would accept St. Laurent, a figure respected but remote. Already he had made a bad start by his experimental entry into the recent Quebec provincial election where his dry, legalistic speeches had done no harm to the victorious Duplessis. Apparently St. Laurent was a lawyer, not a politician, and only a politician of the highest gifts—above all, the gift of homely contact with the voters—could hope to replace King.

Moreover, there were rival candidates who seemed to possess at least some of those gifts.

To begin with, there was Howe. If he could never understand the political process and was destined to smash the Government like a loose cannon on a deck, he had established himself by an economic miracle as the second, or perhaps even the first man in English-speaking Canada. Happily for the nation as a whole, for the Liberal Party, for St. Laurent and himself, Howe was big enough to understand his own limitations. He refused to consider the Liberal leadership and backed St. Laurent with all his nation-wide influence.

King, managing the convention while pretending to be neutral among all the candidates, had to dissuade a generation of younger men—Abbott, who seemed to have every qualification, the formidable and ambitious Claxton, the irrepressible Paul Martin. They were induced to withdraw from the contest in favour of St. Laurent, since their opportunity would recur later on. Gardiner could not be handled so easily. He could not be handled at all.

This singular personage of tiny frame, leather face and battering-ram courage had carved out for himself an almost sovereign state in loose diplomatic relations with the Government and was now determined to possess the nation.

Finally, "Chubby" Power, outraged by the Government's abuse of Liberalism as he understood it, had decided to use his candidature as a protest. After his stand against conscription, he could not be, and did not particularly want to be, leader of the Liberal Party but he could reprimand and warn it, at the cost of any future preferment, which no longer concerned him. The best-loved man in politics had thrown away his career already on grounds of honest principle.

St. Laurent also was prepared for either fortune. He had sought no convention votes. He had approached no delegates. He had not even written a speech. Yet an extraordinary change had come over him. For the first time he had learned to unbend in public. At the age of sixty-six years he was about to establish contact with the people.

King cried like a child as his party said its farewell to him. Gardiner delivered a typically belligerent speech. Power shook the conscience of Liberalism with an outburst of angry eloquence. When his turn came, St. Laurent was standing at the back of the hall, munching a sandwich and scribbling some disjointed notes on an envelope.

The convention had expected and feared from him a formal, stuffy address, a polished lawyer's brief which would read well in print and win no votes in the country. To everyone's surprise, the relaxed and grizzled figure now before the microphone had little to say. In the homeliest language, as if he were meeting a neighbour in the old store at Compton, he remarked that he would not enter "an oratorical contest" but if the party chose him he would do his best.

As convention oratory the speech was worthless. As a revelation of the man himself, so long concealed by shyness, it instantly captured the delegates and, heard by radio throughout the land, astounded the voters. Party and nation wanted an ordinary human being after King's intellectual hermitage. They had found him. St. Laurent was given 848 votes to Gardiner's 323 and Power's 56. This verdict did not seem to elate him. He forgot a reception planned in his honour, left the hall and took his wife to dinner.

The new Liberal leader could not become Prime Minister until King at last resigned on November 15. In the meantime St. Laurent

endured his invidious position with a placid air and a deceptive
silence. Cordial, considerate and crisp, he looked indifferent to
praise or blame but felt both keenly and now thoroughly understood his double load of responsibility.

At home he must prove that a French Canadian could make a
successful Prime Minister, that Laurier's career had not been, as the
gentle despot supposed, a brief aberration which no other man of his
race could repeat. Abroad St. Laurent had realized as soon as King
that war had been followed only by an armistice but, unlike King,
he did not despair of peace and believed that his supreme task was
to protect it, within Canada's frail means. To this end he was already
meditating one of the boldest steps in Canadian history.

St. Laurent's assets, when he formed his Cabinet, were many,
his liabilities few but graver than he yet understood.

King had left him a nation growing economically faster than any
other on earth. The great Canadian boom supported and deluded
St. Laurent for the next eight years. In its glow he appeared as the
image of a natural prosperity which was in fact artificial, temporary
and, in some ways, dangerous. But as long as the boom lasted—for
reasons entirely outside Canada's control—the Government would
doubtless remain invulnerable.

King had also left St. Laurent the strongest party organization
ever known in Canada, an unexampled machine of power built, cog
by cog, since 1919 and now, despite the electoral losses of 1945, in
perfect running order.

Finally King had left St. Laurent a Cabinet not quite as able as
that of wartime—since Ralston and Power were missing, Macdonald had returned to the premiership of Nova Scotia and Ilsley
was on his way to the chief justiceship of that province—but still far
above the Canadian average.

In addition, St. Laurent had succeeded where King had failed in
persuading Pearson to accept the portfolio of External Affairs and
from the beginning regarded the recruit as his heir. Pearson, the
internationalist, had respected King but, distrusting his incurable
isolationism and never liking him as a man, had refused to join his
Cabinet. Only his deep admiration of St. Laurent as a public and a
private person could lure Pearson from the security of the civil
service to the hurly-burly of political life.

There was another major asset in King's estate, though perhaps
St. Laurent alone appreciated it.

In his latter years King had learned to regard the prickly Pickersgill as a kind of preliminary litmus test of his own ideas and the

only speech writer who could put them in his deliberately diffuse and open-ended style. If Pickersgill had become more powerful in the hierarchy than most Cabinet ministers, King was always somewhat sceptical of a youngster who could never be awed by greatness, said precisely what he thought and was often both intolerant and intolerable, sometimes disastrously wrong.

St. Laurent saw much better than King the rare political acumen, the rarer honesty, the earthy humour of self-criticism and the unshakeable courage of an assistant whose mind and body seemed to move on springs. Pickersgill was soon made secretary of the Privy Council and then, by agreement with Premier Joseph Smallwood, was appointed Newfoundland's representative in the Cabinet. The affectionate father-and-son relationship between the old Prime Minister and his young factotum was to have remarkable results.

But of course no other colleague could challenge Howe's rĕgnant position as St. Laurent's essential English-speaking partner. The new Government was a St. Laurent-Howe coalition and thus reproduced the biracial pattern set by the coalitions of Macdonald and Cartier, Laurier and Fielding, King and Lapointe—the only workable system of Canadian government, as its collapse would prove in Diefenbaker's time.

Against the assets of his own ability, his party, his Cabinet, and the big boom, St. Laurent's liabilities were hardly noted but they were serious.

He had taken office at the age of almost sixty-seven years and, though he was still as vigorous in spirit and physique as most men of fifty, his strength was certain to diminish at the very time when, in the iron cycle of events, the boom must end. Even the boom itself contained liabilities that few men understood until it had passed. Meanwhile it assured those mistakes still afflicting us today.

Then there was Howe. He could be reckoned a primary asset and a genuinely great man. Yet this general manager of the boom, with all his business skill, his stern code of honour, his limitless daring, the queer humility beneath his bravado and the warm human affection behind his cast-iron face, could become an onerous liability if the economic and political weather changed.

For the moment, however, St. Laurent was the luckiest of all Prime Ministers and Canada the luckiest of all nations. The only question in the Liberal back room was whether this aura of personal and national success could be translated into votes. All fears on this score were groundless.

Having undertaken his own metamorphosis, St. Laurent, the

remote lawyer, had become overnight a gregarious politician. Very late, he had found his true *métier*. In the election of 1949 the Canadian people, knowing him only by an unpronounceable name, now beheld a man who, with his natural dignity, looked like a Prime Minister and, with his unpretentious, folksy manner, like an ordinary human being.

The contrast between this genial grandfather and the hermit of Kingsmere, between St. Laurent's matter-of-fact speech and King's bewildering circumlocution, was not only a relief; as the public began to note, it marked a change in the whole climate of politics.

If the public sees a leader long enough at first hand its judgment, though hardly conscious, is usually infallible. The public was now seeing St. Laurent at first hand and it was agreeably surprised.

The professional politicians were dumbfounded. Many of them assumed that St. Laurent's public act was no more than an act. Now they began to understand that his real nature was replacing his stiff courtroom pose and his intense shyness. The small-town man from Compton had learned at last to be himself. Even more surprising, outside Quebec, this French Canadian spoke English like everybody else and spoke it in a colloquial idiom pleasant to the ear. Such a man could be trusted by Anglo-Saxons as even Laurier had never been.

When a newspaper correspondent watched St. Laurent talking to some little boys on a railway platform and saw their quick response, a new name and legend were born. "Uncle Louis," said the correspondent, "will be hard to beat."

In one sense "Uncle Louis" was the most misleading of all Canadian legends, a parody of the toughest mind in public life, but it contained some truth. Like all men, St. Laurent had two sides. The soft side was as authentic as the hard and, in the end, was to be his undoing.

Meanwhile, though little understood, he had become the most popular of all Prime Ministers, against whom the slashing, soldierly Drew was helpless. On June 27 the ballot boxes gave St. Laurent 193 seats, or 68 more than King had won in 1945. Liberalism had reached its high-water mark with the largest majority since Confederation. Drew's parliamentary following dropped from 67 to 41.

Now at his apogee, a son of Quebec had almost completely eliminated any sense of alienation in the English-speaking provinces, which was more than Laurier had ever been able to do. As against that, while St. Laurent held a solid Quebec, he held it out of admiration for his success and racial pride in his power, whereas Laurier had enjoyed an almost religious worship. Among his own people St. Laurent was always suspected of being a little too "English" but for the present he had achieved a universality denied to any Canadian before or since his time.

Pickersgill, who served them both, placed St. Laurent above King as a politician and anyone would so judge them as men.

"Partly," says Pickersgill, "this was a matter of generation. . . . Mackenzie King and his generation were not Canadians by instinct; they could never quite take the Canadian nation for granted because they had helped to create it and were deeply conscious of how fragile the creation was, and how divided the loyalties of many Canadians were. For Louis St. Laurent Canada was the only country he knew."

Pickersgill exaggerated the virtues of his idol but he accurately assessed St. Laurent's political method. It was to search for a workable solution of every problem and then, without fanfare or exultation, to make his policy appear not as a dubious innovation but as mere common sense, hardly worth argument. Until he abandoned that method in old age and weariness, St. Laurent not only forestalled divisive controversy but gave his opponents no issue that they could successfully exploit against him.

The atmosphere of competent management and goodwill in Ottawa, as generated by the Prime Minister's personality and nourished by the boom, enabled St. Laurent to undertake a sequence of audacious strokes executed so smoothly and quietly that they passed with little conflict, to change many of the nation's ways forever.

Perhaps the least regarded and most enduring of St. Laurent's many achievements was in the field of foreign policy.

Though he was the product of three centuries of isolation in Quebec, he saw better than King, the instinctive isolationist, that Canada could never be sealed off from the world and its wars. Since the United Nations could not preserve peace, Canada's only chance of survival lay in unlimited co-operation with its allies.

As a practical man, free of King's alternating hope and terror, St. Laurent was among the first Western leaders to propose a North Atlantic alliance.

Few works of Canadian statecraft surpass St. Laurent's success in committing the nation's troops to overseas service at a time of peace with the full consent of his own race. Such a commitment would have been unthinkable a few years earlier and probably impossible for anyone but a French-Canadian Prime Minister. Laurier's thinking had been reversed by his heir, without a political crisis, almost without debate.

There was no crisis and little debate (except among a few English-speaking Cabinet ministers) when St. Laurent led Canada into the Korean War. King had foreseen that war and shrunk from it in horror. St. Laurent took it in his stride as the price of avoiding a world war.

This same doctrine of common sense was applied to domestic politics where all large issues were made to seem small, every bold change obvious and routine. The problems solved and the crises avoided can only be listed here.

It was St. Laurent, much more than King, who had brought Newfoundland into Confederation.

No other Prime Minister had dared to abolish appeals to the Privy Council in London but St. Laurent closed this old controversy overnight by calmly insisting that Canada must accept its national responsibilities, make its own courts supreme and relieve Britain of an unnatural burden. Put in those terms, an audacious reform seemed so natural that no party could seriously oppose it.

St. Laurent appointed the first Canadian Governor General, Vincent Massey, and explained a step deeply repugnant to Canada's Loyalist tradition by saying: "I would not like to think that a Canadian, alone of the Queen's subjects, would not be considered fit to represent her in Canada." King would have writhed in constitutional obscurities, offended half the nation and confused the rest. St. Laurent's disarming appeal to national pride was unanswerable.

Now he stepped into the issue of Canada's constitution where all his predecessors had feared to tread. Again without serious opposition, Parliament took power to amend the constitution in matters of federal jurisdiction because, as St. Laurent said, a sovereign nation should not be required to approach the British Parliament, cap in hand, to settle its own business.

He hoped that the provinces would agree ultimately on a method of constitutional amendment in provincial jurisdiction as well; but since they had failed to agree he did not press the matter. The pragmatist had learned the art of the possible.

King never succeeded in building the St. Lawrence Seaway but St. Laurent quickly persuaded the United States to join Canada in this essential North American project. He launched a huge immigration program; appointed the Massey Commission on the arts, letters and sciences which later issued in the Canada Council; vastly expanded the nation's social services with a universal old-age pension and hospital insurance and all this time piled up budget surpluses to reduce the debt of the war years.

Even allowing for the buoyant climate of the boom and St. Laurent's luck, Pickersgill has not exaggerated too much by concluding that "there has been no comparable record of constructive statesmanship in any other period of equal length in our history."

The climate, the luck and St. Laurent were changing together.

Three momentous events that marked the change and finally destroyed his Government were entirely unforeseen when St. Laurent called his second election on August 10, 1953.

He walked through the campaign as the reliable Uncle Louis, disregarded the unfortunate Drew, who seemed to lose votes with every desperate speech, and won 171 seats to the Conservative Party's 51, the C.C.F.'s 23 and the Social Credit Party's 15. This was a loss of 22 Liberal seats carried four years earlier but the Government still seemed invulnerable. Actually it was beginning to crack.

The first fissure in the mighty wall of Liberalism, as built by King and heightened by St. Laurent, and the first decline in St. Laurent's own vitality were perceived by no one except his intimates who denied these sinister omens even to themselves.

Their immediate occasion, in 1954, was a financial dispute between the federal and Quebec Governments. Finance, however, could not explain the vehemence of St. Laurent's sudden declaration of war on Premier Duplessis. Ostensibly they quarreled about a division of revenue fields. In fact, their quarrel went to the roots of the biracial Canadian experiment and was only the latest version of the struggle conducted by Lafontaine, Cartier, Laurier and Lapointe, the struggle still dividing the races in its contemporary version.

It was said at the time that St. Laurent had stumbled into this strange episode through ignorance, haste or stupidity. The truth is that he had long anticipated and planned it.

As early as 1942 the apprentice politician, in words strictly relevant today but usually forgotten, had declared his concept of Canada as a single nation and bluntly warned Quebec that it "must abandon an illusive dream of a French-Canadian state in North America." He had deplored in his own province "attitudes contrary to my ambition to see this country develop as one Canadian nation and not merely an alliance of ten separate state provinces."

His alarm, more than twenty years ago, was perceptive, as we can see now. He had already surmised in general the events of these times, though he did not expect then that the old theory of an isolated Quebec would penetrate his own party. He knew only that his

concept of a single Canada and Premier Duplessis' concept of two
nations under a common constitution were irreconcilable. The financial dispute between Quebec's rival leaders was merely the latest
expression of the recurring racial conflict. Even so, was it necessary
for St. Laurent to seek a direct confrontation with his enemy?

Some of his colleagues feared it out of political timidity, others
out of wisdom and experience. None of them knew that the Prime
Minister had taken the quarrel into his own hands and intended to
pursue it as he pleased.

He did not consult the Cabinet when he accepted an invitation
to address the Reform Club of Quebec City and he prepared no text.
In this speech, perhaps the most important of his life, he denounced
the whole notion of French-Canadian separatism as a chimera,
flatly rejected Duplessis' claim for larger revenue fields exempt from
federal taxation, said that his Government would stand by the existing tax agreements and told the Quebec people that they could vote
against him if they disliked his policy. In any case, Quebec must be
"a province like the others." As for Duplessis' Union Nationale, it
was using the tax argument as a "screen" to hide its own notorious
sins.

The nation was astonished more by the tone than the contents
of the Reform Club speech. In defiance of race, tradition and ordinary political caution, a French-Canadian Prime Minister had
harshly lectured his own people on their errors—or, as one of his
frightened colleagues remarked, had undertaken a second conquest
of Quebec.

St. Laurent's words sounded brutal, almost contemptuous of
Quebec's deepest instincts. Even his touches of humour (a quality
seldom exposed in public) were strangely rough and irreverent, as
when he recalled his recent conversation with a French-Canadian
priest who had attacked the federal system of children's allowances
as an invasion of Quebec's sacred autonomy and the Prime Minister
had replied: "How many children have you?"

Many French Canadians were appalled and hurt by a ferocity
never seen in St. Laurent before but the Reform Club speech had
made him a hero in English-speaking Canada.

At first he rejoiced in his apparent victory. Then came a sudden
reaction, the reaction of Laurier in 1917, of every French-Canadian
leader who had found himself idolized by another race and doubted
by his own.

In St. Laurent's case the reaction was profound and wrenching
but well hidden from the public. An aging French Canadian had
heard, for the first time clearly, the ancient call of the blood. Also,

he had felt the first intimations of age. If he had obeyed his own inclinations and retired then, before age and misfortune could work their final mischief, the history of Canada would have turned out differently. As he realized later, his worst mistake was to heed the advice of colleagues who, for sincere reasons or merely for their own political convenience, insisted that he must remain as the only leader able to win another election.

A few of his lieutenants urged him to finish the war so well started and complete the destruction of Duplessis. They were shocked when he told them that he was too old for such an adventure. Age certainly was a factor in his retreat but not the governing factor. St. Laurent simply could not bear the thought of separation from his people and the further separation of the races.

As with Laurier, the sense of racial identification, the folk memories of Quebec, the three centuries of labour and stubborn survival beside the St. Lawrence were more important to the Prime Minister, despite his Anglo-Saxon mind, than popularity beyond this precious soil. Moreover, it was evident now that in an open contest with the Quebec government he would lose. Duplessis, a local machine politician, was stronger among his people, and much closer to them, than the statesman in Ottawa.

Events would soon prove that St. Laurent had not changed in the slightest his vision of a Canada united above the clash of races; but he suddenly abandoned, as dangerous to unity and intolerable to his own instincts, his war on the Quebec boss.

That cynical, brilliant and charming man, uncomplicated by any attachments outside Quebec, had waited quietly for his enemy's anger to burn out and was not surprised to receive a conciliatory message from Ottawa.

Since Duplessis would not accept an invitation to St. Laurent's capital, the two men met on the neutral ground of a Montreal hotel suite. There a compromise—just to Quebec and satisfactory to Ottawa—was quickly accepted but Duplessis unquestionably had won, for the time being at least. Or perhaps it would be truer to say that the spirit of Quebec had won.

In any case, St. Laurent retained only the respect and federal votes of Quebec while Duplessis, caring little for respectability, had his people's wry affection, or enough of it to make him unbeatable, the real master of his race in its own land.

These facts and the wastage of St. Laurent's energies were little understood then and soon a larger event obscured them altogether.

Duplessis had wounded St. Laurent personally but he could not destroy the federal Government. That work was left to Howe, who began it in 1955. Quite unconsciously, the great builder, like an absent-minded Samson, proceeded to demolish the towering temple of Liberalism.

He had long been established as the second power in the State, the almost equal partner of its chief, a kind of economic emperor whose decisions were seldom questioned or explained.

King could usually control this wilful colleague. Once, returning to Ottawa and finding that Howe had dared to call the Cabinet together in his absence, King lectured him as if he were a schoolboy. Howe accepted the chastisement and sheepishly told his friends that he had deserved it. Nevertheless, King could not do without Howe and when he proposed to resign because the Cabinet would not support him in a wartime labour dispute all King's talents of conciliation were needed to prevent this catastrophe.

St. Laurent needed Howe, too, loved him and, as a crowning proof of admiration, proposed to make him Governor-General. Howe was inclined to accept this tribute but, on second thoughts, decided to continue the work that he understood and did so well.

Unfortunately he understood only one side of it. The other side, the side of politics, was hidden from him by an impenetrable blind spot. Blindness, not animosity, produced his rift with St. Laurent in 1955.

The origin of the discord was not, as generally supposed, the Trans-Canada Pipe Lines scheme but an amendment to the Defence Production Act under which Howe had long directed the Canadian economy.

His wartime authority had been whittled down already and he agreed reluctantly to some further reduction. After the necessary legislation had been drafted he left Ottawa on a fishing trip. In his absence St. Laurent changed the draft to appease the clamour in the Cabinet and in the House of Commons against Howe's excessive powers. Learning of this retreat, Howe was furious and the old friendship cooled.

St. Laurent had been right. Even in its diluted version, the amendment assured the Government's first serious reverse as Drew saw his chance to revive the sick Conservative Party on the issue of Parliament's rights and Howe's attempt to subvert them. The Government was forced to surrender and limit the indefinite extension of Howe's reduced powers to three years.

In the opinion of Pickersgill, Drew's attack had dangerously shaken the Government and made the Opposition look, for the first time, like a possible alternative.

Anyway, Drew had crushed an incipient revolt against him led by John Diefenbaker, and made himself his party's unquestioned master. He did not know that the Government was more divided than its enemy, or that St. Laurent's physical resources were running out.

Howe provoked the second installment of his quarrel with the Prime Minister by proposing the construction of a gas pipeline from Alberta to the St. Lawrence with government underwriting.

To his amazement, he now encountered an unlikely opponent in Walter Harris, the young, handsome and ambitious Minister of Finance. This potential Prime Minister usually found it difficult to make up his mind but in opposing a government guarantee to the pipeline as financially unsound he was prepared to resign.

For weeks the Cabinet remained split in dubious battle until St. Laurent finally came down on the side of Harris and settled the question. Howe's pipeline scheme was rejected. He thought himself betrayed by his leader, regarded Harris as the saboteur of a great national policy and talked bitterly of leaving politics.

The Harris wing of the Cabinet devoutly hoped he would, but Howe was not the man to quit in defeat. After sulking through the winter, he appeared before his colleagues early in 1956 with a new pipeline scheme which he regarded as the culmination of his life work, the vital test of his honour. This latest project had become as dear to him as the Pacific railway had been to Macdonald.

It was a good scheme, too, as the future would demonstrate. The wary Harris accepted it. Stuart Garson, the meticulous Minister of Justice, drafted the contract. St. Laurent approved it as good business. For personal reasons he eagerly welcomed a reconciliation with his chief lieutenant. The two old partners stood together again. But they stood on quicksand.

Trans-Canada Pipe Lines Limited undertook to carry natural gas from Alberta into the St. Lawrence metropolitan complex and, through a spur line, into the United States. The promotion was heavily backed and controlled by American capital but momentarily lacked $80 million necessary for an immediate start of construction. Legislation introduced in the middle of May authorized the Government to lend the hesitant builders this money on exceedingly stringent terms.

The deal appeared sound in every respect, and so turned out in the end. It was not the contract that guaranteed the ruin of the Government. It was Howe's breakneck timetable.

He insisted that the first section of the pipeline must reach Winnipeg in the current year and wanted the whole work completed, if possible, before an election in 1957. Construction must start by July 1. Money to buy and move steel pipe from an American factory must be available by June 7. Therefore, the legislation must be passed by May 31.

This was Howe's tight timetable. Infatuated with the last of his many useful enterprises, like a youth in his first love affair, he would not consider any postponement. To delay work until the following year was unthinkable. To reveal the timetable in advance was fatal. Yet that blunder, more dangerous than a crime, was committed by the most practical politicians of their trade.

Once Drew knew the timetable, he needed to hold up the pipe-line legislation for only a few days and all Howe's plans must fall. The Government had put its head into a noose and handed the rope to the Opposition.

Foreseeing Drew's inevitable filibuster, though not its larger consequences, the Government prepared to break it by the use of closure, a limitation on debate imposed only seven times, and only once by a Liberal government, since Meighen invented it in the naval debate of 1913.

The decision to use closure and to announce its use from the start was the ultimate, incurable mistake. As the Government should have anticipated, the Opposition would not argue the merits of the pipeline. It would argue the merits of closure. It would fight for the historic prerogatives of Parliament and the freedom of debate. It would stand as the champion of democracy, the Government as the subverter. With a little bit of luck, Drew could hope to make St. Laurent, the great constitutionalist, look like the enemy of the constitution.

As if the timetable were not bad enough in itself, the necessary luck was supplied by Howe, but he could not be held solely responsible for the ensuing calamity. Not without some misgivings and a last-minute change of plan, the whole Cabinet authorized Howe to announce that fourteen days of debate and no more would be permitted. Though fourteen days allowed ample time to discuss the pipeline, or any other issue, a limitation arbitrarily fixed must make the Government seem tyrannical and drunk with power.

Worse than that, because it must re-emphasize the Government's dictation in every day's headlines, closure would be applied, if necessary, at each of the four separate stages in the passage of the legislation.

Drew now held a quadruple noose perfectly contrived to hang

the Government four times over. There was a fifth noose still more deadly which he overlooked, or did not dare to pull.

Thus began the most astounding episode in Parliament's history. It was not a debate on the pipeline. It was not even a debate on the rights of Parliament. It was not really a debate at all because the Government refused to argue for fear of wasting precious time. It was rather a contest of mere sound and almost a riot.

What could explain this total botch by a Government so long dedicated, as it thought, to the parliamentary system and to the constitution, written and unwritten? Two facts, non-constitutional and wholly human, explained everything.

Howe knew that he was right about the pipeline, was sure that the public would endorse it as sensible and regarded the Opposition's manoeuvres as transparently spurious, but in the final test he simply did not comprehend the political process.

St. Laurent, a wiser man, was in no condition to control Howe, lead the Government, fight the Opposition or invoke his own moral authority among the people. He had entered that special cell of torture which no Prime Minister can escape.

For him the torture was peculiarly agonizing and unknown to the public. Perhaps it was unknown even to Howe or any of the Cabinet, since St. Laurent uttered no word of complaint and maintained an air of stoic composure. But beneath his ruddy, vigorous look the old leader was sick in body; he had not recovered from his exhausting world tour in 1954 and was now beset by a private anxiety far more wounding to him than the public blows of politics.

Reporters in the press gallery were amazed to see the Prime Minister sit expressionless, chin on hand, reading a book while the hurricane beat about him. The reporters did not know what was passing in the mind of a desolate leader who had ceased to lead, much less that the regnant St. Laurent-Howe coalition, like any aged giant of the forest, was dying from the top. And least of all could anyone surmise that Drew, the Government's apparent destroyer and successor, was almost finished also in the hour of his triumph.

Like a script written by a mad playwright, the tawdry melodrama rolled on to its anticlimax—from Drew a combination of excellent argument and bruising political invective; from Stanley Knowles, of the C.C.F., a scholarly and killing defence of Parliament's ancient rules; from his leader, M. J. Coldwell, at first a reasoned protest and then a sudden flood of passion shocking in this coolest of parliamentarians; from Davie Fulton a systematic and stealthy guerilla warfare on the Government's flanks, day after day;

from Donald Fleming such an outburst of firecrackers that the Liberal majority, reckless of the most obvious political penalties, ordered him out of the House. When Diefenbaker shouted after Fleming, "Farewell, John Hampden!" and Ellen Fairclough draped his vacant desk with the Canadian ensign the public had been given a symbol of tyranny that the most ignorant voter could grasp.

Several reputations were made in that frenzied fortnight, to flourish later and perish in the end. Drew seemed to be the destined man of the future but already belonged to the past. Diefenbaker, Fleming and Fulton were all assured of high office, and all of destruction. The Government, however, was the immediate and naked victim of its own folly, though Howe surveyed the tumult with boredom and St. Laurent with eyes too tired and pained to see.

Even then the damage might have been arrested this side ruin were it not for the extra folly of the Liberal Speaker, René Beaudoin.

After innumerable rulings, challenges and divisions, the Government, now led by Harris, thought it had got the pipeline bill out of committee on May 31 and could quickly give it final reading. At this point an obscure bit player and parliamentary gremlin tore up the script and stole the show.

Colin Cameron, of the C.C.F., ventured respectfully to suggest that Parliament's privileges had been violated by certain letters appearing in the *Ottawa Journal*. The Speaker agreed that this alleged offence could be debated and he carefully instructed Cameron how to proceed. Harris saw with panic that if the debate continued for only a few days, as seemed certain, Howe's timetable would be disrupted, the pipeline delayed for a year.

Exactly what happened in a night of desperate conferences may never be known but next morning the Speaker reversed himslf, ruled out Cameron's protest and ordered the conclusion of the debate under closure. By that decision he spoiled the Government's last chance of rescue.

He was still on his feet when opposition members ran, shouting, into the sacred centre aisle. The sedate Coldwell stumbled to the steps of the Speaker's dais and shook his fist in Beaudoin's face. Many hoarse voices were heard above the din but the only one that would soon reach the public's ear was silent. "I'm choking," Diefenbaker mumbled to his friend, George Pearkes, and stayed in his seat.

St. Laurent did not move either and watched the hubbub as if it were a passing daydream. Howe looked on it disdainfully as a farce. The Liberal back benches broke into idiot song and then rammed the pipeline bill through on time.

As the mad playwright had written it, the script now lurched to its anticlimax. The pipeline contractors were unable to obtain pipe from a strike-bound American factory. No work started that year. The whole ugly fiasco had been endured in vain.

Only a Government leaderless, insolent and punch-drunk could fail to recognize the depth of the wounds inflicted by a Parliament which, ceasing to be a deliberative body, had become a howling rabble and, in its fury, had aroused the fury of the people. Such was the apparent state of St. Laurent's Government. In reality it was worse than that. It was hopeless if Drew intended to seize the fifth noose.

All other business had been obstructed by the wrangle of the pipeline closure. By June 11 the Government was running out of money and, lacking appropriations from Parliament, would be unable to pay its civil service or the armed forces at the middle of the month.

It must ask for interim supply immediately. If Drew delayed a vote the device of closure could not possibly be applied for a second time in the present mood of Parliament and people. Drew had merely to obstruct a decision for three or four days and St. Laurent would be compelled to dissolve Parliament and call an election. As the practical politicians like Harris and Pickersgill judged their prospects, the Government would certainly be defeated at the polls.

That last risk must be run. On the afternoon of June 11 the Government asked for money and waited in aching silence for Drew's answer, almost sure that he would make his kill.

Why he refused the chance and voted supply has never been explained—perhaps because his business friends and campaign fund backers resented his attack on the pipeline, perhaps because he believed that the Government could win one more election, perhaps because his physical resources, like St. Laurent's, were depleted; or, more likely, because the Conservative machine throughout the nation was financially destitute. Whatever his motives may have been, the office of Prime Minister had slipped through Drew's hands. The fruits of his thirty-year toil, his long service in war and peace, were to be inherited by Diefenbaker, his colleague and enemy.

Having secured money in the nick of time, the Government relapsed into smug arrogance, its mortal disease. Arrogance had led it into parliamentary chaos. Arrogance sustained it now. This was a curious fact, a kind of automatic defence mechanism, since no man could be less arrogant at heart than St. Laurent and all Howe's friends knew his inner humility. The Cabinet's collective arrogance was purely political but it must be tried for its public acts, not its private character. It had fixed the rules of a ruthless game and must live or die by them.

The Liberal régime had managed a successful war, revolutionized the national economy and won five elections. While it might have suffered some passing injury, where had it been wrong in basic policy? On its record how could the voters dismiss it after all its good works? So reasoned the practical politicians.

Oddly enough, one minister who supposedly knew nothing of politics had guessed the meaning of the pipeline. Pearson knew that it might well prove lethal but after accepting the strategy of the experts, he was powerless to save his beloved leader. Probably even Pearson did not see, or refused to see, that St. Laurent had lost control not only of Parliament but of the nation. He must march, with unfailing courage, to the end.

In the autumn of 1956 a third event much graver than the Defence Production and the pipeline debates temporarily masked the Government's true condition and worsened it.

The story of Suez belongs in Pearson's chapter of this book but it ignited the last energies and the finest qualities of St. Laurent.

Canada had been given no advance inkling of Britain's plan to attack Egypt. St. Laurent's Cabinet was in session when the first flash came from London. Paul Martin spoke first in the stunned silence. He said he just didn't believe the news.

St. Laurent's anger against the British Government seemed to make him young again. It did not come, as his enemies would say later, from his French-Canadian blood. It came from his detestation of injustice to any racial minority.

As one who had ardently supported friendship with Britain and was a devoted monarchist by conviction, he felt sickened by the thought of British bombs dropping on defenceless Egyptians, no matter what the provocation might be. And French blood did not abate his anger against Britain's partner, France. The attack on Egypt appeared to him wicked in morals, crazy in world politics, and certain to fail in military terms. His ministers had never seen him so moved and some of them suspected at once that his anger, once it spilled into public debate, might fatally damage the Government among English-speaking voters.

If St. Laurent was furious he was also cold, master of himself and of the Cabinet. He couched his despatch to London in words of stiff formality. They did not hide his sense of betrayal.

The British Government had given him and its American ally no warning. It could not expect him to support an adventure which he considered immoral and insane. Those few who saw his official note were staggered by its contents but even the Conservatives, having demanded its immediate publication, did not publish it when they came to office because, by that time, history had validated all its conclusions.

After Pearson's return from the United Nations, where the Suez crisis was settled on his initiative (as will be told at the proper place), St. Laurent felt relieved though still angry.

So far his public utterances in Parliament had been discreet and good-tempered but when Conservatives like Howard Green attacked him in lurid, visceral language for knifing Britain in the back St. Laurent's colleagues feared that he would speak his mind and regret it afterwards. At least one of them warned him to say nothing that would further inflame a public now bitterly divided by Britain's retreat.

As always, St. Laurent listened politely to this advice and perhaps intended to follow it but the flash point was not far off. The explosion left the Treasury benches gasping.

Why, St. Laurent was asked, had Canada and the small members of the United Nations interfered in the vital interests of the great powers? The old man's voice was steady, his words typically sharp and coherent as he spat out his most famous indiscretion: "Because the members of the smaller nations are human beings just as are their people; because the era when the supermen of Europe could govern the whole world has and is coming pretty close to an end."

The supermen! Whom was the Prime Minister of Canada indicting if it were not Anthony Eden, the Prime Minister of Britain, a figure already prostrate, ill and doomed? In truth, St. Laurent was not thinking of Eden. He was thinking of all the white races and their leaders everywhere who could not see, as he had seen, the long misery, the awakening and the potential power of mankind's coloured majority.

Useless now to attempt an explanation. The damage of the "supermen" speech was irrevocable. In any case, while it grimly prepared for an election next year, the Government had lost all power of expression. Its lines of communication with the people had not broken down by accident; they had withered from lack of use.

Moreover, the Government, by the very success of its policies, had drained its capital of ideas, had hopefully appointed Walter Gordon's royal commission on the economic future to invent new ones; but, as Howe had urged from the start, they would be invented too late. They could only serve to reflect on past Liberal management and to confuse the public, as they confuse it today.

Still the Government did not conceive the possibility of defeat. It had governed well, under King and St. Laurent, since 1935. The nation remained prosperous as the historic year of 1957 began. The Conservative Party had chosen Diefenbaker to lead it but the Liberal politicians regarded him with contempt. While Howe might have antagonized some voters with his pipeline closure, and St. Laurent with his supermen speech, even shrewd advisers like Pickersgill had no doubt about the Government's third electoral victory.

Such men had not only overestimated their own strength and underestimated Diefenbaker. They had completely misconstrued the mood of the public. It was incensed, in many areas, by the closure and the Suez affair and everywhere was tired of a Government too long in power.

Finally, the Liberal strategists misconstrued the national economy and could not grasp the fact that the big boom, that essential ally of the régime, was dying with it.

Despite its occasional ups and downs, the boom had continued without serious interruption since the war. Howe's bold White Paper of 1945, promising perpetual full employment, had been fully confirmed—not by the Government, as it was inclined to assume, but by the hungry world market. Few economists and almost no politicians realized that the titanic growth of the Canadian economy had been bought at the high price of an inflated currency, exchange deficits, capital imports, a towering foreign debt and the wholesale alienation of Canadian resources to foreign investors. Canada, fortune's fool, was living wildly beyond its means.

A larger price, the deep distortion of the economy by the growth of uneconomic industries, incapable of normal competition, had hardly been glimpsed yet. A still larger price—the distortion of the public mind by excessive expectations, its corruption by a sense of superiority over other peoples because they happened to be temporarily poor—had not been suspected at all.

As Harris, the Minister of Finance and of politics, wrote his election budget he was too wise to ignore the Government's danger and frankly expected to be beaten in his own constituency; but he and his advisers continued to regard inflation as a greater risk than deflation, though Howe's experts had already concluded that the tide of economic growth was setting.

Hence, among other honest political mistakes, Harris courageously refused to increase old-age pensions by more than $6 a month while Diefenbaker promised contradictory miracles of sky-high spending with lower taxes and angrily assailed the Government's greatest financial achievement in budgeting for surpluses and reducing internal debt. Harris was so sure of his generally sound policies that he made no serious effort to explain or defend them. The public never understood them until after they had been repealed in favour of the miracles.

The Government, in sum, was dying not from stupidity or failure in any concrete aspect of policy. With glowing health and boundless wealth it was dying from a vague disease, from age, smugness, a sense of its own immortality and a misjudgment of both the people and the nation's true economic position. The fact that Diefenbaker's misjudgment was much worse and would lead almost to bankruptcy within five years had no bearing on the election campaign.

It was Diefenbaker's campaign from the beginning. St. Laurent attempted only the motions, with dignity, fortitude and little effect. He was too tired to do more and his faithful palace guard had warned him not to try. His record of accomplishment, his honourable reputation, the people's real affection for him would be more than enough to extinguish the fireworks of the upstart prairie prophet.

Thus advised by those he trusted, and restrained by his own health, St. Laurent walked through the campaign in numbed benevolence. On the platform, or when he shook hands with the local voters and patted their children's heads, he was still, at the age of seventy-five, an impressive combination of confident statesman and good old Uncle Louis. His speeches were quiet, friendly and sensible, his manner unruffled, but if the crowds saw little change in him they also began to sense that he was really saying nothing.

What was there to say? The Government's record spoke for itself. And surely a hard-headed electorate could not believe the preposterous paradox of Diefenbaker's promises. Doubtless not many voters actually did believe or even understand them. The people's instinct, unconscious and inarticulate, was right, all the same. They knew in their bones that the Government was too old and must be changed.

The wonder, as we can see now, was not that St. Laurent failed to kindle his campaign while Diefenbaker's pyromania had produced a conflagration, but that the Liberal Party escaped a total disaster.

On the night of June 10 St. Laurent awaited the election returns in his Quebec City house. He awaited them confidently before the television set upstairs, without the least excitement, fully intending to hand on an intact administration to his successor at the earliest possible date.

Pickersgill was with him, jumpy and cheerful as usual, then suddenly incredulous as the unbelievable news poured in.

The Maritimes, his own political preserve, had turned to Diefenbaker. St. Laurent had held Quebec, as no leader except a French Canadian could hope to hold it, but the Conservative flood had engulfed Ontario, even submerging Howe, and the West was going, too.

Though the Government had won 40% of the popular vote, the Opposition 39, there were only 105 Liberals in the new Parliament against 112 Conservatives, 25 C.C.F. members and 19 Social Crediters. The next government, whatever its label, must survive as a minority.

These figures mattered little. The election's essential meaning was plain enough—the momentous era of King, Lapointe, Howe and St. Laurent, the era of depression, war, social revolution and boom had ended with its managers that night.

Senator Power heard the first returns in his own home and, as the wisest politician of the Liberal Party, quickly saw that the jig was up. He strolled over to St. Laurent's house to find the Prime Minister unshaken.

What did St. Laurent intend to do? He had an undoubted constitutional right to meet Parliament and test its opinion. If he had loved office as King had loved it he would have attempted to make a deal with the C.C.F. like King's deal with the Progressives in 1925. St. Laurent was not that kind of man. He told Pickersgill and Power that of course he would resign and make way for Diefenbaker.

So he did, on June 21. He sat impassively in the opposition leader's seat through the autumn parliamentary session, delivered a generous speech of farewell to politics, with no word of lament or bitterness and, his labour done, retired to his law office in Quebec.

He never doubted that Diefenbaker must fail. It was galling to be replaced by such a rival but this democratic spasm would pass in due time. For St. Laurent the rest was silence. Nothing became his public life so well as his taking leave of it. An old man's tranquility, the glow of sunset and renewed health of body and mind had returned to the magnificent amateur of politics.

What had he contributed to his time in Canada? While history may give first rank to his work of unity between the races, his imaginative foreign policy and his social reforms at home, they are not his largest monument. Behind all these definable achievements he had given the office of Prime Minister a new size and status, a people's trust, a certain indefinable flavour of justice and honour untouched by partisan quarrel. Few men could sustain those abstract values, more important than any concrete policy. His successor hastened at once to squander what he could never understand.

16: The Lost Prophet

The Conservative Party of British Columbia, convening at Kamloops in 1926, paused briefly to welcome a mysterious young stranger. He was tall, lean, almost skeletal, his bodily motions jerky and spasmodic, his face pinched and white, his pallor emphasized by metallic black curls and sunken, hypnotic eyes. But from this frail, wraithlike person, so deceptive in his look of physical infirmity, a voice of vehement power and rude health blared like a trombone.

As the representative of the Conservative Party in Saskatchewan (where it was then only a wistful aspiration) the stranger uttered the platitudes appropriate to a convention. No one at Kamloops remembered what he said. Of all Canadians active in politics the prairie visitor seemed least likely to become the nation's Prime Minister. Of all possible contenders for that prize he was apparently the least equipped.

The delegates did not hear their guest's name again for some twenty years. They had been wrong in one judgment, right in the other. John George Diefenbaker became Prime Minister in the fullness of time and the vagary of the democratic system but he was never equipped for the office and made of it, considering his opportunities, the most notable failure in its history.

Diefenbaker's tragedy—a tragedy for the man and for the nation that he had misgoverned—came from many causes, the deepest among them lost in the superficial controversy, the spite and adulation, the hyperbole of praise and abuse surrounding his name. We must go beyond the fact of his fall to find the true significance of Diefenbaker.

314

The Conservative Party's long exile in the wilderness had bred a desperate hunger for office at any price and a reckless irresponsibility in seeking it, as prolonged authority had bred irresponsible arrogance in the Liberal Government. Since the departure of Meighen and Bennett, Canadian Conservatism had produced no figure of the first rank, or if Drew could be so reckoned he was not a figure appealing to the electorate and had retired in ill health and despair. Only the consequent vacuum could have allowed the emergence of Diefenbaker, after his many false starts, for lack of a better candidate. And only the mouldering decreptitude of the Government could have elected him.

Yet Diefenbaker's curious record of triumph and bankruptcy (almost including that of the nation itself) was no accident. It represented forces larger and more obscure than he himself ever realized.

It represented, even as he tried to deny it, the shift of Canadian civilization from country to town, from simplicity to complexity, from individualism to collectivism, from the known to the unknown, from the comfortable certainties of the past to the harsh uncertainties of the nation's present and future. By misunderstanding these movements Diefenbaker inevitably mismanaged everything. Few of his enemies understood them any better but they were out of office and he was in it at the time of basic change and therefore must take the blame.

Diefenbaker's record represented not only his own private confusion but the confusion of society at large and the unnecessary chaos of the whole political apparatus which this radical lamb in conservative wolf's clothing stood on its head.

Above all, despite his bewildered humanitarianism and his genuine feeling for the average man, Diefenbaker represented a strange Canadian illusion but, for the moment, fulfilled a vain Canadian hope.

The illusion was a nation's attempt to do more than its means permitted, to consume more than it produced, to build a society for which neither it nor its leader was ready. The hope of doing these things was nurtured by Diefenbaker's oratory, never by his mind, and was hopeless by definition.

In short, Diefenbaker both represented and blindly fomented Canada's refusal to face the facts of its life. The price of this refusal is not fully paid even today.

That his enemies were equally confused and often grossly unfair to him is irrelevant to any serious examination of the Diefenbaker

315

phenomenon. Despite all the conflicting evidence, true and false, the malice, the betrayals and the retrospective judgment of his political post-mortem, the answer to the riddle is quite clear—though Diefenbaker had high talents, he never at any time knew what he wanted to do with them when he had the chance.

For all his patient homework and ceaseless study, he had learned no philosophy of government. He lacked any experience of management in politics or business, any real comprehension of the social process or indeed, of himself. Beyond mere craftsmanship and political ingenuity he had only hunches, sometimes benign, sometimes malignant, always inchoate and disjointed.

As a result, these hunches, once reluctantly translated into action, were nothing more than a wild surmise and, with rare exceptions, unworkable. That was the strangest of all his failures—the failure to make his talents work for him constructively as they had worked so well in destroying his enemies.

A political touch far superior to that of such rivals as Pearson; a sense of public mentality at its lowest common denominator as sensitive as King's and just as feminine; a gift of human warmth, of wit and mimicry; a certain playful boyishness so long as no camera was pointed at him; even an occasional glint of inspiration and always a flavour of killing invective, a leer of insinuation, a sure instinct for crowds and headlines, a kind of weird manic grandeur—all these assets Diefenbaker possessed in abundance as Pearson did not. The pity of it was that Diefenbaker combined them in the end to make a crushing liability. He wanted so much to do his best but could not find the means of putting his abilities to work for more than election purposes, and for them only briefly.

Perhaps these talents of themselves assured his failure. Being purely subjective and ruthlessly egocentric, they distracted him from the public's business to himself. They seemed at first to express the common denominator of Canada and no doubt that was his intention but in truth they were concentrated on Diefenbaker as the chosen man of destiny. In him narcissism, an essential quality common to all leaders of men, became a ravening appetite and finally an obsession, eroding what might have been a great Prime Minister.

His inferiority complex (much like King's) and his youthful humility, those fruits of long disappointment and gallant perseverance, were like a taut bow-string. Released too late by overpowering success, the arrow went straight to his own heart.

Success was written in his stars so long as he remained a critic, an advocate at the bar of justice, the moral conscience of little men, for he had been cut out by nature to be a permanent opposition leader. Failure was inescapable when he grasped power without knowing its uses.

Historians will waste endless speculation on the iconoclast who stumbled into the wrong niche and smashed his own icon but no psychologist is needed to explain the enigma of this man. Diefenbaker could endure failure with majestic courage. He could not endure success. Nor, for that matter, could the nation that first worshipped and then crucified him as fate had ordained from the beginning. The old cycle of hubris and nemesis, so often repeated throughout our politics, found in him its supreme and classic version. Hence the tragedy of man and nation together.

The public facts of his life have been so ably recorded by Mr. Peter Newman in his book, *Renegade in Power,* that they will be drastically condensed here. In any case, the public facts explain little. It is not enough to examine Diefenbaker's personal record. To understand his era we must examine ourselves as well. That examination cannot be pleasant for him or for us.

Two decisive facts of Diefenbaker's life were established at his birth.

He was born at Neustadt, an Ontario village south of Owen Sound, on September 18, 1895, and the sense of being a small-town man, among the poor and oppressed classes, never left him. The ancestors of his father, William Thomas Diefenbaker, had come to Canada from southern Germany in 1816, and those of his mother, Mary Florence Bannerman, from the Scottish Highlands in 1812. Thus he was a Canadian of old and durable stock but his German heritage gave him a lasting sympathy with ethnic minorities. His German name was a political handicap but he carried it proudly like a banner and finally made men follow it.

The intense family devotion of the Diefenbakers, a third fact of importance, grew out of their uncomplaining poverty as they moved to the suburbs of Toronto, where the father taught school, and in 1903, to a Saskatchewan farm north of Saskatoon.

Boyhood close to the soil, to crops, animals and simple folk; the hard chores in summer heat and winter cold; the influence of a dauntless mother and a gentle father; the years in Saskatoon where the father was employed by the provincial government and the two sons, John and Elmer, sold newspapers, John's most distinguished customer being Sir Wilfrid Laurier, who once chatted with him in a railway station; graduation from the University of Saskatchewan in 1916; a lieutenant's commission in the Canadian Army and a short spell of service in England, from which he was invalided home to take his law degree and begin practice first at Wakaw and later at Prince Albert—such were the bare and commonplace facts of Diefenbaker's apprenticeship.

They were not as bare or commonplace as they looked. Young Diefenbaker already had begun to store away the vital reserves of any successful politician—an education through books that no school can provide, an education in human nature to be found only in the close contacts of small towns, best of all in the grimy work of criminal courts. Also, he had learned the habit of frugal living and could never be corrupted by luxury.

Diefenbaker was a born politician. From his first attachment to the Liberal Party of his father, his nomination as a Conservative in the federal election of 1925, his defeat then and again in 1926 against no less a rival than King, Diefenbaker sacrificed everything to politics. Though he was happily married to Edna M. Bower, a vivacious school teacher, and prospered in his profession as one of Saskatchewan's leading lawyers, neither domestic comfort nor money diverted him from the single ambition of his life. Even as a high-school boy he intended to be Prime Minister.

No contender for that office ever suffered such disappointment and none bore it so patiently. Five defeats in federal, provincial and municipal elections could not quench his thirst for power, the certainty of his mission. When the Conservatives of Lake Centre could find no local candidate they nominated and elected Diefenbaker to Parliament in 1940.

His foot was on the first rung of the ladder but Ottawa, busy with the war, hardly noticed, at first, the gaunt new figure in the tiny Conservative Opposition. The trombone voice soon made itself heard, however, always on behalf of the little man. It was still more strident in the opposition caucus which slowly realized that if Diefenbaker wore a party label he was not a Conservative but a grass-roots heretic, his position indefinable.

The seventeen years of opposition seemed a waste for the rebel and lone wolf from the Liberal West. His defeat by John Bracken as a candidate for the party leadership in 1942 and again by Drew in 1948 apparently denied him the only prize he asked of life. In truth these defeats saved the prize for later award. If he had led his party in those days a Government then unbeatable would have extinguished him.

He was not yet the man so familiar to all Canadians later on. The explosion of his ego had not yet occurred to change and warp him.

As I can attest from intimate experience, he was then a man of peculiar humility, eager to learn, candid in admitting his lack of knowledge and direction, always groping, in books, documents, parliamentary debate and private conversation, for the philosophy which he never quite managed to accumulate.

No man in Ottawa was a more delightful, considerate and humorous companion. Those who have known him only as the Messianic prophet and shrill orator of the hustings cannot imagine the personality of Diefenbaker, the private man, in the frustration of failure and almost of exile among his Conservative colleagues.

As a raconteur he had no equal (though his stories were always immaculate, for no man could be more scrupulous in manners and morals than the Baptist teetotaler and devout Christian). As a mimic he could bring to life the ponderous banalities of King, Lapointe's French accent and passionate gestures, St. Laurent's clipped sentences and eloquent shrug, the jumpy movements of Pickersgill and the supercilious look of Drew.

This repertoire was varied and endless. Striding up and down his little office in the Centre Block, Diefenbaker would people it with the entire Parliament from the Speaker to the page boys. His assortment of characters, inflections, expressions and grimaces would have made him a star on any stage. He could have played Hamlet or Touchstone, Macbeth or Lady Macbeth, and once, in the British Columbia Supreme Court, he fell to the floor, clutching his throat, to show how a murder had been committed, until a horrified judge rebuked him.

All this clownery, public and private, had its serious purpose. He was rehearsing a larger role. He was learning to play Diefenbaker.

Here, as one looks back on it, was the beginning of his climb and the assurance of his fall. For Diefenbaker mistook acting for action and gradually came to believe in his own act. Better than any contemporary he could mouth the words and imitate the thoughts of others but, like King, he had no originality of mind. Like King, he lacked a sense of words, the music of language, the ring of sentences; but he learned how to breathe a glowing authenticity into the scripts of speech writers like the brilliant Grattan O'Leary. Thus he made himself an orator before he ever made up his mind on policy and must drown in the flood of his own rhetoric because he had no policy to keep him afloat.

Another element of the strange alchemy now transmuting a minor back-bench critic into a Prime Minister had begun to emerge. Beneath his open gusto on the platform and his geniality in private, a canker of regret, a sense of injustice and a feeling of envy were embittering Diefenbaker's naturally cheerful disposition.

He had some reason to resent his treatment by the Conservative Party since he believed that the convention of 1948 had been dishonestly packed against him and in favour of Drew. He believed, too, that he was a much better man than Drew, whom he disliked and often mocked. Strangest of all in the Diefenbaker chemistry was a secret admiration of King, whose outward methods of smooth compromise he resolved to copy but whose inward genius he lacked.

Both men suffered from the same fear of failure and were similar in their fuzziness of mind. Both could convince themselves of anything they wanted to believe. The testament to this queer association —always unspoken, strictly formal and in King's case contemptuous —would hang eventually over Diefenbaker's bed in the Prime Minister's residence. It was a careless little note from King congratulating the younger man on an obscure speech.

If Diefenbaker's pride in his enemy's praise was pathetic, so, until 1956, was his whole career to date—pathetic in its lonely frustration but valiant in its dogged persistence. He had never doubted that he was the man chosen to reform Canada and now Providence suddenly seemed to confirm his judgment. At last, without warning, the long-awaited reward was offered by Drew's retirement.

Later on Diefenbaker made Conservatism the pale shadow of himself but when the party convention met at Ottawa on December 10, 1956, he was by no means its idol. He had more than sufficient votes, pledged in advance, to win the leadership but he was opposed by much of the party's old guard and traditional campaign-fund financiers, especially by those who accused him of disloyalty to Drew. Besides, the Old Guard suspected, quite rightly, that Diefenbaker was not a Conservative. More serious for him, and for the nation, was the enmity of the Quebec delegation led by Léon Balcer.

The choice of Diefenbaker was guaranteed nevertheless by the undeniable fact that he had a better prospect than any competitor to win the next election, though the prospect looked pretty slight to anyone but him. In giving Diefenbaker 774 votes, Donald Fleming 393 and Davie Fulton 117, the convention made a conscious and wise political decision. Some other decisions were unconscious, their meaning unguessed.

In the first place, the party did not know the man or the purposes contained in Diefenbaker's public figure. That was not surprising since he did not know them himself, apart from the single purpose of electoral success.

Secondly, the party did not know that Diefenbaker would never forgive Fleming, Fulton and the Quebec Conservatives for daring to oppose him or that even in this hour of celebration the seeds of discord had been planted in any future Conservative Cabinet.

Thirdly, the old guard might suspect but the party as a whole did not know that in choosing Diefenbaker it had shifted the centre of its political gravity from the right to the left, from the citadel of Ontario to the agrarian West, from the urban to the rural vote.

The ideology, the direction and the character of the party had been altered more drastically by the choice of Diefenbaker than by any event since Macdonald constructed his Liberal-Conservative coalition.

All these vital facts were lost in the cheers of the delegates. They saw before them the one man who might defeat the Government, who promised to defeat it and sincerely believed his promise, the dauntless man who had endured more than thirty years of disappointment, had never lost hope and, by his courage, deserved his chance.

At the age of sixty-one years Diefenbaker still seemed to express the fire and the dream of youth. Yet his hair, now turned from black to gray, the lines of strength and suffering around his piercing eyes, the kaleidoscopic changes of storm and sunshine passing across his rugged face, the solemn shake of his head and the harsh confidence of his voice all seemed to represent the wisdom of maturity. Youth and age together, the experience and the scars of political war combined with a boy's shining idealism—this was the measure of Diefenbaker's magic.

He had come a long way from the prairie village and the dusty western courtroom. The barren years that would have killed the ambition of most men had only served to corroborate his knowledge of destiny because, like King's, it was ordained by God. He was honourably poor in the world's goods but he had the treasure of his mission. He was enriched by the decay of the St. Laurent Government, the anger of the people, his own vibrant physical health (which a nervous twitch and a slight deafness had not impaired) and a serene domestic life.

Perhaps the greatest treasure of all was his second wife, the former Olive Freeman Power, whom he had married in 1953, after Edna's death. Olive, a sweetheart of his youth, assured the perfect companionship of his age. She comforted and sustained him in his home, stood beside him on the platform and unobtrusively won him countless votes wherever they went together. No other party leader's wife had ever played Olive's role in politics as the image of wholesome Canadian womanhood.

Another fact was significant as Diefenbaker prepared for his hour of test. He had no children by either marriage. Fortune had denied him, as it had denied King, Bennett, Borden and Laurier, that highest of all blessings but the absence of children left Diefenbaker free of domestic distraction, probably of pain also, to pursue his solitary and consuming ambition. How different his career and those of his predecessors might have been with children beside them, and how different the affairs of Canada, is a fascinating thought for students of political psychology.

These imponderables mattered little when Diefenbaker launched the election campaign of 1957. What mattered was the electric shock of the man himself. The nation had watched him with little interest for three decades but now he appeared as a new and unknown force, a dramatic and heroic figure suddenly dwarfing the old men of the tired Government. A neglected cocoon had opened to emit a gorgeous butterfly. The stage was instantly illuminated by an actor striding, after so many false cues, from the wings.

While such metaphors must spring to the minds of all who remember the campaign of 1957, the practical fact was that the Conservative Party had found the greatest political campaigner in the nation's history. St. Laurent's solid dignity, King's humble appeal to reason, Bennett's sulphurous oratory, even Laurier's saintly aura all paled beside Diefenbaker's flaming amalgam of outraged virtue, downtrodden justice and the unconquerable Canadian spirit.

It was not what he said but the way he said it that roused the nation. "Canada first . . . the sacred trust . . . an appointment with destiny . . . equality of opportunity . . . the road to greatness . . ." look flat in print. Diefenbaker's thunderous voice, with his vivid gestures and the mesmeric twist of his face, made platitudes fly like eagles.

The Liberals had given the nation sound management and steady competence. Diefenbaker appeared as the agent of reviving morality, the instrument of a miracle, the common man incarnate. Nothing can disparage the audacity, the spectacle and the undoubted conviction of Diefenbaker's campaign, even if it was for the most part factual nonsense. By ignoring the facts he had come to believe his own words or he could not have said them so well. This was more than a campaign; it was a volcano whose debris overflowed the Government because it failed to take Diefenbaker seriously.

Before he had been on the road a week he completely revised the pattern of Canadian politics. He not only possessed the Conservative Party; he made it the Diefenbaker Party. Not only had he abandoned its Conservative principles and moved it to the left of Liberalism; he had almost abandoned its name, which appeared in the small print of all his publicity beneath the big print of his own.

Not only had he revived the old barnstorming techniques of earlier times, tearing passion to tatters and out-heroding Herod; he had combined these traditional methods of the little western town with the new advertising methods of the metropolis, importing for the first time the depth psychology and market research of Madison Avenue as skilfully deployed by his public-relations expert, Allister Grosart, that ablest of all back-room boys.

Not only had he made himself the personification of the old-fashioned average man; he had revised for Canadian use the foreign cult of personality and, most miraculous of all, had made it look natively Canadian.

This assortment of old and new techniques produced a marvelous work of political invention. That it was phony mattered not at all. Diefenbaker never questioned his own veracity, even if one speech flatly contradicted another, and the voters were not interested in facts anyway. For the volcano had erupted at a moment of history and public humour that must always puzzle the future historians—a moment of collective untruth. And by instinct, not by reason, Diefenbaker knew precisely how to exploit this moment because he shared it with the people.

He dominated the election, as St. Laurent defaulted it, but its historical significance cannot be discovered in personalities or even in the shift, or rather the chaos, of public policy. What mattered above everything and decided everything was the Canadian people's reaction to a social process that neither they nor their leader yet understood.

The big boom was over now, as a few of Howe's experts had vainly warned an incredulous Government. The world market had returned to rigorous competition and many Canadian industries, artificially fattened by the boom, were hard pressed by the new climate at home and abroad. A new kind of unemployment had appeared in the organic structure of a brittle, mechanized society and could not be cured by the familiar methods of monetary manipulation. Economic growth had slowed down and, on a per capita basis, would soon stop altogether.

Canada had no intention of adjusting itself to the changed facts of life. Misled and softened by twelve easy years, it refused to believe that its happy time could end so soon. Instead of facing the facts and overcoming them, it was determined to extend a boom already dead despite all its lingering show of life. When the truth could be disputed no longer Canada became the crybaby of the free world.

In spiritual terms this was the worst and least typical period of Canadian history, denying its people's whole nature, their thrift, their practicality, their cold northern common sense. But it was a period exactly designed for Diefenbaker's use.

As the campaign opened the depth of the economic change was hardly suspected by the best economists, most of whom, in the Finance Department and the Bank of Canada, still thought that inflation was more dangerous than deflation. Diefenbaker's supreme feat was to make them both appear equally dangerous, to prescribe double remedies mutually exclusive and to give this flagrant paradox a look of honest consistency by promising everything at the same time.

If this was economic madness, as the Liberals thought, it did not lack method. Diefenbaker had determined to free his party from the reputation, unjustly fastened on it in Bennett's time, as the party of depression.

His promises may well have been sincere, because he knew little of finance or economics, but they were certainly grotesque. He promised to increase spending on a huge scale, to reduce taxes yet somehow to balance the national budget, thus stimulating business and curing unemployment. In the next breath he denounced excessive taxes as the root cause of inflation, thus turning economic laws into absurdity. Then he denounced the sensible budgetary surpluses of the boom years, and the resulting attack on the war debt and on inflation, as the crime of "over-taxation," apparently believing that the public coffers were fat with superfluous revenue secreted by a miserly Government just to squeeze the people for the fun of it. Using a new set of figures every week, he convinced many voters that they had been defrauded.

He promised higher old-age pensions and better social services for everybody at nobody's expense, since the hidden kitty in the Government's vault would finance all these costs painlessly.

He promised to revivify the Commonwealth by expanding its trade; to divert a large portion of Canada's imports (later fixed as 15%) from the United States to Britain; but always to protect Canadian industry from too much external competition. He even resurrected one of King's old mummies by promising to reform the Senate.

This array of economic impossibilities seemed so preposterous to the Government that it hardly tried to argue with Diefenbaker.

Foolishly it relied instead on the voters' knowledge of simple arithmetic.

Diefenbaker's trick of adding two and two together and making five, or fifty, or five hundred, as occasion required, was nothing new in Canada. All political leaders had used it more or less. Doubtless a majority of Canadians regarded it as nothing more than the customary ritual of politics, the quadrennial visit of Santa Claus, but enough of them believed enough of it, and still more had ceased to believe in the Government.

The true importance of the campaign, however, was not Diefenbaker's one-man victory but his disruption of the party system. As only a few Liberals and not many Conservatives had the wit to see, he made Conservatism the leftist party of reform, the rebuilder of the post-boom era, while Liberalism was thrust to the right as the party of the conservative *status quo*.

That Diefenbaker honestly considered himself the guardian of the future cannot be questioned. That he had no notion of its direction was not yet clear to him or the public. That the Liberal Party needed a spell of opposition to re-think its entire attitude was apparent to a few Liberals, repugnant to most. That Diefenbaker's arrival in office, even with a minority vote and a minority in Parliament, was the greatest achievement of Canadian politics since King's arrival in 1921 no one can deny.

Once Diefenbaker became Prime Minister on June 21 it was certain that he would be given at least a working majority as soon as he could find an excuse for another election but it would not necessarily be an overwhelming majority if Pearson, the newly chosen Liberal leader, avoided some grievous mistake.

As will be recorded at the proper place, Pearson committed that mistake early in 1958. The worst hour of his life, and perhaps the best of Diefenbaker's, provided an unforgettable scene in the House of Commons and seemed to assure the Government an indefinite term of office.

The Prime Minister looked bigger that day than he would ever look again. He listened impassively to Pearson's dreadful speech, his eyes on the ceiling, a hearing aid affixed to his ear and certain documents piled on his desk. He had no way of knowing, and no reason for hoping, that Pearson would demand the Government's resignation and the Liberal Party's recall to power. When that ludicrous motion fell from the opposition leader's lips the House laughed. Diefenbaker's eyes were still on the ceiling, his face immobile, his body slumped in apparent lethargy.

At last he rose slowly and, facing Pearson, mildly congratulated him on his speech. Then as he turned away in scorn from the opposition benches, Diefenbaker's voice changed to a rasping gutteral and he spat out a savage insult: "I congratulate him—but not for courage!"

Now a born actor launched into the superlative act of his life. The alternating thrusts of anger and contempt tore his rival into such minute fragments that their reassembly at any future time seemed dubious. The growls of moral anger and grins of sarcasm manipulated his followers like marionettes who cheered, laughed or fell silent at his bidding.

This performance—extemporaneous, delicious and rather terrifying—was only prologue. Having finally destroyed Pearson, or so it appeared in those ecstatic moments, Diefenbaker applied his *coup de grâce* by suddenly seizing the papers on his desk and flourishing a secret report.

Prepared a year earlier by Howe's deputy, Mitchell Sharp, this document had warned the Liberal Government that the national economy was in decline; and yet, said Diefenbaker, the Government had fraudulently represented business as prosperous and tried to win an election on false pretences.

Such a breach of Cabinet secrecy was outrageous, of course, and unprecedented; but the report had been confirmed already by heavy unemployment and it was murder in politics. Since Pearson had provided the necessary excuse by his ridiculous want-of-confidence motion, Diefenbaker immediately dissolved Parliament, called an election for March 31 and repeated his barnstorming campaign of 1957.

This time he did not need to make additional promises, except his "Vision" of northern development, and relied on exciting generalities—"We'll build a nation of fifty million within the lifetime of many of you here. . . . Adventure, adventure to the nation's utmost bounds, to strive, to seek, to find and not to yield. . . . Instead of the hopelessness and fear the Liberals generate we have given faith. . . . So long as I am in power no person is going to suffer because of the inaction of the Government."

As he waited in Prince Albert, the ritual biography of Lincoln in his hands, the unbelievable news poured in—208 seats for the Government, 49 for the Liberal Party, 8 for the C.C.F. and none for Social Credit. Diefenbaker had won the largest majority on record. Under Pearson, Liberalism had reached rock bottom.

This was the unprecedented triumph of one man as kindly assisted by his enemies. Diefenbaker had been so generally acclaimed the greatest Conservative since Macdonald that no wonder he began to believe it himself. Not only had a clear majority of Canadians decided to "Follow John," as advised by the election slogan; a good many of them almost believed that he could walk on water.

The new juggernaut constructed almost solely by Diefenbaker's hands and wearing an incidental Conservative badge should be good for several terms of office at a minimum. Yet any qualified political mechanic examining the inner gears of this mighty apparatus must see that they did not mesh. For a variety of reasons, generally overlooked, they could not mesh without drastic alteration, and unaltered, must eventually shatter the engine with its engineer.

He was the last to suspect these inner frictions. For at the start everything went even better than he had hoped.

The Cabinet formed in 1957 had given an appearance of speed, efficiency and that youthful enthusiasm long absent from Ottawa.

Diefenbaker had met his fellow Prime Ministers in London, deeply impressed the British Government and been hailed by languishing imperialists like Beaverbrook as the strong man, the true hope of the Commonwealth.

Installed in the East Block, among his precious relics of John A. Macdonald, Diefenbaker worked perhaps harder than any predecessor. He arose at his Sussex Street residence around 5:30 A.M., drank a glass of milk in the kitchen, spent an hour or two alone with his papers, reached his office about eight, took his lunch there on a tray, went home late and used the evening for study. His door was open to countless visitors, his telephone was constantly in use, he found time for frequent speeches all over the country and soon traveled around the world to meet his fellow statesmen.

Various peripheral decisions had been taken at an autumn session of Parliament—a small tax reduction, an old-age-pension increase, agreement to launch the hospital-insurance scheme already arranged by St. Laurent, and substantial aid to farmers—but every central decision was postponed, every point of controversy avoided, even when the Government had won the enormous majority of 1958.

This evasion was not fortuitous. It followed inevitably from Diefenbaker's unique concept of his office.

In fairness (as rarely accorded him by his enemies) history will note that the economic problems now developing and left unsolved by Diefenbaker were not of his making. They came from a process which the Liberal Government had failed to understand, which Diefenbaker understood no better and which still bewilders his successors. They came from the distortions of a rich social system not yet able to distribute fully the abundance of its factories or to keep all its people at work.

Neither Diefenbaker nor any other Canadian knew how to break that paradox in a free society but he had made the mistake (as Pearson did after him) of promising to break it almost overnight. It was not so much the problems themselves as the contrast between promise and performance that alienated the people.

They might have accepted the bread of slow, systematic progress if Diefenbaker had promised no more than that but he had promised the cake of quick, easy solutions and these were patently impossible. The problems could not be seriously approached, much less solved, by his methods of management.

The first, but by no means the last, errors of his administrative system appeared from the beginning. It was to be rule by one man and it might have succeeded on that basis, as it had succeeded for some years under Bennett, if Diefenbaker had enforced it in policy as in ritual.

He asked the unquestioning obedience of the Cabinet and received it because he absolutely controlled the Conservative Party. He fed on the flattery of his colleagues, who supplied it in abundance, and even insisted that they drop all business to welcome him at the airport whenever he arrived in town from his ceaseless travels; but he also demanded unanimity in Cabinet decisions.

That being impossible in any Cabinet, the big decisions were usually delayed, referred to royal commissions or paralyzed altogether. The Government, for all its look of strength, was crippled because it could seldom agree on anything fundamental. As will be shown, it had no policy at all in the nation's most essential business and when it attempted to enforce a policy toward the end this unaccustomed strain disrupted it.

Here a distinction should be made, but is not often made, between policy and ideas.

Diefenbaker had plenty of ideas, some of them grand and exalted. The grass-roots reformer, scarred by the Great Depression and the misery of his prairie neighbours, was resolved to fight the big interests of central Canada who fattened on the poor man's toil (and usually supported the Conservative Party). Though he intended to run the Government single-handed, he regarded himself as the obedient servant of the people and to him the people were the poor, the underprivileged, the helpless.

Hence the curious antinomy of the rugged individualist and lone wolf in his own life who rejected the primary principle, or myth, of his party and believed as much as King in collective action, in the power of government for the general good, in the expansion of the welfare State.

Hence also, under his drive, the welfare State's rapid growth, unfortunately without the means of financing it; the larger intrusion of public authority in the private economy; the evolution, almost absent-mindedly, of the nation's most radical government up to now.

Diefenbaker might be the autocrat and queen bee in his Cabinet but more than any other Prime Minister he was a democrat in his instinct. He believed in the deep, subconscious wisdom of the people, so long as they supported his efforts to serve them.

These efforts failed for the most part because they were only instinctive, and were spasmodic and chaotic in execution. They issued in honest ideals, splendid slogans and some definite social reforms; never in coherent, over-all policy, never with any financial foundation, never with the painful economic changes needed to implement them. Offering the people cake, Diefenbaker expected them to eat it and have it, too.

Another fallacy was Diefenbaker's attempt to govern not by a stern and often unpopular judgment of events but by the precise measurement of his own popularity from day to day, almost from hour to hour.

Grosart, the accurate pulse-taker, who became more influential with his chief than any colleague, measured every spasm of the body politic and reported his diagnosis to Diefenbaker, who then prescribed a remedy; but the remedies were applied to the symptom, not to the disease. They were placeboes and sticking-plasters where the need was surgery. Each treatment placated some group of voters for the time being while the nation's sickness, deep down in the roots of the economy, was not and could not be cured by such superficial palliatives.

Through himself as the people's agent, Diefenbaker tried to enforce a kind of direct democracy, as if by daily plebiscite and Gallup Poll. He supposed that his duty was to give the people what they wanted, thus forgetting Burke's famous dictum to the electors of Bristol—that the duty of government under the parliamentary system is to give the people what they should have, whether they like it or not at first sight, and to accept their judgment at the polls when they have the end results clearly before them.

Instead, Diefenbaker construed government almost as a process of market research, Ottawa as the head office of a nation-wide merchandising chain that must always satisfy the customers whether the product was good for them or not.

Diefenbaker's philosophy, if it deserved the name, was so vague and so little understood, its execution through Grosart and the market researchers so secret, that the public never grasped it, in theory or practice. Even the crudest mechanic could see at once, however, the worst practical flaw in the juggernaut. Diefenbaker had totally misconstrued French Canada.

He had reversed the history of seventy-three years since Riel's judicial murder and demolished the old Liberal stronghold of Quebec; but this was a momentary and Pyrrhic victory. Quebec had voted for candidates calling themselves Conservatives not because it loved them more but the Liberals less, and within two years had regretted the verdict of 1958.

Diefenbaker had revived the old strategy of 1911 by allying the English-speaking Conservative Party with the Quebec nationalists, now known as the Union Nationale, because he could find no strength elsewhere. The alliance, as in Borden's time, was too fragile to resist any serious strain because the Union Nationale régime itself had begun to die.

With his towering prestige, Diefenbaker might have built a real Conservative Party in Quebec. He did not think it important even to try. Unchallengeable in the rest of the nation, he seemed to regard French Canada as peripheral, even expendable if necessary, and proceeded at once to expend it by violating the basic, unwritten law of national politics.

Every successful government (with the exception of Borden's Conservative-Liberal union, a brief wartime phenomenon) had been built on the coalition of an English-Canadian and a French-Canadian leader in almost equal partnership. Diefenbaker did not find, or seriously seek, a Quebec partner. With the exception of Balcer, the French Canadians appointed to the Cabinet were nonentities; and Balcer, as an original opponent of the Prime Minister, was stowed away and silenced in the minor office of Solicitor-General.

For the affront of these appointments Quebec would avenge itself at the first chance, not necessarily in Pearson's favour but against Diefenbaker. By assuming that he could govern successfully without substantial strength in Quebec, Diefenbaker already had fractured an indispensable gear in his machine.

Its most obvious weakness was the collective inexperience of the English-speaking ministers. Diefenbaker could not be blamed for that. After long sojourn in the wilderness the Conservative Party had no leaders of Cabinet experience. The Prime Minister must build at first with the materials at hand. He failed, however, to encourage and promote the excellent material of his back benches where young men of outstanding promise were idle, frustrated and restive.

To be sure, the average ability of the Conservative ministers, and their integrity, easily equalled that of the late Liberal Cabinet; but it is not the average minister, it is the rare exception who counts in the long run, and Diefenbaker could not distinguish the long run from the short. He lacked, and did not seem to want, such potent colleagues as surrounded, supported and frequently saved King.

The Conservative Cabinet included only one man of first-rate potential. Unfortunately Fulton, once a close friend of the Prime Minister, had been judged a rival for daring to seek the party's leadership and now permitting the newspapers to write him up as Diefenbaker's natural crown prince.

The sudden coolness of the Prime Minister drove Fulton into the august silence of the Justice Department. He operated competently and alone, his political talents largely lost to the ministry, his departure to his native British Columbia delayed but now certain.

In the finance portfolio, Fleming, the spokesman of Toronto business, should have been the right hand of the Prime Minister; as such he was immediately amputated. As a contender for the leadership Fleming was suspect and so was his supposed financial orthodoxy. He could seldom see his chief and frequently learned in the press for the first time that Diefenbaker had committed him to some huge new expenditure.

In any case, Fleming, a contradictory person of blustering public manner and private piety, a tiny fighting cock who invariably surrendered in the end, a strange mixture of Galahad and Pecksniff, soon undermined himself by his bold orthodox speeches and his opposite policies.

Howard Green, Vancouver's gaunt and rough-hewn ambassador, was one of the finest men to enter Parliament. He worshipped Diefenbaker and brought a new honesty into the Public Works Department. Later, in External Affairs, he was far outside his depth and his honourable, stubborn resistance to nuclear weapons planted them invisibly in the vitals of the party machine for future explosion.

George Hees behaved as a handsome, grinning playboy who quite frankly intended to be Prime Minister some day, but he made a sound Minister of Trade and loyally supported Diefenbaker so long as the weather remained fair.

The great surprise and major success of the Cabinet was Alvin Hamilton, a composite of buffoonery and rustic shrewdness. As Minister of Agriculture he became the farmer's hero, systematically improved farm life and held the Prairies as a solid Conservative fief.

Diefenbaker's inner Cabinet and operating lever of the administration did not include these prominent personalities. It consisted of the Prime Minister, David Walker, Minister of Public Works, Senator William Brunt and Grosart, all primarily politicians thinking of votes, not administrators thinking of policy.

It was policy, or the lack of it, that split the Government with three distinct and ever widening fissures.

From its first days it was embarrassed by Diefenbaker's promise to divert a large part of Canada's imports from the United States to Britain.

Taking him at his word, the British Government offered Canada a system of free trade and probably was not surprised to see Diefenbaker recoil in terror. But Britain did not expect him to enforce his promise in reverse by raising restrictions against British textiles and automobiles. The great trade-diversion plan was quickly forgotten. Though Diefenbaker undoubtedly felt a passionate emotional attachment to Britain, he demanded a one-sided commercial bargain, thus drawing heavily on his bank account of British goodwill.

The account was further depleted by his entirely honest and effective attack on the racial policies of South Africa. It withdrew from the Commonwealth mainly under his pressure. The British Government agreed with his principles but deplored his methods while the Canadian Liberals, who had been even more antagonistic to apartheid, criticized him for following their advice.

Diefenbaker's final break with the British Government, because it tried to join the European Common Market, Fleming's horrendous warnings against this un-British folly, Green's warning that the United States had cunningly plotted Britain's submergence in Europe, and the ugly climax of the Accra Conference looked irrational at the time. Actually their explanation is quite plain.

Not only did Diefenbaker believe that Britain's policy threatened the unity of the Commonwealth and Canada's prosperity; he also believed, though he could not say so out loud, that the Common Market was a temporary and unworkable experiment, certain to break up within a few years.

After exhausting all Britain's goodwill, he antagonized the United States by a depressingly lukewarm welcome to President Kennedy's grand design of general tariff reductions.

Thus a double quarrel of commercial policy produced the unprecedented spectacle of Canada alienated simultaneously from its two closest friends.

Green, who had always distrusted the United States and was now furious with Britain for its flirtation with the Common Market, rationalized Canada's sudden isolation by announcing a brave new doctrine. No longer, he said, was Canada merely the "honest broker" between America and Britain. The time had come to take an independent line.

In taking it, this excellent and strangely naive man opened a second fissure invisible for some time but ultimately disastrous.

So long as he had Pearson's support in rejecting nuclear weapons for Canada's defence forces—a sort of unwritten, unspoken alliance between Government and Opposition—Green could prevail in Cabinet, even against the tough new Defence Minister, Douglas Harkness. If Pearson reversed himself, Green's whole position must be endangered and with it the unity of the Government. That reverse could not be imagined, least of all by Pearson.

While the fissure of commercial and defence policy was rapidly expanding, the fissure of finance was too wide already ever to be closed by this Government.

Fleming's perpetual deficits, the fiasco of his conversion loan, the high interest rates produced by his gigantic borrowings, the expansion of the money supply to support them, the flight of borrowers to the United States, the resulting growth in foreign debt and eventually the collapse of foreign confidence in Canadian finance all would have been understandable if Fleming had believed in his own policies as a planned stimulus to the national economy. He did not.

On the contrary, he had committed himself to a strictly balanced budget, with no Liberal nonsense like deficits to prime the pump or surpluses to forestall inflation. Against the impossible odds of his colleagues' demand for ever more money, and his chief's genial habit of promising new expenditures without consulting him, Fleming worked patiently, some eighteen hours a day, to balance the budget and by the spring of 1960 announced triumphantly that at last the circle of finance had been squared.

His budget provided for a token surplus and this, he added, in Pecksniff's voice, was the fruit of "carefully designed policies." The surplus turned into a deficit of $340 million and Fleming had to take all the blame. He had been misled by the mistaken estimates of his officials but he never reproached them. Nor did he ever admit a mistake even to himself.

From then on no serious attempt was made to arrest the slide toward insolvency. The deficits continued, not because the Government believed in them but because it lacked the courage to reduce them. Its plea that they were successfully used to counteract business recession, to rekindle economic growth, then at a standstill, and to cure unemployment is disproved by the figures. Often deficits and unemployment increased simultaneously and business improved as deficits fell, in a wild Keynesian parody.

Perhaps the financial fissure could have been disguised sufficiently for the purposes of an election if it had not been for James Coyne. The Government's squalid feud with the Governor of the Bank of Canada has been told and retold; its irony, however, is usually overlooked.

In the first place, when Coyne launched his one-man crusade to save Canada by curbing credit, governmental expenditure and foreign imports he was sincere and moved by a lonely sense of obligation. He was also preaching, as he thought, the true doctrine of Conservatism which the Government lacked the courage to enforce. Therefore, he deserved the Government's thanks and apparently expected to receive them.

Moreover, while such a campaign of heresy by a public servant broke all the rules of official behaviour and appalled his colleagues at the bank, the Government, in Coyne's usually cold judgment, had tacitly authorized and even encouraged him. For Fleming, whenever he was criticized for Coyne's high interest rates, had always insisted that the bank was entirely independent of the Government, that credit policy was under exclusive bank control, though he had said exactly the reverse in his opposition days.

Then Fleming suddenly announced a complete change of policy without the least change of expression. The bank, he said, was bound to carry out the Government's instructions and since Coyne refused, he must go. Coyne, thus selected as the scapegoat for the Government's financial mistakes, would have gone, too, quite peaceably, if Diefenbaker had resisted the temptation to smear all his enemies.

Once the Prime Minister had shifted the ground of argument and impugned Coyne's honour, because he had accepted a large pension increase, the Government was involved in a quarrel as damaging to it as the pipeline had been to its predecessor. The public could never comprehend central banking. It could understand Diefenbaker's sneering description of Coyne as a man who "sat, knew, listened and took."

It was ironic again that the Liberal Party should rally to Coyne's defence while privately rejecting all his theories but the public had lost interest in the merits of the financial dispute and saw only a courageous official pilloried for doing his duty as he understood it.

By allowing a technical controversy to become a human drama, the contest of one fearless man against the massed power of the State,

Diefenbaker had equalled or surpassed St. Laurent's great blunder of 1956.

The statute dismissing Coyne was pushed through the House of Commons and rejected by the Senate, which found him innocent of any wrongdoing. He resigned the same day, his honour untouched. Diefenbaker was smeared by his own brush, indelibly.

Even Diefenbaker recognized the damage of the Coyne affair. To repair it he planned a Cabinet shuffle and the demotion of Fleming to the Justice Department.

The comic events of December, 1961, showed that the old master's touch was faltering. Through friendly newspapers he built his plans up to a climax of public expectation and assured a debacle of anticlimax. What happened in his long confrontation with Fleming is probably known to them alone, but as Fleming emerged, pale and shaken, it was clear at least that he would not accept demotion. And after his friends in the business community had deluged the Prime Minister with telegrams of protest, Fleming could not be demoted. He remained in the finance portfolio at a future price, to him and the country, much higher than demotion.

Meanwhile the charade of Christmas week could not be canceled. Diefenbaker took his colleagues in a body to Quebec City where Governor-General Vanier would approve the Cabinet reorganization amid solemn ceremonies at the Citadel. Alas, nothing came of this grand tableau. Only some minor ministers were shifted. For the first time Diefenbaker felt that most deadly of all weapons, the laughter of the public.

He entered the pre-election session of Parliament with the Cabinet apparently little changed. Yet it was changed, more deeply than the Prime Minister could perceive. In fact, it was mortally wounded —not by the ineffective Liberals but by its own hand.

The price of Fleming's presence at the Treasury could be read in his spring budget. An orthodox financier, who had always promised to balance his accounts, now cut taxes by $130 million and proposed a staggering deficit of $745 million.

This final stroke of irresponsibility was intended as a sop to the taxpayers. To the camel of financial confidence it was the last straw.

Frightened investors withdrew their money from Canada in terrifying flood and Fleming was compelled overnight to turn the last of his many somersaults. Having previously rejected any manipulation of the currency as "a gigantic financial speculation with no assurance of success," he devalued the Canadian dollar to 92½ United States cents, pegged it at the new rate and accepted for the first time the discipline of the International Monetary Fund. These desperate remedies and the suppression of the figures could disguise the dollar hemorrhage for a few weeks. They could not staunch it.

A foreign-exchange crisis of the first magnitude already was under way as Diefenbaker opened the election campaign with an air of unruffled optimism. The familiar theatrical trunk was somewhat battered now. The earlier labels of financial reform, full employment and balanced trade had peeled off but they were replaced by a more impressive slogan—"Canada First."

That old reliable cry of patriotism soon turned, as always, into an oblique anti-Americanism. Diefenbaker's masterly use of insinuation, his hints of dangerous foreign pressures which he alone could resist, convinced a national minority that Canada would be safe in no one else's hands. A majority was shocked by this appeal to naked prejudice. Anti-Americanism had ceased to be even good partisan politics.

Though Pearson was doing it no harm whatever, the Government clearly had passed its point of no return and the nation, still ignorant of its true state, was approaching the point of international bankruptcy.

In a personal contest for his constituency of Eglinton, against a newcomer, Mitchell Sharp, Fleming admitted his own desperation by declaring that Russia desired a Liberal victory. The old American charge that Pearson was soft on Communism could not hurt him but this new low in Canadian politics certainly hurt the Government. Its piecemeal disintegration was apparent at last to everyone except Diefenbaker.

He never doubted the people's verdict. There would be losses, yes, but his huge majority could stand them. His image was too well established to be broken after only five years of office. If Quebec had deserted him, as seemed undeniable, he could do without it. If the nation's hard-currency reserves had started to pour out, the loss could be attributed to the Liberal's cry of "gloom and doom," was not serious anyway and would be quickly repaired by a vote of confidence in the Government. Possibly Diefenbaker believed his own public assurance, on the eve of the poll, that there was no crisis except in Pearson's hysterical imagination, that "we have given you the facts, we have bared the record, we have concealed nothing and shaded nothing."

Considering the real facts—that the Government had failed in all its basic promises, that no problem of importance had been solved and no real economic growth achieved, that Canada was isolated as never before from its British and American friends, and now stood on the brink of insolvency—Diefenbaker's campaign must be accounted the most remarkable of his life so far. His platform sorcery, a little faded by too much use, was still wonderfully potent, the largest of the Government's three remaining assets. The other two were Hamilton's sure grip on the Prairies and Pearson's obvious confusion.

Canada's ballot boxes, opened on the night of June 18, contained no verdict. They showed only that the people had lost their confidence in Diefenbaker and had not given it to Pearson. The popular vote of the Conservative and Liberal Parties, almost exactly equal, gave Diefenbaker 116 parliamentary seats, Pearson 99. Neither had a majority. The nation had voted no-confidence in both parties. The two-party system itself had broken down.

It had broken down in the vacuum of Quebec because Diefenbaker had affronted, and Pearson could not reach, the French-Canadian mind. The latest eruption of Quebec nationalism, led by Réal Caouette, added to small gains in the West, had given Social Credit 30 seats, and the C.C.F., now called the New Democratic Party after its recent marriage of convenience to the labour unions, had won 19.

After losing 92 seats, more than any previous leader had ever lost, a man less self-dedicated than Diefenbaker might have resigned and sought the solace of private life. If such a thought entered his head he did not indicate it. Instead, he rushed to Ottawa and tried to staunch the dollar hemorrhage which he had denied only a few days earlier.

He may not have recognized the depth of the crisis until the polls closed. Clearly his officials did. They were ready with a plan of salvage complete in advance to the last detail—emergency tariffs, cuts in government spending under the pious title of "austerity," loans from the International Monetary Fund, from Britain and from an American Government so long and so bitterly attacked by Diefenbaker.

Until election day Canada had been assured that its affairs were under sound management. Now, cup in hand, it went like a mendicant to its disparaged friends. Happily they knew that Canada was a better risk than its Government and their guarantees of credit ended the exchange crisis.

A broken ankle put Diefenbaker to bed where he had time to meditate, in stunned loneliness, on the ingratitude of the public. It seemed past all understanding but, as he soon persuaded himself, was temporary. Once able to walk again, he re-emerged like a leader

337

who had won a substantial victory—not a decisive victory to be sure, not as wide as a church door, yet enough, provided he could gain a little time. In those dark days he was saved by his courage, his sense of indispensability and his misjudgment of the public mind.

Still deluded as to the meaning of the election, he gained time by refusing to assemble Parliament until the autumn; hurried to another Commonwealth Conference in London as if he still had the right to speak for Canada; lectured the British Government again on the dangerous seductions of the Common Market; and at last demoted the weary Minister of Finance.

Fleming, who no longer cared, was kicked upstairs to the Justice Department and replaced by the popular and able George Nowlan; Fulton downstairs into Public Works; a new senator, Wallace Mc-Cutcheon, was imported, without portfolio, from the board rooms of Bay Street to demonstrate that the Government was financially reliable after all.

These repairs by sticking-plaster could not hide the Cabinet's fissures, least of all the fissure of defence policy which now widened into an outright quarrel with the United States.

The quarrel had begun when President Kennedy visited Ottawa in the spring of 1961. He brought a private working paper, a few typewritten lines, to remind him of points for discussion with the Canadian Cabinet—the desirability of Canada's membership in the Organization of American States, its co-operation in the South American Alliance for Progress, its support of foreign aid generally.

On leaving Diefenbaker's office the President mislaid this innocuous little memorandum. Diefenbaker refused to return it to its owner. Against the protests of his incredulous officials, he locked it away for possible future use.

A year later he was incensed to see in the newspapers a picture of Kennedy entertaining Pearson, with other Nobel Prize winners, at the White House. This honour to his opponent he took as a deliberate affront to himself, an overt interference in the Canadian election, then pending. So he told the dumbfounded American ambassador, Livingston Merchant, and threatened to use the "offensive document" on the platform.

When Merchant reported this threat to Washington he was instructed to inform Diefenbaker that he had made no official report; for had he done so, then of course the President could have no further contact with the Prime Minister. By this old device of diplomacy, an outraged American Government was giving Diefenbaker a way out of his attempt to intimidate the chief of a friendly, allied state.

Suddenly sobered, Diefenbaker promised that the President's memorandum would not be published. Formal relations between Kennedy and Diefenbaker were thus re-established after a breach without precedent but from then on they were formal only and within another year were to become impossible.

Much more than Diefenbaker's manners, and his real suspicion of the United States, had widened the fissure of defence policy.

General Pearkes, a gallant Victoria Cross winner of the First World War, had taken over the Defence Department in 1957 and, scrapping the Canadian Arrow interceptor plane, had arranged to buy American Bomarc missiles in its place. His intention was to arm them with nuclear warheads since otherwise they would be virtually useless. As understood by Pearkes, the decision in favour of American nuclear weapons had been made irrevocably.

This also was the understanding of the United States. It agreed that two of its intended Bomarc bases should be installed north of the border, at Canada's request, for the defence of the Toronto-Montreal metropolitan area. Unfortunately, Pearkes had underestimated his close friend and fellow veteran, Green.

That earnest worker for world disarmament had always nourished a candid and incurable prejudice against the United States. He believed with all his heart that nuclear weapons installed in Canada would discredit it as an advocate of peace and increase the risk of war. So long as Pearson took the same position, and thus protected the Government from serious criticism, Green could veto the nuclear policy now demanded by Harkness, the new Defence Minister.

In his tacit compact with the Opposition on this single issue, Green had underestimated Pearson's ability to change his mind, and knew nothing of the clean split already opening inside the Liberal Party.

While the Government dawdled through the autumn parliamentary session of 1962, announced bold financial policies, repeatedly postponed Nowlan's budget and survived a series of confidence votes with the support of the two splinter parties, three separate triggers were successively applied to the inevitable nuclear explosion of the Conservative Party.

The Cuban crisis presented the first trigger.

Harkness was sickened by the Cabinet's refusal, on the passionate plea of Green, to endorse immediately the United States' quarantine of Cuba, and its further refusal to alert the Canadian defence forces. After forty-four hours Diefenbaker switched from Green to Harkness and joined Canada's other allies in supporting the American position.

The world crisis had eased by then but the crisis in the Canadian Government had only begun. For now the shaken confidence of Harkness could be restored only if he were allowed to acquire nuclear weapons without further delay. As he argued, the Government had already spent nearly $700 million on carriers for these weapons. Was this investment to be scrapped for Green's sake? If so, what was Canada's defence policy?

Diefenbaker gave Harkness no answer. After the Cuban crisis the Prime Minister returned to Green's support; or at least he sought to devise some compromise between the two wings of his Cabinet that represented a deep emotional cleavage of public opinion—on the one hand, the Canadians who viewed nuclear weapons with horror and, on the other, those who were shamed and infuriated by their nation's indecision in the final issue of life and death.

Both sides knew at any rate that Canada's huge expenditures had bought no defence system of any practical use. Moreover, the swiftness of the Cuban crisis had demonstrated the absurdity of the Government's latest promise that nuclear weapons would be obtained if and when they were needed in an emergency. It was clear that no emergency requiring them would leave time for their installation.

As it stood, Canadian defence policy, interpreted by Harkness and Green in opposite senses, was worse than impractical. It had become a farce. For a short time, and a short time only, the eloquence of the Prime Minister, if he were granted a little bit of luck, might conceal the farce until he could decide between his colleagues; but all his luck had run out.

Appropriately enough, an eminent soldier pressed the second trigger. Retiring as supreme commander of NATO, General Lauris Norstad visited Ottawa on January 3, 1963, and, at a press conference, casually remarked that of course Canada had fully committed itself, by solemn agreement, to accept nuclear weapons for its European forces.

The remark was casual only in its setting. In result it was devastating. The man who must know the facts best had flatly denied the Canadian Government's frequent assurances that no such commitment had been made.

Moreover, Norstad had finally tipped the scales in the Liberal Party and convinced Pearson that the commitment must be honoured. Without warning, the opposition leader pulled a third trigger by announcing that a government led by him would immediately accept nuclear weapons.

Now that Pearson had completely reversed himself and abandoned Green, Diefenbaker's position looked hopeless to his friends. He had no defence policy and his Cabinet was obviously at the breaking point. But nothing looked hopeless to Diefenbaker.

After all the shocks of the last six months he was buoyed up by his belief in a personal destiny. As if to confirm it, the economic tide had turned, the country was prosperous and though the rate of unemployment remained the highest in the Western world, it had fallen substantially. The people surely must appreciate the Government's good works—the Bill of Rights, which did not go far but was a brave gesture; the doubled expenditure in social services; the large subsidies to the Martime provinces; the sale of wheat to China and the record income of the prairie farmers; the rapid recovery from the exchange crisis; the stability of prices; above all, the Government's devotion to the common man.

As against all that, of course, stood the daunting fact of the budgetary and trade deficits, the accumulating debt, both domestic and foreign, the alienation of Canada's resources to keep it living beyond its means. And even if Diefenbaker had not made these basic national problems, his own was insoluble. Yet there might still be a way out and at the last minute he saw that chance.

When President Kennedy met Prime Minister Macmillan at Nassau to discuss defence policy, Diefenbaker invited himself to their conference and thus, quite unconsciously, applied his finger to the final trigger.

Still unaware of his danger, he received a vote of confidence from the Conservative Party conference early in the new year and faced Parliament to launch the secret strategy which he had conceived at Nassau.

His speech of January 25 was no ordinary ministerial report. It was a moving, naked confession of his faith, his hope and the anguish of his soul.

"I believe," he said, "the Western world has been directed by God in the last few years or there would have been no survival."

Parliament was hushed by this believer's appeal to a higher authority but puzzled by his secular interpretation of its will. For now Diefenbaker proceeded to construe the Kennedy-Macmillan conference as implying "a change in the philosophy of defence, a change in the views of NATO." Western defence planning was subject to such drastic change, indeed, that the Canadian nuclear role "has been placed in doubt. . . . More and more the nuclear deterrent is becoming of such a nature that more nuclear arms will add nothing material to our defence." Nevertheless, Canada was still negotiating with the United States for a supply of nuclear weapons "in case of need."

What could this mean?

To Diefenbaker it meant a chance to postpone the showdown between Harkness and Green while a new defence policy was built for an entirely new situation.

To most Ottawa reporters it meant that Diefenbaker intended to contract out of the nuclear commitment altogether.

To Harkness it meant precisely the opposite. He therefore undertook a unilateral intervention by publicly "clarifying" his leader's speech. Obviously, he said, Diefenbaker had meant that the nuclear commitment would be honoured. Next day Diefenbaker gruffly retorted in Parliament that his speech required no interpretation.

His quarrel with Harkness was now in the open. A much graver quarrel with the United States was yet to be revealed.

At Washington Kennedy's defence experts had read Diefenbaker's speech at first with unbelief, then with anger and then with panic. It mattered little to them directly that a Canadian Government was disintegrating in full public view, though the process was certainly welcome. What mattered directly, urgently and inescapably was something else altogether, though Diefenbaker may not have suspected it.

His speech of January 25 had taken a few days to percolate into the minds of the United States' European allies. On reading the text they could place only two alternative interpretations on it. Either the Prime Minister of Canada was misrepresenting the Nassau conference which he had attended briefly and from which they had been excluded. Or, as seemed more probable, Kennedy and Macmillan had planned behind their backs an overhaul of NATO, disregarded their interests and violated the whole spirit of NATO. A sudden rumble of anxious inquiries from Europe persuaded the American State Department to take a dangerous step.

Its officials were so inflamed by Diefenbaker's misinterpretations, and so alarmed by Europe's protests, that they did not even wait for Kennedy's approval before issuing a hasty press statement on the night of January 30.

In language uniquely blunt between allies, the statement said that the Nassau agreements, already published, "raise no question of the appropriateness of nuclear weapons for Canadian forces in fulfilling their NATO or NORAD obligations." This repudiation of Diefenbaker was stern enough, especially in holding Canada to its "obligations," but another sentence was savage: "The Canadian

Government has not yet proposed any arrangement sufficiently practical to contribute effectively to North American defence."

Kennedy read these words for the first time next morning and was somewhat shocked. Still, they were only the truth and necessary to reassure the Europeans. Canada had obligations, freely accepted, and it had no defence policy. As a politician Kennedy may have wondered, however (as did the Canadian Liberals), whether this excessively brutal intervention in Canada's business might not help more than it damaged Diefenbaker. Dean Rusk, Secretary of State, who had not seen the statement in advance, tacitly apologized for its wording if it gave "offense," but its contents were not modified in the least. The final trigger had been pulled.

As the American Government may or may not have known, its bullet was aimed at a Government already *in extremis*.

For weeks a rebellion had been brewing in Diefenbaker's Cabinet. Harkness made no secret of his determination to resign unless his defence policy was accepted without any more equivocation. Strangely innocent for an experienced soldier and politician, he expected at least half a dozen other ministers to resign with him. That seemed certain since his associate Minister of Defence, Pierre Sévigny, was equally disgusted, and so, apparently, were Hees, McCutcheon and others.

Perhaps history will never discover how far the rebellion penetrated beyond this hard core when some ten ministers teetered between faithfulness to their party and fear of its ruin by Diefenbaker. The rebellion might be strong enough anyhow to unhorse him if it could find a respectable leader. None appeared. Hees thought himself well qualified but nobody else did and he was still publicly asserting devotion to his chief. Harkness had no ambition, McCutcheon no public following, Sévigny and Balcer no support outside Quebec.

Ill organized and unled, the rebellion seemed to be slipping until, overnight, it was crystallized by the State Department's rebuke and began to reel into a tragicomedy that no playwright would dare to invent.

The Canadian ambassador to Washington recalled "for consultation" as a counter-rebuke to President Kennedy; official business between Canada and the United States virtually suspended; Diefenbaker vowing that he would not "accept external domination" and Canada would never be a "satellite"; the Cabinet rebels shocked by his overt acts of anti-Americanism and resolved to stop them from going further; he still unsure of the rebels' determination and numbers; the Liberals scenting trouble within the Government and eager to exploit it but helpless without the backing of the splinter parties; Parliament droning over routine matters and all the nation's vital affairs paralyzed—such was the interesting state of Canadian politics in the first days of February.

So far the rebels had hoped that Diefenbaker would retire voluntarily. They intended to make Nowlan temporary Prime Minister until a permanent Conservative leader could be chosen. Would Robert Thompson, the wavering Social Credit leader, co-operate in this improbable strategy, keep a caretaker government in office and, if so, on what terms? All Thompson seemed to want at the moment was a resumption of business, an immediate budget and the postponement of an election.

On these reasonable terms the next Liberal want-of-confidence motion could be beaten. The rebels, meeting in the office of Hees, were encouraged but hesitated to strike since it had become clear that Diefenbaker would not go voluntarily. It was by no means certain either that any large part of the Conservative caucus would turn against him.

On Sunday, February 3, Diefenbaker called for the long-delayed show-down. He assembled the Cabinet at his house on Sussex Street, bitterly denounced a "nest of traitors" and demanded a unanimous pledge of loyalty to himself.

Harkness replied in a calm voice that Cabinet, party and nation had lost confidence in the Prime Minister. As for himself, he would resign forthwith.

Though Harkness stood alone as the only minister yet willing to sacrifice his career for a principle, others might follow his example. Diefenbaker realized that danger and, looking at the cold faces around him, saw at last the depth of the rebellion. He mumbled a threat which his ministers understood to mean his own resignation and the appointment of Fleming, the chief victim of his hostility, as a successor.

How much of this was bluff and bravado, or the mere mutterings of desperation, no one could tell. One man at least knew that it must end. Diefenbaker's most faithful friend rushed to his support. Green, who had never been an orator, poured out such an impulsive speech of warning and reconciliation that, coming from this simple, inarticulate man, the words were rather like hot lava from a distant ice field. They sobered the Cabinet but had they united it?

As the meeting dispersed only one rebel had made up his mind. Harkness went home and wrote his resignation. Diefenbaker had called the bluff of the others and was still Prime Minister.

The scene shifted next day to Parliament. There, Pearson had waited patiently. He guessed that the Government was collapsing but had heard nothing of the confrontation at Sussex Street. After many failures, on many non-confidence motions, the moment had come to make his kill, if it could be made. When he moved another motion regretting the Government's "lack of leadership" and "breakdown of unity," everything depended on the splinters. Would Social Credit and the New Democratic Party back his motion?

Thus, on February 4, mysterious comings and goings between the rebels and Thompson; at first his apparent willingness to support the Government, even with Diefenbaker leading it, if a budget was promptly introduced, because an election with "anti-American overtones" would be a "tragedy," as he warned Parliament; then, at the dinner hour, a swift change since he had talked with his mentor, Premier E. C. Manning, of Alberta; an uncompromising demand for Diefenbaker's immediate resignation; a Social Credit amendment to the Liberal motion, attacking the Government in still stronger terms; a magnificent speech by Diefenbaker asking a little more time "to do the things we want to do," promising to fight for Canada's "identity" and pledging himself to govern without "extramural assistance" from Washington—so, through two frantic days, Parliament staggered toward a vote which must save or defeat the Government.

In a last-minute attempt to avoid Conservative defeat, the rebels conceived a queer compromise. Through Hees they offered to make Diefenbaker Chief Justice of the Supreme Court. He refused with indignation. The Government must face the parliamentary vote under his leadership.

Preparing for that test, the reliable Hamilton had organized a trusty claque and it cheered the Prime Minister in the Conservative lobby; but cheers were not votes. As the division bells rang on the night of February 5 the faces along the Treasury benches looked white and haggard. There could be no doubt of the outcome unless Thompson reversed himself.

The Social Credit motion was put to the House. Diefenbaker watched almost the entire Opposition of three parties stand up to announce its lack of confidence in him. The clerk read out the result—111 votes for the Government, 142 against it. For the second time since Confederation a government had fallen in the House of Commons. An immediate election must follow.

The tragicomedy now approached its denouement.

Hamilton, who had kept his head while others were losing theirs, appointed himself stage manager and rearranged the stage. He alone seemed to understand that the next day's events must turn on a tight timetable. If the Cabinet met early, as already arranged, the rebel ministers might unseat Diefenbaker before the caucus could rally around him. It was essential that the caucus meet first and, well indoctrinated overnight, declare loyalty to its leader, thus crushing the rebellion. Diefenbaker saw at once the wisdom of Hamilton's advice and switched the day's schedule. That was a master stroke.

Though held in the morning, the caucus meeting has since been called, with apt retrospection, "The Night of the Long Rubber Knives." If the knives failed to penetrate the image of the still regnant Prime Minister, some of them were made of steel, to be applied later.

Diefenbaker faced his followers knowing neither the number nor the quality of the knives. After the outburst of Sussex Street he was himself again—calm, cheerful, witty and on the offensive. He even offered to resign and was not surprised by the shouted protests of the caucus. A long, windy speech by Hees, explaining his dissatisfaction, fell exceedingly flat. Senator Alfred Brooks, an old intimate of Diefenbaker, brought the caucus sharply to its senses by demanding, in the name of God, whether it had lost them.

This was the cue for a more polished performer who suddenly thrust all the others from the stage.

Senator Grattan O'Leary, a tiny man of swift mind and birdlike motion, had never admired Diefenbaker, had openly deplored his appointment as leader but as an unswerving Conservative and believer in the two-party system had consistently supported the Government, written the best of the Prime Minister's speeches, counseled him repeatedly and would stand with him, sink or swim. In the pinch Diefenbaker's best friend was this old opponent.

That the Government must sink, O'Leary had little doubt. That Diefenbaker had long been sinking it O'Leary knew perhaps better than anyone. Nevertheless, if Conservatism could not be saved from electoral defeat it must be salvaged to fight another day. While Hamilton had assured his chief of solid western support, it was not enough. In the crunch the Irish eloquence of a great journalist rescued Diefenbaker.

Regrettably, no reporter took down O'Leary's oration but no man in that room will forget the surge and thunder of it, the evocation of causes bigger than men, the generous appeal to the rebels, the demand that McCutcheon and others like him withdraw the resignations already in their pockets. Under the orator's heat and passion the rubber knives crumpled, McCutcheon and his resignation wilted together, Hees was close to tears, the rebellion dissolved in merciful catharsis.

346

Following this paroxysm of the Conservative soul, a grinning Hees left the caucus to inform the press that the Conservative Party had united behind its leader and would "lick hell out of the Grits." He was privately convinced, however, that Diefenbaker had promised him, in a whisper, that the defence policy would be revised, the anti-Americanism stilled. Diefenbaker later denied that he had given any such undertaking, and the men around him on the platform agreed with him.

A few days' second thoughts and the anger of his anti-Diefenbaker friends in Toronto persuaded Hees that there had been no change in the Prime Minister's intentions, no improvement in defence policy and no likelihood of the Government's re-election. Despite desperate efforts by Diefenbaker's supporters to stop them, Hees and Sévigny finally abandoned the sinking ship because, as their letters of resignation said, they could no longer stomach the nation's indecision or its quarrel with a neighbour and ally. They hoped in vain that others would join them immediately but at least Fleming, Fulton and Ernest Halpenny decided to leave federal politics after the election.

All except three knives had turned out to be rubber. Yet a Prime Minister with a trio of his leading ministers publicly against him, another trio in ambiguous retirement, almost the whole Conservative press supporting the Opposition, and the nation in a daze, could hardly expect to avoid a total disaster, much less to win an election. These comforting calculations in the Liberal Party ignored Diefenbaker's courage, his platform magic, his sure intimations of immortality.

The old theatrical trunk was badly broken now, all the labels faded, the original contents spilled out, the actor's face deeply grooved by a lifetime on the road, but as he started out again he still had no peer. Once he had escaped the stale atmosphere of Ottawa and burst into the clean air of the country, Diefenbaker seemed to grow visibly, to overtop his plodding opponent and recapture his lost youth.

He must have known that he had no defensible record, no new policy to offer, and could appeal only to the people's cruder emotions. This was no time for debate, consistency or even coherence. Though McCutcheon of Bay Street stayed in the Cabinet and the Conservative Party was well heeled with campaign funds, Diefenbaker still presented himself as the foe of the "Great Interests," the titan wounded by midgets, the faithful public servant impoverished by his service, the martyr of a sacred mission, the only defender of the common man.

The "powerful, the strong and the mighty" sought his destruction. Indeed "everyone is against me but the people." Therefore, he was "going to look into the face of Canada" and had "an appointment with the Canadian people to carry on." Disregarding all his years of office, the Prime Minister remained the instinctive leader of the Opposition. Thus as challenger and aggressor, he charged the Liberals with obstructing the business (including a welcome tax reduction) which he had failed to introduce in Parliament.

If this inversion of the facts was too obvious to be convincing even among the puzzled voters, toward the end of the campaign Diefenbaker found his missing little bit of luck.

An indiscreet statement by the American Secretary of Defence, Robert McNamara, that the Bomarc missiles were of little value except to distract an enemy from urban targets to themselves, gave Diefenbaker a last chance. He promptly denounced as useless and dangerous the missiles installed in Canada by his own Government, against Liberal objection. He warned that these weapons would be decoys for Russian bombs raining on Canadian cities, that Pearson would make his country a "nuclear dump," a "burnt offering."

The fact that Diefenbaker was condemning his own defence policy did not deter him for he was no longer concerned with the people's conscious thought, only with their viscera. He was distracting the public from all the facts. He was attempting, because he lacked any better method, nothing less than a feat of mass hypnotism, an emotional purge. By defying all logic, he almost succeeded and Pearson, unable to compete in this contest of bewilderment, almost failed.

Two necessary ingredients of Conservative success were lacking. Clearly Diefenbaker had lost Quebec altogether and gave it only token attention. He was losing the urban strongholds of Ontario and all the big cities elsewhere. Hamilton's solid rural West could not counterbalance these losses. And on the night of April 8 the greatest one-man campaign ever seen in Canada buckled under the mathematical facts.

Seated gloomily in his private railway car outside Prince Albert, Diefenbaker learned that he had won only 95 seats. Alone he had saved his party from almost certain catastrophe but he had made it the English-speaking party of the farm, the village and the small town. Pearson's total of 129 seats, though 4 short of a majority, represented the growing, decisive power of the metropolis and maintained a bridge into French Canada. Social Credit, with 24, and the New Democratic Party with 17, were still splinters. Without support from one or the other of them, however, Pearson could not govern.

Having resigned, Diefenbaker waited confidently for his successor to fail.

What, then, had the grass-roots prophet accomplished? As Hilaire Belloc wrote of the French nation, Diefenbaker had marched forth and returned after accomplishing only an epic. While he might never grasp power again, he had made a myth to be remembered long after his departure—the myth of solitary struggle, of identification with the common man, of noble failure against a cruel fate, of a mortal beaten only by the gods.

Like most myths, this was largely false. In fact, the significant and costly result of Diefenbaker's rule was the disorder of public business, the break-down of the two-party system—perhaps temporary, perhaps lasting—the loss of national confidence in the parliamentary system itself, and hence the grave damage to the office of Prime Minister.

The vital question confronting Pearson was whether he could repair these injuries, restore the office and heal Canada after the convulsions of its long twilight sleep. His first attempt was spectacular. He made the nation wonder if it had been wrong to dismiss Diefenbaker.

17: The Lonely Extrovert

When Lester Bowles Pearson became Prime Minister on April 22, 1963, he was, next to Diefenbaker, the best-known man in Canada. He was also the least-known man.

Everybody knew his short, chunky figure, the plump boy's face with a lock of hair sprawling across the forehead, the double trade mark of heavy, horn-rimmed glasses and bow tie, the rumpled clothes, the deceptively casual, homespun manner.

Everybody had heard his rather high-pitched voice with its suspicion of a lisp, his graceful, professor's language and occasional indiscreet sallies of egghead wit. A stranger, at first glance, would have taken him for anything except a statesman of the first rank. He simply did not look like a Prime Minister. He looked like Mike Pearson.

If he had little box-office appeal in a profession which increasingly strives to emulate the theatre, and could never hope to appear as every woman's vicarious lover, he was a composite portrait of every woman's son. That, perhaps, would prove more valuable in the end than the Hollywood portrait now so eagerly sought by the synthetic professionals of politics. But despite his gregarious habits and that familiar air of an aging college boy, few Canadians knew the man.

His mind, constructed layer by layer in a series of Chinese boxes, had never revealed its inner contents to any colleague, perhaps not even to its owner. Usually considered a genial extrovert, Pearson was the most popular and the most solitary public person of his times.

This odd paradox of outward candour and inner secrecy had long baffled the men apparently closest to him.

The less discerning supposed that a lucky amateur had won an election but had deeply divided the Liberal Party by his absent-minded blunders. The wiser sort guessed that while he was often confused and fuzzy in his thought, he had deliberately set out from the beginning to reinterpret Liberalism as the true party of radical reform, to put it back again on the left of Conservatism and to continue the social revolution launched by King. Like King, therefore, he must move in circles, conceal his ultimate purposes and unfold them in slow stages lest he alert and unite the enemies of progress.

Both interpretations of Pearson as a politician are too shallow and neither touches him as a man. Certainly he did not succeed in politics by luck or love of the game. Nor did he know his purposes with clarity and plan them even in King's rough fashion. More than King, or any other Canadian politician, he played by ear because he knew no other method, but he differed from most of them in the acuteness of his auditory nerve. Yet both King, the mentor, and Pearson, the pupil, approached the political process with the same general philosophy of idealism and a complete pragmatism of conduct.

While their natures were antithetical and antipathetic, Pearson and King showed a strong resemblance also in their process of thought. Both approached a problem slowly, by circular motion, on hands and knees. Long reconnoitring, often retreat and evasion, preceded final attack. The colleagues of both men could seldom penetrate the thick haze of their intentions or foresee their acts. Both had unlimited flexibility. The elastic stretched but rarely broke.

They were alike in another trait. A man advising either of them went away satisfied that his advice was accepted, only to find it disregarded in favour of an opposite course. Many men who mistook politeness for consent felt betrayed. If charm made friends for King and Pearson, it also made enemies.

Though the work of the pupil, so far anyway, is narrow beside that of the mentor, Pearson is incomparably the better human being. His idealism has sometimes wavered, his pragmatism has been marred by appalling mistakes, a few that could prove to be deadly, but his motives, unlike King's, have seldom been selfish, his methods never brutal. An excessive kindliness to friends, an immoderate humility, a lack of ambition and necessary ruthlessness are, indeed, his largest defects as a leader of men. Still, they have not obstructed some substantial achievements, usually undervalued because he never learned to sell himself in the clamorous bazaar of politics.

Pearson will not be weighed in the scales of history for some time yet. As this is written within his first year of office it is impossible to foresee whether the fourteenth Prime Minister will make himself the sixth success or the ninth failure among Canada's rulers. All we know for sure now is that he is quite unlike any of them—a sport and oddity of the political breed.

As such, he represents, much more than Diefenbaker ever did, the organic changes in Canadian society, and probably he faces its largest crisis. Some of his predecessors failed without serious damage to the nation. The failure of Pearson, or at any rate the failure of his basic principles, could strain the nation to the breaking point. Hence by success or failure Pearson must be a vital factor, a reluctant fulcrum, of our history as it enters a new cycle.

He entered the cycle very late, but perhaps not too late. For even in his sixty-eighth year an abiding boyishness not only saves him from the exhaustion of the daily grind but introduces the energies of youth into government and reflects, as no predecessor has reflected, the spirit of the modern age.

Both his times and his character make Pearson unique. His undoubted intellectual resources and grave weaknesses; the ability to make others love, forgive and serve him; the frequent inability to make up his own mind; the bold inspirations and moments of high courage followed by sudden reversal and infuriating ambiguity; the acute judgment of events combined with continual misjudgments of men; a capacity to build but an absence of that killer's instinct essential to leadership—these qualities in constant flux are difficult to analyze but their origins can easily be traced.

Like all men, Pearson is the product of heredity and environment. In early life, his environment was one of genteel poverty with humble, educated, God-fearing parents; later, of great affairs which he encountered precociously but was marvelously quick to comprehend.

His ancestors, Irish on both sides, had been in America since the early years of the nineteenth century. His father and his grandfather were both Methodist ministers who preached from many pulpits in and around Toronto. His mother's family had immigrated from Ireland in 1824 to Upper Canada where Charles Bowles, his great-grandfather, hewed a farm out of the wilderness. The next generation prospered but in its prosperity maintained a stern religion and ardently supported the Grit policy of reform.

Reverend Edwin Arthur Pearson, father of the future Prime Minister, married Annie Sara Bowles and settled for a time in Newtonbrook, then a village outside Toronto. There Lester Bowles Pearson was born on April 23, 1897, the second of three sons.

In those days, with a salary of about seven hundred dollars a year, a Methodist minister moved from town to town and from pulpit to pulpit, confusing the recollections of a small boy. Lester recalled a happy household, a father devoted to his church yet keenly interested in athletic sports and strongly Conservative in politics. The relationship between father and son was always affectionate but the mother's influence was predominant.

This family, poor in the world's goods but rich in learning, soon repeated the old story which had given Canada most of its leaders. Somehow the three Pearson boys all received a good public-school education in Willowdale, Davisville, Aurora, Hamilton and Peterborough, and then were sent to college.

When Lester enrolled at the University of Toronto in 1913, at the age of sixteen, he was a very commonplace youth, or so he seemed to his companions. Outstanding skill on the baseball diamond was his only distinction and it enabled him, in summer holidays, to earn some money as a semi-professional player. He was a natural athlete who later became a star in amateur hockey and lacrosse.

All his ideas, such as they were, appeared ordinary. He was an industrious student but showed no originality of thought, nor any particular purpose in life. While Diefenbaker, his rival of the future, already had decided to become Prime Minister, Pearson was satisfied to have a good time.

His idea of a good time looks pretty drab in retrospect but it foretold his idea of good government. The upbringing in a Christian home and the example of his parents had permanently fastened on him a strict, old-fashioned morality, a deep religious conviction, a certain innocency, almost a naivety. He never entirely outgrew them.

This attitude of itself would set him apart from the general run of politicians and remind his older colleagues of King, without King's sanctimony. Like King, Pearson avoided liquor, tobacco and all the common vices. And like King, he had a boundless curiosity about everything.

He read as enthusiastically as he played baseball. He had no plan for his life but his professors noticed that whatever he undertook was pushed to a conclusion, and perhaps a few of them detected here the makings of a philosophy. Not to plan ahead but to accept every task as it appeared and to do it as well as possible; not to shine in competition but never to fail if he could possibly succeed; not to violate his moral code but not to quarrel with anyone either if he could help it—such were the instincts of the boy and the methods of the man. For the present, however, he was only an engaging, fun-loving youngster who might make some small mark in life but could not hope to seize its larger prizes.

For Pearson, as for many Canadians, the First World War was the watershed dividing youth from manhood. After two years at the university he enlisted in the spring of 1915 and went to Europe with a hospital unit, expecting to be a hero and probably to be killed.

Instead, he found himself stationed in England, Egypt and finally Greece while his two brothers, Marmaduke and Vaughan, were seeing action in France. Bored by a humdrum life at Salonika, he wangled a transfer to the infantry and, reaching England, was surprised to find himself commissioned a lieutenant on his way to the trenches of Europe.

Before he could be trained as an infantry officer he volunteered for the more dangerous work of the Royal Flying Corps, was rushed through a pilot's training in six weeks and, on his first solo flight, hit a wire and crashed. By the law of averages he should have been killed but that law seldom applied to him. He quickly recovered from the crash, was run over by a bus in London and invalided home unfit for service except as a flight instructor near Toronto.

Later he often said on the platform that his military career had been undistinguished by anything but good luck. Apparently all he had gained by it was the nickname of "Mike" because a tough flying officer rejected "Lester" as fit only for a sissy. Though war had failed to make him a hero, it had introduced him to death and made him a man. Also, it introduced him to Oxford University when he was training nearby and he was determined to return there some day for study.

Meanwhile he was graduated from Toronto University. Still with no plan for his future, he worked briefly in Hamilton and Chicago for Armour and Company to learn the meat-packing business as the operator of a sausage machine and then as a clerk. This experience soon convinced him that he was not cut out for business and revived his longing for Oxford. He got there in 1920 on a scholarship, studied modern history, became the university's best hockey and lacrosse player, and was a member of Britain's Olympic hockey team in 1922.

Following his two blissful years at Oxford, he was appointed a lecturer in history at the University of Toronto where he married one of his students, Maryon Moody of Winnipeg, in 1925. Their son was christened Geoffrey, their daughter, Patricia.

With a salary of eighteen hundred dollars a year and nothing to encourage him but his popularity among the students and his athletic prowess, Pearson's prospects were not bright until he chanced to visit Ottawa. There he was persuaded by his friend, Dr. O. D. Skelton, head of the new Department of External Affairs, to write its stiff entrance examinations, though he had no serious thought of becoming a public servant.

Back in Toronto, he received a telegram from Ottawa but could not read it when his eyes were dulled by drugs after an oculist's test for spectacles. As read by a friendly janitor, the message announced, to Pearson's amazement, that he had led all other candidates in the examinations and was fitted to be a first secretary in Canada's diplomatic service.

That telegram cast the die of his life.

The years at Ottawa as Skelton's trouble-shooter educated Pearson in foreign affairs and also in the economics and the inner politics of Canada, which he then regarded with a humorous detachment.

His pre-war years in London as assistant to Vincent Massey, the Canadian High Commissioner, introduced Pearson to most of the world's leading statesmen and gave him an enduring contempt for stuffed shirts, whom he punctured repeatedly in his dispatches. The London life was gay but he knew it could not last. Returning to Canada for a holiday in 1939, he told King that war was coming. King rejected this warning as absurd. Pearson abandoned his holiday and flew to London. If there was to be another war he wanted to see it at first hand.

He saw it through the London blitz and came back to Ottawa reluctantly at King's request as second man in the External Affairs Department under his friend, Norman Robertson. Then he became assistant to Leighton McCarthy, the Canadian minister in Washington (who once said to me, "I don't mind Mike running the whole legation but I wish, sometimes, that he'd tell me what we're doing.")

When Pearson was appointed Ambassador to the United States and later Under Secretary of External Affairs he had already completed at breakneck speed a career sufficient for one lifetime. He was better known throughout the world than any Canadian had ever been. He was the glamour boy of diplomacy and, far outside the range of his public duties, the chief adviser and universal joint of King's public service.

As his own energies declined, King saw in Pearson a promising successor and urged him to enter politics. Pearson refused because he distrusted King's basic isolationism and what he had seen of politics from the inside. Why give up the work he loved and could do well to become a stuffed shirt himself?

King was right nevertheless and his judgment illuminates today's

Prime Minister. In his young counselor King had perceived a sure aptitude for government but Pearson's talents fell far short of genius, if genius means original thought. Contrary to the later public impression, Pearson was not an originator. He was a skilful craftsman taking the theoretical ideas originated by others and building them into practical policy. He did not build them by magic; he built them by hard work which was, perhaps, a kind of genius.

The Canadian people, proud of their ambassador to the world, regarded Pearson as a prince charming. Apparently he succeeded without effort and grinned his way through life. Actually he was the hardest worker in Ottawa. The casual, carefree man with his feet on the office desk was only the daytime Pearson. Since he detested and avoided Ottawa's social swim, the public never saw the night-time Pearson sprawled on a chesterfield, in pyjamas and slippers, with the secret documents of state littered across the floor while he devoured them and scribbled his notes for tomorrow's official correspondence. More than anything else, the tedious homework of a born student was the secret of Pearson's success.

His kind of success would have been impossible without a bodily health that had never known any illness. This health, the product of playing-field and hockey rink, needed no physical exercise in middle age but suffered no abuse. Pearson liked a glass of whisky before dinner, he sometimes smoked a cigarette without enjoyment until he abandoned tobacco altogether and, having no palate for food, he hardly knew what he was eating.

The vigour of his body was nourished by a knack of the mind. The men around him frequently worried themselves into collapse but he could always relax. He sometimes worried, too, and felt the human situation with a peculiar torment but he could turn off the current of the daily business like a light switch at will. Tired of state papers, he would pick up a detective story, watch a baseball game on television or chuckle over some low comedy.

"My tastes aren't very high," he admitted. Yet he seemed to read every new book of importance and his writing style had a clarity and sparkle which King envied and frequently appropriated.

Pearson, in short, was an almost abnormally normal man, happiest at his summer cottage with his wife, his son, his daughter and later with his eight grandchildren. He could live on two hours' sleep per night at some international conference. More than once he had dressed in a taxi to catch an early-morning plane and often wrote some of his best speeches on his knee while flying over the Atlantic. These were merely the tricks of his trade. His life centred in a modest duplex home and a growing family. He was paid a reasonable salary but money meant little to him and he had no savings of any account until he won $38,885 with his Nobel Peace Prize.

All this labour, normality and domestic happiness could not account for Pearson's rise. All his intimacy with the rulers of the world could not make a Prime Minister. There must be something else behind the public personality. In fact, there were several things.

To begin with, Pearson's charm was irresistible because it was entirely natural, his laughter infectious because he enjoyed it, his wit mischievous but inoffensive because it never wounded, his serious moods impressive because they were genuine. The old cliché that he could walk with kings and not lose the common touch was true enough in his case, for success never tainted his humility, his exuberance hid an incurable shyness and no man, however small, could feel mean in his presence.

These were great gifts in the literal meaning of the word. They had been given to him. He did not invent them. He was not nearly so innocent, however, or so candid as he looked.

A stranger listening to him must be quick to grasp the meaning of his words as they flashed by like a landscape seen from a train window. Viewing his mind in these disjointed segments, you could never be sure that you had seen it whole or remembered it rightly. Statesmen disarmed by his grin began to realize, after he left, that Pearson had got what he wanted without appearing to ask anything. Newspaper reporters, amazed by his indiscretion in great affairs, found on later reflection that he had talked recklessly to hide his thoughts.

What were his thoughts? They came primarily from his own assessment of human nature as never entirely good or bad. Tolerance of men's weakness, including his own, was the key to both his private and his public life.

He could seldom bring himself to hate anyone. Even when he saw that a certain colleague was knifing him, he used to say: "Oh well, everybody knows poor old So-and-So. He can't help it."

Pearson appeared to suffer fools gladly but those who knew him well could watch his mind shut like an iron door if he were bored, while his face showed no change of expression. The door was never opened wide anyway. Those who knew him best learned slowly that the region behind the door was closed to everybody, that the public person was an agreeable but absurd caricature of the real Pearson whom nobody knew. Therein lay his strength as a leader of men; also, his danger.

Out of all these contradictions he had fashioned his own methods, apparently complicated but actually simple. Aware, by trial and error, that no man or policy is perfect, he sought the best he could get. With infinite patience, with a smiling refusal to accept defeat, with continual retreats in preparation for the next attack, he laboured doggedly to devise some compromise admittedly inadequate but better than nothing. He never considered any large issue permanently closed and as a historian understood that history never stands still, that today's wisdom may be tomorrow's folly, that no problem is ever solved without leaving two in its place, that everything, good or bad, must soon pass.

If Pearson had become a deliberate pragmatist of statecraft, he would sometimes take the most desperate sort of gamble, reversing his whole course without notice. He always found a queer fascination in danger as if he were playing a game. An international crisis might terrify but it invariably excited him and instantly summoned all his energies. The veteran fireman loved a fire. Grant Dexter, who knew Pearson as well as anyone, often said that "Mike is happiest when he's clinging to a precipice and just about to fall off." He sometimes did fall off as we shall see, but not often and he always climbed up again.

The conflict between the two Pearsons, superficial and profound, pragmatic and idealistic, was seldom detected even by his intimates. The idealism and discontent issued only in a passing word now and then, an expression of the face; they were there all the same and, with them, a hard core of stubbornness beneath the boyish charm. Once he had made up his mind, he never altered his path by an inch. Such a man was easy to like, impossible to calculate in advance. A few of his companions realized that; more would find it out to their sorrow later on.

Some thought that the deeper region was only a vacuum if it existed at all. They were wrong. It was not a vacuum but whether the contents could ever be projected into practical action, outside his wizardry in foreign affairs, was questioned even by the men who guessed that there was more to Pearson than met the eye of the television camera. That question had become important. Prime Minister St. Laurent could not last forever. Sooner or later his heir must be found.

Pearson did not see himself as the heir when he finally surrendered to St. Laurent's entreaties, accepted the portfolio of External Affairs and committed himself, with the deepest forebodings, to politics. It was typical of him that he brushed off this largest decision of his life with a corny joke. Asked by the reporters when he had become a Liberal, he answered: "Today."

In truth he had always been a non-partisan liberal, standing far to the left of the Liberal Government and moving continually leftwards as he grew older, in denial of the common cycle, but as foreign minister he attempted at first to avoid party politics because they disgusted him. It took him some time, five years at least, to learn that politics are the essential profession of democracy, and the hardest of all professions to master.

In the meantime he was occupied with a series of events too long and complex to be told here. Pearson had become the reliable intermediary of the free world, a diplomat and honest broker trusted as much in London, Washington and the western European capitals as in Ottawa and even more highly esteemed by foreigners than by his own people. No Canadian from Macdonald to St. Laurent had occupied this curious, indefinable position abroad—partly because Canada was so highly estimated and, indeed, vastly overestimated in those times; mostly because Pearson, though no genius in any other respect, had a genius of conciliation.

The name of "Mike," which he seemed to monopolize throughout the world, was a talisman opening every door. His breezy, colloquial language, his habit of discussing international business as if it were no more than a baseball argument in a barber shop set a new style of informal diplomacy. His speeches and the often unwise wisecracks of his press conferences brought the gravest affairs within the grasp of ordinary men. By removing the top hat and pricking the stuffed shirt, Pearson became, among other things, a great international educator.

Underneath all his cheerful banter, those who read his state papers or his reports to Parliament could detect his growing scepticism of mankind's future. Those who talked to him privately knew that he gave civilization no more than a fifty-fifty chance of survival. Seeing better the daily risks of the ultimate accident, he looked into the pit with clearer eyes than any Canadian but he looked steadily because he was supported by some kind of religious conviction which he never discussed.

The stranger who met Canada's foreign minister in some friend's home might find him sitting, cross-legged, on the floor while he explained the fine points of last night's hockey game, or singing some old song beside the piano, but this light-hearted pose could not deceive his confidants. They knew that Pearson laughed lest he should cry.

Anyway, he had no time for tears. Each day was crowded with business.

Since his return to Ottawa he had written St. Laurent's speech first proposing a free-world alliance; and when the alliance had been written into the North Atlantic Treaty, he had proposed, as early as 1951, to expand it into a transatlantic community of free trade.

He had served as President of the United Nations Assembly and would have become its Secretary-General (the job he really wanted) if the Russians had not twice vetoed his appointment (while some Americans were calling him "soft on Communism"). He had almost accepted an invitation to become Secretary-General of NATO and refused it, after long hesitation, only because he could not bear to leave St. Laurent whom he regarded with almost filial affection.

He had steered through the United Nations the establishment of Israel as a state; had prevented an imminent breach between Britain and the United States in the issue of the Korean war; had taken Canada into that war against the objection of some powerful colleagues because St. Laurent supported him; by unlucky chance had chosen the day of General Douglas MacArthur's dismissal to warn the United States that its future relations with Canada could never again be "easy or automatic" and thus, at a moment of high emotion, angered the American enemies of President Truman; had sat with the three-man committee which negotiated the Korean cease-fire; had spent an evening with Nikita Khrushchev in his Crimean palace and, after drinking nineteen toasts, had left in a surprisingly vertical posture, remarking that he had endured "conviviality beyond the line of duty."

With this extraordinary record behind him, all Canadians could take pride in the fame and the non-partisan policy of their foreign minister. Then came the Suez crisis to give Pearson his baptism of fire at home, his first taste of politics in the raw.

Suez is probably the least understood episode of Canadian history and Pearson's part in it the most distorted.

News of the British-French attack on Egypt reached Ottawa in October, 1956. St. Laurent felt outraged. Pearson felt sick.

In the first place, he believed that the invasion was a clear breach of international morality; in the second, that it would drive a wedge between Western Europe and the United States and might well split the Commonwealth between its white and coloured peoples; in the third, that it could not possibly succeed even as a military adventure.

If, he reasoned, Britain and France managed to seize the Suez Canal they could not hold it for long against guerilla attacks without expanding their occupation over most or all of Egypt, and thus antagonizing the West, the Communist empire and the neutrals.

As Pearson saw it, the blindness of the British and French Governments to these dangers was simply incomprehensible but he wasted no time in lamentation or moral lectures. A fire had broken out in Egypt and might soon be a conflagration. Its causes could be examined later. For the present the veteran fireman thought only of extinguishing it.

This threat to peace moved into the United Nations and the Canadian Cabinet devised a rough sort of solution without much hope of success. Pearson was instructed to propose a cease-fire under United Nations supervision, if that seemed feasible, but to use his own judgment. In the special plane carrying him to New York Pearson sat alone and silent, the mask of cheerful diplomacy left behind. He knew that for the first time a Canadian might hold in his hand the peace of the world and, with a little luck, might save it.

Arriving at New York late on the night of November 1, he found the United Nations Assembly in session. The American delegates apparently were determined to pass a resolution, as already vetoed by Britain and France in the Security Council, flatly demanding that they withdraw from Egypt and thus admit an international crime. The delegates of India were threatening that their country would leave the Commonwealth if immediate withdrawal was not accepted. The British delegates were seeking a way out of Suez with a minimum loss of face. No one had yet proposed, while the Suez attack still continued, any practical means of ending it.

Pearson at once rejected Britain's suggestion that the British and French forces at Suez be deputized as agents of the United Nations separating the armies of Egypt and Israel. The Assembly, he replied, would never agree to convert the European combatants into the peacemakers.

The secret history of that night in New York will show, however, that the British delegates did not resent Pearson's intervention. They sought it desperately because he was the one Commonwealth statesman who could hope to deal with an exasperated American Government and was generally trusted by the Commonwealth as well.

It would be said later that he did not oppose the American resolution demanding a cease-fire and thus sided with the Communists against Britain—a legend persisting even to this day. In fact, he abstained from the vote but he knew that the crisis must be brought before the Assembly if it was to be settled peaceably.

In the present tense mood of the Assembly he judged it premature to offer the Canadian plan for a United Nations police force at Suez but he managed to broach the idea by delivering the most painful speech of his life. As the spokesman of the Canadian nation he confronted its classic dilemma, long feared and, until now, avoided. He stood in the middle of a quarrel between Britain and France, Canada's motherlands, and the United States, its neighbour. Neither side was affronted by his intervention. Neither was prepared to move for any effective settlement. The fighting continued in Egypt.

After talking to Pearson, John Foster Dulles, the American Secretary of State, approved the plan for a police force but realized that the United States could not sponsor it without being suspected by its enemies of some imperialist motive. Dulles phoned President Eisenhower on the night of November 2 and, toward dawn next morning, informed the Assembly that the United States would support the Canadian proposal if it were formally introduced. Pearson knew already that Britain could not refuse to accept it. He had broken the log jam. The Assembly resolved to establish the police force by a vote of 57 to 0, the Communist bloc and the combatants abstaining. Within a fortnight United Nations troops, including Canadians, were at Suez and the crisis passed.

Pearson had smoothly executed the greatest Canadian achievement in world politics but his hope that a temporary experiment would become a permanent United Nations peace-keeping agent was to fail. And now, though a popular hero in most of the world, he came home to find himself widely regarded in Canada as a traitor to Britain and France.

Suez had struck to the vitals of Canada's life, ranging many of its English-speaking people behind Britain and many French Canadians behind France.

The Conservative attack on Pearson opened immediately in Parliament. "It is high time that Canada had a government which will not knife Canada's best friends in the back," said the usually temperate Howard Green, whose own knife on this occasion was long, twisted, and unclean. It wounded Pearson deeply.

He fought back with spirit but without any weapons sharp enough to penetrate the Loyalist tradition. For he could not yet tell Parliament all the facts, could only say that at one stage of the Suez invasion the Commonwealth had been "on the verge of dissolution." Nor did he foresee St. Laurent's outburst against the European "supermen."

Suez had assured Pearson Canada's first Nobel Peace Prize a year later. Meanwhile, added to the pipeline debacle, it helped to tip the scales of 1957. In that year's election Pearson was perhaps more of a liability than an asset. At Victoria he made the best speech of his career so far to defend his Suez intervention but the Canadian people were not listening to reason. They were listening to Diefenbaker.

Though Pearson won re-election for himself in Algoma, the prelude to his leadership of the Liberal Party could hardly have been worse. In any case, the prospect of leading the Opposition, or possibly some future government, was repulsive to him. He doubted his own capacity. He detested the back-room deals and the public parade of politics. If his party could agree on any other leader he was almost pathetically eager to escape into one of the many opulent posts already offered to him by Canadian universities and American foundations. Those hopes soon withered.

Unless he fled from responsibility and let his friends down, which was not in his nature, there could be no escape, and when the party convened early in 1958, no doubt about its decision. Paul Martin, with more political brains than his rival and a store of ambition to match them, decided to contest the leadership and may actually have believed that he had a chance to win it. The convention voted three to one for Pearson.

Victory in the convention had been no problem for the new Liberal leader. His only real problem lay elsewhere and he botched it. How he could have managed to botch it so badly, in so short a time, is a question still mystifying to his party but not in the least mysterious.

The man who appeared to be his genial, boyish self on the convention platform and delivered a reasonably good acceptance speech was physically exhausted after a week of hectic preparation and two consecutive nights without sleep. Even if he had been fit to make any decision it would have been difficult enough to decide between the two groups of expert advisers now giving him contradictory advice. In his present state of mind and body he fell between all possible stools.

One group of politicians more experienced than he had warned him that on no account must he give the Diefenbaker Government an excuse to call an early election, which it could not fail to win. Therefore, he must not move a want-of-confidence motion lest it attract the C.C.F. and Social Credit splinters and defeat the Government in the House of Commons. At all costs Diefenbaker must be left in office with a Conservative minority to void his electoral promises and discredit himself.

The second group affirmed just as strongly that the duty of an opposition was to oppose, that Pearson would be destroyed at the start if he refused battle and showed any sign of fear. Therefore, he must defeat the Government, with the splinters' support, and take his chances in an election.

If a personal recollection may be excused here, my own unsought association with this weird affair will serve to illustrate the depth of Pearson's innocence, also his courage.

For reasons never explained or even mentioned, Pearson insisted, through Grant Dexter, that I should interview him on nationwide television after his speech, presumably to complete the day's triumph. Flying up from Washington, I arrived in the press gallery just as Pearson was concluding his remarks and preparing to present, or not to present, a want-of-confidence motion to an expectant House.

Apparently those two alternatives, as argued in the hotel bedrooms all night and pressed on Pearson by his best friends all day, were irreconcilable. It required the agile mind of Pickersgill to reconcile them but his formula had a rather serious disadvantage which neither he nor Pearson grasped—it made the worst of all possible worlds.

The formula was regarded, on the contrary, as so adroit and foolproof, the element of surprise so important, that Pearson did not reveal his intentions even to his party caucus on the morning of the great coup. When he rose in the Commons that afternoon to make his first speech as Liberal leader only Pickersgill, St. Laurent and one or two others knew what was coming.

Pearson paused for a moment and shifted uneasily on his feet. Now that the moment had come his old instinct as a diplomat warned him of danger. But it was too late for retreat. With a solemn face and sudden panic in his heart he proposed that the victorious Diefenbaker resign and hand the government over to the defeated Liberal Party.

The House gasped at this ludicrous proposition and then burst into jeering laughter. Pickersgill's flimsy structure had fallen flat and Pearson was buried under it.

After Diefenbaker had completed the burial by a speech of joyous annihilation, as already recorded, and adjourned the House for dinner, Dexter and I found Pearson alone in his office upstairs. He knew that he had begun his party leadership with the worst conceivable blunder. His face showed the misery of that knowledge but in his valley of humiliation he uttered no word of complaint against those who had brought him there. On that awful night and afterwards he never once blamed anyone except himself.

This was no time for blame or regret. Pearson must face the people on television within the hour—not, as he had expected, to score off the Government but to explain his own debacle.

No preparations had been made for the broadcast, no script or even a note written in advance. What questions did Pearson wish to be asked before the camera? He had been too busy to think about that. What did he intend to say? He had no idea. I scribbled a few questions on an envelope, we drove silently out of town to a television studio and there, without the least preparation, Pearson confronted the merciless electronic eye.

Most men, misled by their friends and crushed by Diefenbaker, would have showed some signs of the day's damage, at least of nervousness. Pearson showed none. In his familiar grin, his witty persiflage and then his earnest discussion of public business, as if he had carefully rehearsed his argument, the watchers across Canada must have seen a man in full control not only of himself but of his party, a confident leader not on the defensive but on the attack. Somehow, throughout this hideous half hour, he could draw strength and serenity from depths never plumbed by his friends.

That was a psychic reserve which might be useful later. It was of little help in an immediate election. And now, as Diefenbaker opened the campaign of 1958, Pearson consummated his own havoc by proposing, on the advice of his expert economists, that income taxes be temporarily reduced by $400 million a year to stimulate business. Thus he appeared to be out-promising a financially reckless Government. While the plan might be good economics, Pearson's "tax holiday" instantly dissipated the Liberal Party's only surviving asset, its claim to responsibility.

Pearson could not win in any case, as he well knew, since obviously the people would give Diefenbaker a majority and a chance to govern. The double error of the no-confidence motion and the tax promise turned defeat into Liberal rout. Pearson had begun his leadership by making the victorious party of Laurier, King and St. Laurent a pitiable rump of forty-eight members in Parliament.

Liberalism might eventually recover from its worst disaster since Confederation, if Diefenbaker made enough mistakes. For Pearson, the architect of this wreckage, recovery seemed impossible. As many of its wisest politicians concluded, the party had chosen the wrong man.

The next two years in the wilderness slowly altered that judgment by revealing a Pearson unknown to the public and probably to himself.

More than once he was tempted to quit and take an easy job in private life. Often he was depressed by the suspicion that politics could never be his trade, and its daily round of speeches, correspondence, manoeuvres and intrigues repelled him. If there had been an acceptable leader to take his place undoubtedly he would have retired. No substitute had appeared. No one wanted his thankless task.

Besides, the Liberal Party, with all its faults, had invariably stood behind its leaders in defeat while the Conservative Party had chosen six leaders in less than sixty years and recently dismissed Manion, Bracken and Drew. No attempt was made to unseat Pearson.

The three front benchers left beside him, Martin, Pickersgill and Lionel Chevrier, were never close to Pearson in a personal way but with their long experience of political warfare they settled down for a long siege. Sometimes they made sorties against the Government and Pickersgill soon proved himself to be the ablest guerilla fighter in Parliament, from whose armour of indignation and mischief Diefenbaker's bullets bounced off harmlessly.

These three could never quite understand their leader. They knew that Pearson's closest advisers were men like Walter Gordon (a friend of his youth), Robert Fowler, Maurice Lamontagne, Grant Dexter and Tom Kent, all men outside politics. The parliamentarians knew also that Pearson offered the party its only chance of recovery, they respected his character and they hoped he would learn his trade. On his side, he forgave their mistakes, encouraged their occasional success and waited for the tide to turn.

It was a lonely time of waiting. Unique among opposition leaders, Pearson had only an intellectual, not an emotional, ambition to be Prime Minister. Until he felt the itch for power in his heart as well as in his mind he could never win office. He could not even lead the Opposition effectively. He could give it arguments, facts and respectability. He could not give it a sense of motion, a hope of success, the vital nutriment of all political parties that live on their appetite for power and eventually die if their hunger is not satisfied.

Contrary to the Government's assumption, Pearson did not waste the time of waiting. All unknown to Diefenbaker, his opponent had begun to undergo a drastic change. After the first reeling shock of his defeat, Pearson's unsuspected stubbornness, the Methodist conscience of his youth and the old habit of doing the job at hand without worrying about tomorrow came to his rescue. The change in him was deeper than that, and quite uncharacteristic.

Not only was he convinced that the Government had begun to undermine the nation but he had acquired a personal aversion to Diefenbaker, the first real enmity of his life. That kind of anger came hard with Pearson, in gradual stages.

During his first two years of opposition the habits of the diplomat and conciliator muted his criticism. To the despair of his colleagues, he usually co-operated with the Government in improving its legislation and smoothing its path. The builder found it almost impossible at first to be a wrecker.

As a result, he did Diefenbaker little harm. All the harm, not yet apparent but already irrevocable, came from Diefenbaker himself. While the animosity between the two men was growing fast, Diefenbaker regarded Pearson with private contempt as being no threat to the Government. Pearson's true feelings toward his enemy were rarely disclosed in his speeches, only in a word of conversation now and then, a gesture or a laugh. He never doubted, however, that Diefenbaker was a national menace.

Anyway, now that he had decided to remain in politics all Pearson's energies were focused on the double task of demolishing the Government and rebuilding the Liberal Party. He had no leisure for the hatreds that sustain but poison so many good men in Ottawa's ceaseless struggle for power.

As an opposition leader, Pearson learned fast, once he decided to learn. Knowing little of finance and economics, he amazed his experts by a quick grasp of their figures, the Government by his knowledge of the facts in every debate. Though they were little noted, his speeches in opposition were frequently polished gems of factual argument, easily shouted down and outvoted but unanswerable.

This work of dull and detailed criticism, sometimes illuminated by a flash of searing sarcasm (as when he called the Government's defence policy "a fog of silence penetrated occasionally by a ministerial platitude") was not Pearson's chief concern. He was satisfied that the Government would destroy itself without much help from him. He must concentrate on the work of making his party electable.

That work was pursued, almost silently, on two levels.

The Liberal Party's organization was placed in the hands of Walter Gordon, who had always been Pearson's intimate since their youthful meeting in Bennett's price-spreads inquiry. Pearson had made Gordon into a public figure in the days of the St. Laurent

Government by insisting on his appointment as a royal commissioner to study Canada's economic prospects. Now Gordon undertook to make Pearson into a Prime Minister and himself into a possible successor.

Having inherited a family fortune and increased it in big business, Gordon applied business methods to politics, which he regarded, with almost childlike fascination, as a game for high-minded amateurs of his sort. That light-hearted air of detachment concealed a strong ambition and some fine ideals but Gordon, as an amateur, had yet to learn the rules of the game as played by professionals and, in learning them, would suffer a ghastly humiliation for his ignorance.

Meanwhile the new Liberal machine was managed in detail by Keith Davey, a young man well trained by the radio industry, and was centred in Gordon's office with branches throughout the nation.

Gordon imitated and improved on the techniques that Grosart had imported from Madison Avenue by secretly employing Lou Harris, who had been President Kennedy's pollster-in-chief and now felt the pulse of Canadian public opinion with a physicians's delicate touch. Both the major political parties were becoming obsessed with the new clairvoyant science of reading the voter's mind and satisfying it when obviously Canada needed strong policies and men ready to execute them whether they were popular or not. And if they were to be strong they could not be popular, as Gordon would find out to his sorrow once he reached office.

Diefenbaker was grossly unfair to Gordon, calling him "the Toronto taxidermist who fills Mr. Pearson with flossy economic ideas"; but certainly Gordon's influence with his chief was paramount, being based on personal affection, and was jealously resented by many Liberals.

Later Pearson persuaded Mitchell Sharp to give up his business career and run for Parliament. The nucleus of an alternative government at last appeared.

On a higher level Pearson was still trying to shift his party's centre of gravity to the left, to reorient its mind as King had done and to bring it abreast of a changing society that the Conservatives failed to comprehend. Like King, Pearson was confused, eclectic and experimental. Since he did not know the answer to the nation's problems, he was ready to grope for new policies at the risk of error and he had not made King's youthful mistake of refining his theories in a book.

His first major experiment (or his latest blunder, as the Liberal old guard considered it) was an ostensibly nonpartisan conference of "liberally minded" men at Kingston, organized by Sharp. This conventicle of assorted dissenters discussed a hopeful hodge-podge of contradictory reforms which the public could not understand very well and generally took to be Liberal policy.

It was not Liberal policy—not yet anyway—but the public hunch was quite accurate. So was the hunch of the party's right wing. The old guard began to see with alarm that Pearson was personally committed, and would increasingly commit Liberalism, to a policy much more radical than that of a radical government. With clumsy, laborious movement, with repeated trial, error and stumbling double talk, he was quietly thrusting Liberalism into the main stream of modern society, as he conceived it.

If the Kingston conference did not clarify his intended reforms, it clarified his political philosophy. In one of his best speeches, and a good example of his own writing style, he said that politics was "the most important of all secular callings," yet it was considered "a rather unworthy pursuit, like running a confidence game or managing a prize fighter in New York. . . . Politics is not magic, black, white or otherwise. It is certainly not an exact science. . . . Politics is an art . . . the search for compromise without betrayal . . . above all, service, and not to self. If it becomes self-service it is degrading and the practitioner's immediate success—for this kind of politics can have temporary success—will not for long prevent or conceal ultimate and lasting failure."

He recognized also in this speech that "our problems have indeed reached new dimensions. We are in outer space and in inner turmoil. We have both cobalt and hydrogen bombs. We can communicate with a satellite twenty-five million miles away but not with a human across a curtain. We can spread political power throughout the nation but we cannot be sure of its responsible exercise."

Pearson's own search for responsibility had begun. It had a long way to go yet, and not in a straight line.

His public statements from Kingston onward; his attacks on the Government's deficits combined with a defence of deficits so long as they were well managed by Liberals; his demand for financial order and impossible tax reductions; his advocacy of private enterprise within an economy planned by the State; his opposition to high tariffs and his argument for currency devalution which would have the same effect—all this mish-mash of opposites was interpreted by the Government as only the deliberate confusion of a party leader on the make.

Of course it was confusion but it was much more than that. Inchoate, blurred and incomprehensible as they looked then, these ideas represented, in their general direction, the true nature of Pearson. By a long detour he had come back to his instinctive position in life. He had found that he was a liberal, in the modern intellectual sense of the word, as well as a Liberal in politics. He stood for the defenceless little man against the great organized power blocs in this age of giantism.

If his specific reforms, his contributory old-age pensions, health insurance, public investment and a vastly expanded welfare State did not yet deserve to be called a policy, they expressed an attitude that might be refined into a policy.

The same could be said of Diefenbaker's attitude but he could not refine and enforce it successfully. Two liberals were at war with the conservatism of both parties. Pearson was winning his war mainly because he did not yet face the hard choices of a man in office and could still talk in riddles. Diefenbaker was failing mainly because the conservatism of the Conservative Party remained too strong for him and he dared not make hard choices.

Pearson at least was clear on one definite point of policy. Though Gordon had persuaded him to urge a devalued currency, as a protectionist device, Pearson boldly advocated a world-wide reduction of tariffs and a drastic expansion of international trade—a concept which he had been the first statesman to call an Atlantic Community.

As a beginning, he had strongly favoured the European Common Market, hoped that Britain would join it and in some of his most effective speeches had denounced Diefenbaker for obstructing this bridge across the English Channel. In economic as in military planning Pearson was an outright internationalist.

That his closest friend, Gordon, was by instinct an economic nationalist apparently did not occur to him. Or if he foresaw a future clash of principle, he assumed that he could always control his friend. Moreover, by introducing Sharp to politics Pearson had given the Liberal Party its ablest contemporary advocate of freer trade. The clash, if it ever developed, no doubt could be adjusted by diplomacy, friendship and compromise. Nevertheless, potential fissures of trade, financial and social policy were opening in the Opposition as in the Government.

What Pearson most needed at the moment was a distraction from these academic theories. He got it, with an unbelievable break of luck, in the Coyne affair.

Here was precisely the sort of situation long familiar to Pearson in many diplomatic encounters. He managed it superbly. Never sympathizing with any of Coyne's tight-money or high-tariff views, Pearson skilfully shifted the whole ground of the argument by defending Coyne's honour and his right to be heard before a House of Commons committee. When Diefenbaker refused to allow a fair trial, the Liberal senators polished off Pearson's job by exonerating Coyne and tacitly convicting the Government of tyranny against a helpless public servant. Pearson was the chief beneficiary of Coyne's misfortune.

Another break of luck was given to the Opposition in the country's financial misfortune as Diefenbaker called an election for June 18, 1962, but it came too late to defeat the Government. In any case, Pearson bungled his campaign.

Having used all his ammunition at the start, he was left with none toward the end. In the jargon of politics he had "peaked" the campaign prematurely. That was not his decisive mistake.

What damaged Pearson most was the obvious confusion of his ideas—the demand for responsible finance on the one hand, the wide-open promises of heavy spending and costly social reforms on the other, the image of a man who didn't know how he intended to govern. The country had lost confidence in Diefenbaker. It seemed to have even less in Pearson.

At this point a sensible public judgment between the two men was rendered impossible by the suppression of the relevant facts. Canada did not know yet, and Diefenbaker flatly denied, that it had reached the verge of international bankruptcy. Pearson suspected a foreign-exchange crisis but, lacking the latest official figures, could not prove his charges against the Government. He may well have lost votes when Diefenbaker accused him of injuring the world's confidence in Canada by his unpatriotic "gloom and doom."

Such Conservative catchwords were meaningless. So, too, was Pearson's promise "to get the economy moving again," a slogan borrowed from President Kennedy's campaign of 1960 and ridiculous in Canada where the economy was now moving in high gear even if the nation's hard currency reserves were running out.

Though Pearson's original campaign posture of "responsibility" was almost obliterated by the pursuit of votes, he knew that none of the nation's problems had been solved, despite the turn of the business cycle, but he could not persuade the people that he knew how to solve them. Diefenbaker simply ignored the problems and attacked the Opposition as dangerous neo-socialists, "a circus of bureaucrats," and "a collection that has never been seen outside a menagerie." Neither man in this duel of slogans was equal to the nation's needs or worthy of its trust. Neither received it.

Yet on election night, as Diefenbaker watched the returns with sickened incredulity, Pearson, despite his bitter disappointment, could claim a unique success. He had taken the Liberal Party at the nadir of its fortunes and increased its 48 seats to 99. Only the upsurge of Social Credit with 26 seats in Quebec, as a protest against both the old parties, had denied him the largest group in Parliament and the chance of immediate office. After only four years' work he had paralyzed the strongest Government since Confederation—and this without the great depression which alone had enabled King to destroy Bennett in five years.

True enough, Diefenbaker had done most of this work himself as the Opposition's unconscious ally, but in all the circumstances Pearson had performed a feat as extraordinary as Diefenbaker's original victory of 1957. Even now, however, when he had proved himself a major domestic politician, many Liberals and most Conservatives still regarded Pearson as a babe in the political woods. All a bewildered nation knew on the morrow of the poll was that it had no government capable of governing, no opposition entitled to govern and, in this state of political impotence, a sudden crisis of foreign exchange.

That dreadful summer tested Pearson almost as much as Diefenbaker. An opposition leader of less diplomatic experience and more personal ambition would have tried to crucify the Government for misleading the people, misrepresenting the crisis, suddenly imposing a phony program of "austerity" and refusing to meet Parliament. Pearson was wise enough to reject these easy tactics. Against the advice of his more ardent lieutenants, he supported the Government's emergency measures and, standing aside, waited for it to die of its wounds.

He never doubted that it would soon die. The only question was the date of its death. He might accelerate it but he must move with extreme caution lest he be accused of damaging the country, at its time of peril, by hindering the Government's work of salvage.

This was a knack of equilibrium that Pearson had learned on countless diplomatic tightropes. Hence, through the autumn session of Parliament, his tentative no-confidence motions to test the feelings of the two splinter parties. Hence his patient attrition when his colleagues demanded a sudden knock-out blow. Hence, too, his one reckless plunge in supporting Social Credit's demand for "debt free" money which he regarded as absurd and, after that motion failed, his quick return to financial orthodoxy.

His greatest stroke was not aimed directly at the Government. It was aimed at Quebec where, as he knew, the Liberal Party would win or lose the next election.

Diefenbaker, having lost Quebec, paid scant attention to Pearson's plan for a royal commission on what he called bilingualism and biculturalism (without explaining exactly what those words implied) but French Canada was listening.

The royal commission might mean much, little or nothing in final result. It seemed to mean at least that Pearson was interested in the aspirations of French Canada which had entered its latest cycle of discontent with the reappearance of an old doctrine now called "separatism."

Pearson's excellent speech, dedicating himself to the principle of a dual Canadian society, was soon submerged by the more exciting political crisis in Ottawa but it might be just enough to tip the political balance in Quebec.

The Fabian tactics of the Liberals in Parliament could not succeed because the splinters feared, as much as Diefenbaker, the prospect of another election. Robert Thompson already was quarreling in his Social Credit Party with his erratic Quebec lieutenant, Réal Caouette. The redoubtable "Tommy" Douglas had been unable to make his New Democratic Party as effective as the old C.C.F. Some stronger crowbar than parliamentary resolutions must be found to dislodge the Government.

Pearson seemed to find the necessary leverage in the issue of nuclear armament but actually it was handed to him, or rather forced upon him, by a then obscure young man, Paul Hellyer. He, more than any single person, accomplished the Government's downfall after a visit of parliamentarians to Europe.

There, as a veteran of the last war, Hellyer was shocked to see at first hand the shaken morale of the Canadian troops in NATO. As fine a force of fighting men as the nation had ever assembled was frustrated and infuriated by its lack of effective nuclear weapons.

Hellyer decided that he must break with established Liberal policy and demand that Canada accept these weapons immediately. Pearson was shocked in his turn but he did not try to muzzle Hellyer, who announced his heresy as a personal view only.

This evident schism in the Liberal Party offered the Government a moment of hope and consolation, a brief moment. Diefenbaker could not imagine that Pearson, having always opposed nuclear weapons with horror, would reverse himself overnight. That was precisely what he now proceeded to do, and he did it alone.

Convinced at last that Canada had committed itself to a nuclear role in North American defence and in NATO, Pearson sat up all night in a Toronto hotel room, wrote and rewrote his thoughts until dawn and next day detonated a mine within the Government.

Two sentences in his speech to the York-Scarborough Liberal Association were as politically disruptive as any ever uttered by a Canadian: "The Ottawa Government should end its evasion of responsibility by discharging its commitments. It can only do this by accepting nuclear warheads." That seemed clear enough until he added in the next breath the promise to exclude these weapons later on, if possible, by agreement with Canada's allies. King had never conducted a retreat so smoothly, squared a circle so blandly or trapped an enemy so neatly.

The reversal was naked and breath-taking all the same.

Only two years earlier a Liberal convention not only had opposed nuclear weapons but had demanded that Canada abandon any combat role in the North American Air Defence Command and restrict itself to "detection, identification and warning" or, as Diefenbaker called it contemptuously, "bird watching."

This policy had been based on a strange moral hypocrisy, which Pearson now repealed by stating the obvious fact, unnoted in the past, that Canada already supplied uranium for American bombs and was morally responsible for their construction. He had come a long way from his original innocence. In the light of the Cuban crisis the original Liberal position now looked dangerous and absurd.

Why had Pearson thus repudiated everything he had said about nuclear weapons for the last five years? His political motives were plain. He knew that his reversal must almost certainly split the Government between the anti-nuclear Green and the pro-nuclear Harkness. The Scarborough retreat (or advance) could not be explained, however, by political motives alone.

In the first place, it was by no means sure that a majority of the voters wanted nuclear weapons. Diefenbaker, a good judge, had made a contrary assessment. He was right in believing that Pearson had taken calculated but grave risks. Many English-speaking Liberal voters would turn against their party on this deeply felt issue. Quebec was still more strongly against involvement in the supreme contest of world power; and in Quebec, where he should have won it, Pearson had lost the recent election.

No, Pearson's reversal was based on a private acknowledgment of his own past errors. He still favoured a non-nuclear defence role but he saw, very late, that it had been excluded by the Government's commitments, which must be fulfilled. Above all, he saw that the refusal to fulfil them had left the nation with no defence policy, the worst of alternatives, and had provoked an intolerable breach with the United States and the NATO alliance. Nuclear weapons, however repulsive, were the least of all evils. Win or lose, Pearson decided to take the clear position that Diefenbaker had so far avoided.

As it turned out, Pearson's reading of the public mind was more accurate than Diefenbaker's. His reading of the Cabinet's mind was quickly confirmed. In short, Pearson gambled everything on his judgment that Diefenbaker's anti-Americanism, as concentrated in the nuclear issue, would prove to be not only irresponsible policy but bad electoral politics. More important, Pearson knew that he had bungled the last campaign and he would not make the same mistake again.

The Liberal strategists believed that the ensuing disintegration of the Government could not fail to elect Pearson with a substantial working majority. While every tangible factor seemed to justify this assumption, certain intangibles invalidated it.

The aura and the oratory of Diefenbaker were still a far more potent force than his enemies admitted, and only a minority of the Canadian people was yet ready to accept Pearson, a far less effective campaigner.

Pearson understood both those dangers. The optimism of his palace guard did not delude him in the least. For all his sunny look of confidence on the platform he never underestimated Diefenbaker or overestimated himself. Several times a day his political managers telephoned him to report assured victories all over the country but he discounted all these predictions. If his natural humility had long been a handicap, it enabled him now to keep his chances in proportion, his head free of self-deception, his energies focused solely on the day's work. After all his disappointments and mistakes, the prospect of victory seemed just too good to be true.

Thus he was angry, though not much surprised, when Gordon's electoral machine suddenly produced a new series of mistakes.

The idiotic flight of homing pigeons, released at Montreal to meet Pearson at London, Ontario, failed to arrive and gave Diefenbaker a useful exercise in derision. A child's colouring-book deriding Diefenbaker in the worst of taste only disgusted the public. A "Truth Squad" led by the actinic Miss Judy LaMarsh followed Diefenbaker to publicize his erroneous statements and quickly became a national laughing-stock.

Pearson quashed these gaucheries as soon as he heard of them.

375

How many votes they had lost him he would never know but he could not afford to lose any. Assuredly, he could not afford any deviation from his plan of campaign.

The plan, of two parts, was powerful in its simplicity—to exploit the confusion of the Government without seeming to rejoice in the nation's misfortune; to present Pearson not as a politician lusting for power but as a serious statesman above the dust and grime of politics, seeking only the nation's welfare.

Curiously enough, this image, as built up by the Madison Avenue technicians, contained some elements of truth. For as he looked at the state of the nation Pearson had begun to fear it more than he feared defeat.

What disturbed him most was Canada's ugly quarrel with the United States which, as a statesman, he considered sheer madness but which, as a campaigner, he must approach with caution. He could not condone Diefenbaker's treatment of Kennedy nor could he seem to side with an American President against a Canadian Prime Minister. He could only insist that the neighbours cease their quarrel. In a happy phrase, he likened the United States to a wife with whom a Canadian husband cannot live easily and without whom he cannot live at all.

Canada's problems, as Pearson described them, could permit no easy solutions and he began to warn the public, rather gingerly, that a Liberal government would have to take some painful, unpopular decisions. His immediate decision to tone down the prodigal promises of 1962 was neither painful nor unpopular since clearly they had served to help Diefenbaker by making him look no more irresponsible than Pearson.

As the nation's business continued to decay, Pearson recognized that responsibility was both good politics in the people's present mood and imperative if the nation was to be saved from still worse trouble. He had reached the sincere conviction that Confederation itself was in danger but this opinion fell far short of an alternative policy.

Pearson concentrated instead on the safe and valid proposition that Canada must have "stable government." While the public agreed, it could not discover what sort of government Pearson would provide. The collapse of so many brave assumptions during the last year had left a Liberal vacuum and the vacuum ached.

It was partially filled by Pearson's new friendship with Premier Jean Lesage, who had done little or nothing to help in 1962 but now assured some Liberal gains in Quebec. Elsewhere it was hardly sur-

prising that a campaign without coherent purpose or specific promises did not go as its managers had planned. Diefenbaker made sure
of that. He endangered the Liberal strategy by suddenly switching
his own to the nuclear issue.

His denunciation of the Government's Bomarc missiles as worthless or, if equipped with nuclear warheads, as decoys to lure Russian
bombers into Canada, was patently ridiculous. Pearson had only to
reply that Diefenbaker had installed the Bomarcs, against Liberal
protests, and if they were no use he should scrap them.

"I've heard a lot of drivel in the campaign," Pearson protested,
"but I've never heard anything so drivelish. What would you think
of a commander who sent a company of men into the front-line
trenches with guns but said: 'We're not going to give you bullets or
you'll be decoys!' "

Nevertheless, Pearson was caught off stride. He had determined,
if possible, to prevent the diversion of the argument to these irrelevancies and to focus it on the nation's real problems. Now Diefenbaker eluded and easily excelled him on the platform. While Pearson
tried to drop the Bomarcs altogether, Diefenbaker, having little else
to offer, thrust them into the headlines every day with mounting
eloquence and his own unique mastery of confusion. So far as
Pearson could see, after he had crossed the country and reached the
Pacific coast, Diefenbaker was succeeding brilliantly.

Moreover, it was abundantly plain that Pearson's new image
had not succeeded, not sufficiently, at any rate, to expunge the unfortunate image of 1962.

He had set out with the primary purpose of establishing the contrast between himself as a practical, responsible Canadian in search
of sound national policy at a time of trouble, and Diefenbaker as
the irresponsible man of power whose policies had failed. That contrast had been pretty well established but evidently it was not
enough. The people who distrusted Diefenbaker were not yet ready
to trust Pearson. With the wisdom of instinct they perceived Diefenbaker's failure and they perceived Pearson's confusion, too, not so
much in his tactics as in his mind. The people were right. Pearson
was confused.

He was confused not about long-run objectives but about short-
run remedies. He still stood to the leftward of Diefenbaker in the
social scale, he was outraged by the spectacle of unemployment at
a time of prosperity, he believed in the power of the State and its
expenditures to correct these evils. On the other hand, a certain
shrewdness surviving from his youth of poverty warned him that the

Mr. Prime Minister

State's disordered finances must be repaired by economy, by extra taxes, or both.

How could the opposite necessities of prudence and fiscal experiment be merged? If any voter could see a logical pattern of policy in Pearson's speeches he was a very percipient voter indeed and saw further than the speaker.

He had greatly improved his platform style, however, and if he could not compete with Diefenbaker's purple passages his occasional sarcasm had been sharpened to a rapier's point. "I would say to the Prime Minister in the most kindly way possible," he remarked with a touch of unexpected venom, "that he must not let failure go to his head." But was Diefenbaker really failing?

At the last minute the Liberal strategists, sensing the public's scepticism, invented their final gimmick and sold it to their dubious leader. He should promise, they said, to give the nation a glorious Hundred Days of Decision. When someone remembered that a similar interval had destroyed Napoleon, Gordon promptly cut the season of Liberal magic to Sixty Days, thereby ensuring his own Waterloo. Pearson accepted the gimmick and thereby committed the worst mistake of his life.

He committed it not because he doubted Diefenbaker's defeat but because he felt in his bones that without some last push his own campaign would fail to win him a working majority.

As in the blunder of 1958, another unseen factor was at work. Pearson had reached the Pacific coast sick from an infection picked up on the road.

At Victoria, the public saw a man in his usual ruddy health. It did not know that he had rested most of the afternoon in bed. He had planned to spend an outdoor week-end at a Vancouver Island country resort and prepare himself for what he already knew would be the most important, and the most dangerous meeting of the campaign. Instead, the doctors put him to bed again and filled him with antibiotics.

He reached Vancouver to receive a sudden gift of luck from his worst enemies, the opponents of nuclear weapons who belonged to no particular party. They had organized such a noisy demonstration that at first their barrage of screaming abuse drowned his voice from the platform. Unwittingly they had changed the whole course of the campaign.

In the sturdy figure standing silent and unmoved before this pandemonium, his wife beside him, their hands joined, Vancouver and, through television, the Canadian people, beheld a Pearson un-

378

known to them. Here was no sleek diplomat of the drawing-room, a professor of history or a dilettante of economics. Here was a fighting man, and a tough guy—tougher than the audience could know since his unflinching look concealed a sick body.

After he had out-shouted the hecklers and reached the audience, its response was electric and flowed like a current across the nation. Still sick and doped with medicine, Pearson flew east next day, accompanied by his new legend of courage, to end the campaign in a crescendo of vigour, confidence and righteous anger.

The public, remembering another legend, supposed that Pearson knew the secret of perpetual youth. What it took for physical energy was a strange energy of the spirit, summoned up in this hour of need from those depths that still puzzle his friends.

Yet his personality, the campaign planning, the machinery, the money, the gimmicks and the Government's disintegration were not quite sufficient to convince the people. Pearson had failed to win a majority by the tantalizing margin of four seats. Still, if anyone could govern with a minority it should be the ex-diplomat who had wrestled so long, as the agent of a small nation, with the majority of mankind.

Such hopes blossomed rapidly as Pearson formed his Government, soon healed Canada's breach with the United States at a meeting with President Kennedy, and opened the magic Sixty Days of Decision.

It was a brief and false blossoming, followed by the deadly frost of the Government's first budget.

Gordon had framed his financial policies with the help of three outside experts from Toronto, had largely ignored the officials of his department and presented his conclusions to the Cabinet at the eleventh hour. A few ministers guessed that his discriminatory taxes on foreign capital were unwise and unworkable but it was too late to change them. Pearson, distracted by other business, accepted Gordon's assurance that his plans were sound and necessary. Without fully understanding it, the Cabinet hastily approved the budget speech and still did not suspect its consequences as Gordon delivered it.

The business world knew better. The stock market fell. Ottawa was bombarded with protests against a budget which was not merely a financial absurdity and a political disaster but, for Pearson, a personal wound. It had discredited his Government and his best friend.

At a moment of humiliation without precedent Gordon remained outwardly serene but inwardly he was crushed. His attempt to save

Canada from foreign economic penetration and move its accounts toward balance had been conceived in patriotism but brought forth in fiasco. The budget was stillborn. After a few days of torture and contradictory explanations to Parliament, Gordon withdrew his major tax on the sale of Canadian securities to foreigners, revised his tax on construction materials, offered his resignation to Pearson and decided to leave politics forever.

King would have let him go without hesitation or regret. Pearson, a kinder and less cautious man, suggested that his colleague move from the Treasury to some other department. Gordon said he must be Finance Minister or nothing. Unable to endure the departure of a fallen comrade, Pearson stood by him. Gordon retained his portfolio but overnight had lost most of his power in Cabinet and party. Instead of a great Liberal asset he had become a burdensome liability. Though his motives were unimpeachable, the amateur had found that politics was a game for professionals.

Did Pearson's decision to retain Gordon come from weakness or strength, folly or wisdom? The Liberal hierarchy seemed to be divided about equally on that question and fortunately the Opposition was also divided. Its fear of another election, and nothing else, saved the Government from defeat in the Commons; but the pitiable remains of the budget, as finally passed, were the first indication of Pearson's basic dilemma, now starkly revealed after a short post-election honeymoon.

Not only had he inherited financial problems that Gordon could not solve; he had inherited a political apparatus out of joint. Not only did he lack a majority in Parliament; he led a party deeply divided within itself and unnaturally distributed across the nation. Not only was the Liberal Party split between its right and left wings (which is normal) but its geography had been turned topsy-turvy, its power centred in the old Conservative and protectionist citadel of Ontario and almost exiled from the old Liberal and free-trade citadel of the Prairies.

In this state of confusion the first of two issues that must settle Canada's direction and Pearson's place in history could be discerned, as yet dimly.

Should the Canadian economy seek growth, affluence and maximum independence by restricting the inflow of foreign goods, services and capital? Or should it expose its business to more international competition, liquidate its soft enterprises, expand the hard ones and thus exploit strength instead of protecting weakness? Specifically, should it welcome or repel massive American investment?

380

Gordon leaned, with unquestionable sincerity, to the side of protectionism. As a patriot he was haunted by the spectre of American influence and inspired by the hope of buying back the nation's alienated resources. Sharp was fully committed to the Liberal doctrine of maximum exports and imports, the freest possible play of competition. So, in principle and a hundred speeches, was Pearson.

The Government, in short, found itself driven back to the original tariff issue. It had split every Cabinet of the past and the resulting illogical compromise had always been announced as a stroke of sheer logic. Another revelation of the same expedient sort could be expected from the Pearson Government later on, but there was a difference this time. Previous governments could delay and equivocate indefinitely. Pearson faced a definite deadline in the negotiations already opening under the General Agreement on Tariffs and Trade, the momentous Kennedy Round.

As forecast in the budget fiasco and then over-simplified in partisan caricature, the argument inside the Liberal Party between the theoretical protectionists and the free traders was made to appear almost irreconcilable, a shattering collision inevitable, but the political process of Canada could not be painted in such harsh tones of black and white, only in the thin wash of water-colours constantly oozing, merging and changing from day to day.

If the Kennedy Round began to accomplish any significant result Pearson doubtless would fit his policy into it on the side of reduced tariffs, as he had so often promised. Given skill and luck, he would somehow reconcile the discordant elements of his Cabinet and party. Given courage, he could enforce his belief in expanding trade.

The business boom of 1963 gave him his first installment of luck, disguised the nation's real economic problems and enabled him to postpone their solution. The larger problems of racial conflict gave him the chance to show his skill and courage. He seized that chance.

Long before he took office Pearson had fully realized that his future, and the nation's, would be deeply affected by financial and economic policy but would be determined in the end by agreement, or lack of agreement, between the English- and French-Canadian communities.

Above everything, behind everything and sure to decide everything, loomed the clash of race. Canada's oldest, largest and most intractable problem was opening again like a poisonous flower and challenging Pearson as no other Prime Minister had ever been challenged. For in its latest guise, French-Canadian nationalism, now ironically called the "Quiet Revolution," did not merely reassert Quebec's sacred autonomy. Pushed too far, it threatened to break Confederation.

That, at least, was Pearson's judgment when he formed his Government. Quite deliberately he chose to present the nation's alternatives in stark terms, as they had never been presented before.

He rejected out of hand the theory that Quebec might withdraw from Confederation but Canada could still live on, like an English-speaking East and West Pakistan, riven by a French wedge on the St. Lawrence. In the strongest and clearest speeches of his career he asserted that the nation must be one whole or it must die, that once severed, its separate parts, including Quebec, must wither and fall piecemeal into the United States. Simultaneously he sought a better understanding with the United States but began to warn it that Canadian-American relations were bound to change in a changing world and that Canada, despite its difficulties, would not disintegrate.

While making the public speeches Pearson was approaching the racial problem by the private methods of the diplomat with no regard to the hobgoblin of consistency that troubles little minds. He was confused at times, he often waffled, he could never be sure that his solutions would work and his changes of mind baffled his friends. Yet in all these strange convolutions there was a larger consistency, if you looked hard enough. Pearson knew what he was trying to do. At any cost in logic or money he was trying to reunite Confederation.

His first step was to reconstruct, from the best materials at hand, the historic political partnership between the two Canadian communities which had been in abeyance since St. Laurent's retirement. As his French-Canadian coadjutor Pearson chose Guy Favreau, promoted him to the prestigious Department of Justice and made him government leader in the Commons.

This was a risky experiment since Favreau, a newcomer to Parliament, had little knowledge of politics. Pearson believed, however, that this brilliant lawyer and experienced civil servant would grow with responsibility.

Favreau possessed not only the useful qualities of learning and intelligence but the essential quality of courage. Moreover, his chunky frame, his plump face, his simple manner and his odd physical resemblance to Lapointe seemed to embody the moderation and shrewd common sense of his race. Seldom had any untried man risen so rapidly in Ottawa but the Pearson-Favreau coalition was no more than an experiment and it began in the worst of circumstances.

By the first of the new year the Government had lived down the budget fiasco and Pearson was manipulating the levers of power with an increasingly firm grip. He had imposed a public trusteeship on the warring labour unions of the Great Lakes, conferred in Paris with President de Gaulle of France, persuaded President Johnson of the United States by telephone to veto a Congressional restriction on Canadian lumber imports and arranged with him to draft a code of reasonable conduct governing the future relations between the two neighbouring countries.

All these steps represented hopeful progress out of the previous summer's morass but the Government was not getting its business through Parliament and the racial conflict had steadily deteriorated. Thus for Pearson the spring of 1964 must be decisive. Things simply could not drift on in this fashion. He knew it, and the deepening lines of his face, the uncharacteristic moments of irritation, indicated the burden of his knowledge. Even his intimates had failed to suspect the change in his mind, his new concept of his office.

He realized now, and admitted occasionally on television, that his first year of power had been disfigured by many needless blunders, most of them resulting from the false premises and the prodigal promises of his election campaign. The broken fragments of the dreadful Sixty Days must be abandoned or reassembled.

If he was to build a coherent national policy out of these ruins and, more important, if he was to meet the crisis of race, he must be more than the chairman of a committee, an ambassador under instructions, a diplomatic handy-man. He must be the undisputed boss of his Government and leader of the nation. A series of sudden overt acts showed to those who knew him best that he had determined, very late, to make himself Prime Minister in fact as well as name.

His resolve issued first in a new defence policy devised by Paul Hellyer to merge the armed services. Whatever its merits might be, this initiative revealed Hellyer as one of Ottawa's strongest men, a colleague who had changed Pearson's mind on the issue of nuclear weapons, a minister who had dominated the military brass of his department.

Pearson's next decision was to intervene unilaterally in the threatened war between Greece and Turkey. Before any other member had offered its services, Canada became an agent of the United Nations in Cyprus.

This initiative, as smoothly managed by Paul Martin, came naturally to Pearson. He had been over the same ground before, in Korea, Indo-China and Suez. However the Cyprus episode might turn out, Canada's prompt action, while other nations hesitated, instantly revived its limping reputation in the world. It helped to repair the Canadian people's confidence in themselves. Doubtless it strengthened Pearson's faith in himself as well.

His third decision overruled the demand of certain colleagues and reckless party managers for a snap election before midsummer on the supposedly popular issue of the Government's contributory old-age-pension scheme, even though it was still half-baked and full of actuarial holes. For unknown to these advisers the Prime Minister had been meditating a new pension scheme and a shift in basic strategy. He was prepared now for his supreme effort to conciliate the French-Canadian race.

Already he had conferred with the provincial governments in Quebec City, had refused (under Gordon's pressure) to meet their financial demands and was appalled by the angry reaction of the Quebec Premier, Jean Lesage. On second thoughts, Pearson saw that his refusal had been another mistake. Under Lesage's thinly veiled threats Confederation was approaching a point of clear and present danger.

As had happened so often before, to so many Prime Ministers, Pearson had misjudged the facts in advance. Having grasped them, he moved stealthily, rapidly and alone.

The overhaul of his entire old-age-pension scheme to make it fit the provincial Quebec scheme, together with an extra revenue concession to all the provinces, were Pearson's personal, single-handed invention. It worsened Gordon's budget deficit, it probably involved federal tax increases and, by guaranteeing the provinces the use of huge pension funds for social investment, it eroded the authority of the national Government. The old, familiar tidal motion of the Canadian system had reappeared again. Power, long flowing to the centre at Ottawa, was flowing now to the provincial periphery.

All these costs in money and power would be justified, Pearson thought, if they produced even the beginning of reconciliation between the Canadian races. He could not be sure, however, when he announced his latest policy to the Cabinet as a *fait accompli,* that he had bought more than a breathing spell in the cold federal-provincial war; but certainly he had stretched the patience of English-speaking Canada very thin. In financial terms he could do no more for Quebec or the other provinces. In symbolic terms he was ready to take larger risks.

The decision to give Canada a new, distinctive flag of maple leaf design was Pearson's alone and one of the most daring ever taken by a Prime Minister because it touched the nation's deepest instincts.

384

Its main purpose, of course, was to satisfy the French Canadians who regarded the Red Ensign as an obsolete badge of British colonialism. But there was more to Pearson's decision than that.

He had become emotionally involved in the flag issue and was resolved to settle it, one way or the other, even if he wrecked his Government and ended his public career. He believed passionately in a new flag, he had promised it in the election campaign and this promise, unlike some others, would be redeemed whatever the risks.

Actually the risks were not half so grave as some of his more hesitant colleagues feared. The electoral arithmetic and blood count in a nation one-third British by descent, one-third French and the remainder of other ethnic origins were favourable to a truly Canadian flag. Pearson never doubted that a majority of Canadians would support it in the end.

Meanwhile he knew that he must face a bitter controversy and lose many votes among the supporters of the Red Ensign, who regarded it as the symbol of Canada's equal partnership with Britain. When this book went to press the flag debate had just begun and its result was unknown.

Much more dubious and disturbing than the flag issue was the outcome of Pearson's financial and symbolic bid for Quebec's loyalty to Confederation or, as his enemies called it, his appeasement of French-Canadian intransigence. Whatever it was called, his policy had now stretched English-speaking Canadians' patience to the absolute limit. There was no question about that in his mind. The only question was whether Quebec would accept his double offer, whether Premier Lesage would see that he could expect no additional concessions, for the present anyway.

Would Lesage finally repudiate and fight the crypto-separatists in his own provincial party, and discipline—or if necessary break with—his chief colleague and rival, René Lévesque, whose views, in Ottawa's opinion, led straight to separation?

Pearson felt sure that Lesage could invoke the natural moderation of the French-Canadian people, that they were overwhelmingly opposed to separation and needed only strong leadership to reject it forever. But such leadership, as in former times of trouble, must come from within Quebec. An English-speaking Prime Minister might reach its mind. He could never hope to reach its heart, especially when its political power was unnaturally concentrated for the moment in its provincial government. Only a son of French Canada could carry his people with him and only Lesage seemed to possess the required stature.

As the federal Government assessed this glamorous, articulate but enigmatic personage, Lesage could join the racial pantheon of Lafontaine, Laurier, Lapointe and St. Laurent and make himself a national statesman, perhaps Pearson's successor; or, refusing his chance, could become the prisoner of his extremists, the Kerensky of his own revolution.

At this writing Lesage's answer is awaited in Ottawa with a misery of suspense, for on it the future of Pearson, his Government and the nation may well hang.

Even if Pearson had bought time in the paramount problem of Quebec, far short of settling the racial conflict which must long survive him, he found most of his legislative program stalled in Parliament and Diefenbaker, his party split by the flag issue and still wrenched by the rebellion of 1962, shrewdly manoeuvring to precipitate an election while still young enough to fight it.

Still worse, the Government's reputation and Pearson's personal image were gravely injured. Some real progress had been made in various directions but it lacked any coherent pattern or clear choice of social priorities. To a nation never noted for gratitude it all seemed bitterly disappointing after the promises of the previous year. Canadians were sated with promises from all political parties and yet, in the returning opulence of the boom, they perversely demanded the impossible and usually blamed the politicians for failing to deliver it.

The people's shaken confidence in the political system reflected an inward lack of confidence in themselves, a gnawing sense of decisions too long evaded but finally inescapable. Pearson was the accurate mirror of this public and private uncertainty. With all his past achievements and his ardent faith in human possibilities he had become, for the time being anyway, the victim of his own excessive expectations, his premature hopes and the numerous mistakes which he confessed and tried to correct. By midsummer, 1964, in fact, the Government's largest asset was not its record but the weakness of an Opposition restive under Diefenbaker and quarreling within itself.

No matter what the endless imponderables of politics may produce, Pearson's larger objectives, if he remains in office, will be unchanged, though he may not achieve them and may end in total failure: the promotion of peace and collective security abroad; the unity of all the Canadian races; the improvement of the national economy; the fairer distribution of its wealth; the expansion of the welfare State within (or possibly beyond) the nation's means.

He is more socially radical, and much more international in outlook than any of his predecessors; but all these fourteen men have pursued the same general objectives, generally by the same amorphous methods. Pearson is new to Canadian experience only in his temperament and circumstances. He happens to be history's journey-man at a time when Canada must grapple with its many-sided crisis in bold advance or abdicate its chosen destiny in cowardly retreat. As an old Canadian, I dare to predict that the nation will advance. So it has always done in every test and, unless its quality has been lost, can do no other.

Macdonald and his Confederation; Laurier, his triumph and his tragedy; Borden, his victorious war and his manly assertion of Canada's independence; King, his management of a second war, his mystical self-worship and his legacy of domestic reform; Bennett, his gallant struggle and the shipwreck of his hopes; St. Laurent, his mastery of two races and his economic prodigy; Diefenbaker, his spectacular beginning and his dismal end; Pearson, his dismal beginning and his unknown end—these passengers of the Canadian caravan have traveled a long road in a young nation.

That march so far is all preface and each Prime Minister in his turn only a milepost. Each pointed bravely ahead to a remote horizon that always faded before him. None knew, no leader or follower can ever know, where the caravan is going.

Index

Index

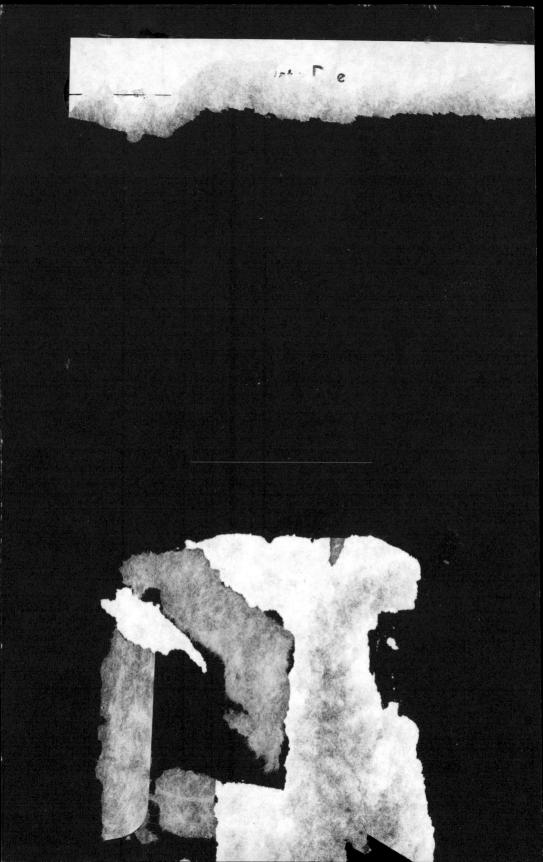